UNCOVERING THE SIXTIES

THE LIFE AND TIMES OF THE UNDERGROUND PRESS

ABE PECK

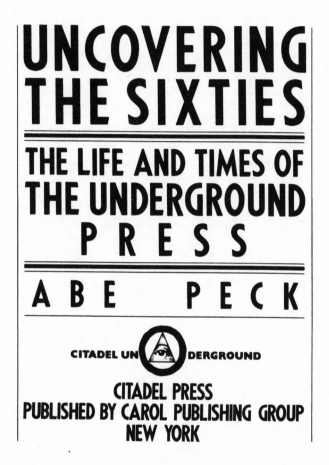

CITADEL UNDERGROUND

CITADEL PRESS
PUBLISHED BY CAROL PUBLISHING GROUP
NEW YORK

CITADEL UNDERGROUND

First Citadel Underground Edition, April 1991

Book design by Margaret M. Wagner

INTRODUCTION TO THE CITADEL UNDERGROUND EDITION

THE REAGAN-BUSH YEARS have not been kind to the memory of sixties protest struggles, which challenged business and politics-as-usual in the United States. Whatever their differences, New Left, black and brown power, antiwar and feminist organizations—known collectively as the Movement—shared a disdain for authority, a zeal for expression, and a mocking mistrust of conventional wisdom. They also shared an acute sense of the shortcomings of mainstream news media, which parodied, trivialized and slighted the efforts of social justice activists, while rarely shedding light on the failures of American society that gave birth to the Movement in the first place.

In retrospect, the rough press treatment the Movement received is hardly surprising. Owned and sponsored by big corporations that were themselves pillars of the American establishment, major media inherently favored the status quo. Rather than challenging government and corporate elites, mainstream journalism reflected their prerogatives.

In this sense little has changed since the 1960s. Far from being independent watchdogs for the public good, our national press corps is cozy with power. Then as now, news bias may have less to do with the foibles and prejudices of working journalists than the onerous nature of the institutions that employ them. More concerned with making money than making sense; mass media companies are incestuously linked with the military-industrial complex that profits mightily from the arms race, the plundering of the Third World, environmental pollution and other social inequities.

With news media functioning like a fourth branch of government rather than a feisty fourth estate, oppositional forces in the 1960s spawned an underground press—a "fifth estate," as a Detroit newspaper was called —which sought to counter mainstream distortions and omissions. The underground press printed news that corporate media were not inclined to publicize, covering protest movements from the perspective of those who marched and demonstrated in the streets.

Whereas corporate journalists were apt to credulously transmit whatever government representatives uttered, the underground press lampooned the official sources that were venerated by America's most influential media outlets. The prevailing assumption in the *Berkeley Barb, Los Angeles Free Press* and hundreds of other underground papers was that government officials lie routinely, matter-of-factly, as it were, and should rarely be trusted.

Had mainstream media displayed such skepticism, U.S. citizens might have learned at the outset that the 1964 Gulf of Tonkin incident was fabricated by U.S. officials to justify a massive military escalation in Vietnam, as the Pentagon Papers disclosed years later. By early 1968, millions of Americans were demanding an immediate U.S. withdrawal from Vietnam, yet still no major U.S. newsdaily called for bringing the boys home. The war ended in 1975 with an outcome sought by the underground press, which had correctly insisted that Vietnam was of little strategic importance to the U.S. and posed no threat to America's national security.

In addition to tweaking the nose of the corporate media by casting doubt on straight news reports, the underground press articulated the themes and passions of a burgeoning youth culture, which evolved at breakneck speed during the sixties. Underground journalism was part of an alternative "multi-media insurgency," as Abe Peck notes, that chronicled the meteoric rise and fall of the Movement and it helped to engender a distinct sense of community that emerged in the mid-1960s.

This was a moment saturated with possibility, and those who partook of that creative groundswell were confident, in the words of Comte de Lautremont, that "storms of youth precede brilliant days." The Cold War had momentarily thawed and students were eager to put their bodies on the line for a variety of causes: civil rights, disarmament, university reform, and so forth. Many were committed to a dual-prolonged radical project. They felt that defying authority entailed a concerted effort to alter policy-making institutions that had been usurped by a self-serving power elite. At the same time, believing that the product could only be as pure as the process, they tried to lead lives that embodied the social changes they desired.

For sixties activists, the quest for social justice was often an extension of the search for personal authenticity. Their emphasis on a high-energy, freewheeling culture formed the bases of a many-sided rebellion whose tentacles reached to stoned heights of ego-melting delirium, a rebellion as much involved with the sexual and spiritual as with matters explicitly political. Nearly everything was being questioned and most things tried in an orgy of experiment that shook the country to its roots.

Various strands of youth revolt were reflected in underground newspapers, where culture and politics overlapped in ways both complementary and problematic. Some rebels subscribed to the notion that "changing one's head" was more important than "changing the system," while others scoffed at the suggestion that transforming personal consciousness could overcome historical forces. Tension between the two camps was played out in the pages of the underground press, which became increasingly strident and obsessed with apocalyptic rhetoric as the decade wore on. By the late 1960s, the "V" sign for peace had given way to the clenched fist of revolution, and the Movement as a whole began to unravel.

Many factors contributed to the demise of the New Left and the underground press, not the least of which involved covert meddling by the FBI, the CIA and other spy agencies. Alternative papers were harassed and "neutralized" in much the same way that dissident political organizations were targeted. Government subversion exacerbated the internecine conflicts that tore apart the Movement, while mounting U.S. atrocities in Southeast Asia and violent confrontations with police at home drove people to the brink of desperation. Although activists succeeded in turning a majority of Americans against the war, the Movement burnt out in the process, unable to master its own intensity.

The saga of the underground press is inseparable from the high hopes and shattered illusions of the 1960s. Abe Peck tells that story with insight, poise and wit, shedding light on the accomplishments and blunders committed during those tumultuous years, whose shockwaves continue to reverberate throughout society. The concerns of sixties activists have not subsided in the Reagan-Bush era. On the contrary, racism, sexism, militarism, appalling extremes of wealth and poverty, media malfeasance, and the abusive powers of the secret state are still crucial issues, inspiring a new generation of rebels who will champion the cause of social justice.

Martin A. Lee
New York City
November, 1990

MARTIN A. LEE is the co-author of *Unreliable Sources: A Guide to Detecting Bias in New Media* and *Acid Dreams: The CIA, LSD and the Sixties Rebellion.* He is publisher of *Extra!*, the journal of FAIR (Fairness & Accuracy in Reporting), the national media watch group offering well-documented criticism in an effort to correct bias and imbalance.

TO SUZANNE

"Life can only be understood backwards, but it must be lived forwards."

SØREN KIERKEGAARD

"Make it wet."

ARTHUR BELL

CONTENTS

PREFACE

DURING the 1960s and early 1970s, a volley of challenges was aimed at the accepted order in the United States. War, racism, class, nationalism, the environment, sexuality, the nature of consciousness, culture, work, lifestyle—all were radically, substantially, sometimes explosively reconsidered. Fire power and flower power; rock festivals and rocks thrown at cops; body counts, body bags, body paint—all became part of the national landscape.

At first, the protest was mainly limited to older survivors of Senator Joseph McCarthy's security dragnet, members of various small Left parties, iconoclastic activists, writers, and teachers. But the escalating war in Vietnam and racism at home drew opposition, and socialism, rock music, LSD, and other forces drew adherents, many of them young.

Initially, this youth activism was physically concentrated in the larger society—in pockets of the segregated South, Chicago's Appalachian-Indian Uptown neighborhood, Newark's black ghetto. Then came protests against an alienating education system. By 1964, meaningful numbers of protesters and dropouts were populating their own communities, off college campuses and in large cities. As the years went by, New York's Saint Mark's Place, Berkeley's Telegraph Avenue, Los Angeles' Sunset Strip, San Francisco's Haight, Chicago's Wells, and Madison's Mifflin streets turned into enclaves as well as addresses.

Some residents belonged to organizations such as

Students for a Democratic Society (SDS), groups that primarily sought to build a New Left, a Movement that would shape fairer, more equitable political relationships in the larger society. Others—"hippies" at first, "freaks" after they'd been bloodied a bit—concentrated on changing themselves via lifestyle, chemicals, and meditation. Members of both constituencies formed food co-ops, legal services, and other institutions that could serve these communities. There was committed activism and a moral spirit there—and also sex, drugs, and rock 'n' roll.

The political Movement and the various lifestyle movements influenced each other, rejecting both an imperial foreign policy and a conformist way of life. But the mass media were shaped by the values and perceptions of primarily white, middle-class, male mainstream writers and editors. Their stories—often distorted, sometimes too correct—only proved how wide the gap was between the two cultures.

Partly as a response to this gap, a new counter-institution developed, as an underground press sprang up to mirror, spark, express, organize, advocate, and hype the strands of protest. Precedents for this press dated back to before the American Revolution, to Ben Franklin and Tom Paine. Again, though, its more direct roots lay in the culture and politics that existed a decade before its appearance, in the dissolving social consensus on what America was about and where it should be going, and in emerging counter-communities large enough to provide readerships for dissident local publications.

In May, 1964—as the United States drew deeper into Vietnam, the civil rights struggle moved toward black power, the Beatles captured America, and the leading edge of a generation called the Baby Boom turned eighteen—the Los Angeles *Free Press* became the first underground paper to publish on a sustained basis. It and those that followed weren't really covert, but their stories provided a dramatically different perspective on the news.

By 1967, twenty or so black-and-white or four-color tabloids were being produced in the United States via cheap offset-press technology and a labor pool of former students. Most emphasized what an underground alumnus named Chip Berlet has called "cultural shock treatment and metaphysical alternatives to plasticized consumerist materialism."

Mainstream newspapers ran crime news and arts reviews and *Dick Tracy*. Underground papers ran demonstration news and rock reviews and *The Fabulous Furry Freak Brothers*, a comic about three amiable "heads" Tracy would have busted for their rampant pot-smoking. The dailies carried ads for pots and pans and suits; the undergrounders sold rolling papers, LPs, and jeans even as they criticized the money economy.

Daily reporters carried police press cards; underground papers printed phony press cards for the next march.

Fledgling, brash underground reporters often lacked skill, and evidence for their conclusions. Their stories could be self-indulgent, even incomprehensible, and could trample the tenets of accuracy and fairness. But they knew that some issues do not have two equally valid sides, and they accepted dissent, experimentation, popular culture, the breaking of class, race, and national boundaries. Their media images were disproportionately influential, and some of their stories proved Berlet's contention that the years 1968–1973 "saw the underground highlight its role as a political muckraker." The papers could offer an honest subjectivity in place of an "objectivity" that ignored its own underlying political and cultural assumptions.

By 1969, the highwater mark of protest, at least five hundred papers served communities and constituencies worldwide, with five hundred to a thousand more dissenting papers in high schools alone. Yet by 1973, the press, like the movements it covered, had both succeeded and withered for reasons that will emerge over the course of this book. Dissenting papers would continue to publish. But as Berlet has noted, "although the political viewpoint remained progressive, there was no longer a mass movement centered around antiwar and anti-Nixon issues and a certain sense of urgency was lost."

Yet from the Beatles' *A Hard Day's Night* to the Paris Peace Accords that ended American involvement in Vietnam, the underground press recorded, and helped create, the period we call "the sixties."

Inevitably, then, this is a book about both the times and how they were recorded by radical participants in them. It traces how movements and communities convinced that their news did not fit into the agenda of mainstream media covered themselves in print. It records the approach-avoidance relationship between the political and cultural wings of dissent. It shows people who, in the words of writer Todd Gitlin, "were happy to be amateurs in the original sense, doing the work for love," and how some of them committed crimes against journalism even as they pursued criminal behavior in high places.

Consequently, this book is less a history of the day-to-day operations of any one paper than a narrative of papers and people encountering key events of the day. The reportorial Los Angeles *Free Press* lends a black perspective to the 1965 uprising in the Watts ghetto. The hippie *Oracle* helps chant in the Aquarian Age at San Francisco's 1967 Human Be-In. New York's gritty *Rat* joins in the 1968 student strike at Columbia

University. The psychedelic yet politicizing *Seed* faces both police and Movement pressure at the 1968 Democratic National Convention in Chicago. Berkeley's feisty *Barb* divides in 1969 over ownership and profit; the *Rat* explodes at the turn of the decade as women refuse to be second-class writers any longer. Papers collectively bellow their outrage after the 1970 slayings of four students at Kent State University. They shudder and wind down as events, and readers, move on in the early 1970s.

This book shows new journalists responding to the causes, adventures, challenges, and repressions surrounding life in the underground press. Occasionally, it compares underground and mainstream stories to show the gulf in perspective and technique that informed their largely exclusive readerships. The recollections of nearly a hundred sources make it a more collective memoir—but, as we learned in the sixties, one shaped by the particular writer.

For me, telling this story has been an act of functional schizophrenia. From 1967 to 1971, I was part and parcel of the underground press. I wrote, edited, typed, swept up, sold papers, and was arrested at the *Seed,* Chicago's best-known underground paper, where I also became involved in the demonstrations surrounding the Democratic Convention. I served on the steering committee of the Underground Press Syndicate, an organization that helped papers share stories and defend themselves against an increasing number of legal assaults. In New York, I wrote for the *Rat.* I covered some of the decade's key events, and gave my time, my heart, my health, to the papers. They gave me my politics, my identity, my crises—and something I never expected during the rush to radical judgment: a subsequent career at *Rolling Stone,* the Chicago *Daily News* and *Sun-Times,* and Northwestern University's Medill School of Journalism. Consequently, this book is both a reconstruction and a revision, one I hope adds perspective while preserving what really happened.

I began my work in mid-1981, reading print and microfilm copies of the *Seed,* New York's *Rat,* the more hippie-oriented *East Village Other,* and the freak-turned-Marxist Liberation News Service. I soon found myself seeking material on the events these papers covered in an array of publications, including other underground papers, the New York *Times,* the four Chicago dailies that published during the period, *Newsweek* and *Time,* lesser-known periodicals, and books published then and since. Despite—or because—of rhetoric, argot, and arcane ideas, memories were rekindled, connections were made.

And yet, I had to struggle to bridge the years. In 1967, I was a hippie whose life in the Psychedelic Now only intensified a young man's feeling of immortality. In 1969, I was a radical who believed that political upheaval was imminent. By 1971, I was leaving the country, convinced that jail or worse awaited me if I stayed. Now I have a family, a career, unexpected happiness, unresolved feelings, some unfulfilled dreams.

As I worked, I recalled the Japanese film *Rashomon,* in which a crime is reconstructed through several very different sets of eyes. Reading the papers only reminded me that, despite our best efforts, there was rarely a single, unified movement of politics and culture, but several sometimes-linked, sometimes-contending worldviews—and a certain amount of simple outrageousness. Consequently, my experiences as a flower child who grew thorns were not the same as those of Red-diaper babies, army brats, Old or New Leftists, ex-mainstream reporters, graphic artists, b.s. artists.

And so, I traveled around the country, interviewing former undergrounders and other participants suggested by the events and sources I was reencountering. I found the underground's foremost comic artist in a northern California farmhouse; Liberation News Service's 1968 London correspondent was at work in a network television studio in New York. Vestigial Yippies occupied a Bowery loft-bunker filled with mattresses and computer typesetting equipment; five miles north, a founding Yippie turned Yuppie networker had literally hung his past in his high-rise closet, pictures of his headbanded self denouncing Phil Donahue peeking out from under the coats. I sat on a lovely rise over Malibu and the Pacific, talking with LNS's onetime man at Columbia about how wonderful the future would be—and on the edge of a Berkeley hospital bed with the *Barb*'s founder, a bitter terminal cancer patient.

Some of the people with whom I spoke remain dedicated to wresting power from the state, more to reforming it. Some feel like failed strangers in a strange land, others lead happy, rewarding, integrated lives. I have tried to incorporate their thoughts into a continuing narrative, enriching it, adding nuance, even contradiction. (Quotes in the present tense reflect statements from these interviews.) Footnotes and a bibliography follow the text, as does an epilogue in which I and my sources assess the underground press and its impact. The conclusions in this book are mine except where noted; at the same time, I want to thank the following for sharing memories, addenda, corrections, anger, and accomplishment:

Judy Clavir Albert, Stew Albert, Vince Aletti, Steve Allen, Jane Alpert, Mick Archer, Frank Bardacke, Dana Beal, Arthur Bell, Karin Berg, Lowell Bergman, Chip Berlet, Walter Bowart, Rita Mae Brown, Bruce Brugmann, Tim Cahill, George Cavalletto, Allen Cohen, Cameron Crowe, Robert Crumb, Clive Davis, Steve Diamond, Lester Doré, Claudia Dreifus, Daniel Ellsberg, Alice Embree, Ken Emerson, Bob Fass,

David Fenton, Jim Fouratt, Allen Ginsberg, Todd Gitlin, Al Goldstein, David Harris, Seymour Hersh, Adam Hochschild, Abbie Hoffman, Alan Howard, Michael James, Flora Johnson, Allen (formerly Allan) Katzman, George Kauffman, Jaacov Kohn, Paul Krassner, Arthur Kunkin, Julius Lester, Susan Lydon, Jay Lynch, Greil Marcus, Dave Marsh, Andy Marx, Cheryl McCall, Tom Miller, Robin Morgan, John Mrvos, Ray Mungo, Jeff (Shero) Nightbyrd, P.J. O'Rourke, Charlie Perry, Craig Pyes, Geoffrey Rips, Tom Robbins, Marshall Rosenthal, Michael Rossman, Jerry Rubin, Bob Rudnick, Sheila Ryan, Terry Sabela Sampson, Ed Sanders, Danny Schechter, Bobby Seale, Irwin Silber, Craig Silver, Peter Solt, Frank Stanton, Andy Stapp, Eliot Wald, David Walley, Harvey Wasserman, Jann Wenner, John Wilcock, Paul Williams, Allen Young, Paul (Simon) Zmiewski, and some sources best left unsung. Rest in peace, Arthur Bell and Max Scherr.

I also want to thank agent Amanda Urban and editor Wendy Goldwyn, who offered constant encouragement and knew that some barriers were only paper tigers.

Todd Gitlin, Richard Hainey, Donna Leff, and Janice Normoyle, teachers and writers about media, critiqued parts or all of the manuscript, as did Jeff Nightbyrd and Eric Probst. Thanks to them for saving me from myself on more than one occasion.

This book became a cottage industry for work-study graduate students at Medill. Phil Apol, Richard Block, Ceci Byrne, Patricia Clark, Beth Duff-Sanders, Gwen Gilliam, Karen Gutloff, James Hussey, Maria Iacobo, Lisa Keefe, John Kennedy, Madearia King, Shari Kochman, Silvia Kucenas, Jennifer Lamb, Kristin Layng, Wendell Link, David Medina, Sara Patterson, Fred Pierce, Karin Roberts, Robert Siegel, Jean Spielman, Ari Soglin, Mike Stanton, Michael Thompson, Craig Tomashoff, Mary Ann Williams, Mike Winklehorst, April Witt, Beverly Wood, and, especially, Katherine Lawson, slogged through tapes, pulled clips, checked facts, and asked more than a few emperor's-new-clothes questions. Cheryl Fox photographed the papers used as illustrations. Thanks also to Carol Ryzak of the Medill staff, and to Jane Shay Wald.

Finally, there would be no book without Suzanne Wexler Peck: wise counsel; keeper of the kids during my long hours at the Kaypro; friend, lover, and wife.

UNCOVERING THE SIXTIES

freethought criticism and satire

The Realist

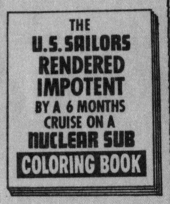

the magazine of
criminal negligence

No. 35   35 Cents

*...beginning our fifth year
of publication...Special
Offensive Issue...featuring
"An Impolite Interview with
an Abortionist"...Lenny Bruce
on "The Great Hotel Robbery"
...William Worthy on "Mass
Media Irresponsibility"...
a report on what happened
when this little magazine
rattled a possible skeleton
in President Kennedy's closet
...a plan for a Humanist
Social Work Organization
...a new game—"Who Would
You Kick Out of Bed?"...
futile fun with farmers,
Adolf Eichmann, God and
"The Realmate of the Month"*

THE U.S. SAILORS RENDERED IMPOTENT BY A 6 MONTHS CRUISE ON A NUCLEAR SUB COLORING BOOK

*...and some Realist
Coloring Books for
Colorless People Who
Have Lost Their
Crayons, bla bla bla...*

1

THE
PROTO-UNDERGROUND

MERICA in 1954 was paradise, said the majority paradigm:

The country was an antidote for the grinding poverty or political repression many of its families had escaped. Millions of working people drove along yellow brick roads toward new homes in the suburbs. Television beamed out a cornucopia of available, no-money-down consumer goods. Finned dream-mobiles decorated the showrooms. "What is good for our country is good for General Motors, and vice versa" was a statement of corporate truth.

The Nazis were a bad memory. The Soviet Union —a threat turned ally turned threat—was held off by everything from the Marshall Plan to the Strategic Air Command. America still wanted to make the world safe for democracy, profit, and Protestant-ethic discipline. Even many Democrats liked Ike; as the TV show said, "Father Knows Best."

Confidence was the national drug of choice.

America in 1954 was limbo, or purgatory, or hell, a second group contended:

Blacks were unable to vote in much of the South, unable to sit at the same lunch counters or drink from the same water fountains as whites. In the North, many of them, and more than a few whites, often were blocked from even standing next to the corporate ladder. A bullyboy foreign policy supported colonial empires and was overthrowing governments from Iran to Guatemala; senators conducted inquisitions in Washington. The economy was fueled by war production, geared to rampant growth. On the heels of Hitler, nuclear weaponry made some fear an even more ghastly Final Solution. The cities were dog-eat-dog, and cultural life was dressed in stifling gray flannel. Sexual repression made horniness *de rigueur.*

Change wasn't exactly blowin' in the wind. The World War I Bohemians were long gone, and a sardonic campus sign of the times— "Conform or Die"—summed this nonscene up. Those who disagreed suffered a "nik" attack: Peacenik. Beatnik. Sicknik.

And fewer and fewer people were Waiting for Lefty. Marxism had lifted Russia from serfdom, freed China from occupying armies and warlords. It represented a hope for a universal, benevolent social order and had informed struggles against fascism, racism, exploitation. But Marxism had also spawned purges, collectivizations, and byzantine politics, and had made "Siberia" more than a place on a map. Most Americans feared its overseas expansion, and the waters of Julius and Ethel Rosenberg's atomic-secrets trial and mid-1953 execution remained heavy, murky. By 1954, the Old Left in America had been reduced to a few caring people with Jobian patience, and some Kremlin groupies.

There also was a set version of American history. In textbooks, media, and ordinary conversation, brave settlers and captains of industry almost always starred over a largely invisible supporting cast of blacks, women, Indians, protesters, immigrants. It was hard to learn that there had been a feminist movement as far back as 1848, urban and agrarian reform movements, a fighting labor movement, a peace movement during World War I, major socialist and communist movements, a number of anarchists (do anarchists have movements?). Similarly, a counterculture had existed earlier in the twentieth century. "This is the greatest place in the world!" John Reed, who'd later chronicle the Russian Revolution in *Ten Days That Shook the World,* had written his parents from Greenwich Village. "You cannot imagine such utter freedom. Freedom from every boundary, moral, religious, social."

But by 1954, such sentiments were only a dim echo, and the protest press was at a correspondingly low point.

The first American newspaper—Benjamin Harris's *Publick Occurrences*— had been shuttered in 1690, after its debut issue criticized colonial life in Boston.

In 1735, John Peter Zenger had been tried for sedition after attacking the monarchy in print. His victory established the press's freedom to criticize members of the government (a legacy that would be largely ignored when the FBI began its campaign against the underground press).

Forty-one years later, Tom Paine had published *Common Sense* to spark rebellion in his native country's colonies. Starting in 1831, Frederick Douglass and William Lloyd Garrison had used the *Liberator* to lobby for the abolition of slavery. During the 1890s, nine hundred or so Populist papers had fed that movement. Scores of socialist papers also appeared, and in 1912, *Appeal to Reason* had circulated 760,000 copies, more than any American radical publication before or since.

Appeal to Reason first published Upton Sinclair's meatpacking exposé *The Jungle* and backed Eugene V. Debs's socialist run for the presidency. But Espionage Act charges, though successfully defended against, drained its resources and energy. Max Eastman's *Masses* had given cultural life to political criticism before World War I—but the postwar "Red Scares" had suppressed it, and Eastman's subsequent move to the Right was not the stuff of Left heroics. One tough anarchist, Emma Goldman, had published *Mother Earth* magazine—before being deported to the then brand-new Soviet Union.

Still, more than a few radical papers continued to publish in 1954. Several were organizing tools for particular Left groups. The Communist Party had been printing the *Daily Worker* since 1924, through Depression, hot and cold wars, and the twists and turns of various party lines. The *Militant* advanced the politics of the Socialist Workers Party.

Growing out of the 1948 Progressive Party presidential campaign of Henry Wallace, the *National Guardian* was an independent Left weekly. The next year, *Monthly Review* had begun critiquing capitalism and the Cold War to a small audience interested in Marxist economic theory.

Other independent progressive or Left media also existed. The *Nation* magazine had been countering government-issue positions since 1865. Founded in 1909 by Robert LaFollette, the Wisconsin-based *Progressive* discussed issues on the Left within an anti-Stalinist framework. The *Catholic Worker* urged on religious pacifists; an editor named Michael Harrington later wrote a book called *The Other America* and helped shake the federal government into launching poverty programs.

Dissent fed into other media, other audiences. In 1949, KPFA-FM had become the country's first listener-sponsored radio station, reaching Left-liberals in Berkeley on its, and their, own terms. In 1953, Left-leaning members of the Mattachine Society had launched *One* magazine (in which homosexual rights meant not being "special in any but one sense"). That same year, *I.F. Stone's Weekly* had appeared, gutsy and well re-searched, but with a far smaller circulation than the daily papers that had rejected both him and his independent politics. Nineteen-fifty-four saw

Dissent begin to explore the ideas that might form a democratic socialism in America.

This alternate media continued a tradition of opposition publishing, concentrated dissenting thought. Some advocated action. All readily integrated their beliefs into their reporting. But publishing in a society generally hostile to or uninterested in class analysis and without a real counterculture, they didn't reach many nonactivists. "We certainly thought we were at the beginning of a long period of real freeze for the Left—a very rough patch," *Monthly Review* cofounder Paul Sweezy would say about those hard postwar days.

THE GREAT THAW of 1954 didn't look to be one at the time. But a cluster of events occurred that year, setting the stage for changes and struggles to come.

On May 7, 1954, 8,000 survivors of the French garrison at Dien Bien Phu surrendered to the revolutionary forces of a Vietnamese leader named Ho Chi Minh. Instead of paving the way for free elections, our government began building a South Vietnam that it later admitted was "essentially the creation of the United States." Over two million Indochinese and 58,000 American lives, $140 billion U.S. dollars, and twenty-one years later, the war would end with the same result an election would have had.

On May 17, 1954, the United States Supreme Court decided in *Brown v. Board of Education* that, ninety years after the fact of Constitutional equality, "separate but [un]equal" education of the races was illegal.

On December 2, 1954, the United States Senate censured Joseph McCarthy, its Red-baiting member from Wisconsin. An army whose loyalty had been questioned had played a role in stopping the senator. So had Edward R. Murrow's televised interview. And so had the *Progressive,* which had published the first major exposé of the senator's smears (ironically, the issue's sales made 1954 the *Progressive*'s only profitable year).

A diplomatic miscue in Vietnam, the encouragement of rights for black people, the end of an American witch-hunt, and the reconsiderations forced by Stalinism. These events (along with other cultural ones to be subsequently explored), hinted that dramatic progressive change might just be possible. Soon this dissent suggested itself in print.

In 1956, a group of veteran activists—A.J. Muste, David Dellinger, and Sidney Lens among them—published a new monthly, *Liberation.* Their March debut contained a "Tract for the Times" designed to end radical rigor mortis by proclaiming a committed, antiauthoritarian, human-scale Left:

Essentially socialist, the "Tract" derided what the authors saw as an often-irrelevant and hypocritical liberalism. Then came what many traditional Leftists would regard as heresy—the notion that the H-bomb, technology, and, yes, totalitarianism, mandated new, even more fundamental solutions.

Demanding economic justice was not enough, the authors declared, if "the average individual finds his life as dull and empty as ever." Marx—more heresy—had fallen short. "In trying to liberate mankind from economic slavery, he failed to see the looming horror of political slavery. . . . A truly radical movement today must take these ethical problems much more seriously than many nineteenth century thinkers did. . . ."

The "Tract" reveled in pluralism: socialism's concern with economic justice, liberalism's insistence on individual rights, the Judeo-Christian "vision of human dignity," the pacifism Mahatma Gandhi had used to free India from colonial domination, elements from American radical history, a commitment to democracy and nonviolence. It revived the idea of a "Third Camp" between Western capitalism and Soviet bureaucratic Communism (one first advanced in *Politics,* a pacifist casualty of the Cold War). It demanded a living culture and an open movement.

The document was an idea-stew, not a program. It was written for those predisposed to socialism, and offered no replacement for class struggle, no key to moving a basically Leftless America. Reader letters soon accused its authors of throwing the Marxist baby out along with the Stalinist bathwater. Nevertheless, *Liberation* plunged into the fray.

On December 1, 1955, a black seamstress-activist named Rosa Parks had begun changing American history by taking a seat in the "white" section of a Montgomery, Alabama, bus. Leaders in the resulting boycott demanding equal seating were seized, black churches dynamited. *Liberation*'s second issue included an article by a young minister named Dr. Martin Luther King, Jr. Racists ensured "good copy" by shooting up his house and bombing his church.

One hundred one Congressmen declared their opposition to integration, but in November, 1956, the Supreme Court outlawed local bus segregation. Movement was in the air. As the "Tract" had concluded, "*Liberation* will seek to inspire its readers not only to fresh thinking but to action *now* . . . concrete resistance in the communities in which we live to all the ways in which human beings are regimented and corrupted . . . experimentation in creative living . . . the freedom of all individuals from domination, whether military, economic, political or cultural."

MAINSTREAM culture also was changing. White collars were predominating over blue. Magazines, television, and radio were beaming big-city values into the heartland. A "new class" of intellectuals, academics, and communicators was rising. Works like David Riesman's *The Lonely Crowd* (1950) had attacked conformity. *Playboy* would later be raked over the coals of sexism and artificiality, but the new magazine represented a more honest expression of (male) sexual longing than did peeking at the topless tribal women in *National Geographic*.

By 1954, Sid Caesar and Imogene Coca's *Your Show of Shows* (1950–54) and *The Ernie Kovacs Show* (1952–53, 1956) had honed an anarchic edge that would be continued on *The Steve Allen Show* (1956–61). "We were all outsiders," one of Caesar's roster of primarily Jewish and Catholic writers would recall. "There was a general unhappiness there, a lot of psychological things. There was total permissiveness."

An adversary culture had not yet developed, and not all these strands would be sequential. But in October, 1955, a new paper brought the cosmopolitian sensibility and a sense of opposition to New York's Greenwich Village.

For decades, the Village had been, in *Voice* historian Kevin McAuliffe's words, "a haven for all that was lowlife and highbrow and offbeat." Alongside Italian groceries and WASPy banks was a cornucopia of Brendan Behan bars, bongo-banging coffeehouses, and shoebox avant-garde theatres; soapbox theoreticians, guitar-strumming folkies, and bop jazzbeaux; dry-mouthed potheads, closeted homosexuals, and black-sweatered teenagers in from the outer boroughs to explore the Land of Cool.

The *Village Voice* wasn't underground wild-and-crazy. It had business-like owners—older guys, one just about forty. It had basically liberal politics, and was printed in black-and-white. The first issue's lead story concerned a trucker-Villager who was suing Columbia University after being expelled from its School of Social Work, supposedly for writing a student-newspaper editorial criticizing cultural narrowness. But from the start, the *Voice*'s pages resonated with the guitars of Washington Square Park, off-Broadway debates about the latest experimental play, and the Village's evolving politics.

The *Voice* established the virtue and viability of inspired amateurism, and proved that a community newspaper didn't have to be just a collection of supermarket ads. "The *Village Voice* was originally conceived as a living, breathing attempt to demolish the notion that one needs to be a professional to accomplish something in a field as purportedly technical as journalism," cofounder Dan Wolf told McAuliffe. Some *Voice* writers were mainstream critics seeking a more flexible, personal writing style, or a more defined audience. Others displayed the knowledge of keen participant-observers. Not all of it was great, but it churned up a dialogue for a community that, it turned out, reached far beyond the Village.

The *Voice* began with a business manager who'd studied Greek and Latin at Columbia and an advertising-sales staff full of poets. But its sensibility, immediacy, and intelligence (as well as its personal and apartment ads) would prevail where five culturally or politically progressive papers had failed. It would supplant a traditional neighborhood paper called the *Villager,* and would eventually become a highly profitable (and provocative) weekly.

The *Voice* articulated the concerns of a post–Silent Generation wider than its readership, one turned off by what Dan Wolf called "the vulgarities of McCarthyism" and "the dull pieties of official liberalism." But though the *Voice* beat the local Democratic political machine and stopped a highway from coming through Washington Square Park, it dissented from the Left as well as the Right. "They genuinely *wanted* to *be* businessmen, precisely because that was the way, as they saw it, to guarantee the very brashness, the independence," McAuliffe would write. "They [Wolf and cofounder Ed Fancher] had both always, genuinely, been turned off by the Left, by the Communists, the Trotskyites, the socialists, the fronts, the fellow-travelers, the hard-core types."

This division between liberal and radical sensibilities was going on at other publications, in trade unions, at universities, and elsewhere. But early on, there was a second schism between two visions of what the *Voice* could become. With a mixture of obnoxiousness and insight, Norman Mailer—investor, columnist, author—was defining in print the nature of something called Hip. The *Voice,* Mailer wrote, should go for the throat of all the plastic establishments even if it consumed itself in doing it. But Wolf and Fancher wanted to come back next week. And so, Mailer's first regular column, in January, 1956, put down the *Voice* as "remarkably conservative for so young a paper." Four months later, he was moving on. "I feel the hints, the clues, the whisper of a new time coming," Mailer wrote presciently. He was no doctrinaire Leftist; his hope was that "the destructiveness, the liberating, creative nihilism of Hip, the frantic search for potent Change may break out into the open with all its violence, its confusion, its ugliness and horror."

Mailer's (ultimately ironic) exemplar of the shape of things to come was a "White Negro" hanging out on life's mean streets. This "philosophical psychopath" mixed the rebel energies of the oppressed black, the juvenile delinquent, and the bohemian cultural dissident. His souped-up romanticism saw angels in the gutters of bourgeois life, dustbin seraphim that would rise up to attack "high culture." Here's his description of Henry Miller's *Tropic of Cancer,* the (male) sexual exorcism that would finally be allowed into this country in 1961: "Down in the sewers of existence where the cancer was being cooked, Miller was cavorting. Look, he was forever saying, you do not have to die of this crud. You can breathe it, eat it, suck it, fuck it, and still bounce up for the next day. There is something inestimable in us if we can stand the smell."

The rift between Mailer and the *Voice*'s more conservative owners was emblematic. "The division was *hip* and *square,* " Marty Jezer would write in *The Dark Ages,* his history of the 1950s. "Square people sought security and conned themselves into political acquiescence. Hipsters, hip to the bomb, sought the meaning of life and, expecting death, demanded it now. In the wigged-out, flipped-out, zonked-out hipster world, Roosevelt, Churchill and Stalin, Truman, McCarthy, Stevenson and Eisenhower shared one thing in common: they were square." The *Voice* would be challenged, even lambasted, by underground papers to come. And the underground press itself would have its own running division—between political, basically New Left, papers and cultural-, rock- and drug-oriented papers. Between what historian Laurence Leamer would call "the fists" and "the heads."

In July, 1954, a nineteen-year-old white Mississippian named Elvis Presley compressed the red clay of the Pentecostal First Assembly of God Church and the rhythms of black America until they exploded with the recorded power of rock 'n' roll. That same year, Marlon Brando played a motorcycle outlaw in *The Wild One.* "What are you rebelling against?" they asked. "Whadda ya got?" he answered.

Blackboard Jungle (1955) fused outlaw generational energy with rocking around the clock. Teens, another movie would say, were rebels without a cause. Youthful energy was seen as erotic, even kinky. Vladimir Nabokov's book *Lolita* (1955) would capture one level of the fascination adolescent sensuality already held for adults. The movie *I Was a Teenage Werewolf* (1957) would offer more grotesque symbolism. "Thus was youth viewed by adults in that day," Albert Goldman would write in his own werewolf biography, *Elvis.* "More importantly, thus did youth regard itself: as a new, perhaps monstrous race"—a race of mass-culture white negroes breaking away from White Castles and white bucks toward some uncharted technicolor territory.

Print technology was still too expensive and unavailable for young people to publish themselves in any great numbers. But William Gaines struck a nerve. Gaines was an older, professional publisher who'd first attracted attention with such E.C. Comics as *Tales from the Crypt*. These were less mice-and-duck fiestas than childhood Holocausts and Hiroshimas, and eventually were supressed by a new Comics Code Authority. By then, though, Gaines and editor Harvey Kurtzman were at *Mad,* which had begun in 1952 as a comic book with sharper teeth than Alfred E. Neuman would later have, and which would rank as an important popular-culture precursor to the underground press.

Mad (and its first cousins *Help* and *Humbug*) was staffed by "generational defectors"—adults who projected their dissatisfaction with the status quo toward younger people whom they saw as not yet corrupted by it (disk jockey Alan Freed, an early exponent and racial integrator of rock 'n' roll, was another one). "What we did was . . . show kids that the adult world is not omnipotent," *Mad* editor Al Feldstein would say. "We told them there's a lot of garbage out in the world and you've got to be aware. . . . Everything you read in the papers is not necessarily true. What you see on television is mostly lies."

Mad's full-length comic stories and parodies pulsed with urban life. "If you were growing up lonely and isolated in a small town, *Mad* was a revelation," Robert Crumb, who spent the fifties growing up in just such a Delaware town before going on to draw Fritz the Cat, Mr. Natural, and other underground comic heroes, would say. "Nothing I read anywhere else suggested there was an absurdity in the culture."

Patti Smith, trash-princess of seventies punk rock, would be more succinct. "After *Mad,* drugs were nothing."

For better or worse, *Mad* probably would influence more underground press writers than Tom Paine, maybe even Karl Marx. And in 1958, a *Mad* alumnus would create the iconoclastic parent of the underground press.

In the lower Manhattan office of the business manager of *Mad* magazine, Paul Krassner had set up headquarters for his new magazine. Though small, this office was actually a nexus of opposition. The business manager, one Lyle Stuart, was already the maverick editor of an anticensorship magazine called, variously, *Exposé* or the *Independent*. Krassner, a *Mad* freelancer and Stuart columnist, was now launching a monthly black-and-white magazine of free-thought criticism and satire. "I founded the *Realist* as a *Mad* for adults," he recalls.

Krassner wasn't black, or an organizational Leftist, or, at twenty-six, a teen rebel. He didn't write poetry. Like many other figures in the early underground, he was a New York lapsed-Jewish nonconformist. A child prodigy (violin), he was maladjusted—if, for example, adjustment meant believing your teacher when she told you that hiding under a desk would save your life during a nuclear attack. Dropping out of the City College of New York with one course to go, he'd hooked up with television's satiric edge by writing for Steve Allen. After a stint with such atheist magazines as the *Truth Seeker*, his interest in the First Amendment— motivated by both a love for free speech and a sense of self-preservation —led him to Stuart's magazine, to *Mad*, and then to the *Realist*.

Beginning with only six hundred subscribers, selling only three thousand of the ten-thousand-copy first run, refusing advertising, Krassner supported himself and the *Realist* by writing in *Cavalier, Playboy*, and other men's magazines. At the *Realist*, he wrote, pasted up, swept up. "I took an atheist's leap of faith. It was like a wolf howling to see if other wolves are out there."

They were. Terry *(Dr. Strangelove)* Southern and cartoonist Dick Guindon contributed. Steve Allen bought a rash of subscriptions. "I am enamored of the *Realist,*" satirist Henry Morgan said, "because even if I throw up at some of its opinions, I am so delighted that it *has* any I'm anxious to keep it around."

Krassner and company began turning the cultural landscape into a free-fire zone, attacking telethons, fallout shelters, political blacklisting, and cigarette ads. At a time when it was heresy to suggest that church and state be separated, Krassner gave super-atheist Madalyn Murray (O'Hair) space to savage hawkish prelates and stringent sexuality. The *Realist* nun zapped people's minds by doing irreligious things in public; Krassner later printed a "Fuck Communism" poster, then giggled while smoke poured out of the ears of both right-wing prudes and rigid Leftists. Sardonic irreverence proved popular; the *Realist* was on its way toward a circulation that would eventually reach 100,000.

Krassner had never read Marx or Engels, belonged to no political group, and his "intuitive anarchism" would lead him down some strange paths. But he felt part of a tradition of independent populist journalism he dated back through George Seldes's *In Fact* to Waco, Texas, and the 1890s, where an editor named Wade Cowper Brann published a paper called the *Iconoclast*. It was not lost on Krassner that Brann had been shot in the back. "From the very beginning, I thought, 'Oh, I just want to have fun, Mr. Rockefeller.' I always wanted to make the *Realist* all satirical, but these carefully researched stories would come along." Then again, reading the *Realist* for hard news was complicated by Krassner's penchant for running fact and "meta-fact" side by side, a tendency that would lead to more than one editorial brouhaha.

Krassner did put his actions where his words were. Inspired by Rosa Parks, the *Realist* covered the emerging civil rights movement. When an article in *Look* claimed that there were no humane abortionists, Krassner found a subscriber who operated as tenderly as possible under the existing (illegal) circumstances and charged by ability to pay. (The story earned Krassner two grand jury subpoenas.) He used proceeds from the Communism poster spoof to send a reporter to Vietnam.

Like Krassner's greatest hero, scathing satirist Lenny Bruce, the *Realist* offered a take-no-prisoners voice. Few if any publications challenged their readers more. Krassner impolitely interviewed Bruce—and American Nazi Party leader George Lincoln Rockwell, in a Q&A preceded by a box saying, "When canceling your subscription please include your zip code." If convicted rapist Caryl Chessman was worth saving from the death penalty, Krassner asked, then how about Nazi mass-murder administrator Adolf Eichmann? "What the readers had in common was an irreverence toward bullshit," Krassner recalls. "Except their own, of course."

THE THAW, and the search for an alternative set of values, was also taking place in another medium—poetry. "This was still a time of cold, gray silence, but inside the coffeehouses of North Beach, poets and friends sensed the atmosphere of liberation," Michael McClure would say about the dawn of the San Francisco Renaissance. "We were restoring the body, with the voice as the extension of the body."

One night in 1955, Allen Ginsberg voiced the *Howl* heard 'round the world. It was in San Francisco, at a place called Gallery Six, where poets and abstract expressionist painters plotted together against objective reality. After Kerouac lubricated a hundred or so witnesses with several gallons of cheap burgundy, Ginsberg, arms outstretched, began firing off bebop fusillades, proclaiming a liberated pansexuality, reciting a casualty list of those "run down by the drunken taxicabs of Absolute Reality," cursing Moloch, "the vast stone of war," the sacrifice-demanding god of "Robot apartments! invisible suburbs!" rising from the asylum to declare everything "Holy! Holy! Holy!" The Beats had been baptized in rapid-fire free association, opposed to both a conformist mindset and the cold formalism of the New Critics.

The critical establishment, many mainstreamers, and some Old Leftists saw the big Beats as deviants: homosexuals, dropouts, drunkards, pill-takers. They could just as well be men of the planet, nonviolent cultural adventurers. "The root," Ginsberg says, "was a matter of extension of consciousness, or awareness or tolerance or generosity." Jack Kerouac was more pyrotechnic in his 1957 stream-of-consciousness, breakout *On the Road*. Beats, he said, were "the ones who are made to live . . . who

... burn, burn, burn like fabulous yellow roman candles exploding like spiders across the stars and in the middle you see the blue centerlight pop and everybody goes 'Awww!' " (The squares said "Nahhh"; *Newsweek* called Kerouac a "tin-eared Canuck.")

Kerouac eventually rejected the "Beat" label and directed equal wrath against the A-bomb and those who didn't respect their parents; Ginsberg embodied the culture-rebel's love-hate relationship with his homeland. "Go fuck yourself with your atom bomb," he wrote in his poem "America," before pleading, "when will you be angelic?" The division over the worth of political involvement prefigured the hippies to come. So did Beat hedonism, male-dominated groupings, and a simultaneously liberated, patronizing, and romanticized view of "spades."

The Beats formed counter-communities, several with magazines: *Beatitude* in San Francisco, *Big Table* in Chicago, and others. Their publications afforded another underground press precedent: Customs and San Francisco police seized *Howl* after its 1956 publication; *Big Table* came out of a censorship squabble at the University of Chicago. Facing authority and general apathy, these scattered efforts were generally short-lived. But they were united by what poet Gregory Corso called "a new art whose objectivity will be the accuracy of its introspection . . . the fury of subjective revolution."

"The hippies," Corso would say, "are acting out what the Beats wrote."

As the fifties became the sixties, poets and painters were fleeing rising Greenwich Village rents, occupying tenements next to Ukranians, Poles, Jews, and Puerto Ricans already living in uneasy détente. Tuli Kupferberg and Ed Sanders became leading bardic publishers in this East Village.

Kupferberg was born on the Lower East Side in 1923, ran away to Greenwich Village when he was eighteen, then drifted back to the old neighborhood. By the late 1950s, he was churning out small offset single-theme magazines. *Birth* ran an issue about Greenwich Village, then covered subjects from children to drugs. *Yeah* exhibited such "found art" as ads for penis enlargers. Silly, perhaps, but sex was still the forbidden fruit of American society, to be freed with everything from humor to avid participation. And Kupferberg was pioneering a go-for-it style of underground publishing. "Do it yourself," he'd say. "All you can do is make an ass of yourself and you will learn something that way too!"

Poets like Kupferberg, Ginsberg, Diane DiPrima, and Allan Katzman (who'd later edit the *East Village Other*) could be found at the Metro Coffee Shop, on Second Avenue and 9th Street, where the energy was as strong as the java. Over at Stanley's bar, on Avenue B and 12th Street, the same crew was joined by underground film-makers fresh from the Charles Theatre across the street, by civil rights activists, by writers Ishmael Reed (*Mumbo Jumbo* and *Yellow Back Radio Broke Down*) and William Burroughs (*Naked Lunch*). A bartender named Peter Boyle practiced a Frankenstein imitation he'd eventually use in a Mel Brooks movie.

Stanley's also was the ex-officio headquarters for Ed Sanders. Born in Missouri, Sanders had come to town to attend New York University, dreams of the space program in his head. "I thought I might go into orbit for the people," Sanders recalls. "Then I found out that there were two kinds of space cadets, and for one you didn't have to have a Ph.D."

Sanders hung out at the *Catholic Worker*, read *I.F. Stone's Weekly* and the *Monthly Review*, then gravitated to the funkier East Village. In February, 1962, the wild-eyed, Zapata-moustached poet began his soon-to-be-notorious *Fuck You: A Magazine of the Arts*. His motto: "I'll print anything."

The mimeo'd magazine was a testosterone-maddened attack on the state of the planet in general, and the Panty-Girdle fifties in particular. A running editorial extolled the precepts of the East Village poet-circle: "Pacifism, unilateral disarmament . . . non-violent resistance . . . multilateral indiscriminate aperture conjugation, anarchy, world federalism . . . the LSD communarium . . . DMT distortion . . . amyl nitrite sniffings . . . butt-fuckings and group-gropes." Poems by Sanders and others had a matching timbre. "It was a healthy thing, and women like Diane DiPrima and Lenore Kandel wrote for it," Sanders says. Both policemen and feminists would disagree.

"Kerouac's later swing to the right and the media's rap gave the Beat scene the image of cool," Sanders recalls. "But people like Gary Snyder and Allen Ginsberg are very political. Cool is for when you're in the coffin." As the Committee for Nonviolent Action (CNVA) and the Committee for a Sane Nuclear Policy (SANE) protested nuclear arms, Sanders did some literal boat-rocking by boarding a Polaris submarine. "No matter how much of a doper, a weirdo, a wild poet, a bard, a flipped-out student, a ne'er-do-well, a Bowery bum, a person, a banker or whatever," he recalls, "you could get a sense of righteous indignation and demand that they stop testing in the atmosphere—and then, some people would say, ban all weapons." When the United States, the Soviet Union, and Britain banned atmospheric nuclear testing in July, 1963, Sanders and others were heartened. Protest "was a way to be righteous, and I think it held a flag up until after Kennedy got assassinated and they immediately started the Vietnam War. It was believing that there were people willing to take certain kinds of risks."

By then, though, a more organized force had come into being. In 1960, Students for a Democratic Society had begun to grow out of the older, more traditionally Leftist League for Industrial Democracy. Two years later, fifty-three people, all under twenty-five, had left Port Huron, Michigan, with a vision of a New Left connecting everything from nuclear war to mass-produced boredom to something called "participatory democracy." "We are people of this generation," their Statement began, "bred in at least modest comfort, housed now in universities, looking uncomfortably to the world we inherit." That December, SDS had launched an *SDS Bulletin,* which would produce much information and more than a few underground-press writers.

Meanwhile, the East Village scene was high on mixed-media possibility. Kupferberg was the mentor of the Revolting Theatre, while Sanders had filmed *Mongolian Cluster Fuck,* which starred some now-famous New Yorkers who today may wish they weren't in it. Poets and artists danced at the Dom, an ethnic hall on Saint Marks Place, and before long Sanders, Kupferberg, and others were in a rock/protest/poetry/eccentric instrument band called the Fugs (named for Norman Mailer's *Naked and the Dead* euphemism for the sex act that was just daring to speak its name). Their repetoire included "Slum Goddess," "Kill for Peace," and other inspired doggerel.

"I was a trained poet," Sanders recalls. "You just barfed out rhymed quatrains like bagels out of a bagel machine." With spirit rushing in where talent might not have trod, the Fugs began a decade-long career. Sanders: "For a joke, the Fugs were OK."

Others were experimenting outside the culture capitals. Tom Robbins, later the author of *Even Cowgirls Get the Blues,* recalls working on a daily paper in Richmond, Virginia, in 1962—and moonlighting:

"I was associated with a *true* underground newspaper. It was called the *Ghost,* and, let me tell you, it wasn't sold on the streets, it just *appeared.* Those responsible for it could have gotten into real trouble. The *Ghost* was exciting, although it was a primitively published rag, radical and eccentric, with no real social force behind it. At that time, we were just inventing the sixties."

By the winter of 1964, though, Ed Sanders was on East 10th Street between Avenues B and C, where men were men and buildings were collapsing. There he turned a former kosher butchery into the Peace Eye

Bookstore, an outpost of adversary culture. Between publishing and getting busted for his work, Sanders noticed something new:

"I was amazed at the spew—I used 'spew' in a benign way—of publications arriving from every section of the country. Before the underground press, there were little political notices in publications like *Grist,* from Lawrence, Kansas.

"Then I began receiving the L.A. *Free Press.*"

THE
FAIRE FREE PRESS

OMENS, NEWS AND PORTENTS . PRESENT AND FUTURE   MAY 23, 1964   PRODUCED FOR THE KPFK.FM PLEASURE FAIRE AND MAY MARKET

DA VINCI'S FOLLY

Opening early this week at the Prima Vera Gallery, the Leonardo Da Vinci Retrospective. After viewing this exposition we feel the grievous truth is that it will mark the pitiful egress of one of the really grand old men of the art game. Excessive puttering in hairbrained gadgetry and Freudian psychology has finally addled our Maestro's faculties. Senility and licentiousness have taken him astray from beautiful Blessed Madonnas to his most recent subject, a cheap, calendar pin-up girl called Mona Lisa.

Last year at this time we sat back, though uneasily, and watched Leo's antics on the Monastery cafeteria mural job. When he put Christ and the Disciples all on one side of the table, we thought, "He's just innovating." When he used goat fat as a painting medium and within a week Christ and the Disciples were flaking away like so much plaster, we shrugged indulgently. All this we could accept as the folly of an old experimenter. But this latest caprice with the brazen Miss Lisa is more insult than we can digest.

Mona Lisa is such a common wench, common as a Rockwell, but more with a tart's look. Her smile leaves no question as to its suggestive prurience. Better Master Da Vinci had struck to Cupids and Virgins. Such a work as the Mona Lisa is pure sensationalism and no could never withstand the test of merciless time. Regrettably such a direction for Leonardo can only bring about his speedy ruination.

Dear Giotto must be rolling over in his grave to think that what he sparked by laboriously scratching a sheep on a rock, has come to this abortive end. We shudder at the emptiness of our generation.

Carmina Burano
CHARLES MONTGOMERY

Old Hell fire and Damnation Giselbertus is after me again. He's stressing portals with demons telling me that the world after is all festering corpses, worms, snakes, claws and teeth. Fat Pope says the Apocalypse will get me if I don't watch out. Which means lay off flesh, wine, and song or there'll be the Devil to pay.

But, you see, I love life. I'm a vagabond student. I travel seeking knowledge and rich, worldly pleasure. I'm poor but free, and Spring is my season. I've been called travelling from a hedonist to a beatnik. Anyway I'm bad, perhaps even mad.

As I journey from hamlet to hamlet, I meet everywhere with the same well meant advice, "find a healthy country wench, settle down to a home and family, join a few clubs and attend the Church of your choice. Start fearing God now and enjoying life less."

I say, "as for me, give me Lord Bacchus and Lady Venus." The tavern is my church, and there is a world of lovely loves to be taken.

But enough of epigrams. I shiver for the silly, Godfearing masses. I must tickle their ribs a bit and warm them with my pagan credo:

To my mind all gravity
  Is a grave subjection;
Sweeter far than honey are
  Jokes and free affection.
All that Venus bids me do,
  Do I with erection,
For she ne'er in heart of man
  Dwelt with dull dejection .
We young men our kingings ne'er
  Shall stern tax render,
Or preserve our fancies from
  Bodies smooth and tender .
O ye young men,
  With the May-bloom shake off sadness!
Love is luring you to join the
  Maidens gladness
Such my verse is wont to be
  As the wine I swallow;
No ripe thoughts enliven me
  While my stomach's hollow.

In The Public Weal
JOHN HAMMOND

Every ship returning from America bringeth increasing quantities of the Indian herb called "Tobacco" which in turn promote ever more widespread indulgence in this novelty. Yet withal the question doth arise, what are the uses of this plant, and further, are such uses beneficial, injurious, or indeed merely innocuous to the user?

One can see many sailors, and all those who come back from America, carrying little funnels made from a palm leaf or a reed, in the extreme end of which they insert the curled and crumbled leaves of this plant and then set fire to them for the pleasure of the aroma. Among the gentry and nobility the taking-in of smoke of this herb by an instrument formed like a little ladle (and called a pipe) whereby it passeth from the mouth into the head and stomach, is greatly taken-up and used in England. Some persons prefer to have their "Tobacco" in the French manner, whereby a pinch of the powdered leaves is inserted in each nostril and inhaled, which practice usually causeth some sneezing.

M. Jean Nicot, formerly the French Ambassador to Portugal, introduced this latter method to the Court of France when he persuaded Her Majesty, Catherine de Medici to try the powder thus, which trial after a sneeze, immediately alleviated Her headache and converted Her to its regular use.

Although the human body is not built to absorb smoke, yet this practice seemingly hath no immediate ill effects, aside from the beginners' occasional attacks of coughing, choking, sneezing, gasping, dizziness, and nausea. Once accustomed to it, however, smoking hath a most soothing effect on the whole body and mind. However, certainly it is that admixtures of flowers, grasses, paper, sweeteners, spices, and 'divers other more unmentionable items can only detract from whatever beneficial or pleasant effect the pure "Tobacco" may have. Yet since smoking hath become the rage many unscrupulous persons have attempted to foist such adulterations or indeed substitutions on an unsuspecting public. Beware of bargains offered in a quiet alley as being "just off the boat." Rather inquire of a regular smoker the whereabouts of a reliable purveyor and even then caveat emptor.

We have but lately received a communication from a reader at Sherwood Forest reporting that the lawyers in Nottingham are again attempting to cheat the public with bows of unseasoned wood. He further maketh bold to suggest that the Sheriff would do well to spend more time putting such frauds in gaol and less time gallivanting around the Greenwood.

We have purchased such a bow and find the complaint to be a true-bill but the bowyers are still safe. Previous complaints from others have likewise claimed that the Sheriff doth not impartially apply the law but rather doth allow his personal prejudice to decide who shall be victim to his law whether they be guilty of any fault or no.

Apparently the Sheriff doth feel that, having a Royal Commission, he therefore hath free rein to function in any way he choose. Let him remember that others of like mind have been forced to resign "for reasons of health." As Her Sovereign Majesty hath insisted, the basis of justice is impartiality, the basis of good government is the public weal.

MAGISTRATE DENOUNCETH FILTH

Self-styled poet, William Shakspur, was arraigned today at Magistrate's Court, First and Hill Street, on charges of disorderly conduct. Upon hearing Shakspur's occupation, Judge Horatio G. Falstaff told the young man to "Get a job."

Shakspur was rearrested after today's demonstration for peddling copies of his book, "Venus and Adonis," which has been termed obscene by Parliamentary Proclamation. At the second arraignment Judge Falstaff said, "I may not know Art but I know filth when I see it."

ENGLAND HATH BEEN SAVED
FROM SPANISH TYRANNY

Harwich, August 1, 1586: The greatest naval engagement of all time hath become a stern chase with the battered remnants of the once mighty Spanish Armada in desperate flight up the North Sea close pressed by our Fleet.

Under the able command of Admiral John Lord Howard and Vice-Admiral Sir Francis Drake we have suffered not the loss of a single vessel of our 150 and but few personnel casualties though the Spaniards under the Duke of Medina Sidonia have lost at least seven of the first line of their 130 ships and all the others are so beaten with great shot as to be scarcely seaworthy; a full fifth of their men being killed and disabled.

If the invasion had succeeded and England subject, France could not have stood alone, and after her the Germans and possibly even the Turks would have come into Spain's grasp. So imagine then: much of Europe, world would resemble we need but look to present day Spain itself.

The Spanish despot, blasphemously claiming to act in the name of Christianity, hath destroyed all freedom within his realm, knowing only how to administrate repression. The working people are cruelly used beyond their uttermost capacity to cater to his whims and they durst not complain. To achieve his ends he and his agents the world over lie, cheat, betray, connive, steal and murder at whim. Yet withal doth he lay claim to honor. Since he believeth himself to be divinely appointed to his odious tasks any question of his action he therefore not merely treason but also heresy and so is to be treated by the infernal arts of the Inquisition. Pity Spain!

Yet, withal, freedom-loving Spaniards, cruelly held down within this realm or having fled this persecution, are remembering the better days before his accession and are joining together to put down the tyrant. This time they shall not die in vain.

Such is our foe which we are pledged to upset and destroy, which act will not only be our victory but a victory for the freedom, decency, and self-respect of all mankind.

PURITAN AGITATION ROCKS LEEDS

Puritan agitation broke out in Leeds today. Rev William Penn, leader of the Middle Sex Christian Leadership Conference, was arrested for leading a sit-in demonstration at Leeds Cathedral. Mastiffs were set on the pickets who bore signs reading, "We shall not be removed," and "Bann the Long Bow."

Inspector R. Crumpkie of Scotland Yard identified the demonstrators as Spanish agents. The famous officer said, "You can always tell them by the way they wear their hair."

2

THE FIRST WAVE

OS ANGELES—MAY, 1964: On February 1, 1960, four black students from a North Carolina college "began the sixties" by insisting on service at a segregated lunch counter. A paroxysm of beatings, dog-bites, cattle-proddings, jailings, even murders followed—evidence of what black author James Baldwin would call "the vindictiveness of the guilty." Black Americans were literally dying to vote, and to eat.

On August 28, 1963, two hundred thousand demonstrators, black and white together, surrounded the reflecting pool between the Lincoln Memorial and the Washington Monument. There Martin Luther King, Jr., predicted that "one day on the red hills of Georgia, the sons of former slaves and the sons of former slave owners will be able to sit down together at the table of brotherhood." Fiery Black Muslim Malcolm X derided the "Farce on Washington."

By 1964, mass nonviolent action and the dictates of sheer justice were forcing Washington to mandate "One man, one vote" and switch to the poor's side in the War on Poverty. But a pungent stew was bubbling with rage and too-little, too-late. In 1963, Baldwin had published *The Fire Next Time.* In 1964, American cities began to burn.

President Kennedy inspired idealism with the Peace Corps, the Alliance for Progress, and civil rights advances. But he angered radicals by backing the disastrous invasion at Cuba's Bay of Pigs and playing

Russo-American roulette to keep Soviet missiles out of Cuba. Nineteen sixty-three saw a nuclear test-ban treaty—and Kennedy's death. Many mourned lost hope; Malcolm X—who himself would be assassinated in 1965—saw "chickens coming home to roost." By 1964, they'd landed.

The former colonies of England, France, Holland, and other countries were consolidating their independence or fighting for it. Frantz Fanon's *Wretched of the Earth* explained the psychology of this Third World liberation, while sociologist C. Wright Mills questioned imperial conduct. But late in 1961, U.S. combat troops arrived in Vietnam, and in 1963, South Vietnamese President Diem was murdered in a coup after U.S. pressure on his government. By 1964, North Vietnamese troops were coming south, and Johnson administration fears of Communism abroad and backlash at home were Americanizing a Vietnamese war.

Students were so numerous that they seemed to constitute a new social class. Activists had organized a Student Peace Union at the University of Chicago, a radical student government called SLATE at Berkeley. By 1964, "the forty-sixers"—the leading edge of the baby boom—were turning eighteen; twenty million others would do so between 1964 and 1970. Only a minority dissented, but "I Am a Student, Do Not Fold, Spindle or Mutilate" became a popular button on campuses.

Censorship was loosening: D.H. Lawrence's *Lady Chatterley's Lover* and John Cleland's *Fanny Hill* had been allowed into the country. Terry Southern's *Candy* (1958) and *The Magic Christian* (1959) had lampooned middle-class sex and greed. Joseph Heller's World War II novel *Catch-22* (1961) would become a touchstone for Vietnam, though in the heat of the war one SDS official would take Heller's protagonist to task for not assassinating his commanding officer. Rachel Carson's *Silent Spring* (1962) had protested environmental despoilation; Ken Kesey's *One Flew Over the Cuckoo's Nest* (1962) had pictured inmates saner than their keepers. Something called "the pill" was on sale, and in 1963 a woman named Betty Friedan had critiqued a less-than-egalitarian *Feminine Mystique*. William Burroughs took literature for a ride on the nova express.

By 1964, Harvard had dropped two professors named Timothy Leary and Richard Alpert (later Baba Ram Dass) for ballyhooing a potent drug called LSD. The Beatles were rocking America, in stereo. A generation gap appeared, and some on the young side began getting by mainly with the help of their friends.

———————————

By 1964, America was a dividing house. A radical politic and an adversary culture had grown. The offset method of printing, which made it possible to paste up typed copy in any pattern and use Pres-Type to fashion all kinds of headlines at a fraction of what letterpress printing cost, was readily available. The stage was set for somebody to make a paper stick to a physical community desiring news and views about itself. Which is what happened when Art Kunkin showed up at the gate to the Renaissance Pleasure Faire, a politely funky tribute to days gone by held just outside Los Angeles.

COATS OF ARMS hung over Lords and Ladies Macbeth, Romeos and Juliets, as they walked to and fro, quaffing Angeleno approximations of mead. With his glasses, wristwatch, and pointed beard, Kunkin looked more like Leon Trotsky at a masquerade party than Robin Hood. But as a metaphor, his outfit wasn't half bad. He didn't want to *rob* the rich, but he hoped that an American-style socialism might link up the freaky kids, artists, and blacks (a few were all three) who were trying to invent themselves on and off campuses, and in the South.

Yet for someone who knew his Marxism well enough to conduct study groups in it, Kunkin was embarking on something of a break with the past. "I was the only leading person of the old radical movement to go into the underground press movement," he claims, more or less correctly. "I wanted a paper that would draw together all the diverse elements in the community, and that would be not only political, but cultural as well. I had been hanging around the coffee houses and the poetry groups, the small theaters and so forth, so I knew there was a whole life there."

At the gathering, Kunkin walked back and forth, hawking copies of the *Faire Free Press*, an eight-page, black-and-white paper he'd put together with a few friends and the support of noncommercial radio station KPFK-FM, the event's sponsor. At first glance, the *Faire Free Press* was just a cool spoof. The outside pages had woodcut-style illustrations and cute stories about a "ban the crossbow" demonstration, the health hazards of a new drug from the colonies called tobacco, and Shakespeare being busted for obscenity.

Inside, though, the lead article dealt with a raid on a theater showing Kenneth Anger's *Scorpio Rising,* a sex-and-biker film that made *The Wild One* look like a documentary about tricycle-riding. Stories also covered Joan Baez's refusal to pay any Vietnam-bound taxes, the jazz world, and a Federal Communications Commission probe of KPFK. Cleverly, Kunkin also included a Los Angeles *Free Press* logo so he could turn the news inside out after the fair.

The hybrid paper sold only twelve hundred out of five thousand copies. But it was a real departure from the single-issue, theoretical, position-paper, or nationally focused approaches of previous publications. The *Free Press* was less a journal than a newspaper about the real political *and* cultural lives of the people who read it. "Some people say the underground press began with the socialist papers of the early 1900s," Underground Press Syndicate coordinator Tom Forcade would note several years later, "while others trace it either to the beatnik little magazines of the fifties or to the *Village Voice*. While it is certainly true that there are some similarities between these early efforts and the current underground press, the latter is a separate and unique phenomenon with a history of its own. That history began with the founding of the Los Angeles *Free Press* in 1964."

Unlike many of those who would follow him, Kunkin had radical roots to both grow on and transcend. Born in New York in 1928, he'd attended the brilliant-nerdy Bronx High School of Science and Greenwich Village's progressive New School for Social Research. World War II's anti-Semitic genocide had led him to radical Zionism, then away from it when his call for a binational Arab-Jewish Palestine disturbed most of his colleagues.

Bouncing around an internecine Left, Kunkin had served as business manager of the *Militant,* the paper of the Trotskyist Socialist Workers Party, and had worked on both *Correspondence* and *News and Letters,* national Left publications with reader-written inserts. By the sixties, though, he was drifting toward settling down. He had his study group, and a socialist-oriented radio show on KPFK, but mostly he was a tool-and-die maker studying to be a history professor.

Then a group of Mexican-American radicals had approached him about working on their paper, the *East L.A. Almanac.* "For the first time in my life, I was writing about garbage collection and all kinds of community problems," he recalls. But after Kunkin, as political editor, chastised President Johnson for ignoring minority issues during a visit to Los Angeles, both he and his bosses at the plant had been visited by FBI agents. In January, 1964, Kunkin found himself out of a job. His former employers, he says, weren't superpatriots, but rather ex-Leftists who dreaded McCarthyism redux.

"I really got pissed," he recalls. "This was the long arm of Washington reaching out to get involved with a paper that had a five thousand circulation. I thought, 'What the hell is going on? What am I doing anyway? I've got to do something!'"

Enter the God of Synchronicity, for the first of its many encounters with the underground press: the FBI had sparked the papers it would later try to extinguish.

Living on unemployment insurance, Kunkin put all his energy into developing what would become the *Free Press.* Despite his Marxist background, he diverged from the precepts advanced by Lenin and other Russian exiles in *Iskra*— the *Spark:* that a (pre)revolutionary paper "combats spontaneity" and *"raises* this movement *to the level of* 'its program.' "

By 1964, Kunkin opposed a top-down model and thought that because labor was so important, the American working class was "locked up." He wanted "a primarily reader-written paper where, when people expressed their opinions, there would be a dialogue with them, and finally the emergence of a program (and party) from what students and so forth were talking about."

And Kunkin set another precedent for most of the papers to come: prior to publishing the *Free Press,* he'd never read the *Masses, Appeal to Reason,* or the other American socialist predecessors.

Most of Kunkin's traditional Left friends shook their heads over Kunkin's new-found "bohemianism." Hipper people also had their doubts. John Bryan, the ex-mainstream reporter whose lusty but sporadic San Francisco *Renaissance* and *Notes from the Underground* had preceded the *Free Press,* would be Kunkin's managing editor between stints at his own *Open City.* His verdict: "a disappointed Trotskyist factory organizer." Kunkin's *Free Press* would be more focused than many of the underground papers that followed it—and less experimental.

Shrugging off criticism, Kunkin saw something that sparked his interest—a single issue of the *Voice.* "I liked the investigative articles, their length, the mixture of culture and community. The *Voice* in a certain sense was the model for the *Free Press.* " Here too, though, he had a cavil: "I had a sharp critique of their relationship to the Democratic Party. The *Voice* developed as the left wing of the Democratic Party, fighting Tammany Hall. They were liberals in that sense, and my whole history in the radical movement had been against alliances with the Democratic Party."

KUNKIN and those who'd follow him also had a basic disagreement with the nature of mainstream journalism.

Professional journalists took on opponents without fear or favor, punched out bad guys, had gone toe-to-toe with Joe McCarthy. Accuracy, fairness, rebuttal augmented their skills. So did "objectivity"—not injecting personal beliefs into stories—as a counter to yellow journalism and other sucker punches. But by establishing the newspaper's underlying values as somehow neutral, objectivity could hit below the belt. Over the years, to cite just a few examples, racism, male-only voting, and no social security had all been defined as objectively true.

Liberal or conservative, American dailies shared what Jack Newfield, then an early SDS supporter, now with the *Village Voice,* called a "rhetoric of objectivity . . . belief in welfare capitalism, God, the West, Puritanism, the Law, the family, property, the two-party system, and perhaps most crucially, in the notion that violence is only defensible when employed by the State." These values, press critic Herbert Gans would later add, projected "the social order of public, business and professional, upper-middle-class, middle-aged and white male sectors of society." Unpopular or unpalatable views usually were ignored or filtered through this belief system.

Objectivity in the midfifties, White House reporter James Deakin would recall, "meant that major governmental news consisted largely of what the government said it was." By 1965, things hadn't changed much. "When I started as a reporter on the San Francisco *Chronicle,* I was on the police beat," Adam Hochschild, later a cofounder of *Mother Jones* magazine, recalls. "I went into the press room at the police station and an older reporter took me to a map and drew his finger around the far upper-right-hand corner—up by Telegraph Hill—and said, 'Sonny, anything in there that happens is news. The rest of the city, unless it's really good—meaning like a double murder or something—forget it.'

"You learn very quickly that when something happens—confrontation, demonstrations, arrest—you head over to the cops. So when something happens in the Mediterranean, you go to the State Department or the Defense Department." Reporters in Vietnam had to keep jabbing to get past the briefings known as "The Five O'Clock Follies." Some didn't try; anywhere from fifty to four hundred American journalists would cooperate with the CIA from World War II until the late seventies, at least.

Many talented crusaders fought for reform, but mainstream journalism rarely battled for fundamental change. "The news consumer is encouraged to sympathize or to rejoice, but not to organize politically," press analyst Gaye Tuchman would write. "News presentations soothe the news consumer even as they reify social forces." Movement goals could be derided in the very language of "victories" versus "defeats," "surrender" versus "liberation," protest "marring" rather than "curing." "They smeared it, they psychoanalyzed it, they exaggerated it," Jack Newfield wrote about the verbal beating SDS took just after its midsixties founding, before things got *really* heavy. "They cartooned it, they made it look like a mélange of beatniks, potheads, and agents of international Communism; they did everything but explain the failures in the society that called it into being."

As the United States' foremost agenda-setting newspaper, and the one that many East Coast radicals had grown up reading, the New York *Times* would be seen as a formidable opponent. The *Times* was the first mass paper to give Students for a Democratic Society major (and somewhat sympathetic) coverage. But, as Todd Gitlin, a former SDS president and underground-press writer turned media critic, has shown, the *Times*'s reporting experienced *a priori* limits when SDS organized the New Left's first major antiwar march on Washington on April 17, 1965.

The march protested American involvement in Vietnam—including the arrival of ground troops the month before. But the *Times*'s next-day lead story stressed personalities, sandals, and beards, not the organization's difficult decision to identify active opposition to the war as a burning moral issue even if it meant dividing its resources and being Red-baited. The *Times*'s story suggested that SDS was confused over how to end the war—even though readily available position papers called for withdrawal. Accompanying pictures balanced fifteen thousand antiwar demonstrators with one hundred prowar ones, and conveyed the message of extremes having little to do with centrist values.

In contrast, the pre-underground *National Guardian* ran two long stories that accepted SDS as a legitimate political organization and excerpted activists' speeches and position papers. "It would be *de rigueur* to observe that the *Guardian* coverage was ideological," Gitlin later noted. "The *Times*'s coverage was no less so."

Writers, and readers, were choosing up sides. Yet the underground press would face its own trials as it tried to merge reporting and radicalism.

In 1964, the *Free Press*'s survival was shaky. Among other things, nearly everyone connected with the *Faire Free Press* had headed back to school. But a small staff willing to work more for love than for money came on, and readers provided many of the articles. Some eclectic socialists gave Kunkin $700. An owner provided office space in a coffeehouse featuring the urban folk music of the day. Arty types liked the listings and reviews; Left friends wrote, pitched in. Despite doubts, science-fiction writer Harlan Ellison and Larry Lipton, whose *Holy Barbarians* had been a major book on the Beats, became columnists. "I'll help," Kunkin remembers Lipton saying. "But I don't think you'll make it."

Early on, Kunkin bounced a check to the printer. Desperate for $500, he heard that Steve Allen was a reader, and offered him part of the paper to keep it afloat. A day before deadline, a messenger arrived with "prepayment for advertising." When Allen later advertised one of his books, Kunkin called attention to it with a front-page teaser: "Why Does Steve Allen Wear Glasses?"

The paper was eclectic enough for the staff to endorse Lyndon Johnson over Barry Goldwater in the 1964 presidential election even as Kunkin called for someone further left. Then, in August of 1965, the *Free Press* broke through. The reason was Watts.

During 1964 and 1965, the civil rights movement had won major victories in its battle to overturn the legal subjugation of American blacks. Lyndon Johnson, a Southern President, had banned discrimination in voting, jobs, public accommodations. But at that creaking rate of change, America's schools would be desegregated in 2054, and black unemployment was far higher than white.

An Omnibus Civil Rights Bill became law in July, 1964, but at the Democratic Convention in August, Johnson and other leaders refused to unseat the segregated Mississippi delegation. That same month, the bodies of three missing civil rights workers were found. That two of them were white helped fuel near-national outrage.

The movement for racial justice had been incredibly restrained. But several cities in both North and South began experiencing violent up-heavals—often a result of police force. On August 11, 1965, five days after President Johnson signed the Voting Rights Act, Los Angeles became a city on fire.

At first, the arrest of a young black driver in the Watts section of town had been peaceful. Then fast-spreading rumors and decades of racism pitted teenagers screaming "burn, baby, burn" against cops wielding "nig-ger-knocker" nightsticks and service revolvers. Stores were ransacked. Black teenagers and police beat guilty and innocent alike. The night sky turned black and orange from smoke, red from flashing police-car lights. The statistics grew: sixteen hundred police, fourteen thousand National Guardsmen; four thousand arrests; thirty-four dead.

The driver had failed a sobriety test, and by prevailing standards, Watts was a criminal riot, which is how the Los Angeles *Times* covered it. "Even by inference," the paper editorialized on August 17, "none should condone the criminal terrorism, or dismiss it as the inevitable result of economic and sociological pressures."

But in its August 20 issue, the first of several dealing with events in Watts, the *Free Press* addressed exactly those pressures. "The Negroes Have Voted!" was the headline over Kunkin's lengthy "post-election analysis." Kunkin stopped short of celebrating any "festival of the op-pressed," as H. Rap Brown would do the next year in Watts by saying that "Violence is as American as the Fourth of July and cherry pie." But though Kunkin deemed the riot "genuinely unfortunate," he blamed the authorities for inaction, and saw the restoration of "the pre-demonstration status quo" as "fundamentally anti-Negro." Instead, he called for a public forum to air complaints, representation of the poor on antipoverty programs, curbs on local bail-bondsmen, and the use of black contractors to rebuild the damage.

Other *Free Press* pieces offered a black perspective largely absent in the mainstream press. A leader of CORE (Congress of Racial Equality) provided a crowd's-eye view of blacks fighting police who called them "niggers." An attorney decried a leadership vacuum in both City Hall and Watts, pointing out that the repeal of a fair-housing ordinance had been "a new fracture in race relations."

"I did a lot of work with CORE," Kunkin recalls. "I built up personal capital in the black community, so as soon as Watts happened there were people there writing for the paper."

Like the mainstream, the *Free Press* didn't do much quoting of those it criticized. Nor did Kunkin's paper overtly criticize violence against innocent whites. But a police sergeant was praised for "great restraint," while some black leaders were scored for ineptitude and corruption. In the main, Kunkin saw the *Free Press* as using its limited resources to set a skewed mass-media record straight.

And the coverage made its mark. When *Time* magazine first noted the underground press in 1966, it recalled the *Freep*'s Watts package as "a commendable series of sociological studies." And by 1967, the National Advisory Commission on Civil Disorders—the Kerner Commission—would be using terms similar to Kunkin's to explain the fires this time.

"*NOTHING* much happened until the fall of '64," Art Kunkin recalls. "That's when the Free Speech Movement began. If I had started then, it would have been easier. But if I had started six months before I did, I might not have survived."

"FSM" would energize students across the country, make Berkeley a protest capital—and spark the Berkeley *Barb*.

"The employers will love this generation," University of California President Clark Kerr said in 1959. "They aren't going to press many grievances. . . . There aren't going to be any riots." To put it mildly, Kerr's crystal ball was cracked. The number of U.S. students would double between 1960 and 1966, and some would seek Left-oriented change. In 1960, students from the Berkeley campus protested capital punishment at San Quentin, and were hosed at House UnAmerican Activities Committee hearings in San Francisco. In 1961, they began going South for civil rights; in 1963, they were among more than seven hundred fifty arrested during an anti-racist-hiring protest at a San Francisco hotel. By fall, 1964, Berkeley had its veteran demonstrators.

The nearly four-month Free Speech struggle began over whether or not students could raise money for causes on campus. Despite pressure from school officials and conservatives about town, students and others refused to obey a regulation that defined conduct on *their* campus and cut them off from the key political battle of their time.

Events quickened when students surrounded a squad car containing an arrested dropout-activist named Jack Weinberg, who'd been soliciting funds for CORE. Weinberg later would provide a slogan for the times: "Don't trust anybody over thirty!"

A twenty-two-year-old senior philosophy major named Mario Savio, who'd spent a summer in Mississippi and headed the Berkeley chapter of Campus Friends of SNCC, emerged as a spokesman for the protest, linking the struggle against tyranny in the South with the multiversity's conformist molding. "There's a time when the operation of the machine becomes so odious, it makes you so sick at heart," Savio said in a gripping post-Thanksgiving speech, "that . . . you've got to put your bodies upon the gears and upon the wheels . . . and you've got to make it stop. And you've got to indicate to the people who run it, to the people who own it, that unless you're free, the machine will be prevented from working at all." Again, these were not words of class struggle, but of alienation from relative privilege in search of some amorphous community that now seemed palpable on the campus.

Through the fall, students occupied parts of the university, taught their own curricula, literally changed their minds. Seven hundred seventy-three demonstrators were arrested; fines and jail sentences would follow. But the students had won the right to political activity, and mug shots became more of a credential than a stigma within political groups, or at communes, bars, and coffeehouses. Strains of protest had been linked. "It is virtually certain, in fact, that, but for the civil rights movement, there would not have been a Berkeley uprising, or a white student movement at all," writes historian Milton Viorst in *Fire in the Streets*. Some activists wanted to turn such ties into an entire worldview. "The very first mission of the American radical is to escape," activist Frank Bardacke would recall in 1966. "The radical must present a counter-vision, he must create new values."

Max Scherr had also attended Berkeley—earning a master's degree in sociology in 1949, a decade and a half before the current crop of radicals. He was nearly fifty now, and had been a lawyer, a union organizer, a civil rights activist, an expatriate (Mexico), and (putting his sociology degree to work) the owner of the Steppenwolf bar on San Pablo Avenue. He'd been on the Left, though less into organizations than Arthur Kunkin. Like Kunkin, though, he'd been thinking of leaving politics behind, possibly for a trip around the world with his "old lady," Jane Peters—until they found a big, colonnaded house on Oregon Street, and decided to stay in town.

Meanwhile, the war intensified. As July became August, South Vietnamese patrol boats launched the latest in a series of raids on territory in the North. Soon after, an intelligence-gathering American destroyer operating in the Tonkin Gulf came under fire. An alleged attack on a second destroyer was unsubstantiated, and even the first was questioned, but President Johnson preempted the hawkish rhetoric of Republican candidate Barry Goldwater by announcing the bombing of a Northern oil port on national television. Congress overwhelmingly endorsed an escalatory "Gulf of Tonkin Resolution," and mass media reported the attacks as fact. No war was declared, but during 1965 U.S. troop strength would rise from 23,000 to 184,000, in part through increased draft calls.

In response, antiwar sentiment increased on the home front. In March, 1965, prowar and antiwar spokesmen addressed students at the first "teach-in," held at the University of Michigan. In Berkeley, a massive teach-in led to the formation of a Vietnam Day Committee whose ranks included an activist named Jerry Rubin. That July, *Ramparts,* the Bay Area Catholic reform magazine turned radical muckraker, turned the spotlight on a prowar lobby of American businessmen, clerics, and politicians.

Out from behind the bar, Max Scherr was impressed by the changes in Berkeley and beyond. But he missed a counterweight to both the boosterish Berkeley *Gazette* and the Oakland *Tribune,* a conservative powerhouse that had helped spark the Free Speech flap by editorializing against on-campus solicitations after students had protested the *Tribune*'s opposition to a fair-housing law. The Free Speech era had produced little magazines such as *Spider, Wooden Shoe,* and *Root and Branch,* and John Bryan, the former San Francisco *Examiner* reporter who would later work with Art Kunkin, had published *Open City Press,* the second community-based underground paper, over the winter of 1964–65. But now the magazines were gone, and Bryan had exhausted his $700 severance pay.

The Berkeley food co-op was supposed to publish a progressive newspaper. But when the *Citizen* didn't appear on August 2, Scherr found himself in an argument at the Med, the coffeehouse hub of Telegraph Avenue.

"You don't have to get $43,000," he said about producing a paper.

If it's so easy, one of the Med's resident cynics answered, why don't you do it?

"OK," the bald, bearded, bespectacled Scherr yelled. "I'll have a paper out by next week!"—or, he later told Peters, "I'll be the laughingstock of Berkeley." But one of Scherr's favorite books was *Don Quixote,* with its impossible dream. And so, on Friday, August 13, 1965, the first *Barb* appeared, its logo featuring a skeletal knight riding a bony horse toward mythic adventure, lance (its tip was the campus bell tower) at full tilt.

If the *Free Press* was Kunkin-earnest, the *Barb* was Scherr-cantankerous. Scherr had thought about calling it the Berkeley *Bias* (as well as, God help us, the *Pinch Penny Prickler*). "I am not seeking the understanding of my readers," he'd say. "I want my readers to feel it."

The first *Barb* looked as if its eight pages had been dragged through an inkwell. Scherr would call it "pitiful," and his debut editorial was almost deferential. "This paper has no pretensions to greatness. It can't afford a professional staff or any news wire. It will not try to go much beyond the black and white borders of Berkeley. And yet," he wrote, "if we do our job well, we hope even to nettle that amorphous but thick-headed establishment that so often nettles us—and to spur into action some of our very own."

Despite its tentativeness, the first *Barb* reflected what would become Scherr's credo: "I'm into all the little movements that are divergent from the mainstream of the culture." In that first issue, a young writer named Marvin Garson began an important underground press stint with a sympathetic story about six sentenced FSM defendants—while a review elsewhere in the paper came out against "romanticizing" the New Left. The Student Union had its own page—"The Free Student." Shortcomings in Berkeley's poverty and Head Start programs were detailed, as were co-op politics and a meeting of the Deacons, a black group whose North Carolina chapter had used guns to fend off marauding Ku Klux Klansmen. Controversial black playwright LeRoi Jones's play *The Dutchman* and the movie *The Umbrellas of Cherbourg* were reviewed. There were ads from coffeehouses and bookstores, and relatively tame personals.

But the main stories had to do with the war—more precisely, the antiwar. On August 12, activists had tried to stop troop trains bearing human cargo through Berkeley toward Vietnam. The next day, the *Barb* told their story.

Dailies waved the flag; the *Barb* denounced "a day of brutality in Berkeley." Demonstrators who believed that an odious war legitimized civil disobedience reported on beatings they and others had experienced. The Berkeley City Council suffered from "guilt by inaction, a subtle form of brutality now central to American life." Nobody from the other side was offered rebuttal; the established papers were criticized for blowing the story. "It was big news," an ex-railroad worker named Bob Randolph wrote, "yet the commercial press ignored the most revealing part of the story—the crudely lettered signs in the windows of one of the trains, put there by some of the troops onboard." Randolph acknowledged that messages like "I don't want to go" and "Keep up the good work, we're with you" had been matched by prowar remarks. But unexpected signs of dissent were taken as a victory.

Scherr had kept his word; now he had to keep the *Barb* afloat. He hit the streets in search of dimes, connections, story ideas, selling twelve hundred issues of a two-thousand-copy press run. One of the people he bumped into was activist Stew Albert, who would write for the *Barb,* only to later oppose Scherr's very ownership of it. "The paper looked a lot like Max—poorly laid out, but very tough," he'd say. Michael Rossman, a Free Speech Movement veteran and chronicler of Berkeley politics, saw a swan in Scherr's ugly duckling; its interrelated radicalism and stories about the new lifestyles were simply "stupendous."

The *Free Press*'s Art Kunkin may have been more active in traditional Left parties, but the *Barb* was closer to the amalgam of civil rights, antiwar, and New Left activities that collectively were being called "the Movement." Members of sectarian political parties didn't like Scherr's italic story lead-ins distancing the *Barb* from "the views expressed below," but got to see their pieces in print. Other radicals crowed about how easy an editorial gatekeeper Scherr really was. "The *Barb* was my little tool," Jerry Rubin recalls. "In 1965–66, at five o'clock on Friday, twenty thousand potential marchers bought their *Barb.* The question of how effective I was as an organizer was to have a story on page one that would make each of those people say to themselves, 'I'm going back to march next week.' You just had to get Max to get a little turned-up, whimsical, adventurous smile on his face and make news in his eyes."

The *Barb* was both grittier and funkier than the *Freep.* Rallies, the Sexual Freedom League, Berkeley life, the emerging Haight-Ashbury community across the Bay, increasingly sexual personals—all set Scherr's eyes a-twinkling, sometimes to the point of overcoverage. The front rooms of Scherr's funky old house became an around-the-clock workplace carpeted with mail sacks and layout sheets. Writers and artists from the campus or the community and companion Jane Peters worked away; presiding over it all was Scherr, often dressed in pajamas and slippers. "The Hefner of the underground," *Esquire* would call him. Around Berkeley, he became "Max."

"The community was encouraged to act by seeing that it had done something of substance," he'd tell underground press historian Laurence Leamer. "That's what a newspaper does. It gives a person a chance to see what he has done, to see how it looks to other people."

IN NEW YORK, a cluster of galleries, experimental theaters, and hangouts was expanding among the tenements between Third Avenue and the East River, 14th and Houston Streets. The scene, the low rents, and the good times, were drawing creative and casual residents alike. There were new problems to deal with: ripoffs, landlords who thought hot water was a luxury, city agencies that rousted artists out of illegal loft spaces.

Walter Bowart hadn't come to New York to put out a paper. At Oklahoma University, he'd been a journalism major more interested in painting, and in the poets and modern artists who drifted through. "Suddenly, I realized there were other people like me," he recalls.

After literally flipping a coin to see which coast he'd head for, the nineteen-year-old Bowart became an artist in a drab neighborhood later known as SoHo. But his career stalled. Perhaps it was talent; he thought it was something else. "I had two strikes against me as a painter: I wasn't Jewish, and I wasn't a homosexual. It was really hard to open doors when you were from Oklahoma and had straw behind your ears."

Nor was Bowart happy with the *Village Voice.* "If Mailer had stayed, it might have been what I wanted. But it was a straight old safe Democratic paper, what you get when a businessman and a psychiatrist go into journalism." Bowart tried to drum up interest in a new paper—first by placing an ad, ironically, in the *Voice,* then while working behind the bar at Stanley's, the East Village art and jazz hangout. In October, 1965, using a New York newspaper strike and $500 he'd saved from bartending, he started the *East Village Other.*

The first issue's editorial spoke of mirroring the opinions of the East Village's "new citizenry" and called for such prudent neighborhood reforms as "rent control, slumlord routing, better business, and safer streets." Yet the monthly's eight debut pages formed a larger surface when opened onto each other, and a headline ran around the edges of page one. The *Free Press* had used the *Voice* as a model; Bowart, heavily influenced by the megatrend media writing of Marshall McLuhan, "thought of a newspaper as a television set."

EVO certainly wasn't the *Voice*. Its articles were less about Tammany Hall than Alpha Centauri, and energetic images sometimes resembled test patterns more than programs. But most of the five thousand debut *EVO*s eventually sold even though the first issue cost a quarter to the *Voice*'s dime (giving pretty "newsgirls" the bar routes helped). Ishmael Reed, the writer who'd put black folk experience through a hip filter, encouraged local literati to get involved, among them Allan Katzman, a balding, Brooklyn-born philosophy major turned poet who would be the only *EVO*ite to work from beginning to end. Journalism, Katzman thought, was "a dead form. Because we didn't know anything about journalism, we had a big advantage."

John Wilcock, a veteran of the London *Daily Mail*, the New York *Times*, and the *Village Voice*, was *EVO*'s news editor—until Bowart nixed a writer's story on the Andy Warhol film *Chelsea Girls*. Wilcock saw some merit in its coverage, but Bowart explained: "I didn't dig the art, I don't dig taking so many drugs that you get all messed up. The crowd around Warhol was that way. The blatant displays of homosexuality were not pleasing to me." When the editorial smoke cleared, Wilcock left to freelance his "Other Scenes" column, which in March, 1968, emerged as a full-scale paper about the international underground scene.

EVO was the first underground paper to be more Groucho Marx than Karl. "I was lumped in with the New Left," Bowart recalls. "But I was probably a Libertarian, even though I didn't know the word." The paper mixed art happenings with drug reports and pictures of LBJ as Hitler. The staff talked about moral crimes or ruthless carnage in Vietnam rather than "imperialism." There were early manifestations of what would become an underground-press trademark: zesty, raunchy comix. And at a time when movie ads in daily newspapers literally had bras retouched and their titles modified to *S— and the Single Girl*, *EVO* featured a soft-core Slum Goddess and *those* personals: "TALL, dark, handsome, 33-year-old white executive wishes to meet with attractive female swinger for cocktails, luncheon and . . ."; "HOUSEBOY Roommate Slave wanted by dominant male of 32."

EVO validated popular culture and mixed media. It covered area happenings while confronting the art establishment. Museums were boneyards, it said, gallery-owners and professional critics a ruling class. The paper also sought an aesthetic for living. "In a world controlled by man for his own joy the difference between art & object disappears," Tuli Kupferberg, the poet-Fug, wrote in one issue. "Life becomes the work. The true work of art is the infinite body of man moving in harmony thru the incredible changes of his particular existence. When the body sings, the world dances."

IN ARTICLES about drugs, seemingly endless profiles of Timothy Leary, and graphics that strove to be *n*-dimensional, *EVO* also expressed the sheer amount of LSD being consumed on the Lower East Side.

LSD had its coming-out party in Basel, Switzerland, in April, 1943, when Albert Hofmann, a researcher for the Sandoz pharmaceutical house, accidentally absorbed a minute amount of a derivative of ergot, a rye fungus. This LSD-25 (lysergic acid diethylamide) transformed the senses of time, geometry, energy, ego, and possibility in ways that could range from profound to paranoiac, depending on chemical purity, the setting for taking it, and the gray matter encountering it. Even its creator was of two minds about it. "The joy of having fathered LSD," Hofmann would write in his memoirs, "was tarnished after more than ten years of uninterrupted scientific research and medicinal use when LSD was swept up in the huge wave of inebriant mania that began to spread over the Western world, above all the United States."

But, Hofmann added, this rapid rise in drug use "had deep-seated sociological causes: materialism, alienation from nature through industrialization and increasing urbanization . . . ennui and purposelessness in a wealthy, saturated society, and lack of a religious, nurturing and meaningful foundation of life. . . . These are the same factors that have led to the origin and growth of the hippie movement that developed simultaneously with the LSD wave. The two cannot be dissociated."

Bowart himself would spend forty days in a "really holy state" that at least one colleague would see as hellish. Nevertheless, many people found LSD a way to sense commonality with others and to encounter seemingly primal images, or even a spiritual oneness. The drug could lend cosmic significance to one of M.C. Escher's Moebius-like graphics or to a song from the new Country Joe and the Fish album. Sex could be transcendent, or extremely silly. It was not a good chemical to consume forty-five minutes before work.

LSD would be criminalized during 1966, but remain so accessible that posters and tickets for rock concerts bore the swirling, flowing images and lettering that stoned people fancied. *EVO*'s copy came to be reversed, shaped into Indian mandalas or nuclear mushroom clouds, backed with half-tone screens whose dot size could be altered until an ordinary illustration resembled a Roy Lichtenstein painting. "There were a lot of visions during those days," Bowart would recall. "There isn't that kind of LSD anymore. It was like E.T., like the whole thing was being directed from an extra dimension. Anything you desired seemed to manifest itself." Other papers would be accused of receiving money from Hanoi;

EVO was more in touch with something it called "the Intergalactic World Brain."

Tim Leary, the renegade Harvard professor who mixed equal doses of the *Tibetan Book of the Dead* and the Blarney Stone, became an *EVO* columnist, urging one and all to "turn on, tune in, drop out." By October, 1966, when the paper was selling fifteen thousand copies on the newsstand each issue, *EVO* had gone beyond not trusting people over thirty to describing the longhairs who were the paper's core audience as representatives of some qualitatively new generation. "Young men and young women seek a voice all their own, for they have a new vision that perhaps older men do not quite understand," one piece said. "Their heroes are not generals, but peace-makers. Their gods are not George Pattons, but Mahatma Gandhis."

Allan Katzman, then: "In this age, we have gone beyond nationalism. The world has gotten so small that the only way to survive is on an international basis. A man can't run away anymore. The nuclear umbrella stretches from one point of the earth to any other. What do I propose to do about it? I propose to put out a newspaper."

During 1965, Bob Dylan, the Beatles, and the Rolling Stones consolidated their hold on young America. Liberals and radicals argued over whether the war was a mistake or was part of the same sickness that had murdered Freedom Riders and overthrown a democratic government in the Dominican Republic. In October, while *Time* trumpeted "The Turning Point in Vietnam," more than a hundred thousand people demonstrated against the war in forty cities (the *Barb*'s headline was "VDC Shatters War 'Consensus,' Greatest Antiwar Protest Ever"). The first draft card was burned; a Quaker immolated himself in front of the Pentagon to protest the war. In November, the American death toll in Vietnam broke one thousand; no real count existed for Vietnamese dead.

In November, it also became possible for people in Detroit to read all about this in the *Fifth Estate,* a self-proclaimed alternative to the mass-press "fourth estate." Its first issue read like an early *Free Press*—which wasn't surprising, since founder Harvey Ovshinsky had worked there for a summer. Its antiwar news was a reprint of a New York *Times* story, and coverage of a local Dylan concert eulogized Folkie Bob instead of hailing Bob the Rocker. Still, that first *Fifth* contained items on marches, the FBI, and the CIA not found in the local dailies. It linked politics and lifestyle, and, hey, what did you want from an eighteen-year-old publisher?

The next month, Michigan got its second paper. Like the *Fifth Estate,* East Lansing's *Paper* also was generated by a young publisher, a twenty-one-year-old Michigan State University Merit Scholar named Michael Kindman. The *Paper* was more campus-oriented than the *Barb*, "an independent alternative to the 'established' news" and to "the bureaucratic minds" running the nation's universities.

These two papers provided and made news to and within their communities. But they resembled what had come before. It was back in California where the last—and furthest-out—of the first-wave papers would make a colorful splash.

South of Golden Gate Park, the Haight-Ashbury area had housed working-class whites (some of them 1930s radicals), poorer blacks, and San Francisco State students in reasonably priced gingerbread Victorian houses. By 1966, they'd been joined by refugees from the waning North Beach Beat scene and an East Bay activism that had helped backlash Ronald Reagan into the State House. The Haight was becoming the epicenter for an emerging Bay Area hip scene, for a new music network stretching from Santa Cruz to Marin County—and for acidheads seeking spirituality, community, and fun.

In late 1965 and early 1966, Ken Kesey, whose *One Flew Over the Cuckoo's Next* had arisen out of some legal experimental trips, led other pranksters in combining LSD, rock, and lightshows into popular Acid Tests and Trips Festivals featuring the Grateful Dead and Big Brother (with a full-tilt "chick singer" named Janis Joplin). As the federal government moved to regulate LSD use, underground chemists pumped out literally millions of doses of acid. Haight, Waller, Masonic—the Haight's yellow brick roads filled with kids and other maturity rebels in search of Oz, meaning, and a haven from what a hit song was calling "The Eve of Destruction." There were instant Indian braves, shamans, Cinderellas, Als and Alices in Wonderland, self-actualized people and parasites. Some were hanging out in a longhaired Fort Lauderdale; others wanted to build a new communal society within the collapsing shell of the old. The community paper that evolved in the Haight came from the unlikeliest of sources. The Maoist-oriented Progressive Labor Party had been among the first groups to oppose the war—and one of the most rigid organizations on the Left. But the Haight had a potential audience of Berkeley expatriates and San Francisco State students, so in the summer of 1966, PLers and others published the first issue of *P.O. Frisco*. It was also the last.

Haight-Ashbury belief systems clashed immediately. The paper's very name was a compromise version of "Psychedelic Oracle," the choice of the local hippies involved in the project. For them, letters from antiwar GIs and stories about possibly using the camps that had held Japanese-

Americans during World War II to intern sixties radicals were just "bad vibes." The paper died—until a group of poets and artists tried again three months later as the San Francisco *Oracle,* with more success.

During its twelve-issue incarnation, the *Oracle*'s collection of artists, poets, and neighborhood gurus would compare their psychedelic swirls, multi-colored graphics, and images of East and American Indians to medieval illuminated manuscripts or the *Tibetan Book of the Dead.* Ethel Romm, a more mainstream reporter, wrote in *Editor & Publisher* that the *Oracle* and similar papers "make a standard newspaper look, to me at least, about as exciting as the telephone white pages." Seen today, the graphics are about as current as cave paintings—and as accurate a manifestation of folk art, in a style that might be called Neo-American Psychedelic. Poet turned managing editor Allen Cohen: "The *Oracle* was designed to aid people on their trips."

From the start, the *Oracle* tried to define a different kind of activism. A "Declaration of Independence" called for "freedom of the body, the pursuit of joy and the expansion of consciousness." *Oracles* brought commune-busting police flowers and flutes instead of bricks. Poet Gary Snyder wrote about his search for a socially responsible Buddhism.

The *Oracle* also was organized differently than the other papers. Hip capitalists Ron and Jay Thelin of the pipes-and-papers Psychedelic Shop, rock promoter Bill Graham, and a drug dealer or two provided seed money, which was augmented by hippies selling papers on the street. But the *Oracle*'s dedication to the politics of free made it oppose financial success. "If anything, there was an interest in not making money," Cohen recalls. "There were offers to put money into the paper that were connected with editorial control and institutionalization. We refused them. There was a very definite feeling that we were entering into a new age, a new potentiality for human beings. And a real definite feeling that everybody had to take LSD."

In the main, the *Oracle* offered dope news for dopers, and became a souvenir for the tourists that soon overwhelmed the Haight. There was news of street fairs, dope busts, the selective charges filed against Cohen and others for selling poet Lenore Kandel's *Love Book,* Ken Kesey facing the music on a pot bust, local entertainment. Increasingly, though, this type of piece gave way to poetry, spiritual messages, personal essays, and especially the emerging Aquarian Age poster art. Cohen saw the *Oracle* as less about "what [Lyndon] Johnson has done, and ugliness like that" than a graphic expression of "a more conscious, loving, intimate, non-alienated world—particularly, a non-alienated America."

The *Oracle* also felt that spirituality, however induced, left Left politics far behind. One reason was summed up in its pages by philosopher Alan

Watts: "whenever the insights one derives from mystical vision become politically active, they always create their own opposite . . . a parody." Yet the paper could become a self-parody. Here's Tim Leary on major LSD manufacturer and Bay Area figure Augustus Owsley Stanley III," a.k.a. Owsley, or "God's Secret Agent":

"In the daily press the Reagans and Romneys merit the adulatory headlines. The O.s, if mentioned at all, are denounced as sordid criminals. But the simple truth is that the Reagans and the Romneys will soon be forgotten."

Nice try, Dr. Tim.

Still, as '66 became '67, the *Oracle* began to realize Cohen's dream of "a newspaper with rainbows being read all over the world." Back East, the story goes, the *EVO* staff had learned that their printer had gone into an unofficial distribution business with five thousand *EVO*s he'd run off on the side. In exchange for burying the hatchet, the printer gave *EVO* several issues printed with four pages of . . . A Free Color!

When the first "color *EVO*" reached the West Coast, it sent the *Oracle* people rushing off to *their* printer. Soon the *Oracle* was multihued, produced by splitting the press's ink fountains with wooden blocks. One issue was personalized by the staff squirting inks from catsup bottles; for another, they added jasmine perfume. Cohen: "We wanted to break the conditioning involved with the linear format of newspapers."

THE FIRST WAVE of underground papers were radical or outré, not revolutionary. The half-dozen were located in big cities and college towns. The early founders had links to socialism or the Beats, but had departed from or never been part of the traditional Left, and were only somewhat involved with the New. To varying degrees, all were concerned with the emerging youth culture. "Ours was a particularly middle-class cultural rebellion," Allen (he's changed from Allan) Katzman recalls. "The masses were content. We were not in Russia after the First World War."

Most of the papers were owned but broke; the lack of money matched a prevailing antimaterialism and minimized any fears of libel suits. Salaries were mostly minimal, but the work was uncompromised and had its counter-community perks and status. The small staffs were overwhelmingly white, male. Like the early SDS, they were at this time disproportionately Jewish.

And like SDS, the papers reflected a commitment to currency that had alarmed Jack Newfield as he surveyed the new members of SDS: "Of twenty-five activists interviewed, none had ever read Rosa Luxemburg, Max Weber, Eduard Bernstein, John Dewey, Peter Kropotkin, or John

Stuart Mill. Less than five had actually read Lenin or Trotsky, and only a few more had ever read Marx." Instead, Newfield's prophetic minority had skipped to the modern half of the syllabus: "Almost all of them had read C. Wright Mills and [Albert] Camus, and about half had read [Paul] Goodman, Frantz Fanon, and Herbert Marcuse." Even here, the choices were uneven: more activists had read the *Realist* than Mill's "Essay on Liberty"—or "The Sermon on the Mount." Seven respondents couldn't remember the last novel they'd tackled.

"Other answers included the autobiography *Manchild in the Promised Land* [Claude Brown]; *Sometimes a Great Notion* [Ken Kesey]; *Candy* [Terry Southern]; *V* [Thomas Pynchon]; *Drive, He Said* [Jeremy Larner]; *Last Exit to Brooklyn* [Hubert Selby, Jr.] and *Making Do* [Paul Goodman]. All the novels," Newfield noted, "had been published within the last two years, and most dealt with the decadence or absurdity of life."

Kunkin knew his Marx, but few of the others did, much less their *Masses* or *Appeal to Reason*, which had more relevance in term papers than in reality. The new protest would be a white-hot but ahistorical assault on a society that activist David McReynolds branded "only rational but no longer sane." But despite the thinness, even the goofiness, of some of its reporting, this fledgling press managed to give new communities a sense of identity. They offered criticism, and debate. They had a sense of purpose, and a sense of decency.

But the papers were isolated, and so in June, 1966, Allan Katzman wrote in *EVO* about the need for an association to communicate "the news that the middle-class press won't print or can't find." Katzman foresaw a hip Associated Press, and more—income-pooling and article-sharing, joint advertising and typesetting resources.

A few weeks later, the organization got a name, for which Walter Bowart's explanation is the most romantic: a *Time* reporter doing the first national piece on the new papers asked what the fledgling combine was called; searching for inspiration, Bowart's eyes wandered out the windows of *EVO*'s office and saw a United Parcel Service truck rolling down Avenue A. "We're . . . ah . . . UPS—the Underground Press Syndicate."

Whatever the origin, the name stuck. The new papers were hardly as underground as *Résistance*, which had published clandestinely in Nazi-occupied France, or the "white weapons" European Jews had surreptitiously distributed during World War II with bounties of 100,000 Reichsmarks hanging over their heads. Only a few would be truly covert: the *Outlaw* at San Quentin; some GI papers; and *Osawatomie*, which would publish the dogma of SDS's seventies Weather Underground remnant. The "underground" tag would limit later attempts to expand audience and advertising. As we shall see, the real underground press would belong to the FBI, CIA, NSA, and other surveillance organizations.

But the appellation had its advantages. John Wilcock: "We all agreed that, though a little grandiose, it was an appropriate image for a new Fuck Censorship press." Now the writers, editors, and artists wanted to get to know each other.

3

THE SUMMER OF LOVE

TINSON BEACH, CALIFORNIA—EASTER, 1967: The call for an underground press gathering had gone out from San Francisco, from the *Oracle,* the most apocalyptic of the new underground papers. Now thirty or so writers, artists, poets, New Leftists, button-store owners, ex–daily newsmen, ex-bartenders, ex–socialist organizers, and freshly politicized hippies from around the country were coming to a house close by the dark blue ocean an hour or so north of San Francisco. Behind the cove stood Mount Tamalpais, which, if you looked at it from the right angle and with the right amount of imagination, suggested the sleeping Indian princess for whom it was named. It was a pretty scene, and it made it possible to forget that the world across the ocean and beyond the mountain seemed to be falling apart—unless you'd been considering the question that the *Oracle's* then-managing editor Ron Thelin had dispatched around the country: "Well, here we all are, Uncle Sam on the verge of death. A sleep-stupor, symbol-addicted environment haunts our hearts, and what are we going to do about it?"

Thelin's letter had suggested a pow-wow of "journalistic tribesmen" who'd "come together for spiritual guidance and fun," and the Stinson Beach gathering was a microcosm of the Haight's big event—the Human Be-In, a convocation called by the *Oracle* and other community groups that had taken place on January 14, 1967. On that day, twenty thousand or so plume-, bell-, flower-, and incense-bearing folk had formed a spectrum of freaks in Golden Gate Park. The Dead, Quicksilver Messenger Service, and other bands had played. Allen Ginsberg, Gary Snyder, Tim Leary, and other neighborhood gurus had spoken. Jerry Rubin had asked for bail money for East Bay political causes while noting that "The police, like the soldiers in Vietnam, are victims and agents." By sunset, when Ginsberg offered a concluding chant and then led the crowd in picking up the garbage, many of those present had had their minds blown, either naturally or chemically.

Oracle reporter Steve Levine was one of them: "Now in this twentieth of recent centuries a generation, considered by many to be the reincarnation of the American Indian, has been born out of the ashes of World War Two, rising like a Phoenix, in celebration of the slightly psychedelic zeitgeist of this brand-new Aquarian Age."

Max Scherr and other Berkeleyites saw a blown opportunity. The Be-In also had been billed as "A Gathering of the Tribes"—San Francisco and Berkeley, freaks and political radicals. "It was badly organized," he'd recall. "The organizers implied that they were against the war, but that they didn't want to bother people on this occasion."

January had also seen a Gathering of the Gurus in a bi-level room on Alan Watts's ferry-houseboat. As the evening unfolded, Watts, Ginsberg, Snyder, and Leary had discussed the emerging scene. Watts, moderating, had explored its underlying consciousness. Ginsberg, moved by a meeting with former FSM leader Mario Savio, had spoken about fusing the politics of being with political action. With Snyder persistently probing what he meant by "dropping out," Leary had talked up hippies as evolving *homo superiors,* certain that "If anything will survive in the whole world, it's going to be Haight-Ashbury, because Haight-Ashbury's got two billion years behind it."

When it was over, the *Oracle* staff had run the 23,000-word transcript, then begun preparing for Stinson Beach.

The Stinson Beach pow-wow—the grittier *EVO* ites christened it "the Hippie Apalachin" after the crime-syndicate summit held in Apalachin, New York, some years before—attracted staff from only a half-dozen or so of the nineteen papers that were now UPS members. But many of the movers and shakers were on hand, among them Art Kunkin, John Bryan, Ron Thelin, and Walter Bowart.

It was a freak-dominated affair. Brown rice and home-made bread were served along with hot dogs and marshmallows. The guest speaker was Rolling Thunder, an Indian who, in black suit and hat, was more conservatively dressed than anybody else. The staff of the *Illustrated Paper,* from Mendocino further north, not only published an *Oracle*-type paper but grew vegetables and raised animals on communal land. Even *Guerilla* out of gritty Detroit centered around an Artists' Workshop headed up by a post-Beat poet named John Sinclair. Some *Oracle* folk suggested naming the fledgling organization the Tribal Messenger Service. Attendees got stoned, sat on the beach, talked about waves and changes. They also agreed to freely exchange articles and subscriptions, and to print a list of UPS members. A "paper" organization had gained substance. The UPS statement of purpose that emerged was nothing less than a post-atomic, postacid repeal of Western civilization:

- "To warn the 'civilized world' of its impending collapse," through "communications among aware communities outside the establishment" and by forcing mass media to pay attention to it.
- "To note and chronicle events leading to the collapse."
- "To advise intelligently to prevent rapid collapse and make transition possible."
- "To prepare American people for the wilderness."
- "To fight a holding action in the dying cities."

In a sense, this brown-rice millennialism prefigured the ecology movement, even the coming population shift from urban areas. But it also presented a profoundly antitechnological strand within the adversary culture, and its ignoring the war and racism put it at odds with the growing New Left.

In the spring before the Summer of Love, the Haight pulsed with communal energy, acid reveries, and the best rock this side of Liverpool. The street-survivalist Diggers fed the hungry in Golden Gate Park; the Haight-Ashbury Medical Clinic and Legal Organization kept them out of trouble. A mailman was known as Admiral Love, the cop on the corner was called Sergeant Sunshine. Strangers smiled on their brothers and sisters. A little-known singer named Scott MacKenzie turned the radio into a road map, telling listeners to wear flowers in their hair en route to San Francisco. Hippies—"free," "loving," "sex-crazed," "dirty"— became the perfect contradictory grist for the mass-media mill. Every publication worth its trendiness dispatched a scribe to the psychedelic front. "The Haight," wrote Michael Rossman, the Free Speech Movement diarist who'd moved in with the flower folk, "was trembling in anticipation of the stellar grubby agony it was about to undergo, victim of America's first full Media Blitz."

Haight cynics joked about bead-wearing *Life* reporters interviewing bead-wearing *Look* reporters. Even *Time*'s somewhat positive story used "color" words such as "disciples," "bizarre," "cult of hippiedom." And the drug experience proved hard to cover, as shown by these honest words from the freelancer dispatched by the *New York Times Magazine* to the Haight:

Only "a fool and a fraud" would write about psychedelics without trying them, he said. But writing from experience meant implicating oneself or one's sources in a felony. "So," wrote Hunter S. Thompson, later *Rolling Stone*'s house mutant, "despite the fact that the whole journalism industry is full of unregenerate heads . . . it is not very likely that the frank, documented truth about the psychedelic underground, for good or ill, will be illuminated at any time soon in the public prints."

Some mainstream reporters praised gentle kids living gentle lives. Mostly, though, there was freakshow coverage, even phony-baloney scare stories about acidheads microwaving their eyes by staring into the sun. And *any* coverage only led kids from around the country to descend on a community already straining to keep from being overwhelmed.

Not all the hype came from the mass press. It was the *Chronicle* that headlined "MAYOR WARNS HIPPIES TO STAY OUT OF TOWN" while *EVO*'s Walter Bowart proclaimed seven-hilled San Francisco to be "the Rome of a future world founded on love . . . the love-guerilla training school for drop-outs from mainstream America . . . where the new world, a human world of the 21st century is being constructed." What curious hippie could stay home after that?

As spring moved toward summer, the streets of the Haight-Ashbury filled with young pilgrims—and with tourists munching on Love Burgers, wearing Love Beads. The *Oracle*'s acid messianism, its reluctance to print "downer" stories—or news in general—rose-colored the Haight. "Moronic optimism" recalls Greil Marcus, a Berkeley-based critic who'd later write for the San Francisco *Express Times* and *Rolling Stone*. The *Barb* was critical too. The problem wasn't LSD, but that "an epidemic of big businesses is threatening to turn Haight Street into a Coney Island that may make North Beach look small time."

But the Haight had a resident critic. Chester Anderson was a street activist armed with a stencil duplicator, with which he pumped out as many as ten thousand leaflets to add "perspective to the *Chronicle*'s fantasies." An ex-Beat, Anderson had been at the Stinson Beach meeting and written for the *Oracle,* including some early rock criticism. (Rock was the glue of the new society, he felt, erasing false categories of art, class, race, privatism, and the gap between audience and performer.) But the paper was too elitist for his taste, and so he founded the Communications Company as a "daily *Oracle.*"

A Com/Co leaflet could be a poem by Richard *(Trout Fishing in America)* Brautigan, a notice that four hundred pounds of free, fresh perch would be available at 4:00 P.M. on the corner of Oak and Ashbury, or a Jeremiad defending the Haight vision:

"HAIGHT/ASHBURY IS THE FIRST SEGREGATED BOHEMIA I'VE EVER SEEN!" Anderson wrote in a February, 1967, flier. "The spades . . . are our spiritual fathers. . . . They gave us jazz & grass and rock&roll. . . . If it weren't for the spades, we would all have short hair, neat suits, glazed eyes, steady jobs & gastric ulcers, all be dying of unnameable frustration. . . . If the Fillmore erupts again this summer—and it most likely will— and we haven't reestablished our brotherhood with the Fillmore's people . . . then they'll erupt against *us* as well as against the Man, AND WE WILL BE BURIED."

An April flier sought to mobilize human resources for the coming deluge: "Gurus/Wizards/Teachers. The kids are coming. The kids are here. MAKE YOURSELVES AVAILABLE TO THE KIDS. . . . Go where they are and teach love. Now—these thousands of kids—is your chance to create the world as you know it should be."

Already, though, Anderson saw that vision slipping away. That same month, he published a screed called "Uncle Tim's Children," directed against the facile proselytizing of Timothy Leary and others:

"Pretty little 16-year-old middle-class chick comes to the Haight to see what it's all about & gets picked up by a 17-year-old street dealer who spends all day shooting her full of speed again & again, then feeds her 3000 mikes [micrograms of acid] & raffles off her temporarily unemployed body for the biggest Haight Street gang bang since the night before last.

"The politics & ethics of ecstasy.

"Rape is as common as bullshit on Haight Street. . . .

"Kids are starving on The Street. Minds & bodies are being maimed as we watch, a scale model of Vietnam. . . .

"Are you aware that Haight Street is just as bad as the squares say it is? . . ."

Anderson slaughtered some of the Haight's more sacred cows. The hip merchants had "lured an army of children into a ghastly trap from which there is no visible escape. . . . Until they start doing something more constructive than selling beads & mandalas . . . fuck 'em. Hard.

"And that goes for Uncle Tim too, who turned you on & dropped you into this pit."

And the *Oracle*? "The *Oracle* continues to recruit for this summer's Human Shit-In. . . . Having with brilliant graphics & sophomoric prose urged millions of kids to Drop Out of schools and jobs, it now offers its dropouts menial jobs [selling the paper]. . . . Groovy.

"If the *Oracle* ploughs less of its money back into the paper & more of it into the welfare of the kids on the Street, I'll grant the possibility that the *Oracle* may be something more than a poorly edited, sleazy, opportunistic rag."

Only "the despised diggers" escaped Anderson's wrath: "the diggers . . . hardly ever talk about love. . . . They're too busy doing it to talk about it." But Anderson didn't escape theirs: they seized his mimeo and he went off to edit a new music magazine called *Crawdaddy*.

> C'mon people now
> Smile on your brother
> Everybody get together
> Try to love one another
> Right now.

YOU COULD HEAR the Haight's siren songs clear across the country. I did in New York, where my bio was an entry in the record of a dividing America.

Born in 1945, I'd grown up in a working-class Bronx neighborhood that assumed Judaism, the Democratic Party, and college. My dad routed trucks and pushed skids in a book bindery; Mom cooked great roast chicken. They were immigrants who wanted their son to do well in the Promised Land of America.

Like Art Kunkin, Todd Gitlin, and Stokely Carmichael before me, I'd attended the Bronx High School of Science. A few kids were into the Young Socialists, but my teen political movement was the Reform Democrats. Occasionally, though, radical jolts hit. At fifteen, I'd been stunned, and energized, by the sight of blacks and whites picketing a Manhattan Woolworth's in the name of Southern integration; this was way beyond my yelling at my dad not to use the word *schvartze* for black people. At seventeen, I'd sat in an older guy's car underneath the El during the Cuban missile crisis; he rapped Kennedy's version of Russian roulette; I was just scared. When JFK was killed, I'd stormed out of a poly sci class at New York University taught by a favorite liberal suddenly defrocked for wanting lessons as usual; getting drunk seemed a better idea. Just after graduating in 1965, I'd returned to campus and a teach-in on the war. Some on the stage said our government was wrong. Were they disloyal, or correct?

The pendulum swung wider. During a nine-month period in my twenty-first and twenty-second years, I'd worked as a graduate student, an insurance salesman, and a welfare caseworker. I'd courted a girl whose mom thought her daughter could never live on a college history teacher's salary. If I was victimized by any establishment, it happened when a professor in a graduate school unjustly accused me of deliberately not handing in a missing exam. Instead of fighting it, I'd dropped out, bored and tired.

No school, no girl, no job. But an engagement and the draft had spurred me to join the only open army reserve unit in town. Now the pendulum yawed; I found myself splitting time between the 11th Special Forces and the Lower East Side. Army and counterculture, the two main experiences of young American men in the sixties. Nothing like spending a Sunday morning cleaning an M-1 while thinking about the hippie excursions of the night before.

It was no contest which lifestyle I liked better. East Village life featured what critic Dave Marsh would term "*serious* adolescence." Forbidden fruits elsewhere were daily events here. Friendships were welded via all-night revelations, everyday epiphanies, Easter be-ins, visceral pacifism. Wasn't it funny when my roommate Eliot's dad walked into *our* place and said, "I just want you to know that I moved out of a better apartment in this neighborhood in 1924!"? It was a good thing he didn't visit a couple of weeks later, when our furniture was toted through a formerly gated window by new neighborhood friends who didn't share our disdain for private property.

We were slumming, purging, searching for noncareer alternatives, having fun. "It wasn't really a deep-seated sense of pacifism or outrage toward the military," Paul (Simon) Zmiewski, a teenaged orphan who found a new family in that Lower East Side apartment, recalls. "It was more like 'Here's a chance for me to get back at parents, government, cops, society, culture, you name it. Them—the big guys, the people in control.'"

By the time the army called me up for basic training at Fort Dix, I was a lot closer to Sergeant Pepper than to the master sergeant.

I don't know whether the army or I would have thought Green Beret training a bigger error. But Sergeant Pepper prevailed; there was nothing to get hung up on. The incoming medical examination got me an honorable discharge for bad eyes, a diagnosis the army celebrated in its inimitable way by giving me a job sticking eensy-weensy screws into eyeglass frames. Some guys in my medical-hold unit were sent off to basic training; one day, we were kept out of our barracks as word spread that someone had cut off his thumb to make sure Vietnam wasn't in his future.

Back in New York, *EVO* was convincing us to go west. Hadn't we sat around listening to Jefferson Airplane and the Dead? Hadn't postcards

told of scenes that shamed our filthy streets? Apprentice Kerouacs, we
bought a used VW van, threw some mattresses in the back, and went on
the road to look for America.

It turned out to be quite a place. In Chicago, we were given shelter
by a writer for the *Seed,* a paper founded just that May by an artist named
Don Lewis and a poster-and-button-store owner named Earl "the Mole"
Segal (he'd been at Stinson Beach). The fledgling *Seed* was a second-
generation mix of *EVO* experimentation, the hip side of the *Barb*'s
community news, and the *Oracle*'s colorful psychedelic graphics. It had
organized a Mother's Day Be-In, where bands played for free and face-
painted Pierrots discovered that they were not alone. It covered the event
with curvilinear headlines and florid rhetoric:

"On the fourteenth day of May . . . Chicago's first Human Be-In took
place as the Midwest's confirmation that She, too, belonged within the
folds of Love that have gathered the tribes together everywhere across
the continent. . . . The crowds relaxed, forgot the cold, the police, the
hate, war, and all the petty flaws that keep men's scattered souls from
uniting in love."

Psychedelic mush, yes. But because Chicago was such a tough town,
a scene developed along the Wells Street hip strip—just like in Seattle,
where the somewhat grittier *Helix* had just appeared, or even swinging
London, where *IT—International Times—*mixed stories about magic
mushrooms and Mao Tse-Tung, the Who and racism in Cuba. Within
a year, three of us five vanmates would be working at the *Seed.*

In Iowa, we city slickers pulled off the road and, laughing with delight,
rolled through amber waves of grain that until then had only been a
phrase in a grammar-school song. Then came the Grand Tetons, the
Grand Canyon, and San Francisco. Psychedelphia.

We freak-danced at the hopelessly misnamed Straight Theatre, and
heard free music in Golden Gate Park. A "white witch" and I made love
in a closet where she'd installed a sleeping shelf. Even an asthma attack
became a strange high: lying in a hospital emergency-room bed, my mind
raced from nor-ephinedrine, one channel recording police radios crack-
ling with ghetto-riot reports, the other straining to read Huxley's *Doors
of Perception.*

During that summer, the *Oracle* published striking graphics and major
poems such as Michael McClure's "Poisoned Wheat," which declared:

> Citizens of the United States
> are in the hands of traitors
> who ignore their will and force

them into silent acceptance
of needless and undesired warfare. . . .

Street people, day-trippers, and tourists pushed the paper's circulation to
117,000, the largest any community undergrounder would reach. But the
Oracle had the Haight's own poisoned wheat to harvest. "Flower power
. . . was a noble experiment," Ed Sanders would write in his million-
selling Charles Manson epic, *The Family* (based on his reporting for the
L.A. *Free Press*). "But there was a weakness: from the standpoint of
vulnerability the flower movement was like a valley of thousands of
plump white rabbits surrounded by wounded coyotes. . . .

"The Haight attracted vicious criminals who grew long hair. Bikers
tried to take over the LSD market with crude sadistic tactics. Bad dope
was sold by acne-faced methedrine punks. Satanists and satanist-rapist
death-freaks flooded the whirling crash pads. People began getting ripped
off in the parks. There was racial trouble. Puke was sold as salvation.
Ugliness was."

One dealer was killed and mutilated; the stabbed and shot body of
high-profile drug merchant Bill "Superspade" Thomas was found in a
sleeping bag dangling off a cliff near Sausalito. The *Oracle*'s plea for
people to stop dealing was futile in a community whose dreams and
economy both depended on the same commodity. The paper's prayer that
the dead men's consciousnesses "return to bodies that will not want for
anything but the beauty and joy of their part in the great dance" sounded
hollow.

The Haight began cracking under the weight of police street sweeps
of dealers, runaways, and the homeless, the peekaboo intrusion of Gray
Line tourist buses rumbling through "the Beaded Curtain," the lenses of
media. But it also crumbled from the ecologic pressure of too many
transients bouncing around on too small a safety net. "The Haight-
Ashbury was appealing," says cartoonist Robert Crumb, who spent the
Summer of Love looking more like a Grant Wood character than a furry
freak. "It was much more open than any other place. But the air was so
thick with bullshit you could cut it with a knife. Guys were running
around saying, 'I'm you and you are me and everything is beautiful,
so get down and suck my dick.' These young, middle-class kids were
just too dumb about it. It was just too silly. It had to be killed.
You'd see them skipping through the park with their bamboo flutes and
their robes, calling themselves things like Gingerbread Prince. And
they had an irritating, smug, superior attitude. If you didn't have
long hair, if you didn't have a bamboo flute, they just ignored your
existence."

The *Oracle* often ignored these problems. "The vibe the *Oracle* projected was a lot more romantic than the reality," Lester Doré, an *Oracle* artist who'd later work at the *Seed,* recalls. "There were no jobs or money. All you could do was sell papers—or dope."

The *Oracle* espoused marijuana and LSD as soul and body medicine while warning people away from heroin and the "body drug" methamphetamine—speed. But not everyone was practicing what they preached. The flowing lines of some *Oracle* graphics suggested a familiarity with LSD. Soon they were joined by jagged lines or intricate curlicues, which suggested that methamphetamine was becoming the drug of choice. The staff began operating on different biological clocks. Acidheads tripped out for eight hours or so; speed freaks went on runs that could last for days, then crashed. At least one contributor, Cohen recalls, took up with the heroin allegedly dumped in the Haight by the Mafia to regain control of the drug trade. "It was so difficult getting all these spaced-out people together," he continues. "We knew we wanted to come out once a month, but we never did. It was always six, seven, eight weeks, and it took a lot of energy to bring the group back together."

The *Oracle,* frankly, was running out of ideas. Cohen, not shyly: "We had a creative problem—we didn't know what else to do. We had brought the format of the newspaper to its zenith and we didn't know where to go in terms of form. So we had basically the problem of 'Can you top this?' We had a content problem too. We'd explored tribalism, astrology, communes, ecology, redoing the cities, and we had a problem of what to do next." After a poem called "A Curse on the Man in Washington and the Pentagon" was scheduled, three dissenters (including one whose dad worked in the Pentagon) quit, claiming that the ode was less than loving. Even success was a hassle. Increased circulation, color work, overtime, the occasional stoning of a printer all made for cash-flow problems.

The *Oracle* and the Psychedelic Shop had opened their doors to the street people, feeding them, talking them down off bad trips. But it was hard to put out a paper with a street-guru and his coterie living in your office and a drug scene that had spread from those Cohen recalls as "creative people" to "the disenchanted, the disabled, the neurotics, the psychotic people who were too young or too scared, and had a lot of pain."

AUTUMN CAME, and the human tide receded, leaving behind a tired community. Hips had died; now it was time for a collective funeral. On October 6, 1967, a year to the day after the California criminalization of LSD and the Haight's Love Pageant, pallbearers carried a fifteen-foot coffin and a stretcher-borne hippie through the streets, pausing at the stations of the Haight's religious crosswalks—the intersection of Haight and Ashbury, the Psychedelic Shop—before setting the coffin ablaze. The marchers called themselves "The Brotherhood of Free Men."

"Death of hippie, son of media," signs proclaimed with a certain amount of truth. But there were two sides to this story. "The people who blame the mass media for the failure of the movement continue to turn handsprings at the sight of a press card." New York *Times*man Earl Shorris wrote from "the gravesite." A Haight broadside agreed: "MEDIA CREATED THE HIPPIE WITH YOUR HUNGRY CONSENT." And so did a new, San Francisco–based publication called *Rolling Stone.* Appearing in November, the oversized tabloid had a crisp look at odds with the *Oracle*'s psychedelic approach, and centered around rock 'n' roll as both music and an agent of change. The Haight scene, *Rolling Stone* said, had "become trapped by the publicity that the messianism had created. Words had become labels, ideas become slogans, art become advertising." The ceremony had "no weight. . . . It will take more than the funeral to rescue the vision."

In other cities, acid communities were also reaching watersheds. Linda and Groovy, a tripping couple, were murdered on New York's Lower East Side. Hippies complained about the extensive media coverage, but the deed had happened. In Boston, acid authoritarianism was dominating a paper.

"I tell you I am the greatest man in the world and it doesn't trouble me in the least," wrote Mel Lyman in the *Avatar,* a clean-looking broadsheet that first appeared in June, 1967. The *Avatar* ran astrolo-chat, and sex, drug, and legal-defense news, all of which attracted attention in student-heavy Boston.

In the fall, the paper answered the arrests of some fifty of its street-sellers with a blistering centerfold of artfully drawn four-letter words that won a First Amendment battle and raised circulation. But the paper's core consisted of pronouncements from Lyman, who headed a cult of personality that lived communally in the city's Roxbury area. Lyman provided a unique version of objectivity: "I am the truth and I speak the truth," he proclaimed in a debut statement called "To All Who Would Know." "My understanding is tinged by no prejudice, no unconscious motivation, no confusion."

The Haight's ideal of self-actualization was proving hard to come by. Acidheads had reached out toward some Cosmic Force; now some were tumbling through the universe, and some found an anchor in charisma abetted by psychoactive drugs, The *Avatar* chronicled Lyman's entry into that late-sixties growth industry, the Great Guru Sweepstakes. Soon he was writing as many as three rambling columns per issue, which were accompanied by pages of pained "Letters to Mel." When more news-oriented editors printed an issue without Lyman's endorsement, members of his Fort Hill commune seized and scrapped the 35,000 offending copies.

The last *Oracle* appeared in February, 1968—number thirteen if you counted *P.O. Frisco*. The newsiest story centered on a Masonic Auditorium symposium between Alan Watts, psychologist Carl Rogers, and futurist Herman Kahn (Allen Cohen rankled at Kahn's remark that mainstream society could handle 30 percent of its people reducing their lives to the "child's game" he saw in the Haight). The issue also contained the *Oracle*'s swan-song: "Freak out, come back, bandage the wounded, and feed however many you can, and never cheat."

Cohen and the others had become alienated from the revolution against alienation. "I was an editor trying to get all this material out—not living what I was feeling. The paranoia was all around." As the *Oracle* fell apart, the Haight's jackals began picking at its bones. "Things started disappearing," Lester Doré remembers. "One day all the typewriters were gone." The paper just petered out; Cohen moved to the enchanted forests of Mendocino, joining a community of about twenty people out to rediscover the alleged intimacy, nonmaterialism, and matriarchy of Stone Age culture. Consensus opinion-making did develop, and Cohen wrote *Childbirth Is Ecstasy,* a book on natural delivery. But that community, like the Haight, eventually foundered, in this case over the twin agendas of the women's movement and fundamentalist Christianity. The Stone Age wasn't the Age of Aquarius, either.

Other Free Cities, other papers, would try again.

THE FIFTH ESTATE

Vol 2, No. 9 (35)
Aug. 1-15, 1967

10¢

15¢ OUTSIDE DETROIT

city ablaze

by Harvey Ovshinsky

On Sunday, July 23, at 3 o'clock in the morning, the DOORS' "Baby Light My Fire" was the number one song in Detroit.

It couldn't have been more appropriate.

At 3:30 a.m. a large crowd of black people watched as their brothers and sisters were arrested for drinking in a blind pig.

At 4:00 a.m. they stopped watching and began throwing things. The rest is history.

As of this writing, 40 people are dead, 2,000 are wounded and 3,500 people are in jail.

It started with mass looting in the inner city, but soon spread quickly into other areas. It was black and white together as looters gave way to arsonists and arsonists gave way to snipers. Young children watched as their parents broke into hardware and grocery stores. When the paratroopers came in with machine guns and tanks the looting stopped. Not so much because the people were afraid but because there wasn't anything left to loot.

When the fires started on Sunday afternoon, Mayor Cavanagh asked that suburban fire departments come in and help out. Several times the fire fighters were forced to leave the area because of heavy sniper fire. At first the fires were limited to clothing, furniture and grocery stores, but on Monday the shit hit the fan.

Hands of arsonists left the ghetto and by late Monday many homes and businesses in Northwest Detroit were gutted by fire, as were most on the East and West side.

As this paper goes to press, over 1,300 fires have been set, 50 firemen wounded by sniper fire and everybody wants to know why.

Cries of "outside agitators fail in deaf ears for this reporter.

The looting was interracial and unusually cordial and friendly until the paratroopers began firing. Teenagers joined with black militants in arson and sniping, six whites were arrested for firing on troops and while many deaths were blamed on snipers, the black and white residents of the ghetto say that the troopers were responsible for most of the killing.

In a discussion with FIFTH ESTATE co-editor Peter Werbe, one black militant acknowledged that residents were arming themselves and in his words "getting themselves together."

Fighting between snipers and troops reached fantastic proportions as armed assaults were made on police precincts, command posts and even the downtown headquarters housing presidential assistant Cyrus Vance.

Bands of Negroes, armed with army machine guns kept two police precincts from functioning for almost an hour as they lay siege to them. Also on several occasions guardsmen and police were forced to abandon entire sections of the ghetto due to sniper fire.

Not outside agitators. Just plain folk. Plain folk, some white, most black, who were angry at America. Plain folk who set Detroit on fire and made Watts look like a Love - in.

picket at lbj speech

Lyndon Baines Johnson, 36th President of the United States of America, the man who sends troops to Vietnam, Santo Domingo, the Congo, and now our own hometown is scheduled to speak in Detroit on August 2nd.

Peace activists across the country have promised that Johnson will be met with demonstrations wherever he goes as long as he continues the war in Vietnam. And if Johnson is not frightened away by a little rioting the major peace and civil rights group plan a large reception for him in the form of a giant picket line.

He is scheduled to speak to the Association of County Employees at Cobo Hall in downtown Detroit, 2:30 p.m. on the 2nd. In the event LBJ doesn't appear an administration representative will speak in his place and the demonstration will still be held.

Be there and tell Johnson to get out of Vietnam now!

"get the big stuff"

by Peter Werbe

"The chickens are coming home to roost" Malcolm X, Nov. 22, 1963

Malcolm was right, of course, and the chickens have come home so many ways since that grim day four years ago. Malcolm's own death, riots across the country and now the biggest chicken of them all -- the Detroit riot. Detroit always does things up in a big way.

The destruction, looting, killing, and violence have been chronicled to such an extent that no repetition is necessary here.

This newspaper has concentrated its observations on the hippie, new left, and avant garde community it serves.

The geographical center of that community -- the Warren Forest area near Wayne University -- was relatively untouched by the holocaust.

The FIFTH ESTATE office at Warren and John Lodge was unharmed as were the adjacent offices of the Artists' Workshop, Trans - Love Energies, and the Detroit Committee to End the War in Vietnam. Our newspaper office sported a "soul brother" sign and two large banners were hung from Trans-Love reading "Peace on Earth" and "Burn, Baby, Burn.

Hippie and political residents of the Warren Forest area reacted to the situation just like their poorer neighbors -- they took whatever wasn't nailed down.

They joined the Negroes and Southern whites in cleaning out the stores on Trumbull and Forest, which now lie in ashes, the Krogers on Second and Prentis and other stores. Looters came back laden with goodies, swapping stories of harrowing experiences with the guardsmen and bartering goods that they had in excess. The mayor was certainly right about the "carnival atmosphere." Everything was FREE.

Kee Halonen, a resident of W. Hancock, described the scene as that of integrated looting. "There was complete cooperation between the races in their common endeavor," she said. "There were children carrying toys they never would have been able to afford."

Detroit's Communications Company, which distributes leaflets in the area

(continued on p. 8)

4

THE SUMMER OF DETROIT AND VIETNAM

S TINSON BEACH—EASTER, 1967: Apocalypse and the Summer of Love weren't the only concerns of the first underground-press gathering. A minority of writers closer to political activism, the New Left, and in some cases Students for a Democratic Society, spoke about political action, social responsibility, and the antiwar and black-power movements.

A roster of events nationwide since the summer before explained why: civil rights activist James Meredith shot and wounded in Mississippi; ghetto riots in the North; an armed Leftist group called the Black Panther Party challenging police brutality in Oakland, California; the Fermi nuclear reactor faltering seriously enough to inspire a later song called "We Almost Lost Detroit"; the creation of a National Organization for Women; a Cultural Revolution convulsing China. In February, the Los Angeles *Free Press* had published "The Student As Nigger," in which a teacher from Cal State, L.A., blasted a situation that left most students with "no voice in decisions which affect their academic lives." The next month, *Ramparts* had unmasked CIA funding of the National Student Association in violation of its own charter; the exposé (the kind too often lacking in underground coverage) ended that relationship and radicalized part of the campus press.

More than four hundred thousand American troops were now in Vietnam, but the antiwar movement was making itself felt. When military commanders asked

Lyndon Johnson to intensify the bombing of North Vietnam, he replied, "How long [will] it take five hundred thousand angry Americans to climb the White House wall . . . and lynch their President?"

On the second day of the conference, the editors had shifted to San Francisco and the *Oracle*'s Haight Street office. With the move came a change in spirit, one that became noticeable when Max Scherr showed up and greeted a second speech by Rolling Thunder with less enthusiasm than the Indianophiles'. He wasn't alone. "In fact, this is pretty much where the division comes," John Wilcock would write that April in UPS's first publication, a roundup of the Stinson meeting. "On one side are the two *Oracles* [S.F. and L.A.], *EVO* and a couple of others; on the other, the *Barb*, the L.A. *Free Press, Fifth Estate,* etc., with papers like *IT* [London's *International Times*], Mendocino's *Illustrated Paper,* Texas's *Rag,* and the *Canadian Free Press* [Ottawa] in between."

At Stinson Beach, the UPS paper that most prefigured those to come was the *Rag,* represented at the gathering by several writers, including the increasingly important Thorne Dreyer. The *Rag* had become the South's first undergrounder after an editor from Michigan's *Paper* came through Austin, Texas, in 1966. It published only monthly, and had a circulation of only two thousand or so. Like the other papers, it didn't express a consistent ideology, certainly much less than such "party papers" as the *Insurgent* (the W.E.B. DuBois Clubs' monthly magazine) and the *Challenge* (Progressive Labor), or even SDS's *New Left Notes,* founded the previous winter.

But the *Rag* was the first independent undergrounder to represent, even in a small way, the participatory democracy, community organizing, and synthesis of politics and culture that the New Left of the midsixties was trying to develop. More specifically, the *Rag* reflected the variant of SDS politics that had appeared in 1965 under the rubric "prairie power." As the name implies, prairie power developed in the heartland of America, and was less the radicalism of "Red-diaper babies" raised by 1930s Communists than a politics that often was accompanied by a break with conservative parents.

Staff writer Jeff Shero, an air-force brat turned activist, had helped desegregate the restrooms at the University of Texas, an action with what was probably the sixties' best slogan—"Let My People Go." In 1965, he'd become SDS's national vice-president as part of prairie power's rise. "Your mother didn't say . . . 'We supported the Republicans in the Spanish Civil War, and now you're in SDS and I'm glad to see you socially concerned,' " he'd tell SDS historian Kirkpatrick Sale a few years later. "In most of those places it meant, 'You *Goddamn Communist.*' There was absolutely no reinforcing sympathy . . . the commitment in those regions was stronger than it was in the East."

Shero had edited the *SDS Bulletin*, but the *Rag* was involved in covering and creating a radical-hip community, not the Austin branch of SDS. It both protested the war as a systemic expression of American policy and cosponsored events such as Gentle Thursday, be-ins during which the old jet parked in front of the University of Texas ROTC building was decorated with "MAKE LOVE, NOT WAR" and "FLY GENTLY, SWEET PLANE." And in keeping with SDS's ideas about egalitarianism, the paper did away with the idea of a strong founder-editor, instead putting information in the hands of a person known as "the funnel" while retaining collective decision-making on stories.

"Austin's a very funny scene," Dreyer, whose lengthening hair still had a bit of a ducktail to it, wrote in UPS's post-Stinson roundup. "There aren't the real ideological-philosophical splits between politicos and hippies that exist many places. We probably have the most political hippies and the most hip politicos around. Guess it's kind of the result of us against THEM . . . hardly a week passes that some beatnik doesn't get bashed on the head by a beer bottle."

But that was the exception to a split starting to run through the underground press. In one camp were the hippies. At the *Oracle, EVO,* the *Seed,* and elsewhere, most staff members believed that changing oneself was a prerequisite for changing society. Right action meant living the politics of nonviolence and sharing, and many writers used (or rationalized their use of) drugs as tools for internal and social change. There were hippies and *freaks*—Diggers barged into the Stinson house to lambaste the *Oracle* for not organizing the Haight community—but both groups wanted to be left alone by both the government *and* any radical party.

Political radicals—"politicos" if you were being derogatory—turned the process around. Sharing was fine, they felt, but established interests would not voluntarily end the war or cede power. Within UPS, *Win* and *Peace News* were American and English voices of pacifism, more concerned with nonviolence than creative page layouts. Max Scherr was covering marches and issues in the *Barb.* The *Free Press*'s claimed fifty-thousand-copy circulation was based on blending a lucid Living Arts section with the latest antiwar coverage, not on psychedelic graphics. And events in the so-called Great Society and changes within the movements soon would encourage or pressure all the papers to politicize.

On April 15 in New York's Central Park, the Spring Mobilization to End the War in Vietnam drew a throng that the police, always conservative in such matters, estimated at between 100,000 and 125,000. The largest antiwar demonstration to date spanned the range of dissent from suit-and-tie mainstreamers to pacifist hippies to National Liberation Front supporters. There were chants: "Hell, no, we won't go!" "Hey, hey, LBJ, how many kids did you kill today?" Several thousand hips held a be-in in the park. Seventy, a hundred, perhaps two hundred draft cards were burned. At a sister demonstration in San Francisco, fifty to seventy-five thousand people heard speaker after speaker call for unconditional and immediate withdrawal from Vietnam.

Again, underground and mass-media coverage of the events diverged widely. A lengthy New York *Times* story on the April 15 rally showed that the antiwar movement was now large enough (and the Mobilization, a coalition of liberal and radical groups, legitimate enough) to attract coverage. But the soberly written story offered few connections between the rally and events in Vietnam or within the antiwar movement. It took no overt position on the war or the march, and though the lead centered on protesters gathering to denounce the war, the principle of balanced coverage gave nearly as much space to a much smaller number of counter-demonstrators as to the remarks of speakers who'd addressed at least a hundred thousand people. Antiwar activists were rarely accorded this kind of "equal time" whenever administration spokesmen defended Vietnam involvement. Then again, the Yippies would exploit the mass press's commitment to at least perfunctory rebuttal during their organizing for the 1968 Democratic National Convention.

An editorial on the day of the march noted that "some of the original sponsors have quite rightly withdrawn because they do not want to be associated with speakers and marchers who depict the U.S. as the epitome of evil and the Vietcong guerillas and their North Vietnamese allies as the epitome of good." It offered no comment about the unity that had led to a march of this size, instead criticizing demonstrators for a "moral . . . double standard."

The *Barb*'s coverage of the San Francisco march offered another perspective. It was less detailed than the *Times*'s report, and an entire story nitpicked the *Times*'s plausible crowd estimates. The main story was a lively, first-person account of a "counter-action to the war, the visible embodiment of human love and joy." Counter-demonstrators were quoted to an audience that would laugh off remarks such as "you lousy bunch of chickens." Here too there was no Vietnam backgrounding; in the *Barb,* opposition to the war was *a priori.*

The *Barb,* in an unusual move, also ran an editorial. Surprisingly, it too warned about Leftists—the "dinosaur leaders" who sought to "manipulate" demonstrators involved in "a new stage in the evolution of mass man." Country Joe McDonald, the lead singer of the acid-cum-protest-rock band the Fish, offered a telling comment: "Man, I learned one thing that afternoon. There's more than one revolution."

It was the *Guardian* that talked about colonialism. The underground press of 1967 was closer to the counter-napalm prose of Ed Sanders, the Fug. "It makes us puke green monkey shit to contemplate Johnson's war in Vietnam," he'd say that summer. "Lyndon Baines is squirting the best blood of America into a creep scene."

The April demonstrations turned isolated antidraft protest into a Resistance whose members thought it better to burn paper than people. "We, the undersigned men of draft age," one statement of noncooperation had read, "believe that all war is immoral and ultimately self-defeating. We believe that military conscription is evil and unjust. . . . We urge and advocate that other young men join us in noncooperation with the Selective Service System."

Refusing both induction and deferments, resisters faced five years' imprisonment and a $10,000 fine. But their protest—the principled tip of an iceberg of exemptions due to drug, psychiatric, and sudden physical disabilities—made them feel empowered rather than isolated.

In May, *Resist* began publishing out of Palo Alto, California. Produced by members of the Peace and Liberation Commune, a three-house network of a dozen activists with interests from Buddhism to political organizing, the eight-page mimeographed mini-tabloid was designed to be a monthly organizing tool that would keep Resistance chapters in touch with each other. "We were putting out propaganda," recalls David Harris, the former Stanford University student-body president who was en route to becoming the decade's second-best-known resister (after Muhammad Ali). "There was Information that would substantiate our position and create draft resisters. Part of the reason we put it out was for credibility: 'Of course we exist, we have a magazine.' And we had a press. Ex-students who'd been reading for years now had the capacity to print things other people would read."

This would, after all, be Vietnam Summer as well as the Summer of Love. Vancouver's brand-new *Canadian Free Press* covered acid and rock, but in May, a writer named John Kelsey caught the changing times in a story called "Is Love Obscene?" "There's no future playing one-two-three-O'Leary, even though it's fun," he argued. "Love has little meaning for a Filipino Huk, who's seen the CIA and Suharto kill about a million neighboring Indonesians, and who knows that if he doesn't keep his knife sharp, he's next.

"Storm troopers don't love back, see, they just walk on your prostrate, flowered face."

Hippies, a less rhetorical Jack Newfield said in the *Nation,* were too intent on seeking pleasure to effect change. "They lack the energy, stability and private pain to serve as 'the new proletariat.' . . . Bananas, incense and pointing love rays toward the Pentagon have nothing to do with redeeming America. . . . The effect of acid activism is to make them fugitives from the system, instead of insurgents against the system."

Yet "acid imagination" soon produced the underground's most outrageous single story.

DESPITE their growth, underground papers had small staffs and circulations compared to the mainstream press. Hundreds of stories cried for a new perspective, but few writers had the wherewithal to travel to Vietnam, and most underground reporters were young white dropouts with some college education but little journalism training. Advocacy could slip easily into unverified onesidedness. Some writers did able power-structure research, but the police and various governmental agencies usually were regarded as less credible sources than the hip in the street. Undergroundpress writers sometimes saw things more clearly than those enmeshed in mass society. But when a story was right, it often had more to do with intuition than investigation. A few stories bypassed the research entirely, and tried to shock readers into rethinking their ideals and immediately acting on them.

The most notorious "zap" appeared in the May, 1967, *Realist.* Entitled "The Parts That Were Left Out of the Kennedy Book," the piece purported to represent excerpts deleted from William Manchester's JFK biography, *The Death of a President.* The last entry had "Jackie Kennedy" allegedly corroborating an incident on Air Force One as it ferried the assassinated President's body from Dallas to Washington:

"That man [Vice President Lyndon Johnson] was crouching over the corpse, no longer chuckling but breathing hard and moving his body rhythmically. At first I thought he must be performing some mysterious symbolic rite he'd learned from Mexicans or Indians as a boy. And then I realized—there is only one way to say this—he was literally fucking my husband in the throat. He reached a climax and dismounted. I froze. The next thing I remember, he was being sworn in as the new President."

The final paragraph included an author's note: "Is this simply necrophilia or was LBJ trying to change entry wound into exit wound by enlarging?"

Realist editor Paul Krassner had written this scandalous satire. The repercussions were immediate. The magazine's regular printer, an independent socialist, refused to print the piece; his wife asked Krassner how he'd feel if Jackie Kennedy committed suicide after seeing it. The *Realist* was banned in parts of Boston. Subscribers canceled. A United Press International columnist called the story "slime . . . senseless hatred . . . that makes the truly concerned and serious opponents of the Vietnam War look bad by association." An editor at *Holiday* magazine threatened to punch Krassner out. A *Realist* supporter said that the CIA had planted the story. Robert Scheer, then *Ramparts'* managing editor, worried that the credibility of factually true *Realist* exposés would be undermined.

But *Ramparts* editor Warren Hinckle sent a telegram: "Brilliant dirty issue." Cops came by with complaints, stayed to read. A Minneapolis *Tribune* columnist used Krassner's story to criticize Manchester's alleged "exercises in grief." Nazi leader George Lincoln Rockwell, whom Krassner had interviewed, saluted his "balls of steel" and offered a perverse accolade: "For a Jew, you shoulda been a Nazi."

Talking on the telephone with someone Krassner said had identified himself as Manchester, Krassner explained that he'd run the piece "To satirize certain things about the assassination, its aftermath, the hypocrisy, the exploitation . . . the quest for power." (Manchester later denied speaking to Krassner.)

At least one reader reconsidered the question of taste in one of the follow-up letters published in the *Realist:*

"I don't cancel my subscription to the *Chronicle* because I read every day of the horror, the obscenities, the crimes committed by LBJ. . . . That grisly image was *not* burned children in Vietnam, crying mothers, bombed villages or starving black kids in Oakland."

"Metaphor is a kind of truth," Krassner explains. "The people that believed that, or even considered it, had to suddenly face the fact that they believed their president was crazy. So it was a metaphor for what was going on in Vietnam, and here."

The piece was journalistically irresponsible, and uncaring about Jackie Kennedy's feelings. It was also compelling, the story most often recalled by those interviewed for this book.

Legal segregation had been smashed. Laws protecting civil and voting rights were on the books. But actual discrimination in jobs, housing, and social attitudes endured. Martin Luther King's ideals of a fair, integrated society secured by nonviolence were increasingly challenged by either a separatist Black Power movement or a Black Panther Party allied with other radicals willing to accept internationalism, coalition, militance, even armed struggle. Both became the subject of a values collision between underground and mass media, and within the underground press itself.

SNCC (Student Nonviolent Coordinating Committee) chairman Stokely Carmichael had found sit-ins far more realistic than socialist rhetoric. Beaten and jailed in Mississippi, he'd lobbied for SNCC field workers to be allowed to carry guns for self-defense. He'd seen the Democratic Party's decision not to replace segregated Dixiecrats with an integrated delegation at its 1964 National Convention as a betrayal. West Indian by birth, he'd been influenced by nationalism and pan-Africanism, Guevara and Fanon. "SNCC's Third World orientation," Carmichael profiler Milton Viorst has noted, "drew it inevitably to the conclusion that Vietnam was a colonial war, conducted by whites against people of color." Many black militants began seeing whites as enemies—or as fickle, manipulative friends.

By mid-1966, Martin Luther King had been frustrated by the explosion in Watts and his failure to make headway against a wily Mayor Daley in housing-segregated Chicago. A black SNCC worker had been murdered in Alabama after using a whites-only restroom. SNCC had encouraged draft resistance against a society seen as racist both at home and abroad, and had organized a separatist Black Panther Party to challenge the Democrats for elective offices in rural Alabama. At SNCC's spring 1966 convention, white activists had been instructed to organize within their own communities. At a July rally after the shooting of James Meredith, Carmichael, by now SNCC's chairman, had proclaimed that "The only way we gonna stop them white men from whuppin' us is to take over . . . Black Power!" King had immediately denounced the slogan —"equally as evil as white supremacy"—but by December, the last whites were off the SNCC payroll.

The summer of 1967 was the proverbial long, hot one. From July 12 to 17, twenty-six people were killed and over a thousand arrested in Newark, New Jersey. From July 23 to 30, forty-seven hundred paratroopers and eight thousand national guardsmen occupied a burning Detroit. The immediate causes were the arrest of a black cabdriver for allegedly assaulting a policeman and a mass arrest at an after-hours bar. But radicals saw insurrections against pervasive racism, charged liberal elites with being incapable of effecting massive social change or fending off a police state, espoused a just transfer of power from white establishments to oppressed black communities. Underground-press writings showed how much velocity rebellion had picked up in the two years since Watts and the L.A. *Free Press*'s reasoned coverage. Sounding like a torch-bearing Emily Post, Harvey Ovshinsky wrote in Detroit's *Fifth Estate* that the looting had been "interracial and unusually cordial and friendly until the paratroopers began firing." The riot-rebellion "made Watts look like a Love-in." Forty were dead, two thousand injured.

Speaking in Watts a few weeks later, H. Rap Brown, the new SNCC chairman, declared America to be on "the eve of a black revolution." His speech also excoriated an institution he now identified as "the White Power Press." "Their job over the years," he said, "has been to make black people enemies of black people."

Brown's speech was reprinted in the Los Angeles *Open City*, just as a speech by Lyndon Johnson or Governor Reagan might appear in the Los Angeles *Times*. (The daily paper, though, might have also run analytical sidebars.) But the rise of Black Power also meant that even fewer blacks would write for the underground press. "Over the long run it didn't work out," Art Kunkin said about the integrated team that had informed the L.A. *Free Press*'s Watts coverage. "They were in a black nationalist phase even then, a little suspicious about working with white people." As a result, underground papers would have to report the issue across a gap intensified by racial separation. Which made the coalition-building Black Panther Party all the more attractive.

These Black Panthers were not the same group as Carmichael's Alabama separatists. Soulful, tough, they were coalescing in black communities around the issue of police brutality. The organization had gathered strength at Merritt College in Oakland, where the party took root in June, 1966. In October, its leadership had promulgated a ten-point program demanding community control, full employment, decent housing, no exploitation, liberated education, an exemption from military service and an end to police brutality, freedom for jailed black men, juries of real peers, and a U.N.-supervised plebiscite to determine black people's national destiny. In May, 1967, an armed cadre had visited the California state capitol in Sacramento, to demand rights—and media attention.

The Panthers got it. A *New York Times Magazine* story published that August (written by a *Ramparts* editor named Sol Stern) was knowledgeable and quoted Panther leaders at length. Most mass-press stories were hostile, though, and even sympathetic coverage usually assumed that electoral politics was the only acceptable means for social change, not armed protest by a tiny number of radicals, no matter how many people they said they represented. Few if any articles *supported* the Panthers and their revolutionary goals—and support was what the Panthers (like all but the most masochistic news subjects) really wanted.

The Panthers had begun their own paper in April to gain an unfiltered forum for their ideology and to raise money through mandatory sales by the rank and file. The *Black Panther*'s circulation would eventually pass eighty-five thousand, and it and the white underground press would promote the Panther leadership as first-name icons—Huey, Bobby, Eldridge.

In July, the *Black Panther* reprinted an article from *The Movement* that seconded Rap Brown's assessment of mass media. The story discussed guidelines written by a California news director on how broadcast media should cover ghetto "disorders." In the event of upheavals, the press was directed to police command posts, where they would receive secondary-source information from law-enforcement officials. "Reports should be calm, objective, and present the 'overall picture,' " the guidelines said.

"They intend," the *Movement/Black Panther* story countered "to be objective without presenting any of the views of one side in the conflict. . . . There is no Guideline that says 'seek out the causes of the riot and find ways of ending the oppression.' . . .

"The press," the story concluded, "is a conscious tool of the police. "The press, too, must be battled and opposed."

Which is what happened when the National Conference for New Politics convened in Chicago in late August. Almost immediately, the conclave of two hundred or so antiwar, civil rights, and community groups found itself in disarray. Half the black delegates refused to meet with even radical whites, and the Black Caucus that consented to do so demanded a bloc vote equal to that of the much larger white membership. Reparations, some whites agreed; white guilt, others countered. Eventually, bloc voting was accepted, which meant that any issue supported by united blacks needed to receive only one of twenty-eight thousand "white votes" to carry. The conference also foundered over whether the radical movement should stress opposing the war abroad, or overcoming racism at home, or Trying to Change It All. One of the thirteen points ratified at the conference condemned Israel for its role in the recent Six-Day War, which irritated many (but not all) Jewish radicals.

Writing for the hometown, We-Are-All-One *Seed,* Cynthia Edelman granted the horrors of racism and noted that it had made black militants better organized than their white counterparts. Still, the gathering's politics saddened her:

"People who do not wish to think in any terms but a united race of deliciously various skin color were forced once again to accept a division," she noted. Then she slipped into apocalyptic prose. "The NCNP has shown us at least one thing: the time is shorter than we knew, and we must decide *now* what we will do personally to restore humans to the path, before the Universe blots us out as too stupid to remain on a ravaged earth."

How? "The best idea I heard was to have a spontaneous pot party in the last plenary and turn everybody on."

The divisiveness, though, was made to order for the conservative Chicago *Tribune.* Its chronicle of chaos was often correct, if punctuated with phrases about "Black Power fanatics" and white "capitulation." But other articles ballyhooed the presence of "seven Reds" whom the paper declared to be the vanguard of hundreds of Communist Party puppet-masters. The story quoted extensively (with accompanying photo) from copies of registration forms "made available" to the *Tribune,* and from statements by "federal and local security officers who are closely observing proceedings of the convention." Before the conference was over, black militance, Movement tumult, and police-oriented reporting gave the paper another story—one of its photographers was punched around after a Rap Brown speech.

"Straight media" was a receding phrase. Soon "pig media" would be set in underground type.

5

THE FALL OF THE PENTAGON

WASHINGTON, D.C.—OCTOBER 20, 1967: The large loft was filled. Liberal-to-Left college editors talked politics, or decried campus apathy. People from many of the nearly one hundred underground papers forged during the Summers of Love, Vietnam, and Detroit laughed together or argued. A Washington *Post* reporter and several observers condemned by their ties were asked to leave—after all, radical writers weren't being invited to sit in with mainstream publishers or police chiefs. And underground-press people tried to talk about a service that would both syndicate and generate radical news.

Two months before, the underground editors had met amid the furor of the National Conference for New Politics to discuss such a service. Their papers illustrated the growing range of the dissident press: the civil-rights-oriented *Southern Patriot;* the Chicano *El Gallo* out of Denver; New York's socialist *National Guardian;* and, in a dose of cross-media participation, New York listener-sponsored radio station WBAI. Now the media hype of an Underground Press Syndicate was on the verge of becoming real.

The loft gathering was a journalistic accompaniment to the march on the Pentagon, where perhaps a hundred thousand members of what Norman Mailer would christen the Armies of the Night would "Confront the Warmakers." By now, whiffs of fear were in the air. In June, police forces had crushed a peaceful antiwar demonstration at Los Angeles' Century City, a dark moment the rock group Buffalo Springfield sang about as having drawn battle lines and caused paranoia to strike deep. In Oakland earlier the week of the conference, demonstrators had been beaten by police and had felt the sting of a new drug called MACE. "The caravan will pass through some very hostile territory and many will die on the trip," a detachment of California heads told *EVO* before moving out toward the Pentagon. Everyone survived, but *Easy Rider*–type snuffings already seemed all too possible.

But in Oakland, protesters during Stop the Draft Week had fought off small police detachments, had even overturned cars. En route to being indicted (and later acquitted) as one of the Oakland Seven for felonious conspiracy to create a public nuisance, resist arrest, and trespass, a thoughtful radical named Frank Bardacke was addressing a key question facing activists: could they end the war without alienating the people needed to build a mass Movement?

Bardacke was the radical who the year before had declared the need to escape to a counterculture. Now, he was writing, the hip promise was dissolving into radicals "playing with guns as a way to forget their own hopelessness." Worse, he felt, the Left could neither offer America an alternative nor even keep its draft resisters free.

The Oakland fighting had been less a moral attempt to engage the white middle class in antiwar dialogue than an exhibition of radical toughness aimed at previously ignored young blacks and *workers*. But this tactic had come at the expense of being labeled "vandals." So be it, Bardacke now was prepared to say; "If we can actually convince them that we can cause chaos in this country as long as the war continues, so much the better. We may have even stumbled on a strategy that could end the war."

In the Washington loft, though, the birth of a news service was experiencing its own chaos. Some of it was fun, as when the *Oracle*'s Allen Cohen and *EVO*'s Walter Bowart engaged in an impromptu poem-off. And Bowart's claim that the underground press was the real voice of what was coming to be called "the youth culture" fell on receptive years:

"I am told that the editors present here today represent more than fifteen million young readers," he said, using a reader-to-copy ratio that assumed each paper was read by an entire commune. "Fifteen million people who have yet to exercise one iota of the social, economic, and political majority they possess, for, as you know, fifty-one percent of the population of this country is younger than twenty-seven years of age. That's a lot of frustrated energy."

But Bowart encountered resistance when he shifted to the Underground Press Syndicate. In the six months since Stinson Beach, UPS had picked up two-score-plus members, and its policy of free reuse of material gave readers a sense of national movement and smaller papers enough material to fill their pages. Still, all UPS enrollment required was sending a letter to New York. And UPS's sharing of articles had fallen into the culture-politics rift. Bob Rudnick, then UPS's coordinator: "The first thing I wanted to do was a news service, so I starting sending out mimeo'd news items. I stopped because the peace-love papers really resented political news, and didn't want to contribute any money to UPS."

Now writers from member papers denounced UPS as not only an *EVO* puppet-show but a scam that diverted money due them from record, book, and movie ads. Rudnick soon found himself in the rear of the room, drinking apricot brandy while the arguments raged.

Despite all this, the thin, energetic guy up front thought that a news service could happen.

Marshall Bloom, Denver-born scion of a furniture-store family, had emerged in radical circles the year before, when, as editor of the *Amherst Student*, he'd condemned the awarding of an honorary degree to then-Secretary of Defense Robert McNamara. While president of the London School of Economics' Graduate Students' Association, he'd led protests with enough gusto for an Anglo-American newspaper to bellow "Bloom Go Home." Some of his best friends were SDSers.

At the same time, Bloom, like many Americans in his early twenties, was familiar with the hip side of things. His hair was billowing into an "Isro" (a Jewish Afro), and a Sergeant Pepper frock coat draped his cranelike body. In the value system of the day, LSD made more sense to him than LBJ.

Bloom had recently been fired as executive director of the United States Student Press Association (which operated the College Press Service) for publishing a scathing attack—in the organization's name—on the CIA's funding of the National Student Association. (He'd also spent thousands of USSPA dollars to bring underground writers to a National College Editors Conference.) Now, with things heating up, Bloom had formed a New Media Project to link antiwar and countercultural papers. A prototype of the thrice-weekly packets the service would mail to its $15-a-month subscribers (black and gold ink on magenta paper this time around) explained why Bloom was calling it Liberation News Service—LNS: "After resistance comes liberation."

From the floor, Ray Mungo watched the spectacle with growing pessimism; clearly, this assembly was too untogether to cooperatively *own* its own service, as Bloom had originally planned. A slight, bespectacled twenty-one-year-old with a smile that overcame its less-than-perfect orthodonture, Mungo had grown up in a dreary Massachusetts mill town, been a scholarship parochial school student, and edited the Boston University *News*. A short time later, he'd become the All-American Nightmare: a pot-smoking pacifist who'd burned his draft card on Hiroshima Day, had called for the impeachment of LBJ, and had sent a reporter to Vietnam while editor of his college paper. The confidence of being part of something larger than himself—the baby boom, an international struggle for justice in Vietnam, LSD's seemingly primal images—left Mungo self-assured, even cocky. That summer, he'd returned from a Czechoslovakian meeting with "the Vietnamese" proclaiming, "We are the Americong"—as in American Vietcong.

"From Vietnam, I learned to despise my countrymen, my government, and the entire English-speaking world, with its history of genocide and international conquest. I was a normal kid," Mungo would write in *Famous Long Ago,* the poetic if one-sided memoir of LNS's power struggles he'd conceive just two years later, which, for him already would be "after the revolution."

This fall, though, he'd dropped a Harvard fellowship and quit the student press association to hook up with Bloom. They were an entry, BlooMungo, the News Brothers. Of the two, Mungo had even less use for the mainstream press. And though he'd later recognize that some LNS pieces were better passion than fact, he felt (and still feels) that writing experientially could make for an honest journalism. He also knew something else: Young people were attracted to the underground press not just to implement "critical social change" but because they were terrified at the prospect of "working at dumb jobs for constipated corporations."

The early LNS would be more family than collective, with Bloom as daddy, Mungo as the older brother, and deadlines met via some inspired chaos Mungo called "magic." Stories were written by staff on LNS's one electric typewriter, sent in from a network of literally worldwide contacts, or reprinted from UPS papers. After being printed on a small in-house press, packets containing news stories, shorts, and features would be dispatched to underground papers, political groups, a few mass-press editors, and other subscribers. The articles reflected the values of "politicized freaks." Good stuff: personal liberation, resisting unjust laws, pot and LSD, adventure, the right to an abortion, Karl Marx—again, leavened with doses of Groucho. Bad stuff: the war, American imperialism, materialism, dogmatic thinking, boring schools, hard drugs. "Originally, LNS was quite a collection of free souls," Mungo recalls. "They were anything but violent, committed as much to the revolution of consciousness as to the political revolution. We sincerely believed that we had a new Utopia building."

But on the day before the Pentagon demonstration, Mungo sat in the Washington loft as charges and countercharges swirled in the air. "It was clear on first meeting our constituency that LNS was to be an uneasy coalition."

It would shatter within a year.

Bloom and Mungo approached the Pentagon demonstration respecting such National Mobilization organizers as David Dellinger, *Liberation* magazine's pacifist editor, and Rennie Davis, the bright young New Leftist. But they had drawn closer to Jerry Rubin, the Berkeley activist brought onto the Mobilization team to attract the outlaw young many political radicals had dismissed. Rubin and his friend Abbie Hoffman, a SNCC activist turned Lower East Side street organizer, were making a dadaistic call for the levitation of the Pentagon, which Bloom and Mungo found more realistic than any serious attempt to breach the building's defenses. Like Rubin's writing, Bloom's predemonstration call, widely reprinted via a prototype LNS packet, had been part prediction, part myth-making:

"Something's happening but you won't know what it is, General Jones, because you think that only angry Mothers and bearded students march, and that hippies stay in Haight-Ashbury and the East Village. Look out your window on Oct. 21 and freak out at what will be marching toward the Pentagon. . . . Swamis, Indian men, people with water pistols (passed out free), noise makers, hundreds of skulls on poles, flower banners. . . . Guzzle another shot, mutter to yourself that hippies aren't supposed to be political, and feel what it's like to be exorcised as an evil spirit, General."

When Bloom's piece ran in the Chicago *Seed*, it became another milestone for me. My Summer of Love trip to California had ended with a mindless contretemps at the Mexican border after a Tijuana day trip that left one of my van-mates convicted of possession of a switchblade and the rest of us innocent but broke. Now I was in Chicago, a textbook salesman living at a hotel where most of the residents wore hot pants and most of the men were named John. A workaday haircut and brown company Chevy made me resemble an undercover cop, but I was soon a regular at the aptly named Headland, the hole-in-the-wall headshop that we'd stumbled into during our cross-country trip.

I tried to keep working in the mainstream, really I did. But like Mungo, I was allergic to corporate life, and was developing a healthy loathing for the war. One October day, I found myself in Headland, talking with Jim, one of the owners, and with "Treeman," a friendly, mushroom-haired local lifeform who worked behind the counter.

"A bunch of freaks are going to demonstrate against the war at the Pentagon," I said.

Dressed for hip success—stovepipe hat, fur vest, embroidered shirt, blue sunglasses, black pants with gold piping—Treeman raised his voice. "The war sucks. We should go. I hear they're gonna levitate the Pentagon."

And so, the brown Chevy headed east, the odometer ticking off mile after mile impossible to explain on home-office expense vouchers. in a last burst of conscientiousness probably more dangerous than anything we'd encounter at the Pentagon, I, the insured driver, drove all the way there (and back), my eyes brighter than the headlights.

Soon we were climbing a Virginia hill toward the Pentagon, where there was something for every opponent of the war. Flower people used M-1s and M-14s for vases. Allen Ginsberg, Ed Sanders, and other shamanists chanted "Out, demon, out" to the strains of flutes, whistles, and bongos. Demonstrators bearing red, yellow, and blue National Liberation Front flags breached a side door, only to be beaten back by, among others, U.S. marshals who'd protected activists in the South just a few years before. People shared food, water, solidarity, each other. There were 647 arrests. The building didn't rise, but the spirits of thousands of demonstrators did. When we returned to Chicago, I began writing for the *Seed*.

Not surprisingly, LNS and the New York *Times* disseminated different versions of the Pentagon demonstration.

In numerous reports, *Times* reporters worked an unfolding story, moving from citing only the police estimate of fifty thousand demonstrators to also mentioning the one hundred fifty thousand figure provided by Dave Dellinger. They accepted, then challenged, military reports that the teargas used had come from the dissenting side of the barricades.

But *Times* reporters didn't join the rebels (at least in print), and their stories focused on arrests and permit deadlines while barely mentioning the war-related issues underpinning them. A profile on Dellinger acknowledged his pacifism, then homed in on his police blotter.

This absence of the politics behind the protest was standard. But it also reflected the trouble policy-makers at many dailies were having finding a place to stand. "Other than stopping the bombing," *Newsweek* wrote on the eve of the demonstration, "the nation's editorialists seem at a loss for advice." With the exception of reporter John Kifner's astute sidebar on the peace movement's new militance, the *Times*'s news stories offered only perfunctory quotes from administration hawks, disaffected doves, and militant Leftists alike.

James Reston's post-mortem analysis, however, expressed a real disappointment over a divided America:

"This was a sad and brooding city tonight," Reston wrote, "because everybody seemed to have lost in the anti-war siege of the Pentagon this weekend. The majority of the demonstrators who marched peaceably and solemnly to the banks of the Potomac were unhappy because the event was taken over by the militant minority. The leading officials of the Government were troubled by the spectacle of so tumultuous a protest against their policy in Vietnam and by the repercussions of this demonstration on their relations abroad. . . .

"Even the pugnacious young activists who battled the marshals and soldiers at the Pentagon were not satisfied at the end, for they had not won support for ending the war or defeating President Johnson, but may very well have done the opposite."

In contrast, LNS's own nine-story-plus-photos Pentagon packet was dispatched to a hundred papers, with a potential (but doubtful) readership of one million people. It mixed freak and radical perspectives, politics and celebration, and, most of all, demonstrators' experience. Two sympathetic GIs told about life on the other side of the fixed bayonets (admitting that other soldiers were hostile to the protest). Ray Mungo reported from jail. Demonstrators were hailed as politically correct and morally superior. Mainstream reporters were criticized for blowing the story—even as LNS covered their confronting an army spokesman on the tear-gassing story. There was a preview of sit-ins to come.

Thorne Dreyer, the Austin *Rag* writer, served as LNS's James Reston via a state-of-the-art New Left "analysis"—overtly political, exhortatory, didactic, and mildly profane, "On October 21," Dreyer began, "the white left got its shit together. . . . The gala Pentagon confrontation, long billed as a move from 'protest to resistance,' was a dramatic and intense political event."

Dreyer evaluated the Pentagon demonstration via a new underground-press standard—the militance of Black Power:

"Black America has gained new respect for the white left'," he wrote, quoting a black spokesman. And he cited a higher revolutionary source. Ernesto "Ché" Guevara, who'd helped Fidel Castro make the Cuban Revolution, had been killed in Bolivia just two weeks before the Pentagon demonstration. The New York *Times* had carefully verified his death with pictures and fingerprints, and quoted a general saying that Guevara had admitted failure before his death. But many American Leftists saw Ché as a hero who'd made the ultimate sacrifice, and Dreyer now invoked him as a caution against emerging military macho:

"Some of the demonstrators on the front line wanted to force more violent confrontations with the soldiers. It seemed to many of us that this was suicidal and would prove nothing. One is misreading Ché Guevara by concluding that a guerilla fighter confronts a superior military force in positional combat."

The *Movement* agreed. "We are convinced," its post-Pentagon summary read, "that power throughout the society is illegitimate and will continue to be basically unresponsive to public opinion and normal political pressure. That conviction forces us to a conclusion of resistance. But what they advocated was "not a revolution, because entrenched power is too strong to be broken."

YET THE CURVE toward armed conflict was rising.

On October 28, 1967, the Black Panthers' goal of community control of police collided with the Oakland force they denounced as racist. A shootout left one policeman dead; another officer and Huey Newton were wounded.

The confrontation propelled Panther party and underground-press coverage toward what would come to be known as either "struggle-oriented journalism" or "propaganda," depending on who was dropping the names. In the *Black Panther,* Minister of Information Eldridge Cleaver offered a blistering polemic. The police were "gestapo dogs . . . wretched jackals" who employed "murder, brutality and the terror of their image" to keep black people down. Liberation from bondage, Cleaver said, required breaking their power. He claimed unity: twenty million blacks agreed that Newton was not guilty, was a political prisoner, was right. "There will be no more reports of black people being massacred or we want to hear more reports about more dead cops shot down by black men. . . . there can no longer be a double standard."

When LNS reprinted Cleaver's article in its packet of December 15, 1967, it also ran a piece by a white writer from Berkeley that attempted to build support for the Panthers. Yet the reporter felt the need to defuse some of the stories and cartoons in the *Black Panther*. Depicting the shot police "as two limp white pigs with bullet-holes in them," he wrote, "may give a wrong impression." Meeting the Panther leadership, he said, showed them to be reasonable men acting in self-defense.

In 1968, Huey Newton would be convicted of voluntary manslaughter; the conviction would be reversed. A 1974 murder charge would be dropped after juries deadlocked; charges the same year of being a felon in possession of a pistol produced a three-year sentence that remains on appeal. Late in 1967, though, an underground writer was arguing that larger political Truth overshadowed the legalities—or reportorial details —of the situation. "Whether Frey [the dead policeman] shot first or not (the lawyers seem to think the case will hinge on this) is irrelevant; his death was self-defense on Newton's part. The case is not a criminal, but a political one." In the famous Panther buzzphrase of the time, one would be "either part of the solution or part of the problem."

After the Pentagon demonstration, LNS took a deep breath and declared its position vis-à-vis the daily press:

"Liberation News Service provides a totally different alternate medium," it said, "for those of us who are fed up with hearing there were 'some 25,000 to 40,000 demonstrators' when we ourselves saw at least twice that many; hearing them say that 'police acted with appropriate restraint' when we saw the guy next to us getting his skull busted just because he had long hair; hearing that we . . . are 'sincerely working for peace' and that we are 'supporting and defending democratic government in Vietnam,' when we see our government destroying a countryside, waging an undeclared war of attrition on helpless women, children and farmers in the name of one totalitarian puppet regime after another, with no sane end in sight . . . IF YOU TOO ARE REALLY UPTIGHT ABOUT ALL THIS, and want to get the truth to as many people as convincingly as truth can be . . . then we want to help *you*, because if there is to be any truth and humanity found in today's American Press, . . . it is going to be up to us in the college and underground press to print it, and keep printing it until we win or fold."

"End of pitch," the statement was signed. "Om shanti."

LNS stories covered protests in Iowa and New York and Saigon. When four radicalized sailors jumped ship in Japan, LNS printed their statements. When "Dow Shalt Not Kill," an article about the noted napalm producer by historian Howard Zinn, created a stir, LNS created twenty thousand pamphlets. Danny Schechter, who'd previously written about the civil rights movement, met Bloom while in England doing research on the CIA's covert support for various foundations; soon he was LNS's London representative. Exchange agreements with SNCC's new Afromerican News Service and the radicalized Student Communications Network provided access to stories about blacks other than Movement figures, and allowed for on-campus distribution around the country. LNS excerpted the work of Wilhelm Reich, the sex theorist whose books had actually been burned by government officials here in America. SDS's politics of resistance and Tim Leary's LSD religiosity ran side by side. There were tips on securing still-illegal abortions. And there was lighter news: one story chronicled the shipment of $7.1 million in pickles to South Korean kimchee fans soldiering in South Vietnam.

In December, LNS moved into a house that soon became headquarters for much of the Washington movement, including the Washington *Free Press* and *Gordon Free News,* a *junior high school* underground paper. Sharing space with each other, and with the Four Horsemen of the Underground—politics, sex, drugs, and rock 'n' roll—made the LNS staff *tight.* Woodrow Wilson Fellows and clever runaways worked seventy-hour weeks for the same $15 the honchos pulled down. Demonstrations and druggy intermissions alike were soul-food for thought. "We wanted to be stoned, wasted, and free," Mungo recalls. "We were proud of being individuals."

LNS staffers were radical outlaws, honest within their collective even as they hustled the world at large. While the rank-and-file sought five-finger discounts at the local supermarket, Bloom and Mungo worked the white-collar scams. "We were criminals, man," Mungo admits with a smile. "Bloom, if I may say so, was an expert thief. We felt like it was revolutionary activity. We were liberating urgently needed 'materials.'

"Essentially, we weren't stealing," he recalls. "What we were doing was being granted credit that we couldn't pay for. Bloom was a fast talker and could wear a three-piece suit. He'd walk into a hardware store and pick up two hundred dollars' worth of stuff and hand over his business card and say, 'I'm Mr. Bloom from the New Media Project; put it on my account.' No clerk in the world could stand up to him."

Ripoffs or Robin Hoods—it depended on where you stood. A long LNS story argued that the summer's looting had not been antiwhite but a popular redistribution of wealth. But like most poor and anti-class-structure underground media, LNS was located in a low-rent district, and it wasn't long before some sticky-fingered residents of the surrounding ghetto gave the service a chance to practice what it preached. So what? "We felt," Mungo recalls, "that the black people deserved our TVs and our stereos."

Through scams and ingenuity, LNS survived to get the word out—but paid a price that would be charged against other media in years to come. "We were inherently doomed," Mungo says now. "We were burning our bridges behind us as fast as we could go. All the papers were. And pretty much all of them went under, unless they got creepy and profit-oriented."

There was another problem: accuracy. "We were not sticklers for accuracy—neither is the underground press in general, so *be advised,"* Mungo would write in *Famous Long Ago* at the end of the sixties. "But our factual errors were not the product of any conspiracy to mislead the young, but of our own lack of organization, shorthandedness, and impatience with grueling research efforts. . . . All we say: tell the truth, brothers, and let the facts fall where they may."

Time has hardened Mungo's judgment about LNS's reliability, or lack of same, "We would print anything some crazy person sent to us," he now says. "It wasn't true simply because some hysterical person wrote it down thinking that it was true. They exaggerated it and nobody checked it out. The facts were wrong a lot of times. We were sloppy, our research scarcely existed, and we didn't have money to pay reporters. The stuff that was seriously political had to be more careful, and certainly there was a lot of truth to it. But even that stuff, I'm sure, made factual errors because of inept reporters. After all, we weren't dealing with paid professionals, but with a bunch of crazy enthusiasts."

ANDY STAPP had grown up uneventfully middle-class and Presbyterian in Philadelphia. As early as 1962, he'd become involved with Youth Against War and Fascism. Paul Krassner might interview Nazi George Lincoln Rockwell in the *Realist;* Stapp had demonstrated against him, picketed U.S. Army and Marine public information offices, and worked on YAWF's paper, the *Partisan.* By 1965, Stapp was actively antiracist, anti-imperialist, anticapitalist, a member of the Maoist Progressive Labor Party. "The same senators and political elements that were the biggest loudmouths on Vietnam were the racial extremists and connected to U.S. business interests," he says.

In August, 1965, Stapp had commemorated the A-bombing of Hiroshima by protesting at the gates of the White House, where he was arrested, beaten, and jailed. In May, 1966, just shy of twenty-three, he'd talked his way around having burned his draft card and enlisted to organize within the army. He wanted more than an antiwar movement. He wanted socialist revolution. "Ché Guevara believed this is a people's war against imperialism," he recalls. "I shared that."

Stapp had told his barracksmates that the war was wrong, and, when soldiers seemed receptive, that socialism was better than capitalism. He says he never had trouble. "It was a captive audience; you don't go home at night from the army, and I had a very good idea of what I wanted to do there."

In August, 1967, Stapp and YAWF had begun developing the idea of an American Serviceman's Union. When it was released at Christmas, the ASU's eight-point program called for collective bargaining, a federal minimum wage, free political association, election of officers, no saluting or "sir-ing," and "the right to disobey illegal and immoral orders." No officers allowed.

Stapp organized for the ASU—and the official reaction put him on permanent latrine duty. Then, during his third politically motivated court martial, he came into contact with the *Bond,* the Berkeley-based GI paper that was one of sixty or so which would publish on or near military bases here and abroad, some covertly. A typical GI paper was black-and-white, and contained partisan news reports on Vietnam and the military, defenses of GI rights, attacks on especially loathed officers, and cartoons that showed soldiers turning their guns on overly gung-ho officers or on the plutocrat behind the general behind the officer behind the sergeant. Distribution was haphazard, advertising usually nonexistent. Demand and disciplinary action ran neck and neck.

All of the GI papers were antiwar, but could have divergent politics. Using the divisions suggested by sixties underground-press author Robert Glessing, several "Trot" papers—those influenced by the Young Socialist Alliance, the Student Mobilization Committee, and other Trotskyist groups—limited protest to the war per se. "Independents" such as Chicago's *Vietnam GI* and the San Francisco Bay area's *Ally* would approximate SDS's broader anti-establishment politics.

The "militants" wanted highly radical change, and Andy Stapp moved the *Bond* in that direction after its exhausted staff simply shipped everything to him in New York. "They had been writing about me, and in the end, they asked us to take it over when we set up the American Serviceman's Union as a formal union. The *Bond* was simply packed up and the mailing list was sent to us." By the time Stapp was undesirably discharged in April, 1968 (the verdict was later reversed), the *Bond* was the paper of a two-thousand-member ASU.

"We wanted to use the *Bond* as a vehicle to build the ASU," Stapp recalls. "That made us a national organization. The Pentagon is an international organization."

ASU membership would peak at twelve thousand. But what if the army had adopted its program?

"Paralyzed the army is what it would have done," he replies emphatically. "This was not a reformist goal, but what I went into the army for. And it was paralyzed to the point they could no longer conduct a war in Vietnam."

A TURNING POINT in the war began during Tet, the lunar New Year of the Vietnamese calendar. Its nature would be argued long after the fighting ended.

On January 30, 1968, some 84,000 Viet Cong and North Vietnamese troops began a two-month attack on thirty-six provincial capitals, scores more district capitals, fifty hamlets, and twenty-three bases. The streets of Saigon filled with fighters; sappers blew the outer wall of the American embassy compound.

In reality, South Vietnamese and United States forces won a battlefield victory over the forces that Stapp and other radicals called "the Vietnamese." From January to March, 3,895 U.S. and 4,954 South Vietnamese troops died, versus anywhere from 40,000 to 60,000 North Vietnamese and Viet Cong soldiers (including perhaps half the Viet Cong forces).

Yet Tet proved that American power would not be decisive in Vietnam. American nuclear or conventional weapons, if used with total ruthlessness and without political consideration, could have turned North Vietnam—or the entire planet—into a Dead Zone. Instead, U.S. policy settled for "gradual escalation"—a peak of 542,000 American troops reached during 1968, aerial bombardment exceeding the total tonnage dropped during World War II, the Operation Phoenix program's assassination of 20,000 or more actual and alleged NLF cadre, widespread defoliation by the poisonous Agent Orange.

It wasn't enough. "The Americans," one Hanoi official had predicted to a Canadian diplomat in late 1965, will "be so fed up with the war that they would be ready to quit, not in defeat, but in disgust." The NLF and the North were led by dedicated, sometimes ruthless socialists who enjoyed wide popularity; the South's governments were often corrupt and unrepresentative; United States policy was divided on why we were in Vietnam in the first place. Ten years later, an American colonel in Hanoi to help implement the peace accords told a Vietnamese counterpart that North Vietnamese troops had never beaten American soldiers in the field. "That may be so, but it is also irrelevant," his counterpart replied.

Tet decimated Viet Cong cadres (North Vietnamese regular army troops became increasingly active in the war). But, coming just two months after polls showed a plurality of Americans against the war for whatever reason, the image of Tet—fighting in the capital; a pointblank execution sent round the world via Eddie Adams's AP wirephoto—were stark. Many mainstream reporters would be criticized for overestimating the Viet Cong's military prowess during Tet. But if this happened, it was in reaction to the constant official propaganda about imminent U.S. victory the generals and politicians had been handing out.

Tet only entrenched the underground press's various positions. Flower papers abhorred the carnage; overtly socialist papers saw a confirmation of eventual victory for the people's warriors in the black pajamas. As reporters, the *Barb* staff erred in deriding General William Westmoreland's military conclusion that "the enemy's well-laid plan went afoul," and in claiming a military victory for the NLF. As predictors they fared better. A New Year's greeting from Ho Chi Minh cited the "daily massacring [of] Vietnamese people and burning and demolishing [of] Vietnamese towns and villages—as well as the dead Americans and lost billions of dollars.

"In a word," Ho wrote, "the U.S. aggressors have not only committed crimes against Viet Nam, they have also wasted U.S. lives and riches, and stained the honor of the United States."

Making the revolutionary's wishful but inaccurate claim that "the entire Vietnamese people" were "united and of one mind," Ho said that they would fight on against U.S. imperialism. "We shall win and so shall you," he concluded. It was a link many New Leftists prized—and one that recalled Frank Bardacke's conundrum: how did one end the war without putting the Movement at odds with much of America?

RAT

SUBTERRANEAN NEWS

LIBERATED
DOCUMENTS
PAGE 8

may 3-16, 1968
n.y.c. 15¢ outside 25¢

HEIL COLUMBIA

6

KING AND COLUMBIA

WASHINGTON, D.C.—FEBRUARY, 1968: The United States Student Press Association was having its first big meeting since Marshall Bloom's expulsion the previous summer. No funky lofts here; $10,000 from the Washington *Post* corporation provided, among other things, downtown hotel space. But radicals were a part of campus life, so Abbie Hoffman and Jerry Rubin had been asked to address the four hundred or so college editors on hand. Even LNS was allowed a booth.

Then all hell broke loose.

Amid a sober debate between campus hawks and doves, the visiting editors were stunned by a filmed barrage of napalmed babies and rumbling bombbursts.

Before they could recover, a police sergeant announced that the film had been smuggled into the country. The perpetrators had been apprehended. Anyone remaining in the room would be arrested.

As editors stampeded for the door, one of them experienced an emotional flashback of a Vietnam tour of duty. Concerned editors gathered around him. Dialogue about the war intensified.

In the main auditorium, Senator Eugene McCarthy was speaking, a month away from almost defeating LBJ in the New Hampshire Presidential primary and sparking a campus crusade. As McCarthy finished his speech, Jerry Rubin rushed at him.

"CONG CRACK JAIL IN HUE: FREE 2,000," read the front page of the newspaper Rubin waved at Mc-

Carthy. What, Rubin yelled, did the senator think about that?

Eugene McCarthy was too polite for his own good.

"That's very nice," he said.

McCarthy was a decent man who wanted to end the war. But being a liberal rather than a Viet Cong supporter made him an object of radical ire. And so, as Rubin, Ray Mungo, and other rads screamed at McCarthy, the auditorium's rear doors swung open for the Death of Hip reincarnated. Self-styled "freemen" carried a casket toward the stage, then tipped a sea of McCarthy buttons and an American flag onto the floor.

The policeman and the flashbacking student were guerilla-theater actors. The "zap" had been designed to raise consciousness about the war and censorship. "They [the editors] believed they were going to be arrested for seeing a fucking film," Jerry Rubin would say. "They believe they live in a Nazi country. They accept it." The event had been compelling, polarizing, fun. And if most of the collegiate editors had been more embarrassed for Gene McCarthy than about the war, some had been radicalized. Early in 1968, the idea that a militant minority might stop the war was gathering strength.

The Beatles, the Rolling Stones, the San Francisco Sound, Jimi Hendrix, made music that trembled with liberation, music that some FM-radio disk jockeys were melding into free-form segues. The anarchistic Living Theatre and numerous local troupes literally left the stage to try to turn audiences into activists. In January, SDS-oriented film-makers around the country had formed Newsreel, a national collective that would depict events from the Movement's point of view. The underground press was an integral part of this multimedia insurgency. Fed by outrage and outrageousness, political protest and a generational landslide, the papers stood conventional reality on its head. Peace-marchers were more moral than peace officers, acid cooler than alcohol. "From the outside looking in," Oz's Richard Neville would write from England in his book Play Power, "the radical youth Movement seems out to destroy civilization as we know it. From the inside looking out, it is civilization which is destroying itself."

And in topsy-turvy America, the dissident press was succeeding. According to Marshall Bloom, LNS packets were circulating to one hundred twenty-five underground papers, eighty "peace" papers, and seventy-five or so college papers. Advertising and circulation were up; readership estimates now ranged from the Wall Street Journal's 333,000 to Bloom's hefty 4.6 million. Millions of young Americans would serve in Vietnam or vote for George Wallace, but the underground press was helping to define the images of sixties youth as radical. "America now finds itself split into two camps, two life cycles," *EVO*'s Allan Katzman told the San Francisco *Chronicle*. "A cultural evolution is taking place that will sweep the gray-haired masters into the garbage heap. Wisdom and time are on the side of youth." And, undergrounders believed, on the side of the papers. Marvin Garson, the ex–Free Speech Movement activist who was starting the crisp San Francisco *Express Times*, agreed. "It's going to get bigger all the time."

Over the next few months, the underground press would offer increasingly radical coverage of racism, the war, and the nature of the university.

On the night of February 17, five thousand people, most of them black, were in the Oakland Auditorium to celebrate Huey Newton's birthday. Newton was in jail, charged with murder in the Panther-police shootout of the previous October. But on the auditorium stage, Stokely Carmichael was giving him a searing birthday present. With church cadences and street-corner riffing, stallion eyes and wrath-of-God finger-pointing, the former SNCC chairman turned Black Panther's Party prime minister promulgated "A Declaration of War" that threatened both white racists and a largely white underground press.

Carmichael laid down his version of what the Movement was and who was in it. The white man—"the honky"—had slaughtered red men, dropped A-bombs and napalm on yellow men. Now, Carmichael said, there was a real possibility of genocide against blacks. Preventing this, he said, required a proud black united front capable of both love and hate, one that could "restore to our people the humanity and the love that we have for each other."

Voting he dismissed as meaningless. Poverty programs offered crumbs. "We have no alternative but to fight, whether we like it or not. On every level in this country, black people have *got* to fight, *got* to fight, *got* to fight."

Had Huey Newton killed the cop? Carmichael cared only that blacks were willing to fight to "Free Huey." Blacks, that was, for Carmichael disagreed with the Panther call for a rainbow coalition (the phrase began in the sixties) of socialist blacks, browns, and whites. "Poor white people are not fighting for their humanity, they're fighting for more money," Carmichael declared. "No matter how much money you make in the black community, when you go into the white world, you are still a nigger, still a nigger, still a nigger. . . .

"It's not a question of Right or Left," he concluded. "It's a question of black."

Carmichael's speech, one of the decade's most forceful, was reprinted in an early issue of the San Francisco *Express Times*, whose key editor,

Marvin Garson, was by turns magnetic, talented, and erratic. Proceeds from Barbara Garson's scathing antiwar, anti-LBJ play *Macbird* helped pay the rent.

Less spacy than the *Oracle*, less knee-jerk than the *Barb*, the *Express Times* had more nuance than many underground papers; its typewriter keyboards contained "??" and well as "!!" Its coverage of Carmichael's speech ran over two issues. "Cold print lacks both the rhetorical devices and the general emotion of the speech as delivered—which was magnificent," the paper noted in introducing its text. The next paragraph was more rueful. "The general sentiment of staff people who heard the tape in our office was, 'Too bad he's so groovy.'"

In a story called "The Red and the Black," Garson addressed Carmichael's points. He allowed that genocide against blacks was possible. After all, one strain of black history included slavery and lynchings, ghetto conditions and ghetto risings, the killing of three black students in Orangeburg, South Carolina, just two weeks before the speech. "Better safe than sorry," Garson opined about organizing for self-defense, "as the experience of European Jews showed."

But what was this "honky" business? There was, Garson continued, a difference between the "white race" and "white racism." Hippies and antiwar activists might not be John Browns, he said, but they were far from genocidal. "The great majority of white people," Garson continued, "are not yet spoken for. . . . A black power movement that identifies 'the white man' in general as its enemy will thereby throw the political battle to the forces of genocide."

After criticizing Carmichael's anti-Zionist (and anti-Jewish) references, Garson sought common cause: "when Carmichael says, 'We're fighting for our humanity,' he is absolutely right. But when he goes on to identify the human and the anti-human with the colored and the white, he trips all over himself."

The rebuttal was a spirited defense of the integrated spirit that had existed during Mississippi Freedom Summer. But Carmichael's speech turned out to be the relative calm before yet another firestorm.

On March 2, the government confirmed the perniciousness of racism.

"Our nation is moving toward two societies, one black, one white—separate and unequal," said the thick *Report of the National Advisory Commission on Civil Disorder*. This finding of the Kerner Commission bolstered underground arguments. The main reason for the 1967 battles in Newark and Detroit had been systemic white racism, it said. "Important segments of the media," it continued, "failed to report adequately on the causes and consequences of civil disorders and on the underlying problems of race relations."

But it was not a call to militance. "Violence," it concluded, "must be ended—in the streets of the ghetto, and in the lives of the people."

On April 4, James Earl Ray fired a bullet into the heart of that entreaty, leaving Dr. Martin Luther King, Jr., dead on a Memphis balcony. Eleven days of black rage followed; thirty-five blacks and four whites died. In Washington, Lyndon Baines Johnson made radicals retch by intoning King's "We shall overcome." In Chicago, Mayor Richard J. Daley promulgated a tougher line: shoot to kill arsonists, shoot to wound looters.

In Chicago, the year-old *Seed* had attracted a few thousand readers to its mix of flower power, hip-neighborhood news, and increasingly colorful psychedelic graphics that included quite a few nubile young women. I was coming around to the office more and more often, joining the other writers in expressing our hopes that humanity was evolving toward some noncompetitive, nonbelligerent world. We were less organizers than liberals and freaks in the middle of a magical mystery tour. A cop or two threatened to break the arms of our street-corner sellers; the Chicago *Tribune* bought our printer, dropped our business. But our readers—the usual blend of freaks, radicals, kids, sympathetic liberals, weekend hippies, curious suburbanites, and horny businessmen—sent letters, supplies, and money that indicated we'd touched their lives.

We understood the thrust of Black Power, but in our hearts we were pacifist integrationists. In one article, a hippie told a black that he would not "pick up the gun." A regular contributor, a black writer named Ernest Thompson, asked street bloods to recognize "the flower child" as "undoubtedly the best friend the Negroes have ever had." Sometimes, though, our positions took telling detours. When young blacks trashed stores on the hip strip, the *Seed* defended "a reflex action to the shit they have to take every day." When kids threw a brick through *our* window, editor Valerie Walker denounced "the black equivalent of Nazi storm troopers."

Prepared before the assassination, the inside of the next issue contained a typical mix of freak-dominated news and views, plus the paper's hallmark rainbow graphics. The front cover was uncharacteristically simple: a black-and-white photo of King, with reversed-out excerpts from his "I Have a Dream" speech of less than five—no, five thousand—years before. The back cover held a short poem damning his killers, and a brief report from a white kindergarten teacher—one of the new publishers' wives—about the prayers her forty-five Mexican-American kids had said that day.

A shocked Valerie Walker wrote about being the only person wearing a black armband on a boarded-up street, a mourner for nonviolence. I wrote a screed:

"Moderation was slain in the streets of Memphis," it began, relatively quietly. "Peace was struck down by a slug from a hunting rifle. Brotherhood, slowly dying concept in a sick America, was administered a coup de grace. . . . We all died in that emergency room." Apocalyptic visions followed: armed suburbanities, outgunned National Guardsmen, reactionary Congressmen, black and white cops confronting each other in squad cars, teachers explaining "how things have progressed since November of 1963." Lame-o hippies were excoriated for not caring, as were black militants who would "push whitey to genocide and then scream, 'I told you so' as they mace you." My answer: none—except that I'd just learned "that the Statue of Liberty puts out."

The *Seed* was expressionistic, purgative. Other papers were more analytic about King and his murder. In Atlanta, the *Great Speckled Bird* had just been formed by academics, organizers, and draft resisters who'd worked with the Southern Student Organizing Committee. They believed that white southern intellectuals were capable of linking up not only with oppressed minorities, but with the labor movement.

Published just after King's slaying, the *Bird*'s third issue bore the slogan "Don't Mourn, Organize" to unite King's fate—and contribution—with that of an earlier radical, Joe Hill, the IWW (International Workers of the World) martyr of a half-century before. The *Bird* also fought to save King's work from being coopted. An excerpt from one of his last speeches called for a unilateral cease-fire in Vietnam, a statement that had alarmed some liberal integrationists. The main story, by ex–SSOC chairman Gene Guerrero, Jr., critiqued both liberalism and the local media:

"King was a gentle man who spoke of love and of nonviolence, but he spoke even more often of the deep sickness gripping this country. . . . Now that Dr. King is dead, his dream is being smothered by those who have been making pious sermons on nonviolence, gentleness and heart-searching, but who offer no meaningful programs to end the burning and the killing both in America and Vietnam."

More militant radicals had seen King as passé, the riots that followed his death as the next link in a growing chain of mass insurrection: Harlem '64, Watts '65, Detroit '67, Memphis '68 . . . But the King death-spasm would be the last mass black urban explosion of the sixties. There were too many dead, leaders and citizens alike. Too many burnt-out neighborhoods. No widely shared ideology. No mass desire to take the fight downtown—or a harrowing appreciation of the firepower that would await such a move.

And yet, black struggle was far from over. Two days after King's death, police and Black Panthers again shot it out in Oakland. Bobby Hutton, the party's seventeen-year-old treasurer, was killed. Four cops and three Panthers, including Minister of Information Eldridge Cleaver, were wounded. In the *Barb,* Panthers talked about savage repression, while police described a "planned ambush" against officers. The story's title projected the *Barb*'s opinion: "In Cold Blood: How They Killed Him."

Again, the Panthers were Leftist, militant, internationalist, dynamic, located in real communities, willing to make coalitions with whites, influencing a sizable number of white Bay Area activists. Blacks faced endemic discrimination, were organizing, had politics, were dying. King and Malcolm X were dead; nationalists dismissed whites. Panther battles with the authorities demanded attention, even respect. Consequently, white activists offered support, dedication, veneration, a desire for reflected glory, and encouragement beyond the Panthers' means to deliver. Inflated revolutionism would energize the Movement—and leave outgunned Panthers out on a limb and superheated rhetoric in the pages of the papers.

VIETNAMESE PEASANTS were opposing the world's most powerful military machine. Blacks were dying in American streets. Radical students supported both, but seemed passive by comparison. Pressure was mounting for them to become more militant, to organize and stir their peers to action.

In April, the student movement began what would be two years of escalating protest, which would end with reform of universities, the flight of key leaders, and a tragedy at Kent State University.

Specifically, activists at New York's Columbia University resented the on-campus presence of the Institute for Defense Analysis and a plan to build a university gym in a park bordering Harlem. After a month or so of relatively polite protest, SDS and black activists led perhaps a thousand students in an eight-day occupation of five campus buildings. Files were seized. Demonstrators fended off athletes and members of a conservative Majority Coalition. H. Rap Brown, Stokely Carmichael, Tom Hayden, and Abbie Hoffman lent their presence.

The Columbia demonstration was a watershed not only for SDS, but for LNS and a new New York paper, the *Rat.* It also indicated limitations and excesses that would grow with time.

LNS remained a forum; its dispatches ranged from Todd Gitlin's report on a Cultural Congress in Havana to a spoof on rhetoric which claimed that the Rolling Stones gathered no moss because they "lacked roots among the people." Response to LNS packets was just as diverse. The business manager of the *Utah Daily Chronicle* canceled his subscription "to the most distasteful literature that we have ever received in our office." The National Liberation Front's European ambassador sent word that "I appreciate very much the work being done by your news service." So did four hundred other primarily Left and freak subscribers—especially when LNS writers covered Columbia from inside the occupation.

The administration, the police, some students, and the mainstream press denounced theft, vandalism, and educational disruption on a campus where the names Sophocles, Plato, Aristotle, and Demosthenes were literally carved in stone. LNS dissented. "A new, more fluid style of revolutionary activity on the American campus has been introduced by Columbia University students, who held physical control of the campus for a week," was the lead to its "Columbia: The Revolution Is Now."

The series of overnight stories were written by an LNSer and Columbia student named Steve Diamond, who'd lived in Panama and come to think of journalism as "adventure" after seeing his parents string for newspapers during anti-imperialist demonstrations. Augmented by student reporters in each building and two LNS photographers, LNS's pieces outlined demonstrator demands (IDA off campus, gym out of the park, no ban on indoor demonstrations, amnesty). One also pictured "several beautiful American would-be Ché Guevaras with long hair and beards" smoking President Grayson Kirk's cigars while ensconced in the office from which files would be taken.

Though convinced that the rebels were right, Diamond's stories did credit police with being relatively restrained—at least until the final bloody arrests. They also largely omitted the guns brought onto campus by black militants and the provocative tactical ideas at least one visiting leader had offered to "intensify the struggle."

Diamond's supportive dispatches not only were widely reprinted in the underground press, but attracted interest from a mass press that was being shut out of a part of the story. Black students had established a media pecking order, with black reporters for black media getting preference, and scribes for the conservative New York *Daily News* not getting anywhere. LNS, *Rat, EVO,* and Newsreel had "the white exclusive." Soon *Life* and *Look* began calling LNS. "There was a whole debate," Diamond recalls. "Could we get *Life* magazine to print the story the way we wanted it?" Eventually, LNS stayed close to the Movement, giving

Ramparts its material for a package whose coverage included Tom Hayden's escalating call for "two, three, many Columbias."

Columbia also made Jeff Shero's *Rat* the underground press's hottest publication. Shero, a veteran of SDS's *New Left Notes* and Austin's *Rag*, had written briefly for LNS, then was approached by some New York radicals. *EVO* was too hippie-dippy, they said, the *Guardian* too national and rigid. What about a paper that appreciated both SDS and LSD?

Slow-talking, workshirted, love-beaded, trim-bearded, radical, and humane, Shero drawled his assent and began raising funds among New York's radicalized literati. In an age when the *New York Review of Books* would put a molotov cocktail on its front page, he collected $3,000 by convincing well-off liberals that stopping the war transcended the need for stock shares or tax-deductible receipts.

The first, twenty-four-page *Rat* appeared on March 4, 1968, tough and scraggly. In each issue, a logo-rodent hoisted a cartoon rifle in the general direction of the week's prime editorial target. Aimed at radicals, politicized freaks, and opinion-leaders, the *Rat* sought to synthesize New Left politics and the countercultural lifestyle. It covered and fomented demonstrations, offered information on draft counseling, free universities, and rock concerts. Headlines proclaimed "THE YEAR OF THE HEROIC GUERILLA FIGHTER," and on layout nights, the Motherfuckers street-tribe swirled into the *Rat* office like so many wild boar to produce compelling pre-Punk graphics that merged Indian motifs and M-16s on the two-page spread Shero had ceded them. Their slogan—"Armed Love"—wasn't quite flower power.

Shero saw Lower East Side longhairs as an underclass living by its wits, but divided his readership with stories such as how to rip off free subway rides. Anti-people, some radicals said. The IRT needs every penny it can get, put-upon liberals added. The *Rat* countered with three cheers for chaos: "it becomes not only moral but liberating to throw a monkey wrench into the machine. . . . We do everything we can do to destroy their system, and in the process attempt to build something new based on our humanity."

And so, when students found correspondence in Kirk's files linking Columbia to outside corporate interests, Shero called his girlfriend, Alice Embree, who worked with NACLA, the North American Congress on Latin America. Early the next morning, "Alice from Dallas" appeared to spirit the papers away. They had only one problem: the building was surrounded by police. Shero reared back and threw the rolled-up documents frisbee-style. Embree closed in, reached out—and caught the papers face-first. Black-eyed but unbowed, she scooped up the files and raced off.

"HEIL COLUMBIA!" the *Rat*'s front page proclaimed as a swastikaed helmet loomed over "TPF [Tactical Police Force] LIBRARY." Inside, Shero, other staffers, and injured students recounted the occupations and arrests (720 by month's end), while Embree and others called the Institute for Defense Analysis a cold-war think-tank and analyzed the files' disclosures about the university's business relationships. A boxed article explained that *Rat* was running the papers "in the belief that information which concerns the public welfare should be made available to the public and should never be maintained as the privileged right of those who wield power over us all."

"I think they were incredibly revealing of connections with the power structure," Embree says. "Now we'd all say, 'Of course.' But that was a revelation, just as the Pentagon Papers were a revelation."

Threatened with legal action, NACLA returned the files, but published a pamphlet called "Who Rules Columbia?" For Shero, the Columbia strike was a journalistic coup: "Politics was alleging something, and journalism proved the political allegations."

A "second occupation" fizzled after 177 activists were arrested for protesting disciplinary actions taken against leader Mark Rudd and others. But Columbia marked a turning point for the student movement and the underground press. "Columbia was [seen as] part of a power structure linked to the same forces that were waging war in Vietnam, and oppressing black people," recalls Allen Young, a Red-diaper baby who'd studied journalism at the school, attended the Pentagon demonstration between shifts at the Washington *Post,* and was emerging as a New Left opponent of Bloom and Mungo at LNS. "We viewed the disruption of university life as a necessary step. For life to go on as usual in the face of the horror of the Vietnam War was unacceptable and immoral."

Columbia also increased polarization between underground and mass media. Vehemently opposing the demonstrations, the New York *Times* called on the school "to turn once again to its mission of teaching, research and public service." Radicals wondered why, in SDS chronicles Kirkpatrick Sale's words, "none of what SDS had been saying about the university's missions of slum-lording, war complicity, autocracy and public disservice had reached its ears." They also saw the *Times* as compromised by, among other things, its publisher serving as a Columbia trustee and its assistant managing editor writing a front-page story.

"In fact, the great newspaper and wire services of our time can be and are mobilized daily to serve the interests of the great corporations and the Federal government," Allen Young charged then. "While imaginative reporters and editors take great pride about exposing the small lies about our society (muckraking), the big lies about class relations and imperialism go unchallenged."

At Columbia, mass and underground coverage told opposite stories. The daily press denounced theft, vandalism, and the interruption of academic proceedings while largely ignoring, denying, or defying the specific claims. The *Rat* was a proud coconspirator in theft, and applauded the rejection of "liberal, peaceful change." Though demonstrations were not planned against people, underground media used inflamed images— "Revolution," Nazi symbols, talk of destroying the system, the gun-toting *Rat* himself. Underground articles were as much commercials for revolt as attempts to make events politically comprehensible.

But Columbia was an attempt to organize *energy* as well as goal-oriented politics. "We manufactured the issues," Mark Rudd later admitted. "The Institute for Defense Analysis is nothing at Columbia. And the gym issue is bull. It doesn't mean anything to anybody. I had never been to the gym site before the demonstration began. I didn't even know how to get there." At Columbia, occupied buildings became communes where, Jeff Shero wrote, "participants by the hundreds realized new concrete possibilities in their lives and were forever changed. Alliances between black and white, between the campus and the community, the exaltation of people over property . . . ideas found only in radicals' fondest pot dreams slowly emerged into realities."

And *the* dream seemed to emerge in May, when street-fighting, anarcho-communal students nearly took power in France. "The more I make love / The more I make revolution!" "We are all undesirables!" "All power to the imagination!" The slogans sounded very familiar.

In the wake of Columbia, SDS membership burgeoned across the country, and nearly two hundred antiwar demonstrations occurred on campuses during the rest of the spring. But, again, at a price. "These images," Todd Gitlin would write, "helped render the street-fighting style legitimate *within* the movement as they helped render it anathema for the audience *outside* . . . The [mass] media unintentionally helped polarize the society between revolutionism and embattled reaction."

Action and dreams, leaders and sensationalism, questions of mass and radical media—the stage was being set for Chicago and the Democratic National Convention. Tom Hayden and SDS would advance the power of student revolt. Rennie Davis, David Dellinger, and others would continue the broader-based National Mobilization Committee to End the War in Vietnam that had marched on the Pentagon. The McCarthy kids, "Clean for Gene," would back the Minnesota senator in his drive to liberalize (but not radicalize) the presidency. But it would be the Yippies

—the Youth International Party, most closely identified with Abbie Hoffman and Jerry Rubin—that would grab the spotlight, in large part because it chose to fight its battles on the field of media. The Yippies would capture and divide public imagination, test the ethics of organizing via media, end flower power as a factor in the papers, and fuel the most divisive debate in the history of the underground press.

7

CHICAGO: HIPS, YIPS, AND POWER TRIPS

EW YORK—NEW YEAR'S EVE, 1967: The group of stoned activists partying in Abbie Hoffman's New York loft listened attentively as he and Jerry Rubin laid out the idea they'd hatched over Christmas vacation.

They were quite a duo. At thirty-one, Hoffman was a former SNCC worker who'd chosen life on the Lower East Side over what he saw as a plodding, unimaginative New Left. The previous August, he and a dozen other Diggers had tossed money onto the floor of the New York Stock Exchange to suborn acquisitiveness. He was a clever street hustler, capable of stirring hippies to action. Some straighter organizers thought him anarchic.

Almost thirty himself, Rubin had been moved enough by Fidel Castro's revolution to visit Cuba in 1964. Returning to Berkeley, he'd been active in the Free Speech Movement, and had cofounded Berkeley's Vietnam Day Committee, the one whose troop-train action had been featured in the first issue of the *Barb*. Aware that hippies were an ever-growing constituency, he'd spoken at the Human Be-In, and won twenty-two percent of the vote in Berkeley's 1967 mayoral race on a platform that included the legalization of marijuana. When called before the House Committee on Un-American Activities, he'd appeared costumed as a soldier in the (second) American Revolution. With Hoffman, he'd created the intriguing mumbo-jumbo about levitating the Pentagon. Some radicals and hips thought he was his own most important product.

Now in the loft, the dynamic duo talked excitedly about an idea they'd hatched over Christmas vacation: an outrageous event that would use media to bring hordes of freaks to the 1968 Democratic Convention. They batted it around, and then Paul Krassner, ever quick, exclaimed a name: "Yippie!"

The Yippie chieftains didn't have many Indians. But at the Stock Exchange and, especially, the Pentagon, Rubin and Hoffman had shown how radicals could use resistance and a range of media to build support. "We announced we were going to close down the Pentagon, and Lyndon Johnson said, 'I will not allow a small group of disrupters to close down the Pentagon.'" Jerry, who'd spend thirty days as the price for learning these media lessons, recalls. "Thank you, Lyndon Johnson. You just told three million people that we are protesting on October 21." But Jerry Rubin was an equal-opportunity operator: "I manipulated the Movement enough so that they went along with it."

Signed by twenty-five "hip Leftists" involved in organizing, radio, theater, rock, and the papers, the original Yippie announcement was distributed via LNS on January 16. "Join us in Chicago in August for an international festival of youth, music, and theatre," it began. It promised "making love in the parks . . . singing, laughing, printing newspapers, making a mock convention, and celebrating the birth of FREE AMERICA in our own time."

Then it turned vaguely militant:

"The life of the American spirit is being torn asunder by the forces of violence, decay, and the napalm-cancer fiend. We demand the Politics of Ecstasy! We are the delicate spores of the new fierceness that will change America. We will create our own reality. We are free America! And we will not accept the false theatre of the Death Convention."

But the Yippies had a problem: they didn't know anybody in Chicago. Reenter the God of Synchronicity. Just before the birth of the Yippie myth, Paul Krassner, soured on the gray skies of New York City, had placed a small notice in the *Realist* requesting that anybody with space in the hinterland contact him. Reading Krassner's complaint in Chicago, I exercised the countercultural view of private property and wrote to volunteer an acquaintance's farm as the site of Krassner's new office. Instead, I got Rubin talking about a groovy festival to be held in my newly adopted town.

Seated in my apartment—the top floor of a three-flat building furnished in Standard Dropout, Middle Tapestry, and Primordial God's-Eye —Rubin became Jerry as he talked quietly but enthusiastically about a festival of youth, music, and theater in Sweet Home Chicago! And if it just *happened* to coincide with the Democrats' convention, well, as the release had said, "the two are, of course, entirely unrelated."

In that living room, on that night, Jerry described a nonprofit Woodstock one year early. But if his confrontational fingers were crossed, my arm wasn't twisted when I said I'd be Yippie's man in Chicago. Naïve, flattered, I nevertheless hated the war, disdained straight society. The Yippies weren't some boring Leftist sect, but all-American rebels who, instead of arguing over slices of the pie, wanted a whole new menu. And the whole thing sounded so exciting! Hadn't the tail end of that release said, "Chicago is yours! Do it!"?

LATE WINTER saw momentum building for protest in Chicago. The Coalition for an Open Convention organized around finding an electoral alternative to Lyndon Johnson. The more radical Mobilization called for militant, nonviolent action to force an end to the war. Names, connections, boldness, and publicity soon ranked the Yippies alongside the other groups. Their claim of representing the alternative culture soon led to tension over political involvement, and violence. A series of *EVO* articles caught the opposites: "There is a gathering storm of sheer rage," American Buddist philosopher Alan Watts wrote, "in which almost every important political group from the Birchers to the New Left is fascinated with the forces which it hates and is bereft of psychic energy for any constructive action. Apart from a few high dreamers like Buckminster Fuller . . . and Marshall McLuhan, no one seems to realize that an entirely new world is technologically possible in a very near future."

Early in February though, Jerry, a popular figure at *EVO,* cited the death of Ché Guevara as evidence "that if we want change we are going to have to risk our lives. . . . When guerilla war breaks out in the city, and cops and blacks start shooting, are we going to hide, or are we going to take sides?"

Then, on the twenty-first, Tim Leary sat in a lotus position on a red cloth in the *EVO* office, incense and candles on either side, and proclaimed a press-conference alliance "between the Peace, Black, Flower and Women's movements in this country . . . a life force of peace, fun, love and laughter against the menopausal, metallic, middle-aged minds that run this country."

In the *Seed,* Jerry became more internationalistic. "The Yippies are with the Vietnamese peasant guerilas wherever they are, and the black and other struggling people of America." His Chicago vision: "A kid turns on television and there is his choice. Does he want to be smoking pot, dancing, fucking, stopping traffic, and going to jail or does he want to be in a blue uniform beating up people or does he want to be in the convention with a tie strangling his throat making ridiculous deals and nominating a murderer [LBJ]?" Then an organizational hedge. "You probably don't agree with this description of Yippie, but that's because you are a yippie, and you have your own fantasy."

On February 27, six weeks after thirty students at the State University of New York at Stony Brook had been arrested for alleged drug possession and/or use, a hundred or so Keystone Kop Yippies staged a predawn raid on the campus. It was the first big Yippie media event, and the press, of course, was invited.

The story was in the eye of the beholder. The New York *Post* found the guerilla theater creative. *EVO* acknowledged student apathy, but ballyhooed "the Year of the Yippie." "There may," *Newsweek* added, "be some laughs yet in the U.S. this summer."

The *Times,* however, could only find students and faculty opposed to the action. And the *Post*'s Max Lerner, a traditional liberal, muttered that Chicago would attract "every crackpot . . . disruptive force in American society that thinks it has a pipeline to absolute truth." He thought all radical protests counterproductive; Mayor Daley, he predicted, would keep to his "sensible distinction between allowing demonstrations and dissent but drawing the line at violence and plans for it."

Not surprisingly, the Yippies preferred the 'puff of a story' that appeared in the *Post*'s news section of March 18.

"THE YIPPIES—that's Y for Youth and Ippies for Hippies—will hold an enormous music festival in Chicago during the Republican [sic] convention. . . . They plan mad antics which with their thousands of young adherents will compel the networks to cover them."

The Yippies were flamboyant, but not stupid. They'd seen dissidents ignored because of politics that were unpopular or overly precise or too pure, or because of boring presentations. And they'd been misquoted and misperceived (and sometimes all too correctly perceived) enough to think of media interaction as a combat zone. As a New Left writer named Norman Fruchter would say:

"The opposition spokesman is presented as a commodity, interrupted by commercials. He or she is defined as potentially civilized, prepared to sit at a table, answer questions, smile at the mediator." The result was a presentation depoliticized even before the questions were asked.

The Yippies attempted to avoid that trap in several ways—including some that outraged Fruchter and others. They staged actions and used symbols—music, clothing, drugs, energy—that spoke directly to the constituency they wanted to reach. Aware that most straight-press reporters couldn't tell Jefferson Airplane from the Jefferson Memorial, Yippies claimed to speak for a united counterculture.

Yippies also understood that once enough steam was built up to convince media gatekeepers to cover a story, the premise of fair comment ensured that most reporters would, however they set up their articles, report back what Yippies "claimed" or "alleged." Scruffy Yippie anarchists thus could blurt out in the nation's journals that 500,000, 1 million, 3 million people were heading for Chicago.

Thus, a relative handful of Yippies was able to garner national attention, and Yippie energy would arguably draw more people to Chicago than more sober protest. But pipers lurked among those note pads and TV cables, demanding to be paid.

Like most advertising, Yippie projected the most popular and salable messages—"everyone is a leader"; "the Festival is whatever you want"; "let's have a party"—whether or not they were the most accurate. Jerry, later: "It was mutual manipulation. To interest the media I needed to express my politics frivolously. . . . If I had given a sober lecture on the history of Vietnam, the media camera would have turned off."

Also, since Yippies had neither the money nor the politics to buy sustained commercial time (which wouldn't have been sold in many outlets anyway), a different currency had to be used—hype. If 100,000 people were today's magic number, then 110,000 better be coming tomorrow. If today's release announced a love-in by Lake Michigan, then tomorrow's had to talk about kidnapping delegates to Wisconsin. Exposure became the measure of success, and Yippiedom an exercise in "Can You Top This?" Up the establishment! Up the figures! Up the ante! The dissidents who'd blamed *Time* for media-burning the Haight now wanted to use *Time* to bring people to Chicago.

And despite the egalitarian rhetoric, the most mediagenic Yippies set the agenda without any feedback or control from below. Not exactly participatory democracy.

As time went on, the underground press began testing the New York Yippies. Who'd made them leaders? What were the ethics of media organizing? Would the event be a Festival? riot? hype? "It was important to perpetuate myths in the underground press, so I have to say I tried to manipulate it," Jerry admits. "The underground press was easier and harder to manipulate [than the mass press]. Easier because some of them shared a vision, so you could say, 'Let's go further with this vision.' Harder to manipulate because they were more cynical. They were aware of the vision." All this began to bother some early sympathizers. Paul

Williams, who'd started the rock magazine *Crawdaddy,* visited the Yippies' New York office and found "a celebration advertised as a Festival of Life but no doubt fantasized as the Storming of the Steps, 1917." Williams was turned off. "Six-column-a-day habits," he called the media fixation; nobody wanted to go cold turkey.

But Williams added, "Not that we had anything better to suggest."

The first major underground criticism came from Michael Rossman, the Free Speech Movement veteran whom Jerry had asked to help coordinate the Yippie protest. Instead, Rossman declined and issued an ethical critique that appeared in the *Barb* and elsewhere that March.

"The Yippie thing really troubles me, man, because it's deeply and dangerously irresponsible," Rossman wrote. "The brilliant formless Yippie publicity, in waving the magical beckoning symbol of our Music, projects grooving and warmth, and does not warn that joy there must be won from within—not absorbed from others."

Rossman worried that "fledgling kids" would be unprepared for and disillusioned by official violence. "If there's any ethical principle we can fix for our actions in this fractured time, it's that we must keep straight with our own. . . . This sort of organizing, however spectacular, is neither moral nor efficient, effective."

"The article was more mealy-mouthed than I felt," Rossman says now. "I had some regard for Jerry at that point, but I saw just the worst kind of organizing. It was totally irresponsible."

Jerry responded with an upbeat letter to the *Express Times,* which also had run Rossman's piece. By then, though, the responsibility question had gone public, with a bang.

March 22 was the vernal equinox—springtime in New York—and the Yippies were taking their act uptown, to Grand Central Station, in the heart of Manhattan, where they'd gathered before. This time, six thousand potential Yippies appeared. Incense burned. Balloons climbed toward the ceiling. A demonstrator climbed onto the big clock above the information booth and celebrated the Eternal Now by removing its hands. The police were not amused.

Despite "several arrests" by "a blue wedge of belligerent beef" (the actual total was close to fifty), a piece of *EVO* cheerleadering claimed victory for the forces of spontaneity.

A less underground but very knowing reporter disagreed. His name was Don McNeill, he was in his early twenties, and though he wrote for the *Village Voice,* Abbie Hoffman thought of him as a talented comrade. With five stitches in his head from being rammed into a plate-glass door by four cops who didn't like the *Voice,* McNeill launched an across-the-board critique of "astonishing" police brutality and a planning failure by both the city and the Yippies "that borders on gross incompetence and irresponsibility.

"The Yip-In was," he warned, "a pointless confrontation in a box canyon, and somehow it seemed to be a prophecy of Chicago."

These pieces stung, but Jerry took the long view. "All opposition was really creating the myth of Chicago. As long as Chicago was accepted as a legitimate activity that people had an opinion about, I won." Bob Fass, WBAI's talk-show pioneer and an early Yippie, disagrees. "I think it cut down on the reservations for Chicago. What terror does is terrorize."

Immediately after the Yip-In, a Movement summit conference in Lake Villa, Illinois, proved to be an exercise in disunity. Black groups went their own way. The National Mobilization—"the Mobe"—wanted a programmatic, nonviolent, legal, *political* protest. That struck at least one Yippie as hopelessly *passé*. "America is dead," he yelled, "and yet you're getting involved in a dance with a dead lady." *New Left Notes* ran a long SDS putdown called "Don't Take Your Guns to Town" that accused the Yippies of using talk of rock and pot as lures to put kids "up against bayonets." Eighteen months later, one of its cowriters would himself be rioting in the streets in the Weatherman faction of SDS's Days of Rage.

But the Yippies had their counter-media supporters. Goateed, moustached, bespectacled, Julius Lester was the intelligent columnist for the more traditionally Left *Guardian,* and one of the few blacks writing in the underground press. Now he articulated much of what had first attracted me and the other *Seed*lings to the Yippies. The Yippies, he pointed out, had helped politicize hippies (who, he agreed, may have always been political), projected an alternative lifestyle, and did not engage in the nitpicking common on the Left.

Lester then described *his*—and the *Seed's*—version of Chicago in August. The Yippies were aiming "not at the Democratic convention as the other political organizations will be doing, but at the youth . . . on strike against the way of life America was presenting them. . . . Once you're in a liberated zone, you'll fight to keep it from being reclaimed. The Yippies are a liberated zone."

More public events, though, were sweeping everyone along:

March 31—Lyndon Johnson, the immediate symbol of America's Vietnam involvement, announced that he was dropping out when his term was up.

April 4—Martin Luther King, Jr., was murdered and urban riots broke out. Radicals saw rebellion. There were still five months left before the convention.

April—Dr. Benjamin Spock, "the baby doctor," and four other responsible intellectuals were under indictment in Boston for conspiracy against the draft. So were seven organizers of Oakland's Stop-the-Draft Week. In Washington, a rider to bill HR 17893—"the H. Rap Brown Law"—made it illegal to cross state lines with the *intention* of inciting a riot. In Chicago, twenty of the seventy people who attended the first local Yippie meeting were arrested after four raiding narcotics agents found a small packet of marijuana that may or may not have been there before they arrived. The next day, the *Tribune* reported that hippies had been seen making the "V" sign, which, it proclaimed, meant "I have pot."

In an "Open Letter to Mayor Richard Daley," I recognized his power to crush any pre-Convention organizing, then asked, "Do you wish to be known as the Mayor who revolutionized Chicago?" Before that letter could be printed, the April 27 Peace March was crushed. After several thousand members of groups such as Women for Peace gathered by the Civic Center to quietly protest the war, the police simply ripped into the crowd.

Years later, a Chicago cop turned San Francisco jeweler told me how things had looked from his side of the plaza:

"Each one of us was told that we had to make an arrest. I couldn't believe it. There was nobody bad there. When things got really heavy, I grabbed this shrimpy little kid from the U of C. He started to yell, but I yelled louder, right in his ear: 'Don't worry, I won't come to court.'

"Some of the coppers were tossing people *up* into the squadrols [trucks] so their heads banged off the door lintels. I managed to get my kid in without him getting smashed. Fuck, *I* got hit on the shoulder.

"I quit pretty soon after. That was it for me."

But mayoral bellowings about "hoodlums and Communists" were cited in the daily press with little or no rebuttal. And there were more subtle forces at work: *before* the event, the city desk at the liberal *Sun-Times* was instructed to tack any peace-march news onto a VFW Loyalty Day Parade story. Though the peaceniks drew more people and were involved in violence—two usual standards of importance in news coverage—the story still centered on the hawks.

The *Seed* ran four pages of atrocity tales. The subsequent blue-ribbon Sparling Commission Report severely criticized police conduct. Both were widely ignored.

May 2—Twenty-six people were arrested at the Electric Theatre rock hall after a phalanx of police marched in, declared the existence of "fire law violations," and proceeded to clear the hall of some fourteen hundred people on hand to support the Digger-like Free City Survival Committee, which included the Yippies.

Mother's Day—A march from the hippie haven of Lincoln Park delivered an apple-pie peace offering to the 18th District police station. Several men in blue muttered about hash brownies in disguise, so it was all the zanier when they suggested that we take them to Saint Vincent's Hospital around the corner. There, Sister Gertrude graciously accepted them and an impromptu $18 collection, with a Yippie button pinned onto her white habit. Nobody was killed.

There was at least one dissenter: Abbie Hoffman, veteran of various police scuffles, wrote a leaflet distributed at the parade. Its key sentence, directed at the cops: "Shit pies next time."

A couple of weeks later, the shit hit Abbie's fan from a new direction.

Rolling Stone had begun publishing the previous November in San Francisco, the music-and-lifestyle creation of Jann Wenner, a twenty-one-year-old former Berkeley student who'd strung for NBC and worked on *Sunday Ramparts.* By the time he started the magazine, Wenner, like his mentor, San Francisco *Chronicle* columnist Ralph Gleason, had "a general disbelief in American politics" but was "not really enchanted anymore with radical politics.

"The bankruptcy of both sides was what I was seeing," he recalls. "There must be a way out," he'd thought, "and rock 'n' roll is it."

If Wenner was not a part of the New Left, then neither was his magazine an underground paper. *Rolling Stone* rarely advocated demonstrations, much less confrontation. It was a for-profit publication. It looked cleaner, sparer, straighter than nearly all the undergrounders. Wenner kept it out of UPS, not seeing very many articles he wanted, not wanting to give up some of the adept reporting he was printing.

"The *Barb* was exciting and lively, the *Oracle* was peculiar," he recalls. "But the pieces I was choosing from in assembling *Rolling Stone—Melody Maker, Ramparts, Downbeat,* the London *Times* a little, maybe a little *New Yorker*—had nothing to do with the underground press. I wanted to do something professional-looking, with professional standards, something primarily about rock 'n' roll."

"He didn't like the prose," recalls Greil Marcus, who went from the *Express Times* to *Rolling Stone.* "He didn't like the look. He didn't like the people. He didn't like the way it was done. His values were, 'Put out something that looks good, that's readable, that tells you something in the first paragraph and wraps it up in the last and knows that getting across the story is what's important.' So he never for a minute wanted to be considered part of the underground press. And *Rolling Stone* never was."

In its May 11 issue, *Rolling Stone* came out smoking against the Yippie "shuck."

"A self-appointed coterie of political 'radicals' without a legitimate constituency," editor Wenner wrote in a front-page story called "Musicians Reject New Political Exploiters," wanted to stage a convention protest "as corrupt as the political machine it hopes to disrupt." Almost a decade younger than the New York leadership, Wenner attacked them as reckless, out-of-it media-trippers. "Rock and roll," he concluded, "is the *only* way in which the vast but formless power of youth is structured."

Though exaggerated in parts and passive about the war, the editorial was in touch with some ideas held by large numbers of young people: that the wondrous notes pouring out of stereos were powerful enough to change society on their own, that politics of any kind was corrupt, that Left ideas were both implausible and impossible to implement, that "progressive violence" was no better than "official violence."

"There were three people who were Yippies, except the newspapers were so dumb they were making like this was some big movement," Jann says. "Their whole existence depended on the coverage they were getting. The only way they were going to get people to Chicago for the Convention was to claim it was a rock 'n' roll event.

"I was speaking to some musicians or their representatives, and they would say, 'We're not coming; someone's using our name without permission.' So we took the lead in calling the bullshit. It was reckless to encourage all these people to come thinking it was gonna be a Festival of Life, this harmless thing. I thought Abbie and Rubin's activities were extremely destructive, and I was right."

Abbie Hoffman would see *Rolling Stone* as destructive, lacking radicalism, outflanking the underground press, sapping its advertising. His view of Jann Wenner? "The Benedict Arnold of the sixties."

They'd have a few more go-rounds before it was over.

JUNE— In Chicago, nothing was happening with our request for demonstration permits. The New York Yips thought of pulling out—until a Palestinian nationalist named Sirhan Sirhan gave America its second Kennedy assassination on June 5. The *Seed* saw another sign of how sick the country was. Abbie Hoffman saw "the fastest recount in history." Jerry's later comment: "Sirhan Sirhan is a Yippie."

The gap between flower pacifism and street militance began to yawn. "It's hard to say Festival of Life anymore without reaching for flowers that aren't around," Jerry said in New York when I visited him for a

Seed story after he, of all the heads in the East Village, had been busted for pot. His vision of post-Chicago America: "Total instability, every day a minor revolution, wave upon wave of mass action, the breakup of institutions, a lot of friends in jail, angry, bloody demonstrations, fierce confrontations for power between right- and left-wing forces, mass disruption in high school and colleges.

"And you are there."

In truth, we Chicago flower folk had toughened up a bit, suing for permits to hold free concerts, forcing police to cease mass street sweeps of hippies by organizing several hundred people for a "Bust-In." I even adopted the nom de plume Abraham Yippie. But as the summer went on, city officials alternately threatened, cajoled, or ignored us. And when we saw Abbie pencil in "Riot" as Wednesday's main event, we couldn't tell if it was a prediction, a caution, a desire, or an obituary. Blithe remarks about "twenty to thirty killed, six thousand wounded" didn't help. Obviously, we'd been totally naïve to think we could pull off a peaceful counter-event in this environment. For a while, I'd adopted the nom de plume "Abraham Yippie," but maybe we weren't Jerry's kind of Yippie: "the Marxist acidhead, the psychedelic Bolshevik." Corny as it sounds, we really did feel connected to all those unknown freaks Out There who might be slouching toward Chicago in search of Peace 'n' Love.

I was the *Seed*'s editor now, and early in August I wrote a statement that voiced the ideas of myself and most of the *Seed* staff, Dave from the Hip Job Co-op, and the guys from Headland:

"The word is out. Many people are into confrontation. The Man is into confrontation. . . . Chicago may host a Festival of Blood. . . . But people are still into the Festival flash. . . . The only way to end the sham is to withdraw our permit request. . . . New York Yippies have told us to expect a lot of static for this decision. That's cool. We refuse to pose as front-men for an alternative that no longer exists. . . .

"It was a chance to pull off a freaked-out fun-fest in a large city. It probably was the last chance for a long time. . . . There are many reasons to disrupt the Death Gala. If you feel compelled to cavort, then this is action city. There is no reason to wear flowers for masks. . . . As individuals, we may join in trying to stop Hubert the Hump. As a group, our advice is—

"Don't come to Chicago if you expect a five-day Festival of Life, music and love."

It was one of those Summer Specials Chicago seems to import from Equatorial Africa, muggy enough to send the mosquitoes out on strike.

Less than three weeks before the convention would nominate the presidential candidate of the incumbent war party, it was even steamier in the *Seed* office, on North LaSalle Street. For one thing, the storefront's plate-glass window didn't open, and the place had no air-conditioning. For another, the door was closed lest several large men parked outside in large-antennaed cars take over-zealous notes. But what was making the atmosphere hot enough to fry eggs on the light table was the debate raging between two groups of protesters.

There was Jerry Rubin, moustached, T-shirted, a scale-model lion roaring about safety in numbers. There was Abbie Hoffman, curls tumbling over his forehead, making eloquent comparisons to the far worse repression civil rights workers had faced in the South, arguing for a stand against the war, yelling, "When you bite the tail of the tiger, you just don't let go!" There was Paul Krassner, the *Realist*'s impish publisher, more of a peacemaker, but still angry. People were dying in Vietnam, they said. How was our pulling our application going to end that?

Across the room, near a full-sized cardboard National Guardsman festooned with Yippie bumper stickers, sat our gaggle of peace creeps, heads, *Seed*lings. We cited Bob Dylan's line about how those who lived outside the law had to be honest with each other. Was the crackle in the air love vibrations, or the adrenaline that comes from jolting history by rioting for change? If the latter, why were people being strung along with talk about a festival?

The thunderstorm blew back and forth. Someone suggested that we could use an arbiter. A call was made. Time passed. And then Tom Hayden arrived.

Hayden was the BMOC—big man of confrontation: He'd cofounded SDS, organized in Berkeley and in the Newark ghetto. He'd been a visiting professor of radicalism at the Columbia University occupation, and had gone to Hanoi before it became Lefty-fashionable. Now the slippers he was wearing suggested that he was not thrilled to be out mediating a dispute between two sets of *freaks*.

Hayden sat quietly, tightly. Then, looking in Jerry Rubin's direction while talking about me, he rendered his verdict in three little letters: "CIA." Such was the nature of our unity, and our trust.

Eventually, a compromise was hammered out. Most of the *Seed* and Free City organizers—myself included—decided to keep their names off any permit request. The New Yorkers, some Free Cityites, and Paul Simon, my old roommate turned *Seed* artist, would file a new permit request. Everyone vowed to stay involved. Everyone agreed to advise those who wanted a festival not to come to Chicago.

THE PERMITS were never issued. The Mobe, Yippies, even the more mainstream Coalition for an Open Convention went to court in Chicago, where they proved Lenny Bruce's old adage about how in the Hall of Justice the only justice was in the hall. The most successful litigant received an appearance date for three weeks after the convention. Already, everyone in Chicago had the fever.

The lead article in the August 5 *New Left Notes* had SDS officer Mike Klonsky cautioning that the convention would be "a case of 'Let's light the fuse and see what happens.' " SDS, he said, should eschew mass actions in favor of organizing Eugene McCarthy's campaign workers.

And how was this sober message headlined?

> Hot Town—
> Pigs In The Street [picture of beefy cop]
> But the Streets Belong to the People! [clenched fist]
> Dig It

The crescendo was building to August 26 and the convention.

August 20—Soviet tanks began crushing the flowers of Czechoslovakia's "Prague Spring." Even as Fidel Castro spoke out against "deviation" among socialist countries, several *Seed*lings picketed against the invasion outside the Polish embassy on Chicago's Near North Side.

We nearly came to blows with a "go back to Russia" type who didn't read our signs.

August 22—A seventeen-year-old Indian kid named Dean Johnson was shot dead on Wells Street. The police said he'd fired first; the New Yorkers claimed a martyr.

August 23—Pigasus, the Yippies' presidential candidate, was arrested in the Civic Center along with six human pals. In fine form, Treeman, now of both Headland and the *Seed,* visited the Chicago Humane Society. "I lost my doggie," he said. "It's black and white and has a curly tail."

The last round of preconvention articles proved that Yippie was still in the eye of the journalistic beholder.

In the "Chicago" issue of the *Realist,* Abbie Hoffman wrote that mythic media distortion had been "the lifeblood of the Yippies," but it was now time "for a greater degree of precision." Having said that, he reiterated the fairy-tale version of the event. The "huge rock-folk festival" was still on, with thirty or so bands still coming. "We have had several meetings . . . and it remains but to iron out the terms of the treaty . . . for us to have a bona fide permit in our hands." Reason would prevail, he wrote. Violence was in nobody's interest.

At the *Seed,* we worked for twenty-four hours to make sure that the cover for Volume II, No. 12, was just right. Our most ambitious effort to date, it was an eight-page foldout with multiple images auguring the imminent convention. Cook County Jail was self-explanatory. The front gate of the International Amphitheatre, where the delegates would gather for what we were sure would be war-business as usual. A map of the hippie haven at the south end of Lincoln Park, where we'd hoped the Festival of Life would be.

Over it all hovered a nude pregnant woman—a typist when not undressed for the Cause—in solarized purple and green. "Don't fear the birth of the new," a fragment from the *Tibetan Book of the Dead* intoned.

Chicago's four daily newspapers were running stories about the Democrats' agenda; the *Seed* ran the demonstrators' agenda. The daily papers quoted police sources about the danger of violence; the *Seed,* also leery of violence, ran a service story called "What to Do in Case of Arrest." The dailies covered the latest debates over the Democratic war position; the *Seed* called Humphrey a joke, McCarthy a false hope, Nixon a threat. Its candidate was a pig, but at least he'd withdraw the half-million-plus American troops in Vietnam.

The *Seed*'s convention issue contained a last debate. I reiterated why we had warned off the unwary. Abbie Hoffman countered with an epitaph for a generation of flower papers:

The *Seed* is "not a Movement paper, but a family affair. That's not a putdown. The *Seed* is a movement paper that teaches by example— LOOK, WE ARE A FAMILY—HERE IS OUR SOUL—WE DO OUR THING—YOU DO YOURS. It's an important message. But . . . the *Seed* is the last in the line of flower papers. Gone is the San Francisco *Oracle,* gone to the hills; gone is the L.A. *Oracle,* off to the seashore; gone is the Boston *Avatar.*"

The new generation of papers, Abbie continued, were "Tougher— that's it, TOUGHER. . . .

"How can a newspaper such as the *Seed,* which is supposed to be in the Zen tradition . . . persist in labeling things political or apolitical? . . . Joy is picking flowers in the woods. Joy is punching a cop when he steps on your toe. . . . Joy is saying no and living no to a government grown old and evil. . . . Joy is just another name for an American liquid soap. Bubble! Bubble! If you want to have the most together, exciting, intense time of your life, you can have it in Chicago."

We agreed on one thing: "Abe and the other *Seed* people wouldn't miss it."

"WE GOT THERE early and said, 'Look, there really are Yippies coming,' " Paul Krassner recalls. "We were never really sure. It was all propaganda."

When the players finally took the field, the projected half-million Yippies had shrunk to ten thousand protesters, including Mobe folk, neighborhood kids, and numerous police agents. The Yippies had attracted massive coverage—but mostly as zanies or barbarians. It had been judged too weird, or scary, or manipulative, or wrong, or another wearying protest, or not the rockfest Yippie had pitched. Demonstrators were outnumbered by six thousand regular army troops, six thousand Illinois national guardsmen, many of Chicago's twelve thousand police, various undercover agents.

The underground and alternative press had divided oddly around the Yippie plans: *Rolling Stone* and SDS's *New Left Notes* against; *EVO,* the *Barb,* and especially the *Seed* flip-flopping; the *Rat* and LNS gung-ho. Now a *Ramparts Wall Poster* called on "those who insist on change to mobilize and enact it." *Rat* "Convention Specials," fifty thousand of them, were pseudomilitary, targeting police stations and hotels, companies complicit in the war effort, and "the High Finance Kings of the Democratic Party." "We are coming to Chicago to vomit on the 'politics of joy," Tom Hayden wrote, citing Hubert Humphrey's campaign slogan. Liberalism was morally bankrupt, he said. So, the future legislator said, was the Democratic Party, whose convention "is not only undemocratic in nature, but under the control of war criminals." Humphrey would not succeed in bringing American values to Vietnam, but instead would bring the war to America. "We want the army to occupy Chicago not to begin a war, but to reveal the truth about our system," he said. Any violence would be due to governmental "negligence and brutality."

During the week of the convention, demonstrators massed in Lincoln and Grant Parks and on Michigan Avenue, and attempted to march to the Amphitheatre. Before it was over, hundreds of convention delegates also marched. The police rioted. "Daley dozers"—national-guard Jeeps with concertina wire laced to their hoods—furnished the proper motif for the image of "Czechago."

Undercover police from the city, the federal government, the army, were everywhere. They followed and threatened us, and some served as agents provocateurs. One masqueraded as a biker and became Jerry Rubin's bodyguard. Their work is still a source of litigation in Chicago.

Yet there were odder moments.

Ramparts staffers had their hotel bill deferred after editor Warren Hinckle complained that he'd seen a man in the next room wearing a headset and monitoring his calls.

Ed Sanders's experience was more bizarre.

After the police first cleared Lincoln Park, Ed saw that his anarchist-joyfest vision might require a few alterations. So the poet-Fug journeyed to the sports department at the Marshall Field department store to make a purchase—a football helmet.

Suddenly, he had company: the Red Squad agent assigned to follow him. "Ahh, Mr. Sanders, I've been on your detail for twelve hours and my replacement is going to meet me here, and if you leave right now, I'll miss him and I won't be able to go home for another couple of hours."

Sanders thought for a moment, then answered, "All right, we'll wait."

The favor was returned when Ed had his difficulty with "the honey." A friend of the heroic Yippie guerillas had journeyed from New York with this quintessential marijuana extract. When police and reporters couldn't find key Yippies, they suspected covert activity; often, though, their disappearance was due to complete stonedness.

Which is why Ed, dazed and confused in Lincoln Park, found himself being helped toward his hotel by none other than his police tail. The agent saw that they were walking across normal green park grass; Ed perceived "a giant frothing trough of mutant spinach egg noodles."

"That," he recalls, "was not conducive to orderly social change."

Neither were the occasions when Tom Hayden, Jerry Rubin, Abbie Hoffman, and Rennie Davis were seized or beaten.

The battles of Michigan Avenue were the ones watched on televisions across the country. But for *Seed*lings, at least, the elemental struggle took place in Lincoln Park on the night of Tuesday, August 27.

After two days of skirmishing, contending spirits were vying in the darkness where the Festival of Life was to have shone. Gathered behind a large wooden cross, a score or more ministers stood and called for peace, both in Vietnam and in Chicago. The night before, a priest had had his skull fractured by a rampaging cop; other seminarians and ministers had been clubbed. Now the clerics were back, putting their bodies on the line in the name of "collar power." Their Passion Play was about to begin.

Nearby, a few-score acolytes of an Eastern religious experience older than Christianity sat in a circle, "Ommming" for peace. (A few skeptics on the fringe sang, "Ommm, Ommm on the range.") More powerful forces—demons, if you were on this side of the line—were about to present themselves.

Midway between the two drives defining the park stood several thousand demonstrators, breakers of the 11:00 P.M. curfew, alternate convention delegates unified by police nightsticks. Most were nonviolent; a few were new crusaders in a people's army that fantasized fighting fire with fire. Demonstrators gathered behind picnic tables and overturned trash cans, some applauding when a rock shattered the glass of a scouting police car. Anticipation, fear, anger hung like fog.

When the police arrived, their centerpiece merged East and West in an awesome, tacky metaphor. In the Indian religions the "Ommmers" preferred, Juggernaut was a huge cart-drawn idol of Krishna that crushed anyone in its path. The police Juggernaut was a dump truck with tear-gas sprayers mounted on it. Its acolytes were scores of cops with a mantra all their own: "Kill, kill, kill." For the police, this was a war to reinstate authority, a class war, a gang war, a style war all rolled into one. Their most common epithets were "Commie" and "pussy."

Ommers became tear-gassed coughers. The ministers' wooden cross—along with some of the ministers—was beaten to the ground. The peace people ran as fast as sandals, boots, and sneakers could carry them, a hard rain of nightsticks spurring them on. Radical affinity groups coalesced, fought back. I saw the power of flowers wilt, first by gas, then when the guy next to me—a hardened street-hippie out of *A Clockwork Orange*—lobbed a trash can through the windshield of a trapped squad car.

Over the course of the week, *Seed* people hit the streets, parks, Movement Centers, hospitals, and jails as both writers and demonstrators. On Wednesday night a *Seed* stalwart nicknamed "Walrus" and I were manning the phones when we heard a sharp crack and saw the office's picture window become a spider web. Like an idiot, I ran to the door, unarmed as always, to see who had shot at us. The only car visible, blue and white with lights on its roof, cruised slowly up the street.

Hundreds of civilians and a lesser number of police were injured, six hundred sixty-eight people were arrested. Compared to Vietnam, the violence in Chicago was minimal. But it was unprecedented, and was made real as newsmen paid a price for doing their job. The police department whose brochure had celebrated "the excellent rapport between the Chicago police and newsmen" now engaged in a celebrity version of Beat the Press. What a roster! Dan Rather slugged while on camera. Mike Wallace removed bodily from the convention floor. Smaller fry smashed on the streets. News executives from around the country filed protests; reporters' stories recounted nightstick justice. Others went further. Hugh Downs used the word "pig" on the *Today* show. Walter Cronkite talked about "thugs" before Mayor Daley, in *Newsweek*'s words, "overwhelmed the newsman as if Cronkite were a Republican alderman."

"The whole world is watching," the crowds had chanted in front of the Conrad Hilton Hotel. But where radicals saw—or in some cases encouraged—systematic violence by the authorities, mass media depicted an aberrational event. Chicago's *American* followed a columnist's "Horrifying View of the Police State" with a front-page postconvention interview of Police Superintendent James Conlisk edited by his PR man. Chicago *Daily News* columnist Mike Royko, no radical, turned his tough prose on the cops; the *News* later gave eight pages to a Mayor's White(wash) Paper printed as a mailer that could be sent to disgruntled out-of-towners. The *Sun-Times*'s coverage intensified after top editors witnessed the carnage; an editorial entitled "The Police and the Press" seemed more perturbed that reporters had been beaten than that bystanders had. Demonstrators hardly counted.

Beaten reporters also inspired a telling editorial called "Bad Judgment by the Police" at the conservative Chicago *Tribune,* where rhetoric focused on "hippie mobs" and a story about shattered windows neglected to mention that they'd been broken by police pushing demonstrators through them. The editorial denounced "rowdy demonstrations [by] young punks." It sympathized with police who were "tired" (their arms, no doubt) war veterans facing off against antiwar, antidraft demonstrators.

Even the *Tribune* acknowledged that "strong security, however, does not require the police to beat up newspaper reporters and photographers who are lawfully trying to cover a news event."

But it concluded with a statement with which many radicals readily agreed: "The press is not an enemy of the police force; it is the policeman's friend."

The convention's politics were also filtered through a centrist news mesh. In pages of text and color photos, *Newsweek* lashed out at "Mayor Daley's beefy cops, who went on a sustained rampage unprecedented outside the most unreconstructed boondocks of Dixie." But the magazine wrote radicals out of antiwar history. The strong vote for a stop-the-bombing plank at the convention was, *Newsweek* said, "a clear index of just how far the doves had come since Gene McCarthy began his lonely crusade nine months ago." Not how far radical doves had come since twenty thousand people demonstrated in Washington—in 1965!

As the event ebbed, many younger reporters gnashed their teeth over what was called the Great Retrenchment in their papers' relationships with the authorities. In October, some would launch the *Chicago Journalism Review* to examine how mainstream news was reported in their "shops."

"It was a no-win situation for the authorities," Abbie Hoffman recalls, "No matter which way they moved, there was going to be a cataclysmic event. Had the authorities given us permits, there would have been a large festival."

In the wake of the protests, radicals declared gains. Political business as usual had not been allowed to occur. The cost of staying in Vietnam had gone up. Police brutality, nearly invisible when used against minorities, had been exposed. Liberal spokesmen would blame the protests for the election of Richard Nixon, but liberalism's own failure to move beyond its New Deal laurels and its reliance on a war economy had made it vulnerable.

"The whole world was watching," media-kiddies had cried, and millions would agree when the *Official [Walker] Report to the National Commission on the Causes and Prevention of Violence* concluded that there had been "unrestrained and indiscriminate police violence." Half the young "forerunners" in a Yankelovich survey now called the U.S. "sick"; two-thirds believed Vietnam was a mistake; a majority preferred Ché Guevara to Lyndon Johnson or Richard Nixon. Hundreds of thousands of college students called themselves "revolutionaries," as did perhaps twice as many graduates, dropouts, older people, and high-schoolers.

The SDS-aligned *Movement* assessed medical teams, legal-defense committees, and other convention counter-institutions. "The battle for Chicago will be remembered in heavy years to come as the beginning of a Revolution," *EVO* editor Allan Katzman wrote, his arm still in a sling from shaking hands with cops in Lincoln Park. Colleague Bob Rudnick belched out rock-and-bottle doggerel:

> "I hit my first cop with a rugged red brick
> broke a store window and rioted
> running wildly free down Chicago streets. . . .

It took me a dozen years to hear the rest of the story.

In the current decade, Jerry Rubin and I went out for dinner, then returned to his apartment. He'd gone from the Youth International Party to tossing parties for people who want to combine business cards and flirting. In his closet was a past life: a rock 'n' roll poster, a picture of Jerry the headbanded firebrand eating Phil Donahue alive.

"We were not just innocent people who were victimized by the police," he says. "We came to plan a confrontation, to make Chicago a moral center of antiwar protest for the world."

That "we" had gotten him into trouble with other activists, so he shifted pronouns.

"What I wanted to do was to embarrass America internationally because of what America was doing in Vietnam. My job was to make America pay for what it was doing in Vietnam, and therefore stop it. I don't even know if I hid that factor—did I?"

My eyes rolled as I recalled the original "Let's have a party."

"Of course. But 'let's have a party' didn't mean 'let's just have some ice cream.' Let's have a party that expresses our values, which are: Don't go to Vietnam. Don't work for the large corporations. Don't do everything our parents say. Let's show that we stand for life."

Then the conversation turned personal.

"We manipulated you in the sense that our goal was national, not local. I think we thought, 'Abe is very, very creative, very smart, but he wants to mother all the kids in Chicago and protect them from the big, bad New York organizers. What's wrong with that guy? We're letting him be part of the team here, an international and national leader, and he's worried about the possibility of a little blood. At least this time the blood will have political impact, instead of regular police violence.'

"I didn't quite understand—I thought there was a lack of consciousness on your part. My feeling was that you didn't have that international political view."

What about the deceit of hiding confrontation under the guise of a proto-Woodstock?

"That's true," Jerry admitted. "We did want a confrontation. Chicago was a tiny bit of violence when you compare it to anything—a couple of heads, not even that, really. But I think that it was like a [vaccine]. I think that I felt then that America had to have on national TV a violent purge in which it came to terms with its own violence. It didn't understand dropping bombs on the Vietnamese because war is *accepted* violence. But somehow police beating up kids in the streets . . ."

As Jerry paused for a second, I remembered how he had assured a *Seed* writer that the police would never hit sixteen-year-old kids over the head. To hear Jerry tell it now, though, he knew it all the time.

"How do we get our image across?" he asked. "We are going to be culturally outrageous, and they're going to come after us with clubs. And then we're going to say, 'Hey, we're trying to be culturally outrageous —do you get beat for that in America? And how does that relate to the Vietnamese violence, and the violence against black people who don't fit white middle-class standards?' We had a specific plan. We achieved our plan. We were right. We should be heroes."

Not everyone agreed with that admixture of strategy and commitment, manipulation and hubris. "I was naïve," recalls Ed Sanders, who'd sent me a nasty telegram after the *Seed*lings backed off. "It looked like Woodstock a year before it happened. But we had a couple of guys who believed in Pizza Street, that bloodshed was OK."

After the convention, seventy percent of respondents to a national Harris Poll backed the police. Backlash would help Richard Nixon into the White House. Imagery, violence, militancy, and isolated celebrity increasingly elbowed past humane organizing. "The guy who hits the hardest, moves fastest, begins to look like the biggest revolutionary cock," Todd Gitlin, always wary, wrote. "It doesn't seem to matter whom he hits, where he runs."

It was important to press the authorities on Vietnam and the rest. But Chicago was a cusp. Before it, the Movement was against America's war in Vietnam; after, segments favored a war on America. Before it, the papers were open to a range of views; after, they were more politically aware—and more rigid. Within three weeks, this nonviolent person was babbling in the mainstream press about whether he'd be carrying a flower or a gun.

Two issues after the convention, the *Seed* cover showed a pig dressed as a cop.

8

REVOLUTION?

ONTAGUE, MASSACHUSETTS—AUGUST 12–13, 1968: Eight hundred miles from the cultural and political storm gathering in Chicago, twenty-eight radicals charged from the night shadows. Walkie-talkies crackled. The invaders poured into the red seventeen-room building perched on sixty acres of hilly farmland. A baseball bat or two, an iron rod, a knife came into view. "Where's the deed?" a Liberation New Service staffer demanded. "Where's the money?" another yelled. Even verbal resistance by the building's dozen or so occupants was met with slaps, or worse.

Through the night, members of LNS and SDS, the *Rat* and Newsreel, searched the house for documents, the garage for a printing press. When they left, it was with the deed and a check for $6,000 of the $15,000 they'd come for.

What was the target? A usurious bank? A Dow Chemical napalm facility? An ROTC armory? No, the enemy was punched-out, bloody-nosed Marshall Bloom, the freak who'd heisted his own news service to keep it from falling into what he saw as heavy Left hands.

The LNS brouhaha was a variation on a rift that had divided Leftists from the Russian Revolution through the Spanish Civil War to the streets of Paris just a few months before. Were radicals—and, by extension, the underground press—to celebrate personal freedom or engage in centralized political struggle? Was all political control the enemy, or only capitalism? Was the radical journalist or artist or film-maker supposed to serve the muse or serve the people, touch the sky or off the pig?

At the turn of the century, in *What Is to Be Done,* Lenin described a revolutionary publication as "part of an enormous pair of smith's bellows that would fan every spark of the class struggle and of popular indignation into a general conflagration." This paper was to be used as an organizing tool around which "a regular army of tried fighters would systematically gather and receive their training."

Some American radicals concentrated on fusing artistic freedom and political commitment, with varying success. The *Masses,* its editor Max Eastman wrote during World War I, was "a magazine directed against rigidity and dogma wherever it is found, printing what is too naked or true for a money-making press"; soon revolution's cleansing fire would create new ground for artistic accomplishment.

But as John Reed, who covered the Bolshevik revolution and was a radical official in New York, pithily noted, "This class struggle plays hell with your poetry." Even as the *Masses* promoted a hundred causes, its writers argued over whether "pure" or "proletarian" art offered creative salvation.

The government ended the *Masses'* debate by banning it from the mails and indicting its editors for conspiring to obstruct the draft. But in 1921, Eastman again tried to bridge art and politics in the *Liberator.* Artistic "work has to be playful to be creative . . . very free and irresponsible," he wrote. "It cannot, I think, submit to the official control of a party." Yet, he declared, that was precisely why artists, humorists, poets, musicians, and the like were "more in need of guidance and careful watching by the practical and theoretical workers of the movement than the members of any other trade."

Eastman was not able to cross his own bridge. In 1928, he resigned from the *New Masses* after editors read his critique of Marxism and "ordered all such heresies to cease." A decade later, after denouncing the artist's lot in the Soviet Union as a choice between surrender and "social misery," he successfully sued the *Daily Worker* for libel after it accused him of serving British intelligence. His renunciation of socialism followed.

By June, 1968, when LNS moved to New York from Washington, Ray Mungo was closer to the later Eastman than to Lenin: "We were the crazy people's news service, the forebears of the New Age," he recalls. "And then came this other group who all thought they were in this army and had to obey rules and march around."

For Mungo and Bloom, the Beatles' *Yellow Submarine* was becoming more important than Chairman Mao Tse-tung's *Red Book.* Obviously a partisan, Mungo divided LNS into two camps. The freaks of the Virtuous Caucus supported the revolutionary National Liberation Front of Vietnam, but were personally nonviolent, mellow decentralists. The Vulgar Marxists were communal socialists who seemingly wanted to join the NLF, and who were packing LNS in order to take it from its founders.

The Marxists, though, saw the freaks as erratic, not charismatic. "It was very much the distinction between democracy and magic," says George Cavalletto, who'd dropped out of a Columbia University Ph.D. program to head LNS's New York bureau, and who espoused a one-person, one-vote arrangement. "The almost religious quality of [the Bloom faction's] experience of life legitimized what in other terms might have been a ripoff," agrees Sheila Ryan, who'd angrily found herself doing more typing than research, and who married Cavalletto while they were at LNS.

That summer, tension built over everything from story selection to money the members of both factions had put into the service. But the sides were too equal for any purge, and LNS's thrice-weekly schedule continued to grind down people in both camps.

And then there were the Beatles.

By mid-1968, the Beatles had moved from the moptop simplicity of "Love Me Do" through John Lennon's budding complexity on "In My Life," George Harrison's sitar on "Norwegian Wood," the alienation expressed in Paul McCartney's "Eleanor Rigby," and the techno-psychedelic flowering of "Sgt. Pepper." Even more than Dylan, the Stones, or Hendrix-Who-Kinks-Dead-Airplane-Doors, the Beatles were providing the sound-track for scenes in some great generational movie. But Steve Diamond, LNS's man at Columbia, had read in a music trade magazine that the group was having trouble showing their third movie, *The Magical Mystery Tour,* because it was a bit too freaky.

Not one to be bothered by freakiness, Diamond called the Beatles' New York representative and asked if LNS could show the movie for a benefit. The God of Synchronicity was on his side: just the week before, George Harrison had spoken to LNS in London. And so, a rambling interview about good vibes scored a film from the group that was becoming "more popular than Jesus." *Magical Mystery Tour* wasn't *A Hard Day's Night* or *Help!* But on the night of August 22, several thousand people would flood rock promoter Bill Graham's Fillmore East rock hall to see it.

As Diamond ran around Manhattan firming up the benefit, he began shifting his allegiance to the Bloom faction. A piece he had written claiming that the Bolivian Communist Party had sold out Ché Guevara had been rejected by at least one LNS Marxist as "too divisive." And there was a more immediate flashpoint. At one of the seemingly constant meetings, a truly Vulgar declared that "Marshall Bloom was a frustrated homosexual who uses the news service as his genitals."

Bloom, both supporters and detractors agree, was "a gay celibate." But homosexuality, if sub rosa, wasn't foreign to LNS, and the underground press supposedly supported individual liberation more than mainstream society. The gender-oriented attack left Diamond livid: "In my young mind, that was a low fucking blow."

The freaks wanted to get off gray New York streets, out of gray Movement politics. They felt guilty about turning their backs on the Vietnamese, the blacks, but agreed with a letter sent by the *Express Times* challenging the assumption "that serious stuff has to appear gray and doctrinaire in order to be correct [as] a debased conception of politics." Mungo had already relocated to a Vermont farm.

And so, the freaks invoked the spirit of the ripoff. Hadn't creative financing fed LNS's Washington operation? Hadn't a disgruntled editor at Boston's *Avatar* just heisted and destroyed thirty-five thousand papers printed by a rival faction? Hadn't radicals recently invaded New York public television station WNET in search of public access—with LNS's subsequent editorial approval? Now Bloom used $5,000 of *Magical Mystery Tour* advance ticket money to gain title to the Montague farm and, on the morning of the benefit, the freaks ransacked their own offices and began their own Magical Mystery Tour.

Conscientiousness was their undoing; intending to keep on publishing, the freaks had filed a change-of-address card with the postal authorities. Discovering it, the outraged radicals headed north to their raid. The deed and the check were voided as soon as the raiders left. But the theft, the use of violence, and the pressing of criminal charges by the Montague folk rocked the Movement and the underground press.

An Associated Press thumbnail described LNS as printing "news from the hippie point of view." Packets from "LNS/NY" and "LNS/Mass" were more detailed.

Even-tempered and analytical, the New Yorkers called the relocation an unprecedented violation of Movement principles. It had left them with a hard choice: press charges, give up, or forcibly return the mailing lists and money "to collective possession." Committed, opposed to the idea of ownership, not wanting to recognize the "illegitimate legal authority of the system we oppose," they'd chosen repossession. A tag-along person had flipped out in the heat of the moment, they admitted, but overall there'd been only minimal violence.

Charges of "SDS propaganda," they wrote, manifested "latent anti-communist paranoia in a movement that is supposed to have gone beyond that." And the New Yorkers denied being heavy-handed apparatchiks. "Our perception of politics is that personal liberation is an integral part of the revolutionary process in 20th-century America—personal liberty expressed in poetry, graphics, photography and joy in media."

The real issue, LNS/NY said, rested with an SDS-inspired moral imperative toward collectivity. With seventeen full-time people, the service "could only expand and serve the movement in a larger way if it were identified not with a single individual, however talented, but with a staff that functioned collectively."

A packet from the Massachusetts-based "Liberation News Service of the New Age" also was appearing in subscribers' mailboxes. Ray Mungo opened with a back-to-the-land credo that independence, even survival in "a nation at war," lay in the countryside. Then a seven-page main story printed on colored paper expressed the freaks' position. LNS, they said, was not just about providing a mirror image of mainstream news. "We wanted our very essence to signify the New Age, a new way for journalists, artists, and photographers to share, grow and create together."

Instead, they said, the idea of an eclectic, even contradictory, news service had been challenged by nose-to-the-grindstone socialism. This, they felt, justified the heist, while "pursuing a family in a quiet house in the dead of night like a lynch mob is not revolutionary."

The Massachusetts contingent closed with an admonition: "Accept No Substitutes."

The underground press now had a divided news service. The remaining *Magical Mystery Tour* money was tied up by injunctions and legal fees. The raiders faced charges of kidnapping and larceny, and when they were reduced to disturbing the peace, Sheila Ryan complained that a male-chauvinist judge had fined the men twice as much as the women.

LNS was less than a year old.

THE HIP SCENE wasn't dead; arguably it was more popular than radical politics. In the wake of the Democratic Convention, underground papers ran new lifestyle-oriented writers, artists, and stream-of-collective-consciousness poets. The *Seed*'s postconvention issue also announced local boutiques, head shops, and rock halls, and new albums by Janis Joplin, Canned Heat a.̣d Blue Cheer, Ravi Shankar, and Peter, Paul, and Mary.

But the Summer of Love had turned into convention summer. The war in Vietnam raged on, and heads at home had been bloodied. Huey Newton's police shootout case had concluded, at least temporarily, with a two-to-fifteen-year sentence for voluntary manslaughter. And Bloom, Mungo, and other hip forefathers were moving off center stage. "By '68, some of us were real bored," *Avatar* acolyte and *Crawdaddy* founder Paul Williams says. "Even the New York *Times* was writing about rock 'n' roll. It sounds elitist, but you're in early, you beat the drum, and then the administrators take over."

Other hips had harsher reasons for checking out. With gallows humor, the *Seed*'s masthead listed staffers who'd been gassed, Maced, freaked out, rejected, inspected, and vivisected during the Chicago protests. Copublisher Colin Pearlson, a commercial photographer who'd sailed to America from Scotland and smiled on flower power, now placed an ad seeking people interested in completing his new forty-five-foot sailboat and heading out on a world cruise. George from the headshop, my impish ex-roommate, had harbored the Yippie pig and pulled the *Seed* through more than one seemingly insurmountable printer's bill. Now he was readying himself for India and "the Maharishi's crashpad."

The day after the Democratic Convention's conclusion, a leather-jacketed guy named Michael James came into the *Seed* office. Mike had grown up in a Connecticut suburb, and his neohillbilly accent belied an education at upscale Lake Forest College. He'd played football there, had worked in SDS's JOIN (Jobs in Our Neighborhood) project in Uptown, Chicago's poor-white Appalachia, and had been very active in the convention streets.

I'd published an article of Mike's called "Take a Step into America" that asked freaks not to ignore working-class people. The *Seed* staff was trying to step as far out of America as possible, but James's piece had been energetic and humane, worth running. Now I told him that I was bitter about the convention carnage. Michael was confident; reaching across my rickety wooden desk, he took my right hand and bent two fingers outward to form a peace sign. "That's over," he said. He bent the fingers back, then turned my hand so it formed a raised fist. "That's what's happening now."

Not surprisingly, the underground papers that debuted after the convention were more politicized than their predecessors. In September, *Kudzu* appeared, astoundingly, in Jackson, Mississippi, offering "Subterranean News from the Heart of Ole Dixie" and a crude cover drawing of the tenacious vine whose name it aptly bore.

"We feel that the youth culture is the major happening of this decade, and will prove to be one of the major events of the last part of the twentieth century," a staffer named David explained inside. Yet *Kudzu* knew its roots. "Past generations of educated Southerners have allied themselves first with the big planters and slaveowners, then with the carpet-baggers and Yankee merchants, then with Northern big business, lastly with the corporate liberals. We have broken with this tradition, and we now strive to ally ourselves with unemployed and working class whites and with the black movement for liberation."

Kudzu's debut issue offered stories about Bob Dylan and Jefferson Airplane, Eugene McCarthy and the NAACP, the Chicago convention and the FBI. "We do not subscribe to the Old Left doctrine that we must become fake workers in order to manipulate a revolution," the editorial concluded. "We cannot organize workers any more than whites can organize blacks or blacks organize whites. We must remain true to our identity as long-haired intellectuals. . . . We do not seek a narrow, violent political revolution. We seek a much more profound revolution, a revolution of a whole culture."

Founded the same month, Cambridge's *Old Mole* owed more to SDS, which now had nearly 100,000 members and over 350 chapters, and was influential at LNS, the Washington *Free Press,* and several other papers. The *Old Mole* featured power analyses of Harvard University, Movement stories, reviews of Newsreel films. Its first cover, mostly type, cited the Revolution, and roughly quoted the source of its name: "We recognize our old friend, our old mole, who knows so well how to work underground, suddenly to appear: The Revolution"—"Marx."

At the *Seed,* we still favored freak news, sometimes-crude comix, and four-color graphics that were stunning when they weren't off-register. Increasingly, though, there was news of grape strikes and draft resistance, of black and student protests. A speech by Mike James denounced capitalism and called on young activists to go forward and fight. In an "Open Letter," I called for postconvention unity between brigadistas and astrologers: "freaks and politicos and greasers and blacks erased their labels and became a united force. . . . Black flags, red flags, NLF flags waved high: fifty stars had no answer."

And yet, our near-injurious visit to a George Wallace rally showed that any mass redneck-hippie alliance remained hostage to their prejudice and our elitism. A story on proposed election-day demonstrations was called "Here We Go Again." An analysis of the Movement was laid out around a photo of Frank Zappa seated on a toilet. Our goal remained an alternative society, an amalgam of free stores, clinics, and the like for an age that would produce postindustrial plenty or apocalyptic collapse. Our politics were less those of the poet Mao than of the poet Gary Snyder, who wrote that "The conditions of the Cold War have turned all modern societies—Communist included—into vicious distorters of man's true potential."

Which, in the post-Chicago atmosphere, were less and less Movement values. In October, several SDS-oriented longhairs opened a Chicago branch of *Kaleidoscope,* the Milwaukee-based paper founded late in 1967 by a former Milwaukee *Journal* reporter named John Kois. Kois was one of the shaggiest editors in the underground—*Rolling Stone* writer John Burks would describe him as either "a small bear or a medium-sized cave hermit." But Kois had developed a solid paper with an arts section that appeared in spinoffs located in Madison, Indianapolis—and Chicago.

The first Chicago *Kaleidoscope* had a cartoon cover but talked about "a newspaper from the people and for the people." When the two staffs met to sniff each other out, a young but veteran alumnus of JOIN and SDS (and heir) named Skeets Millard laced into us: Where were our politics? he asked. In November, *Second City,* a paper produced by traditional Leftists that favored nuts and bolts over purple haze, asked the same question of both papers. "*Second City* is not intended to be just another 'underground paper,' " it harrumphed. "*Second City* is intended to be a voice of the Movement in Chicago."

But this divisiveness had its bright side. By Thanksgiving, Chicago had three community papers of dissent publishing regularly, plus SDS's *New Left Notes. Seed* and *Second City* people found each other's papers irrelevant. But *Second City*'s publisher distributed the *Seed,* keeping the money in the Movement family. New York had the *Rat,* the *Guardian, Win, Liberation,* numerous special-interest and party papers, an emerging network of high school underground papers—and *EVO,* which was circulating sixty thousand or so copies a week. The L.A. *Free Press* was closing in on a hundred thousand. Sixty or so of the most important papers now belonged to the Underground Press Syndicate; hundreds more were available across the country.

The two LNSs were going through a similar sorting-out. "We were the outlaws of the Movement," politico-turned-freak Steve Diamond recalls. "In a way, that was the best thing that ever happened, because we were then given this opportunity to attempt to live out some of our attitudes and ideas—live collectively, live a self-sufficient existence, learn how to get it on in a group, learn how to survive in an antimaterial life."

Autumn leaves and love affairs, newborn animals and new crops, were real changes for those experiencing them. But increasingly, the New Age didn't jibe with the New Left. Diamond: "Nobody wanted to know about communal living in the country, about organic food. It was, 'Be in the city, in the streets fighting the man.' " LNS/Mass wasn't where the action was. "Do you think that the *Seed* needed to hear from us third-hand from somebody in Chicago rewritten by us upstairs in the farm-house and rushed down to the garage and sent out two weeks later?

"We were out of the mainstream. The question was, were we big enough to accept it?"

LNS/NY, meanwhile, pumped out packet after packet. There wasn't much about alternative lifestyles, Mexican and Cuban posters superseded underground comix, and its reprinting of "The Internationale" probably didn't run in many papers. But LNS reported on napalmed peasants in Vietnam and napalmed draft files in Milwaukee, on student sit-ins in the U.S. and murdered students in Mexico City, on the threat of Wallace and Jerry Rubin mocking HUAC wearing black pajamas and bandolier to a hearing on the "convention disorders."

LNS ran SDS leader Bernardine Dohrn on revolutionary Vietnamese women; other articles covered protests at the Miss America pageant by a new group of activists—feminists. Seeing youth as a neo-Marxian class, LNS/NY chronicled the battle between East Village freaks and rock promoter Bill Graham for a community night at the Fillmore East (backing the protest, but noting that the people's representative belonged to a wino-liberation front).

In his "Outside Agitator" column, Ralph J. Gleason reiterated that the Beatles were not only "more popular than Jesus" but "more potent than SDS." In "From the Other Side of the Tracks," Julius Lester was more radical.

Lester had different influences than most underground writers. "Let's start with the fact that I'm black," he says, recalling college in the South at the dawn of the sit-ins. But he wrote for the *Realist* and pointed out flaws in the liberal peace Movement for the *Village Voice*.

When he began his *Guardian* column in 1967, Lester's goals were to bridge the black and white movements, and to be a "Movement critic." His reasoned thought and personal tone led LNS/NY to begin syndicat-ing his column in the summer of '68. Almost immediately, he defined the fulcrum on which protesters uneasily perched in the wake of the Chicago convention.

Recent events, Lester wrote, showed the dedication of many white radicals and the need for a black-white alliance. But the situation was dangerous, and not just because of the authorities. Leftists were "in danger of falling victim to our own words. We have proclaimed . . . that the revolution has begun and if red flags are a sign of revolution, then indeed it has. . . . A revolution, however, is not *the* revolution and too many of us mistake the former for the latter."

What was real, the man who'd backed the Yippies said, was an uprising against cultural values. "It is a revolution which has seen the young go into the streets to confront the present with the new of their uncut hair, the new of their multi-colored clothes, covering less and less of their bodies (which are real and good and beautiful and yes yes it is nice to touch each other, isn't it?). They have been willing to accept the consequences of their new lifestyles of lying on the grass openly passing joints, of saying no to the government's immoral demand for two years of your life in a uniform to fight a war, of repeatedly placing their bodies in the streets."

But that, Lester continued, was not the same as challenging an economic structure that remained intact, "leisurely chewing up millions of people every day.

"We defeat ourselves by calling what we have brought about 'revolution,' " he continued. "We have not begun to approach that day when we have seized power, held it and begun to create a system that is based on a sense of community. . . . The system will not disappear because we say 'fuck the system.' "

True enough. But around the underground, cursing was easier than changing. "Don't vote for shit," the *Express Times* advised its readers re the impending presidential contest featuring Hubert Humphrey, Richard Nixon, and George Wallace. Many underground papers were following the Black Panther lead and writing about the "pigs." Even the formerly peace-and-love *Seed* ran a cover showing a porcine, Mayor Daley-esque policeman.

For Lester, this was an ethical error. "It is the deed we must hate, not the doer of the deed. The policeman acts like a beast, but to call him a beast, 'a pig,' is only to negate the potential of man that is within him." Lester also saw another problem: if a radicalism cut off from most Americans went to war, it would be exterminated.

Lester, however, soon found himself at war within the Movement— for criticizing Stokely Carmichael and, especially, the Black Panthers.

The Panthers were bidding to become the Movement's vanguard, an idea the nearly all-white underground papers increasingly supported. "The Underground Press is sometimes smitten by the please-Stokely-rape-my-sister syndrome," wrote Richard Neville, editor of London's *Oz*. But, he continued, this "partly compensates for the attitude of the overground press over the past few hundred years."

There also were real political reasons to support the Panthers. They had a program, and some support in black communities where police brutalized as well as protected. Militant pride could be a stunning alternative to despair. They were socialists, not black nationalists. And they were under attack, which made any criticism, even if constructive, seem potentially racist.

Late in 1968, Lester, who'd favored the Yippie media guerillas, wrote a column which warned that mass media would select the Movement's leaders, get them "caught up in the glamour of their own image," set distorted priorities. "No matter how easy it may seem, one cannot use the media to one's own ends. Whatever gains are made are ultimately illusory. In present-day America, the media can be nothing but an enemy of revolution."

Even opponents would agree with this part of Lester's critique. "More systematically than any other black group," former Black Panther Party Communications Secretary Kathleen Cleaver would write in the 1980s, "the Black Panthers exploited television's powers . . . to counter attempts by authorities to discredit and dismantle the organization." But not without cost. "Justice for blacks," she concluded, "remained invisible, overshadowed by television's emphasis on violence."

Many mainstream reporters did oppose or distort radical positions, but it could be argued that CBS didn't sell guns to the Panthers, NBC didn't carry them into the California State Legislature at Sacramento, and ABC didn't script those remarks about barbecuing, skewering, or otherwise "offing the pig." Lester's 1968 disapproval, though, went even further: after bows to Mao and Fidel, he dismissed Black Panther Minister of Information Eldridge Cleaver as "an ex-convict rapist-revolutionary who can write."

Such comments, LNS's Karen Wald retorted then, were slanderous, and "incredibly impolitic . . . just when the total forces of the state are gathering to put him back behind bars."

Lester, now: "The attitude was that the Panthers were untouchable, and I had been very aware of a lot of defects." He recalls one Panther leader pulling a gun on a famous black author in the New York offices of SNCC. "I was also very aware that to come out and start writing all that would put me in personal danger. So I held off from doing it for a long time, until I couldn't do so, and all hell broke loose."

On November first, the tonnage of explosives dropped on Vietnam exceeded the total for the entire Second World War—the bombing halt that followed was taken as just a pause in the disaster. When Richard Nixon won the 1968 Presidential election, Chicago *Kaleidoscope* taunted "scared-shitless liberals," and the cover of *Other Scenes* featured all the candidates' names tumbling out of someone's ass. LNS's story was more sober: "Movement activists voted with their feet in the streets, on campuses and in cities around the country," it began, "but in most cases, they failed to attract much support from other students and young people." However, the impulse toward militance was growing. When LNS/NY reported an early-October explosion at the Institute of Science and Technology at the University of Michigan, it credited "urban guerillas" and headlined the story "Michigan Liberation Blast."

"The revolution is not yet," Julius Lester had written. "The seeds have been planted, but . . . the system plays for keeps. It will destroy us or we will destroy it." At the *Seed* in November, we received a harbinger of authority's response.

During the LNS split, we'd sided with the freaks but continued to subscribe to both services. Several times a week, packets arrived—along with position papers, poignant essays and pragmatic survival tips, rants and raves, and enough verse to leave a manila envelope with the words "No More Goddamn Hippie Poetry" scrawled across it hanging heavily behind my desk.

One unmarked, mimeo'd, yellow letter had an odd edge to it.

". . . And Who Got the Cookie Jar?" it was headed. Signed by "a former staffer," it labeled the LNS split "a real kindergarten performance" by "cats" and "girls." Bloom, it read, "has always been a bit of a nut. . . . He's managed to turn LNS from an efficient movement news service into a complete mess."

After praising SDS, the memo concluded, "It's a bad scene when a good movement organization engages in civil war. . . . The situation was stupid, stupid, stupid."

Maybe so. But in reality, this letter was an FBI plant designed to keep the flames of the heist from cooling, cooling, cooling. On September 9, the office of Director J. Edgar Hoover had alerted the Special Agent in Charge (SAC) of the FBI's New York office about "an excellent opportunity to take advantage of the split to further disrupt the underground press and to attack the New Left." (That same day in Los Angeles, the FBI decided to mail copies of the *Free Press* and *Open City* to their landlord in the hope of a dual eviction.)

On October 7, the FBI's New York office had responded with a plan "designed to take advantage of the recent split in the Liberation News Service" by mailing out the best of several fraudulent letters "to various 'peace groups,' New Left organizations and individuals." The suggested texts came with an apology: "The letter is written in the jargon of the New Left, necessitating the use of a certain amount of profanity."

Two weeks later, the director's office approved the fraud—cautiously. "You must take all necessary steps to insure that the Bureau is not identified as the source of this letter."

At the *Seed,* we decided that the letter's language was too hey-bop-a-ree-bop to be authentic, and didn't run it. But even if Big Brother was clumsy, the letter hinted that he was out there, up to who knew what?

9

PARANOIA STRIKES DEEP

DALLAS, TEXAS—NOVEMBER 15, 1968: Once upon a time, he'd been Brent LaSalle Stein, descendant of a family of printers that could trace its way back to 1539 and the court of Francis I of France. After listening to Buddy Holly's "That'll Be the Day" and the Beatles' "A Day in the Life," smoking pot, and dropping LSD, he'd become Stoney Burns and begun publishing an underground paper called *Notes from the Underground,* and then Dallas *Notes.*

The paper was a local variant of the basic underground mix circa 1967—until *Notes* made news with a story that Texas Congressman Joe Pool had been arrested on charges of drunken driving after his car hit a carload of soldiers. Before long, Pool was telling the Dallas dailies that the underground press would "slander and libel everyone who opposes these traitors in their attempt to destroy American government." He also used his position as a member of the House Un-American Activities Committee to investigate various papers.

The Pool piece hadn't hurt *Notes'* circulation, which climbed into the low five figures. But now, for the second time in two weeks, the twenty-five-year-old editor was being arrested, ostensibly for pornography. This second bust brought the total of confiscated material to four typewriters, some cameras, a desk, a drafting table, business records, and copy for the next issue. "I didn't know what to seize and what not to seize, so I just took everything," one police officer said.

The raids drove two editors off the *Notes* masthead. The U.S. Supreme Court eventually would order the state of Texas to redraft its obscenity law, but the mushroom-haired Burns would be busted dozens of times more. And *Notes* was not alone. No less than twenty-eight papers, Underground Press Syndicate director Tom Forcade was writing, had recently been subjected to "a raw deal."

Forcade knew that most editors had taken police attention as proud proof of both establishment lameness and the headway they were making. But his list, as expanded by LNS, suggested selective enforcement of existing laws, an attack on radical virtues turned mainstream crimes, and illegal use of force and entrapment.

- Editors at Bloomington, Indiana's *Spectator* and other papers had been convicted of draft resistance.
- The staff of *Kudzu* had been beaten—by deputy sheriffs.
- Milwaukee *Kaleidoscope* editor John Kois's car had been firebombed; publication of an interracial sex photo would net him a fine and probation.
- In Saint Louis, an undercover policeman had infiltrated *Xanadu* and busted the paper's editor for marijuana possession.
- In Vancouver, British Columbia, the *Georgia Straight* was charged with criminal libel against a judge.
- Despite the bravado of a connect-the-dots sequel to an "obscene" cunnilingual cover graphic, *EVO* editors worried about fearful newsdealers dropping the paper. In Austin, Texas, printers were putting black boxes over items in the *Rag* that stirred their prurient interest. In Los Angeles, the cost of defending against a crotch-shot record ad and a poem would put John Bryan's *Open City* out of business even though the convictions would be reversed on appeal. In England, *Oz* would have a celebrated obscenity trial.

In Chicago, I was about to be arrested in connection with the *Seed*'s Christmas issue.

The three-color front cover of the twenty-four-page *Seed* featured Santa Claus crucified on a dollar sign (inside, a smaller Santa bore Ho Chi Minh's face and the holiday message "Ho Ho Ho.") The contents fused counterculture with radical politics. Stories supported striking California grape pickers and a fugitive Eldridge Cleaver, and previewed the anarchist Living Theatre, which used Artaud's techniques, chants, and body games to break down the barrier between audience and performer. Dr. Hip(pocrates), the underground's Ann Landers, opined on clitoral stimulation and birth control. Eugene Feldman, an older white man who'd been into civil rights way before it had become fashionable, contributed his regular Black Heritage feature. Reviews discussed an antidraft guidebook and Abbie Hoffman's *Revolution for the Hell of It*. My editorials plugged the new *Second City* and *Kaleidoscope*, as well as the *Chicago Journalism Review*. Two full-page ads from Columbia Records tried to titillate our paranoia by suggesting it was wise to "know who your friends are."

And then there was the centerfold.

"Memories and Memories to Look Forward To" was the work of Karl-Heinz Meschbach. The moustached East German refugee's accomplished drawings had become characteristic *Seed* centerfolds. The current bio-graphic melded Berliner barbed wire with Chicago convention nightsticks, and surreal and sexual images.

Laid up with asthma, I hadn't seen the picture until my girlfriend, the delightful hippie-mystic Mary Sunshine, brought a *Seed* home. "This is great," she said as we eyeball-tripped our way across it.

"It really is," I echoed.

Then I uh-ohed.

There, in the lower right quadrant, bounded by the words "Make Love, Not War," a young lady was in intimate contact with an erect male member, close by none other than . . . Mayor Richard J. Daley.

"Could be trouble," I said. Mary smiled and shrugged.

Suspicions aside, a healthy editorial I probably would have run the picture. The graphic artfully celebrated the freedoms and lack of same in Meschbach's life, and for an editor unilaterally to spike copy in the underground was generally seen as an ego trip rather than a reasoned judgment.

In any event, two weeks later I arrived at the *Seed* to find a police vehicle parked outside the dry cleaner on the corner.

"Stick-up," I thought, worrying about the owner, with whom we had a friendly if apolitical relationship.

In our office, I found out what was really up.

"Abraham Peckolick, you are under arrest," said a representative of "the obscene matters squad," who'd previously come by to purchase an offending issue. Also on hand was Robert Pierson, the undercover agent who'd successfully posed as a biker to become Jerry Rubin's bodyguard during the convention festivities.

The college-dropout vendor who'd made the sale was already in the van, charged, as a local liberal bookseller would be, with selling obscene material. But the police were hierarchical. If I merited being arrested not only for "providing obscenity for sale" but for "being reckless in my editorial responsibility," I deserved a ride in a cruiser instead of a bumpy old truck.

We were bailed out after six hours of goofing off and being interviewed for newspaper stories, some of which sympathized with our questions about whether sex was more obscene than war, or why we'd been singled out for arrest when Loop newsstands were full of horny-porny magazines. An outraged Meschbach published a scathing letter to the head of the police Prostitution and Obscenity Unit, extending "my gratitude for your unsolicited critique of my graphics." A slightly off-register *Seed* cover collaged our heads into a picture of scarlet-letter Puritans in stocks.

The American Civil Liberties Union and lawyer Elmer Gertz (who would win a landmark libel suit against the John Birch Society) took our case *pro bono;* one ACLU lawyer began a pseudonymous legal column in the *Seed.* In March, a circuit-court judge proved himself to be Solomon in disguise. The graphic was obscene, he ruled; the entire issue, however, "although trashy, was not obscene." Case dismissed.

Actually, I'd had some light moments with the authorities. Before the Democratic convention, FBI agents had visited my old building in the Bronx, where Mrs. Schwartz, our next-door neighbor, gave them the lowdown: "He always used to hold the elevator door for me." Aside from Meschbach's bruised palette, the "obscenity" arrests had simply sold some extra papers. And when we'd burnt our deposit slips and unused checks to protest the closing of the *Seed*'s account by a local bank, at least the FBI did some accurate reporting:

"They carried signs which stated 'LSD not LSB,' 'Lake Shore Unfair to Freaks,' 'Be Leery of Lake Shore Bank, 'America's Seediest Bank,' and 'Poop on Lake Shore Bank."

But after I spoke to FBI agents investigating police brutality at the Democratic Convention, I was subpoenaed to appear before a federal grand jury without benefit of counsel. There I was badgered with questions only about radicals, not about police. Later, the FBI inquired whether I should be indicted under the "Rap Brown" antiriot statute. A new underground press was on the rise.

LIKE THE EARLY LNS, this new underground press was headquartered in Washington, D.C., with offices across the country. As in UPS, its members exchanged stories, information, and staff. But instead of revolutionary broadsides, it dispatched phony letters, divisive manifestos, even bogus newspapers. This press even had its own three-letter acronyms: FBI, CIA, NSA, IRS. It eventually would force the Underground Press Syndicate to leave Arizona, and hit LNS with tax audits, a fire, a phony packet containing a divisive antisemitic article, and as many as a dozen informants planted around (and in?) the service. Some papers fared even worse. State spying was undergoing one of its periodic expansions. The Palmer Raids of 1919–20, with their thousands of arrests and beatings and hundreds of deportations, had been so full of anti-"Bolshevik" frenzy that the government subsequently curbed domestic intelligence-gathering. But World War II, the Cold War, and McCarthyism had nourished a new apparatus increasingly independent of restraints. Authorized in 1956 by Director J. Edgar Hoover for use against the Communist Party of the United States, the FBI's COINTELPRO (Counter-Intelligence Program) had cast a red net far and wide. "The FBI," the Final Report (1976) of the Senate Select Committee to Study Government Operations later said, "went beyond excessive information-gathering and dissemination to the use of secret tactics designed to 'disrupt' and 'neutralize' domestic intelligence targets."

Ironically, COINTELPRO's first major sixties target had been the Ku Klux Klan, in response to the civil rights murders of 1964. Then a multi-agency network of FBI, CIA, and local police had been directed against everyone from the still-tiny number of armed-struggle advocates to pacifist civil rights activists and antiwar senators. The FBI had acted to frustrate the emergence of any "real Mau-Mau" or "messiah" capable of unifying black America. Not content with calling the Nobel Peace Prize–winning Martin Luther King, Jr., "that burrhead," Hoover had assigned numerous agents to search for Communists under King's bed and women in it. According to the Select Committee, "a non-violent man was to be secretly attacked and destroyed as insurance against his abandoning non-violence."

Continued polarization had led to new COINTELPRO categories. In 1967, as some had proclaimed insurrections in Detroit and Newark, the FBI had initiated hundreds of actions against such "Black Nationalist Hate Groups" as the pacifist Southern Christian Leadership Council. The Black Panther Party had been expressly targeted (233 of 295 "actions") for "crippling" via infiltration, disinformation, provocation, and aggravation of conflicts between it and other black groups, and between blacks and whites.

The confrontation at Columbia University had led to a third classification: the New Left. Starting in May, 1968, hundreds of break-ins, smear campaigns, telephone taps, mail "covers," "disinformation" plants, and encouragements of right-wing groups had been initiated against whomever the FBI decided was part of the New Left.

The CIA also spied on the movements. In 1966, it had agreed to share information with the FBI. In February, 1967, positing fears for its own installations and staff, it had begun Project Resistance, which, even though the CIA was not supposed to involve itself in domestic spying, would turn into a six-year campaign to dampen campus radicalism. "There was no mention of, or apparent concern for, direct influence or control of the 'New Left' by agents of hostile foreign powers," the Select Committee concluded. "Instead, the stress was almost entirely upon ideological links and similarities, and the threat of ideas considered dangerous by the FBI."

In August, 1967, Operation Chaos had intensified antidissident efforts. Using FBI and CIA intelligence reports, the government had started a Rabble Rouser Index of activists. By 1973, a National Security Council Watch List of domestic dissidents with foreign connections would bear three hundred thousand names. Army Intelligence developed its own hundred-thousand-name list; the Internal Revenue Service compiled eleven thousand names of its own. Twenty-six thousand activists were targeted for rounding-up in case of some undefined "national emergency."

As the voice of the various movements, the underground press was COINTELPROed even when its writers and editors were not committing illegal acts or doubling as Movement activists. As early as 1966, the FBI had placed an ad in the L.A. *Free Press* designed to discredit the Communist Party. In February, 1967, upon learning of *Ramparts'* plan to publish its blockbuster story linking the CIA to the National Student Association, CIA officials had asked the IRS to examine the magazine's tax returns, an event which led to Operation Chaos. When *EVO*'s request for an airplane pilot to drop two hundred pounds of flowers on the Pentagon during the October, 1967, demonstration resulted in an airport full of police, it was because the ad had been answered by the FBI.

In May, 1968, the FBI had issued a series of interoffice communications (Airtels) suggesting that "information can be used through friendly news media to vividly portray the revolutionary-type actions and militant nature of the New Left movement."

The agency and local Red Squads would quash articles unfavorable to them and feed information damaging to various underground papers to mainstream reporters. Some daily reporters and editors were sympathetic to elements of underground-press style and were vocal about First Amendment rights. But far too often, the established papers showed a commitment to freedom of only their own presses. "The underground press was largely right about government sabotage, Washington *Post* Watergate investigator Bob Woodward would say in 1974, "but the country didn't get upset because it was the left that was being sabotaged. The country got upset when the broad political center, with its established political institutions, came under attack."

The attacks on the movements and the underground press had come together on July 5, 1968, in a memo from the director of FBI to "SAC, Albany." The text boiled two months of suggestions into a twelve-point plan for "Disruption of the New Left."

The memo called for instigating or exacerbating conflicts, selective drug arrests, and raising suspicions that leaders were FBI informants. More specifically, it called for "the use of articles from student newspapers and/or the 'underground press' to show the depravity of New Left leaders and members." Articles and anonymous letters were to be sent to deans, parents, and other potentially upsettable parties. It again suggested the use of "friendly media" to isolate radicals from other students or soldiers.

The memo closed with a helpful hint:

"Be alert for opportunities to confuse and disrupt New Left activities by misinformation."

Much of what was collected was junk, hearsay, newspaper clippings, duplicate documents. But COINTELPRO and the other programs took the movements at their most revolutionary word. Black-bag burglaries, constant surveillance, and selective enforcement ground activists down and warped our behavior. "I've had more trouble out of parole officers and the Department of Corrections simply because I've been relating to the Movement than I had when I was committing robberies, rapes, and other things I didn't get caught for," Eldridge Cleaver said that November.

BUT THE FBI was not content with monitoring, or even penetration.

"As students, we feel the war in Vietnam is a political and military travesty, foisted on the American people by an unsympathetic administration . . . unmindful of the will of the people. This situation we can and should deal with at the polls. The truth of the situation here at IU, however, is that this dissatisfaction with national policy is being used by a few to seize the university and to strike at the heart of the democratic system."

The words were from the second issue of *Armageddon News,* an underground newsletter that began appearing in Bloomington, Indiana, in the fall of 1968. The editor of the *Spectator,* the campus's first underground paper, was being tried for draft resistance. The staff of *Armageddon News* consisted of FBI agents operating out of the Indianapolis office.

Armageddon News followed a strategy of using mock media to paint radicals, especially campus radicals, as a disruptive minority. And the FBI took perverse pride in its work. On October 11, a letter from the director's office to SAC in Indianapolis panned *Armageddon News's* first issue: "subsequent material must contain a more sophisticated approach. . . . Your leaflet should be prepared ostensibly by students who, while disagreeing with the Vietnam War policy and so forth, nevertheless deplore subversive elements on and off campus who are using these issues for their own purposes."

Practice must have made perfect. On January 17, 1969, the FBI's San Antonio office sent a letter to Washington that proposed countering the active SDS chapter at the University of Texas at Austin with "a one-page, throw-away document which could be printed or mimeographed to expose or point out the identities of New Left individuals who are causing disruption and on specific occasion point out the background of some of these individuals." Soon after, the *Longhorn Tale,* named for the school's mascot, appeared on campus, produced by the same office that would pressure the *Rag's* printer into dropping the paper.

A third phony paper, the *Rational Observer,* also began publishing at American University, in Washington, D.C.

Not content with trying to destroy LNS, the FBI also began its own network of news organizations. The Pacific International News Service was set up in San Francisco. Chicago's Midwest News was ignored by local underground papers, but afforded army intelligence agents entree into media events. As we'll see, the New York Press Service was the FBI's big hit, especially during the trial of the Chicago Eight.

On November 5, 1968, the day Richard Nixon was elected the thirty-seventh president of the United States, the God of Synchronicity had J. Edgar Hoover distribute a memo designed to intensify the attack on the underground press:

"One of the most important aspects in our current investigation of the New Left movement involves the movement's propaganda activities," it said. Agents were ordered to scrutinize both organizational and "anarchist-type" underground papers, both to keep up with the radical Joneses and to "take advantage of situations which could embarrass the New Left movement and counter New Left propaganda." Field offices were asked to file the paper's name, publisher, printer, circulation, finances, staff, "subversive connections," "foreign ramifications," legal imbroglios, relationship to any news services, and any licensing information.

Again, the authorities answered their own question with more than surveys. Printers and advertisers were pressured. Staff members were defamed, beaten, arrested. The Red Squad attended *Second City*'s first-issue party, and police supported right-wing violence against that paper and San Diego's *Street Journal* and *Door*. One of Tom Forcade's repression reports claimed that the percentage of underground staffers involved in drug arrests was 100 times that of the general population, a figure that, if true, was unjustifiable even by the herculean pot-smoking at the more psychedelic papers. By 1969, UPS was reporting that sixty percent of the several hundred papers loosely grouped as "underground" were experiencing major repression. Some failed to survive.

In its actions against "Black Nationalist Hate Groups" alone, FBI instigations contributed to deaths through provoked battles between the Panthers and black nationalist organizations, Eldridge Cleaver Panthers vs. Huey Newton Panthers, police vs. Panthers. Thousands of arrests and hundreds of court cases would tie up activists, lawyers, and scarce resources even while securing an extremely low conviction rate. It would take the 1971 "liberation" of COINTELPRO files from the FBI's office in Media, Pennsylvania, to provide even activists with hard evidence of police repression. And as Allen Ginsberg has pointed out, despite numerous exposés, only a handful of FBI figures would be convicted of crimes —and then receive presidential pardons.

Yet both government and Movement saw things differently at the time. "It was my assumption that what we were doing was justified by . . . the greater good, the national security," one participant in the FBI's mail-opening campaign later testified. The Senate Select Committee explicitly allowed for domestic intelligence. And Movement innocence wasn't always complete:

"We did illegal things at the College Press Service," former underground writer Chip Berlet recalls. "We were very heavily involved in the underground of AWOL soldiers. We printed phony IDs that got people out of the country. We saw that as part of our role as underground journalists."

Berlet is a major investigator of repression against the underground press.* During the 1960s, he began his radicalization in Newark by

---

*Geoffrey Rips's and Angus Mackenzie's work in the PEN American Center's *UnAmerican Activities: The Campaign Against the Underground Press* also has helped inform this book's repression information, as has David Armstrong's *A Trumpet to Arms: Alternative Media in America*. See notes following the text.

marching to mourn Martin Luther King, Jr.'s, murder. He then wrote and edited for the University of Denver campus paper, the undergroundish CPS, and Denver's *Chinook* and *Straight Creek Journal.*

"We thought that if we were getting away with illegal things, which we were, that they [the authorities] couldn't be too good at what they were doing," Berlet says. "Yet there was a real sense of us versus them, that we were the voice crying in the wilderness and the government was going to get us."

Various repression researchers have assigned causal importance to police repression in killing the underground press by driving staff away, bleeding off financial resources, and making its journalism so shrill that readers and staffers alike abandoned it before it could mature. "The paranoia was everywhere," Berlet agrees. "You expected that your office was being broken into, and it turns out that it was. You expected that people were spying on you, and indeed sometimes you could see them —they would be out in cars looking at you."

Yet he stops short of crediting the government with kayoing the papers. "Being paranoid, exhausted, scared contributed partly to burnout," he says. "Some publications probably were hounded out of existence. But I don't think the repressive apparatus was the cause of the underground press's demise. I do think that the underground press would have flourished considerably more had there not been this repression.

"When I did my civil disobedience and lay down in the middle of the road, I had no doubt that they were going to arrest me. It was naïve to think that you could kick the shins of the government and not expect to be kicked back. I can still manifest outrage at being carted off, and at my trial, but I never understood the political viewpoint that the state doesn't have the right to protect itself from attack.

"The repression was wrong, and it was blatantly unconstitutional," Berlet adds, "but I think it was to be expected." After all, activists knew that the Vietnamese and other struggles had faced far more repression than theirs.

Actually, the number of underground papers would continue to grow until 1970 or 1971, and underground spokesmen saw repression as the inevitable death-throes of a dying regime. Tom Forcade:

"The Underground Press Syndicate papers, as advance scouts for journalism in Amerika & the world, often find themselves in conflict with the last vestiges of honky mentality. . . . uptight Smokey-the-Bears of the totalitarian forest rushing around with para-legal shovels and axe-weilding blue meanie henchmen, stomping out the fires of a people who have found their voice and are using it."

It wouldn't work, Forcade predicted. "The fires are too many and too big."

Berkeley Barb

VOL. 8, NO. 20, ISSUE 190, MAY 16-22, 1969
2042 UNIVERSITY AVE, BERKELEY, CA. 94704, 845-1940

15¢ BAY AREA   25¢ ELSEWHERE

PIGS SHOOT TO KILL-- BYSTANDERS GUNNED DOWN

Property of the Regents
The University of California

NO TRESPASS

Any Equipment
Property Left on These Premises
May Be Deemed Abandoned

10

STREET-FIGHTING MEN?

MADISON, WISCONSIN—THANKSGIVING, 1968: A year and a half ago, twenty or so people from a few small papers had traveled to Stinson Beach, California, for the Underground Press Syndicate's first meeting. There an Indian had pronounced them children of the future and warned that evil lurked in a five-sided building outside Washington, D.C.

Later in 1967, writers and editors marching on that Pentagon had expressed their anarchy and booed *EVO*'s efforts to administer the Underground Press Syndicate.

In the summer just past, several-score underground pressmen had visited Iowa City as the eyes and ears of counterculture communities. The number of longhairs across the country, LNS's Marshall Bloom had declared, proved that a peaceful victory had been won.

Now, back in the heartland, a self-professed Radical Media Conference was convening.

Dissident media were growing, diversifying. *Vocations for Social Change* listed progressive jobs. HIPS—the High School Independent Press Service—coordinated teenaged dissidents at four to five hundred papers. GI journals merited their own press service. The *Black Liberator, La Raza,* and *El Grito Del Norte* sought to organize blacks and Chicanos into a self-determining rainbow coalition.

The "youth culture" press was solidly international, from London's witty *International Times* and colorful *Oz* to *Actuel* in Paris, *Puss* in Stockholm, *Om* in

Amsterdam, *Eco Contemporáneo* in Buenos Aires. The counterculture of Czechoslovakia's suppressed Prague Spring lived on in a real-life underground press.

Together, the papers surprised even their editors. When John Wilcock visited Zurich, Switzerland, for his *Other Scenes,* he and the editor of *Hotcha* were amazed to find that many images in their sheets were identical. It wasn't a lack of ideas, Wilcock recalls, "just the same reaction, the same viewpoint, automatically."

The Madison conference came together under a similar rhetoric of solidarity. It was the largest underground-press meeting yet: two to three hundred delegates from sixty or so of the hundred fifty community-based papers and other radical media outlets that now existed. The conclave was sponsored by UPS, LNS, and Newsreel, the SDS-oriented makers of movies on Movement themes that formed the meeting's largest delegation.

As usual, much of the gathering consisted of editors exchanging shop talk. But a major discussion centered on what now was being called "the bourgeois media." "There is a consensus on one thing: the mass media is the enemy," Thorne Dreyer, the Austin *Rag* writer who'd helped cover the Pentagon March for LNS, now reported for the more politicized LNS/NY. "It is an institution of the ruling class of this country, and, as such, serves capitalism's ends."

Mass media, the Newsreelers argued, were inherently counterrevolutionary and printed the radical side of the story only when needed "to create the illusion of objectivity." Radicals and radical writers should boycott them, they said. Other attendees countered with what Dreyer called "the softer line"—that an Eldridge Cleaver interview in *Playboy* or a story on SDS in *Life* reached people without access to underground media.

No real solutions were formulated about media relations, or such topics as the role of advertising in allegedly radical media. And, Dreyer admitted, Newsreel itself had become an issue to some of the writers present. Its members weren't "print people." The group had held its own first national meeting coincident with the conference, and its closed caucuses had seemed standoffish. Dreyer noted an "obsession with street militancy."

Still, Dreyer judged the gathering a success in words that noted a shift in the balance between freak and political concerns. "The level of discussion, of political sophistication, was far above that at previous conferences," he wrote. "The scene has changed . . . as individuals began to experience the emptiness of lifestyle ('freakiness,' dope) as a definition of reality. As people realized that you can't build a 'community' of beautiful people in a rotten, capitalist society. And it occurred with Columbia and Chicago—with the death (and cooptation) of 'do your own thing,' with the beginning of revolutionary consciousness.

"At Madison," Dreyer concluded, "one thing became clear. There is no more underground press—the media of the revolution is rapidly evolving."

Not everyone was happy about this shift.

Trinidadian by birth, New Yorker by choice, Lennox Raphael— whose play *Ché* would later be busted for coitally depicting the United States sticking it to Latin America—went to Madison for *EVO*. The rectitude he found left him glum and angry:

"MASSES, MASSES, THEY, THEY, THE WORKING PEOPLE," he wrote about the political mantras he heard, "they slip up on the care and feeding of their own minds, illumination, dreams, their private persons, deny that every revolutionary must come before he mans the barricades." The papers were just as bad, he continued, "too dull, flatirons of defense."

The months to come would offer radical highs—and growing disputes over whether dissidents were out on a limb or not militant enough. The underground press would talk about revolution, yet be accused of lacking purpose. By June, 1969, the New Left's largest organization would be in shambles; Movement and countercultural papers alike would combine radicalism, rudderlessness, and rigidity in an increasingly volatile mix.

THE TENSION in underground media reflected one in Movement politics.

By now, the underground's early, relatively polite, calls for integration and peace were sometimes echoed in the mainstream press. But Richard Nixon's election campaign had required the Thieu government not to sign a Vietnam peace treaty. The just-announced bombing halt was a sham; the secret bombing of Cambodia was just a few months away. Countless Vietnamese lives and twenty thousand American ones—and $60 billion—would be wasted trying to defeat a guerilla force nearly all the underground papers now actively supported.

Propelled by ideals and adrenaline, frustrated by reality, radicals lived in a topsy-turvy world where honor students fought cops while government officials rationalized mass destruction. "I know a cat who tattooed across his head, 'Born to Kill,'" Eldridge Cleaver said in a speech reprinted in *Ramparts*. "Whereas Lyndon Johnson doesn't have any tattoos on his head, he has blood dripping from his fingers."

Two hundred black people had died in riots and insurrections, by police brutality, in urban guerilla warfare. Parts of seventy-plus cities had been occupied by national guardsmen. Serious demonstrations had taken place on two hundred or so college campuses. Movement veterans symbolically walked the Ho Chi Minh Trail and raised fists at the Mexico City Olympics. Increasingly, nonviolence was seen as defending the status quo. Protest literally exploded, and the papers' best and brightest portrayed bombings of draft boards and ROTC offices as legitimate counterviolence. "The campaign of revolutionary sabotage," SDS veteran Andrew Kopkind wrote just before the Madison conclave, "grows logically from very real conditions."

Activists cried from teargas, danced in the streets, relished power taken, sometimes surprisingly, from an unsure dean or an overzealous police chief. Inherited credos melted into shed-your-class/race/nation/religion adventures. "We lived, really, in a lot of ways for each other," Todd Gitlin recalls. "We could not carve out personal careers. We evaluated things not according to personal benefits. And we lived *with* each other."

But the Movement also was deluded by its "success." Its claim to an antiwar majority equated National Liberation Front supporters, nonviolent liberals, and hawks disillusioned by a lack of further escalation. Its ideas butted heads with the endemic American suspicion of socialism. Moving rapidly, often reflexively, some advocates of Marxism began using it increasingly as catechism instead of as an analytic tool. At underground papers, former students with good language skills tried to write revolution into existence. "The next step in the evolution of the revolutionary process will be the move from self-defense to aggressive action," the *Guardian*'s Julius Lester wrote early in 1969. Snipers in East Saint Louis approximated the NLF in Vietnam, he said, and a mid-1968 ambush of police in Cleveland was more important than the Detroit or Watts rising.

"I think what I was hoping for is precisely what I indicated," Lester recalls, "namely, movement toward organized guerilla activity leading to revolutionary change. What I could not see was that [it] was not the beginning of something new but isolated activity by a few who had taken the revolutionary rhetoric of the late sixties to its logical conclusion. The statement [and deeds] misread how willing, capable, or even sympathetic the majority of people were to such actions. They weren't sympathetic at all."

Lester's misreading was typical. In a Man of the Year poll held by the L.A. *Free Press,* the most mainstream of the major underground papers, Eugene McCarthy edged Eldridge Cleaver by one vote. But Richard Nixon was president and Cleaver was in Algerian exile. In the papers, somberness began matching exhilaration. "Nineteen hundred and sixty-nine has come," Julius Lester wrote in a more subdued column. "The enemy is exposed and no one seems to know quite what to do about it. For along with that depression has come a feeling of frustration which is more and more causing us to fight among ourselves, to squabble, to disintegrate into factions."

The lifestyle and consciousness movements also hung between successes and limits. In the *Rat,* William Burroughs, the author of *Naked Lunch* and other prehip attacks on bourgeois lifestyle, saw possibility. "When I was in college in the thirties, there were only two alternatives, either you were a Marxist or you were supporting the establishment. But these people are not, by and large, Marxists. . . . Ché Guevara, and Castro, really, their tactics date back to the nineteenth century."

Former Free Speech Movement activist Michael Rossman had written about "America's prototype VOLUNTARY YOUTH GHETTOS"—Berkeley, the Haight, the East Village. "A new culture, in the full strength of that term, is being born among the young of technological America," he'd proclaimed. Papers in these hip zones adapted ideas from "The Post Competitive Comparative Game of a Free City," a Digger manifesto calling on communards, Black Panthers, hippies, and revolutionary gangs to create a network of food co-ops, medical centers, and other counter-institutions. The *Seed* and other papers ran pages of resource information that helped people live better—and, in the case of drug-help services, may have saved lives.

Yet a community largely populated by the prematurely retired proved economically baseless. Advice on ripping off the phone company and subway alienated straighter folk—and sometimes rebounded. The *Seed* spoke of $400 stolen from the high-energy rock band MC-5 by "revolutionary thieves." Seattle's *Helix* reported that James Cotton's blues band had been robbed of $2,000 and two saxophones.

Soon Liza Williams of the L.A. *Free Press* was denouncing "The Bullshit Revolution," whose activists were "about as free as prisoners who rattle their bars and write slogans on cell walls. Their whole time is spent in avoidance of things, landlords, cops, tax men, bills, warrants, girls who love them, anything, anything which would make them pause for a moment and evaluate their position."

Marjorie Heins, who'd written for the first *Rat,* now questioned whether counter-institutions could make a difference. "Free City has disappeared," she wrote sadly in the *Express Times.* "The Movement is suffering under immense pressures of paranoia and persecution. . . . We're in limbo. . . . Hippie beads in Bergdorf's seem more depressing than encouraging." She offered less a revolution than an exodus: "We will know when to slip away and let those murderous fools rip themselves to pieces."

That feeling had spurred Marshall Bloom and friends to relocate their part of Liberation News Service in rural Massachusetts. For them, city life was too heavy, too frustrating, over and done. The war, nuclear weapons, and general rootlessness suggested a coming apocalypse. Psychedelic drugs could create an awareness of the earth as a united entity, a sensibility also suggested by that do-your-thing compendium, *The Whole Earth Catalog*. Many papers were printing a new column called "Earth Read-Out," which Keith Lampe, a former Yippie muckamuck, filled with news and musings about something called "ecology."

But LNS's resettlement came at the expense of Movement involvement. While LNS/NY challenged "the pigs," LNS/Mass raised goats. Increasingly, those in Massachusetts were less worried about what was printed in the papers than about which burned best in the fireplace, or whether the New York *Times* or *Peking Review* was tops in toilet paper. Over Christmas, 1968, the ink froze in the printing press. In February, 1969, despite Marshall Bloom's remonstrances, his service spluttered to a halt with packet number 140. "We simply didn't have anything more to say," Steve Diamond later wrote, in his *What the Trees Said*, "other than perhaps get some land, get your people together, and see what happens."

The cities remained the places where most of the action was, and the papers there continued to offer a range of counter-information and counter-ideas. Some of them ran counter to each other. A January, 1969, *Rat* pictured a freak in a tree sighting a rifle, and the slogan "The Revolution Has Come/It's Time to Pick Up Your Gun"—along with a reader letter saying that "the revolution must be within each one of us. There can be no peace, no love, no freedom, no equality by one power structure replacing another." Both Movement- and freak-oriented papers mixed stories of damaged draft boards with the "Revolutionary Letters" of poet Diane DiPrima:

> but don't get uptight: the guns:
> will not win this one, they are
> an incidental part of the action
> what will win
> is mantras
> the sustenance we give each other
> the energy we plug into
> (the fact that we touch
> share food)

the buddha nature
of everyone, friend and foe, like a million
earthworms
tunneling under this structure
till it falls.

Energy surged as well as ebbed, and a new generation stepped forward. David Fenton was among them. A tall, thin kid who looked a bit like a teenaged Dick Van Dyke, Fenton had been a student working on a New York high school undergrounder called *Sans Culottes*. When his teachers went out on strike, he attended "liberation classes" at the Bronx High School of Science, then dropped out of what by normal standards was an excellent school, and into taking photographs at LNS/NY.

"Part of it was just the excitement of not having my mother tell me to be home by midnight. And part was a sense of belonging to this community of people who were innovative, and who were trying to stop this killing in Southeast Asia, and who were much freer with each other than most people I knew."

THE MOVEMENTS offered freedom. But early in 1969, growing militance and the espousal of Marxist-Leninist tenets again raised questions about the nature and purpose of art in a time of political struggle.

"All too often I cannot listen to music," Lenin, an admirer of Beethoven, had written. "It works on one's nerves. One would rather babble nonsense, and caress the heads of people who live in a dirty hell and who nevertheless can create such beauty. But today one should not caress anyone's heads—one's hand would be bitten off. One must beat heads, beat unmercifully."

Art, Marxism-Leninism said, should represent the materialist interest of the proletariat, a class with no stake in the current social order. Consequently, the correct art form was realism.

At its worst, such thinking led to Joseph Stalin's 1932 criminalization of nonrealist art in the Soviet Union. But during the sixties, struggle-oriented art also included the extremely attractive, semi-abstract posters of armed revolutionaries produced by OSPAAAL (Organization of Solidarity of the Peoples of Africa, Asia, and Latin America). Newsreel's film on the Columbia strike brought audiences roaring to their feet, screaming "Strike! Strike! Strike!"

Now a small but increasingly loud voice on the Left wanted underground press men and women to be class-based revolutionaries rather than artistic outlaws. In the spring, 1969, issue of Montreal-based *Progressive*

Books and Periodicals, J. S. Thompson criticized "vagabond journalists
. . . promoting bourgeois decadence as a way of life. The hopeless
contradictions of imperialist culture drive these vagabonds to try for
nothing less than eternity, an eternity of 'free' music and 'free' media.
. . . The petty-bourgeois functionaries of imperialist culture . . . have set
out to eliminate the 'squares.' " For Thompson, "avant garde" was a curse.

Advocates of a new culture were just as adamant. "I don't like most
People's Art," wrote the *Express Times'*s Sandy Darlington in "The
River," his music-and-culture column. "All art is for people, so if you
slant it in some way to make it more appealing to 'people,' that means
it's honkified, simplified, sanforized, cleaned up. Art that is cleaned up
may be quite soothing. But it's fake."

Neo-Marxist Herbert Marcuse would offer a third perspective. Why,
he'd ask, did Greek tragedy remain great even though it was produced
in a slave society? What about Eros? Thanatos? Beauty? Art, Marcuse
thought, could inform both capitalist and state-socialist societies, oppose
patriarchy, renew the environment, develop a new sensibility and morality. Marcuse even opened the Pandora's box of class analysis. Under
advanced industrial capitalism, bourgeoisie and proletariat had much in
common. Thus, "Revolutionary art may well become An Enemy of the
People."

No topic better illustrated this debate than underground "comix."
Strange strips appealing to a hip audience had appeared in various college
humor magazines, and relatively tame comix had run in *EVO* as early
as 1965. By late 1968, a potpourri of styles and subjects had evolved, and
the artists had developed a symbiotic relationship with the papers. The
artists—whose characters got high, had sex, fought cops, lived together
—found a compatible outlet; the papers got lively, inexpensive material
that entertained regular readers and attracted new ones. "Underground
papers printed any crazy thing you did," recalls Robert Crumb, the
creator of Fritz the Cat, Mr. Natural, and other characters. "A lot of these
guys had given up on getting into the *New Yorker,* but the underground
press said, 'Great stuff, give us more!' They didn't pay nothing, but you
just felt so glad that somebody would print your stuff with no censorship
at all."

Some comix were juvenile, obsessive blurts, celebrations of the illegal. Others were bright, satiric alternatives to mass culture. On TV,
The Mod Squad turned a Watts rioter, a runaway, and a spoiled middle-
class kid into cops. The antiwar *Smothers Brothers* comedy show soon
would be canceled for *Hee Haw.* At the movies, *Bonnie and Clyde,*

Easy Rider, and *The Wild Bunch* deflected energy into necrophilia. The mass press was conceptually at odds with radical victories.

In contrast, underground comix offered radical-hip life on its own terms, presented cathartic violence, hinted at what it would be like "to win." *EVO* ran Spain Rodriguez's *Trashman,* the continuing story of a revolutionary who fought the police. Crumb's *Fritz the Cat* was an affable, horny scoundrel, his *Whiteman* a paranoid specimen of repressed racism and sexuality, his *Angelfood McSpade* a black female reflection of the artist's own angst over lust and race. Gilbert Shelton's Fabulous Furry Freak Brothers celebrated pot and fraternity. Ron Cobb of the L.A. *Free Press* was the underground's Herblock, drawing telling panels about robot police, or a television-toting middle American searching for an electrical outlet in a postnuclear wasteland.

Some characters defied mainstream comparisons. S. Clay Wilson's bikers, pirates, and lesbians went beyond *Candide* into a grotesque realm of member-chopping violence. The *Inner City Romance* of Guy Colwell, a former draft protester, portrayed humane young radicals living in liberated, integrated situations.

Again, there were splits. Emory, the *Black Panther* cartoonist, filled his space with stark images of wounded and dead police-pigs; most underground cartoonists hoped that the Rapidograph would be mightier than the rifle. Skip Williamson, who'd copublished a comix magazine called the *Chicago Mirror* and now ran much of his work in the *Seed* before anthologizing it in *Bijou Funnies,* found comix more persuasive that rhetoric, but feared mixing them with revolutionary culture because they "deal with the cliché situations created by a decadent society." Harvey Kurtzman, whose work at *Help* and *Mad* had prefigured the comix, was more skeptical. "I think they're more interested in the battle than what the battle is for," he'd tell comix historian Mark Estren. "In any one of the revolutions we know about—Russia, China, Cuba—Shelton and Crumb would be the first ones they'd have to get rid of."

Jay Lynch agreed. Because he'd been hassled by police during the 1968 convention, Lynch would collaborate with Williamson and draw *Conspiracy Capers* on behalf of the Chicago Eight. But he lacked his partner's enthusiasm for the struggle. Radicals "were the underdog and should be defended," he thought. Yet "it would be an awful country if they seized power." Inversely, some radicals blanched at Crumb's exaggerated renditions of black and female anatomy even if they were a protest against sanitized liberal images or all-too-accurate reflections of male libido.

When SDS convened in June, 1969, for its national convention, Paul Buhle was there. Buhle, a Wisconsin surrealist who edited the SDS-backed *Radical America* magazine, believed that, "like any potentially subjective cultural mechanism, comix serve art best to destroy an old view of the world and to replace it with a new one." At the convention, though, he was told that his magazine's comix issue was so just much "petty-bourgeois radicalism."

REAL-LIFE militancy continued to increase. On May Day, 1969, thousands of demonstrators gathered before the federal courthouse in San Francisco. Cries of "Free Huey" rang out as speaker after speaker demanded bail for the imprisoned Black Panther leader. Then a bulletin: "a pig" had been killed in the city's Mission District. The crowd cheered.

Increasingly, the underground press conformed to life during wartime. "Shangri-la, shangri-la," Judy Clavir Albert (a.k.a., "Gumbo") recalls about her meeting with women guerilla fighters in North Vietnam. "Revolution at work, social relations, the position of women, struggle on all fronts. A rose-colored-glasses experience, and one which I completely love, and won't give up even though I probably would have learned more with a more critical approach." Abbie Hoffman saw "a society 100 percent commited to revolutionary struggle, heroic in every sense of the word. I mean, my image of Vietnam was always a farmer with a rifle shooting at a jet plane." The Black Panthers, LSD, rock music —all enjoyed similar status among their constituencies. "It felt good to be the revolutionary vanguard in the U.S.," Todd Gitlin recalls. "It made me feel important. Cubans took you seriously; the Vietnamese thought you were heroic."

This euphoria among many Movement leaders and radicalized underground-press writers was matched by the realization that criticism, even telling the whole truth about a demonstration or an AWOL soldier, could be used by the Movement's enemies. Abbie Hoffman: "Just as it's the duty of the capitalist press to protect the capitalist system, it's the duty of the revolutionary press to protect the revolutionary system." Chip Berlet: "There was no second thought about it. It was just, 'Sure, this is wrong and I may even personally disagree with it, but it's the Movement and we can clean our own house.' "

Here and there, political radicals began using a word new to the underground press. "Our journalism is designed to propagandize," LNS's Allen Young said then.

"We used to get a little propaganda bulletin from North Korea, which was really just outrageous," Young, whose view of Marxism has changed for the bitter, recalls. "And because the right line was to support Kim Il Sung and the North Koreans, I would try to pick out a couple of little news items that I could rewrite into acceptable American journalism. I got a certain sense of amusement that I could do that. But there was certainly no journalistic integrity in it."

"Reflex journalism" appeared in grimmer situations.

Art Kunkin recalls being in the Los Angeles *Free Press* office, looking over a reporter's article about a memorial observance of Martin Luther King, Jr.'s, assassination. He was stunned; there was no mention that a black nationalist had shot at a speaker, or that a guard had accidentally fired a shot into the ceiling of the room where the event had been held.

Why not? Kunkin asked.

We didn't want to criticize the black movement, he says the writer replied.

"This is incredible," Kunkin recalls himself saying. "It displays the divisions of the black movement, and the inadequate preparation of the guards. This story ought to be written before somebody gets killed."

The issue was locking up, but Kunkin managed to reword a photo caption to include the incident. Shortly afterward, two Los Angeles Black Panthers were killed by local black nationalists. The situation had been exacerbated by FBI disinformation pitting the two groups against each other. But softsoap journalism didn't protect the Movement from its enemies.

Not everyone embraced open sloganeering. When an LNS piece on the NLF's underground press celebrated "the typewriter and the gun, the propagandist and the soldier," San Francisco's *Good Times* (successor to the *Express Times*) ran it under the headline "THIS ARTICLE IS PROPAGANDA." But even the best reporters felt constrained. "There were criticisms of Cuba that I somehow never got around to writing," Gitlin recalls, "and I wrote the enthusiastic stuff."

"We weren't journalists," Allen Katzman says. "We were revolutionaries."

IN APRIL, 1969, an empty lot in Berkeley became a People's Park. Corn-and-sandbox socialism now bloomed on land seized, not purchased, from a university that had paid $1.3 million to outflank the hairy hordes of Telegraph Avenue. Frank Bardacke, one of the Oakland Seven on trial for his organizing during Stop the Draft Week, went to the library, did some research, and published a broadside called "Who Owns the Park?" that the underground press soon picked up.

Printed over a screened picture of a rifle-toting Geronimo, it accused the "rich white men" who directed California's education of purchasing stolen land. "When the University comes with its land title," the manifesto concluded, "we will tell them, 'Your land title is covered with blood. We won't touch it. Your people ripped off the land from the Indians a long time ago. If you want it back now, you will have to fight for it again."

Depending on who looked, People's Park visualized a new society, or was a tactic for further polarizing Berkeley via inevitable confrontation, or constituted an act of mass trespass. In any event, hundreds of police picked up the gauntlet on May 15. In the month-long battle that followed, scores were shot, the campus was gassed, a (white) bystander named James Rector was killed. Berkeley became a combat zone, complete with street-fighting, curfews, States of Disaster, States of Emergency.

Like the city, Berkeley's media polarized. The *Gazette,* the Oakland *Tribune,* and the San Francisco dailies denounced the theft of property and the resultant violence. To the *Barb,* which had called for Park volunteers, property itself was theft. Its pages were filled with eyewitness reports (all glancing Leftward). "None of the straight press could cover us," Max Scherr later said. "We just had it from every angle, except the police angle."

The National Federation of Republican Women threatened to boycott downtown San Francisco if the *Barb* continued to be sold there. The *Barb* office was teargassed. Then-governor Ronald Reagan and Max Scherr denounced each other. After Rector was killed, the paper called on Berkeley to "Rise Up." Circulation rose to ninety-three thousand.

At the *Seed,* a third anniversary found tensions over politicization also rising to the fore.

At twenty-nine, Marshall Rosenthal had been on the edges of Chicago's Beat scene and Michigan's *Paper.* An ex-professor of business turned bearded vegetarian, he'd come to the *Seed* after the Democratic Convention with a days-of-chaos poem that made the back cover. His "epiphanies" talked about traveling the country, about Bob Dylan finding peace within himself. He'd sensed "terrible vibes . . . evil emanations" from the "stupid, meaty, blank-faced thugs" of the Red Squad— but also denounced "the shit" of declaring Sirhan Sirhan a Yippie. "He is another casualty, another symbol of how the world madness for killing and oppression creeps into each of us and affects, in the most odious manner, our weakest brothers."

Marshall had come to the *Seed* to write, and had found an antidote for the loneliness that seared his mind. Now he was alienated from the revolution against alienation.

"Are we staying here fourteen mad hours a day for something beyond ourself?" he wrote in his diary one depressed night. "For 'the world'? To change the WORLD? Watch it brother—I heard you say that. . . . And what are we—this little part of the world—doing? Well, we are blowing grass into a dog's nose. We are digging garbage. We are fucked up in our relationships with the ones we love the most. We are having abortions, and taking body-warping drugs. We are conning advertisers and counting money and buying and selling. We are crossing the street to avoid the beggar, and shouting 'Hooray' when a cop is shot. We are going to totalitarian conventions, and we are feeling important. We are wearing buttons and accepting titles. Oh yes, we are the world. Sixty thousand dollars went through our hands in a year, and we argue about whom to bail out of jail for $75."

Marshall was betwixt and between, "I'm certainly not at one with the radicals, nor the establishment . . . I need orderliness. I am truly getting older. When, and if, Abe leaves there will have to be someone to do Movement shit, or drop the Movement and move closer to a magazine of the arts. Do such things survive?"

In June, 1969, he was put to the test.

"The Movement is like Flash Gordon movies," I complained in a seven-page, week-in-the-life article, "where eighty-seven different nationalities live in the same neighborhood without being able to understand each other." I'd covered a Black Panther speech, a bogus arrest at SDS's national office, the death of a Young Lord. I meditated on the cooptation of "the Dodge Rebellion," and of Mayor Daley throwing a free rock concert in Grant Park less than a year after the proposed Festival of Life. I recited the litany of *Seed* annoyances: the cracked light table, the backed-up toilet, the lost articles and unmixed inks, the brother and sister who might or might not have quit.

Nixon had been on TV, I wrote. "As he says, 'not a civil war blah blah blah,' some kid from Topeka takes a slug in the chest from an AK-47 . . . some 4'8" eighteen-year-old with a five-letter name that has no vowels learns that he will never be nineteen." Two Supreme Court justices, a cabinet officer, and several local officials had been accused of malfeasance. A crewman of a captured spy ship joked about "yellow slant-eyed bastards." Forty-six U.S. helicopters had been shot down in Vietnam in a week; fifty people had been shot in Berkeley by "peace officers."

"Who," I wanted to know, "was directing this movie?"

I had no answer, so I left my second army in two years. "Private Abraham Peck of the People's Army of the United States . . . is applying for furlough. He wishes to spend his summer . . . breathing clean air and trying to establish diplomatic relations with the planet before some asshole turns it into an ashtray. We are the people our parents warned us against, and that is a good thing. But I don't want to become someone that I warned me against."

Marshall was the new editor, and the June entries in his diaries explained why: "Abe himself was caught up in his own ambivalence and dilemma, which he projected on all of us. 'Art and politics' is one way to state it. Which is the road to travel through these confusing times? Well, Abe himself was unsure, torn at all times, suffering great anguish . . . attempting to make final judgments on every page of the issue . . . acting out the reverse of everything he espoused: the *Seed* as family.

"On the last night," Marshall continued, "Abe said, 'We won't get this together.'

" 'It'll somehow fall together as it usually does.'

"His answer was a scowl and a fearful sneer: 'Let's see if you're that optimistic when you're editor.' Well, I'm both today, and I'm feeling so good."

I would return in four months. Marshall would leave within a year. Such was life on the underground-press roller coaster.

THE STRESSES at the *Seed* were but a hippie microcosm of a far more profound split also taking place in Chicago from June 18 to 22.

Over the decade, SDS had advocated participatory democracy, opposed the war, pushed for racial justice, based its actions on solidarity, trust, and hope. It had moved from protest to resistance and, at Columbia University, to occupation and defensive militance. But the rage, stridency, Korrectness, and governmental surveillance of the last six months had taken a toll that would greatly sadden SDS historian Kirkpatrick Sale:

"How ironic it all was: at precisely the time of the greatest explosion of the American left in all of the decade, SDS, its leading organization by every index . . . was gradually but unmistakably isolating and diminishing itself, losing its student constituency, its women, its alumni, failing to connect with the high schools, the soldiers, the workers. The SDS revolutionaries were on the barricades, but they had forgotten to look behind: their troops were no longer following."

Even as Red Squad and FBI agents spent their Wednesday clicking photographs outside the crumbling Coliseum south of the Loop, some fifteen hundred SDSers arranged themselves factionally within the cavernous hall. Would a Progressive Labor Party (PL) hewing to a rigid model of Maoist working-class revolution take over SDS? Would young workers and minorities, formed into a Revolutionary Youth Movement led by Black Panthers and inspired by revolutionary Vietnamese, prevail? Or was the wave of a violent, bring-the-war-home future marked by the title of the six-page story in *New Left Notes'* convention issue: "You don't need a weatherman to know which way the wind blows"?

Ironically, the first test of sectarian strength came when PL succeeded in barring members of the mainstream press instead of admitting them for a fee and a pledge that they would not tell government officials about what they'd hear (a New York *Times* reporter had just testified about SDS before the House Internal Security Committee). Soon rival claques chanted radical chapter and verse. Black Panther visitors charged "counter-revolution"; Progressive Laborites retorted with charges of Redbaiting. Youth-movement proponents walked out; by Sunday, there were at least two SDSs.

The *Seed* ran a cartoon in which two screaming demonstrators argued whether the "Neo Trotskyist Progressive Socialist Radical Action Club for International Peace" or the "Socialist Progressive Club for International Democracy Thru Radical Prototrotskyist Action" held the correct line. But our detailed summaries lamented the internecine warfare. On my way out of the *Seed*, I warned against throwing out the baby with the bathwater, saying that, despite the propensity of many SDSers to use women's liberation as a political football, ignore youth culture, and turn politics into theology, SDS remained the dominant organization of the white left. In another piece, a writer named Bernard Marshall struck closer to the mark.

"SDS had been irrevocably factionalized in thorough imitation of Left-wing politics of the Twenties and Thirties. The New Left as embodied by SDS is dead. SDS will no longer be a forum for varying ideas and a testing ground for political practice. This means that SDS (all factions) will wither and become even less of a voice for student unrest than it had been over the past year or so."

Former SDS president Carl Oglesby soon summed up the Movement's preceding half-year in a *Liberation* magazine article called "Notes on a Decade Ready for the Dustbin": "the attempt to reduce the New Left's inchoate vision to the Old Left's perfected remembrance," he wrote, "has produced a layer of bewilderment and demoralization which no cop with his club or senator with his committee could ever have induced."

But it would be the CIA, part of the apparatus that had done its best to hinder SDS, that tied SDS's collapse to a mass stumbling by the papers. "The 1969 SDS national convention, which split SDS into a number of opposing factions, signalled the downfall of the underground press," it would note in a 1973 report. "Lacking national focus and leadership, each paper was forced to define its role and develop its own political line based on what remained of the radical youth movement, its own readership and financial backers. Most papers vacillated during the ensuing months and many more folded in the process."

11

FROM COUNTERCULTURE TO OVER-THE-COUNTER CULTURE

NEW YORK—AUGUST, 1968: Jeff Shero looked forward to
seeing Janis Joplin. The head *Rat* had known the white
blueswoman since 1963 and the University of Texas,
when he'd been a civil rights activist and she a post-
Beatnik with a raspy, compelling voice. A half-decade
later, they were both in New York, two figures of the
new culture. After Martin Luther King's murder, the
underground editor had heard the new queen of the
San Francisco Sound sing a wonderful memorial version of "Summertime."

Rock 'n' roll was rock now, urgent, middle-class
yet rebellious, radiating what life could feel like if
only people got together. Amid racism and war, the
best of the musicians hailed black roots, celebrated
protest and community. "Like a Rolling Stone," "Satisfaction," "My Generation," "A Day in the Life,"
"Purple Haze," "Down on Me" were stunning songs,
vinyl diary entries marking a listener's first apartment,
demonstration, orgasm, trip.

On this day, though, Janis was holding court at the
Chelsea Hotel. Shero, confident as always, put in a call,
got through, and popped the question:

"Hi, this is Jeff from Austin. How 'bout an interview?"

"Well, honey," he recalls the voice at the other end
drawling, "I'm talkin' to *Time* and *Newsweek*. Why
do I want to do an interview with a li'l ol' hippie
publication?"

Shero had an answer: "Rock music is part of *our* culture."

"Hell," Joplin replied, "millions of people read *Newsweek*. I'd rather do that."

After the call, Shero gut-checked himself. He was an embarrassed radical heavy dusted off by a celebrity he'd known back when. He felt bothered by what he saw as an ego trip from someone he liked. And he was upset by the gap between a rocker and "the community."

He would not be the only upset radical. Over the next year, the underground press would continue an up-and-down love affair with rock music, live off its money, honeymoon at Woodstock, and be challenged by new, more polite suitors, corporate logic, and, perhaps, the FBI.

Besides Ralph Gleason at the San Francisco *Chronicle,* Al Aronowitz at the New York *Post,* and a handful of others, most mainstream writers cared more about a Beatle's hair than his guitar. In fact, the Chicago *Tribune* had covered the first Rolling Stones tour of America with the headline BARBER GIVES SCARE TO FIVE FUZZY SINGERS and a story that claimed "they wear their hair, they vow, two inches longer than the Beatles."

Mainstream magazines didn't do much better. *Cheetah* had begun in the fall of 1967, "born looking like today, speaking the language of today." Nine months later, it was yesterday's news. In March, 1968, *Eye* had come into view. But articles such as "Sexy Nice Girls in Their Summer Underwear" misread what was going on. Within a year, the Hearst Corporation shut *Eye.*

The traditional left had its own problems with rock. Though countless thousands of young people were playing electric guitars all over America, folk remained the Official People's Music. Older Leftists either decried cultural decadence or saw rock's energy as a cooptable middle-class fantasy that didn't affect the means of production.

Consequently, magazines had arisen to put rock at the journalistic center of a shared odyssey. *Crawdaddy* and *Fusion* favored musings on how an LP or concert had led the writer to encounter Truth itself. "The music was the most tangible part of our lives," says Paul Williams, the slender essayist who'd founded *Crawdaddy* in January, 1966, while at Swarthmore. "It was a revolution: 'We're taking over and we're something you've never seen before and this is ours.' The Beatles' new records were always different, and the bands themselves were making discoveries."

Most underground papers also danced to the music. But they spoke less about notes and scales than chimes of freedom, aural aphrodisiacs, or boot-stomping music for a people's army. In an issue of the *Seed* that also covered New Left demonstrations on campuses and at the Pentagon, a piece about Jimi Hendrix by surrealist Franklin Rosemont expressed rock's claim to radicalism (or was it vice-versa?):

"Music . . . which does not *revolt* is only the auditory reflection of oppressive ideology, the echo of imperialism. . . . Revolt is only very partially political. It must be poetic and sexual, total, putting everything at stake: all or nothing. . . . Jimi Hendrix, who refers to himself as 'apolitical,' ruthlessly attacks not only imperialism but the entire foundation of oppressive Western civilization."

Some underground rock writing was intelligent; too much simply said "oh, wow!" or "right on!" "Like a primordial group ejaculation, the Moby Grape unleashed their wrath and sound," a writer had declared in *Rat*'s first issue in March, 1968. "Not one girl left Hunter College a virgin," a distaff *Rat* reprise of a Hendrix concert had said. Often reviewers just threw up their hands—and their critical faculties: "It's impossible to talk about Janis or at least to convey what she's like to someone who hasn't seen her," still another *Rat* writer gushed.

Now *Rolling Stone* was emerging as an alternative to both daily and radical papers.

"We have begun a new publication reflecting what we see are the changes in rock and roll and the changes related to rock and roll," the hybrid newspaper-magazine had announced in its November, 1967, debut issue. "*Rolling Stone* is not just about music, but also about the things and attitudes that the music embraces." In addition to its coverage of the Death of Hip, the San Francisco-based biweekly's first issue had criticized Monterey Pop Concert's booking policy, covered the music scenes, and reviewed records. Both publisher/editor/driving force Jann Wenner and his mentor Ralph Gleason had been unimpressed by other attempts to cover the rock world. "*Cheetah* had some good articles, but the name was terrible," Jann recalls. "A high-gloss, slick magazine like *Eye* was just completely wrong."

Wenner was a rock fan, rock critic, a member of the rock culture. From the start, *Rolling Stone* had placed rock at the center of things, not as a spoke on a Movement wheel. In May, 1968, Wenner had run "Musicians Reject New Political Exploiters," his attack on the Yippies for attempting to use rock to lure unsuspecting hips to a violent scene in Chicago (described in Chapter 7). He would quote Ralph Gleason's belief that writing for the underground press required only "a typewriter and a lot of speed."

Criticism was a two-way street. Some underground editors praised the energy and depth of *Rolling Stone*'s coverage; many dismissed its reportorial distance as wishy-washy, reformist. *Rolling Stone* was against the war, but rarely advocated protest, much less confrontation. Rock stars could be closely scrutinized—or treated as fantasy objects seemingly made accessible (which they were early on). The underground claim that "the music belongs to the people" was more rhetoric than reality, but *Rolling Stone* rarely muckraked the music business, and didn't question its basic corporate structure. If necessary, underground editors were willing to see their papers consumed by revolution; *Rolling Stone* was its own worthy cause.

AT THE END of August, the Beatles released their first single on their own Apple Records. The "A" (designated-hit) side was "Hey Jude." But the flip side made at least as much noise. "Revolution" drew a hip line that the Beatles would not cross. They might want change, they'd listen to plans for it. But quote Chairman Mao and talk about violence, and you could count them out.

John Lennon's own politics were hazy, and he'd wavered between having the lyrics count him "in" or "out." But he'd made his choice, and the record immediately triggered support and criticism throughout the underground press.

"The more political you are, the less you will dig the Beatles' new song, 'Revolution,' " Ralph Gleason wrote in a piece distributed by a still-eclectic LNS/NY. "American activists are going to have to deal with this if they insist on the idea that the Beatles embody the youth movement and that is by radical definitions revolutionary."

Almost immediately, the *Barb* fired back: Even naming the song "Revolution" was worthy of *1984;* the song itself sounded "like the 'hawk plank' adopted last week . . . at . . . the National Demokratik Death Party.

"They spend a verse putting down Chairman Mao. O.K. He has lots of bad points, but . . . nowhere in the song is the U.S. or British establishment attacked, or even criticized, only the people who attack or criticize the establishment."

Gleason, the *Barb* said, had "bad politics." But the *Barb* inadvertently supported his allegation about radicals being closet squares. "Revolution," the paper said, featured "shitty piano"; "Hey Jude" was "a boring love song." Political listeners, the *Barb* concluded, would do better with the Stones' "Street Fighting Man."

LNS/NY not only ran Gleason's piece, but picked him up as a columnist. Yet it also headlined a story "LNS Supports Rolling Stones in

Ideological Split with Beatles." Like the *Barb,* LNS implicitly ignored the talk in "Street Fighting Man" about compromise solutions.

At the *Guardian,* cultural ideologist Irwin Silber took the hardest line: "who ever said the Beatles were revolutionaries in the first place? The record companies, the press agents, the promoters, the managers—the whole greedy crew of artful dodgers who figure you can peddle revolution along with soap and corn flakes and ass and anything else that can turn over a dollar."

"Our goal is not to get our message out on 10 million Columbia records," Silber later wrote, "but to take over Columbia Records and make it a part of a people's socialist system based on human need and human expression."

But many underground papers owned their expansion, maybe even their existence, to record-company advertising, and many writers—especially in New York and Los Angeles—lived off the industry they criticized, making their rent by selling free records, eating many of their meals at record-company events. It wasn't quite clear who was taking over from whom.

A HALF-DOZEN LONGHAIRS circled a stereo, staring into space or into their own dreams. Placards bore messages: "MUSIC IS LOVE," "GRAB HOLD!" and a third, larger than the others—"THE MAN CAN'T BUST OUR MUSIC."

"The Establishment's against adventure—and the arousing experience that comes with listening to today's music," a disembodied voice said.

"So what? . . . The Man can't stop you from listening. Especially if you're armed with these"—meaning "the first shot fired in the [Charles] Ives revolution," and Terry Riley, Inc., "the only legal trip you can take."

Albums courtesy of Columbia Records.

"The Man Can't Bust Our Music" ad appeared in underground papers and music magazines late in 1968. It was commercially clever, but soon proved embarrassing. Then-Columbia president Clive Davis worried that it identified the General Motors of rock "much too closely with the counterculture." *Rolling Stone* lampooned CBS's "identity crisis." Underground papers pointed out that cool records did not deter the police from their appointed rounds.

CBS continued advertising in underground papers as a vehicle to reach a young, hip audience. "I'm one of the people responsible for funding the underground press," says Jim Fouratt. Coming to New York as a teen,

Fouratt had become, in rapid-fire sequence, an actor, a beaten peace demonstrator, a Lower East Side activist armed with a mimeo machine, a coordinator of the massive 1967 Be-In, and an eventually disillusioned Yippie. Now he was at Columbia Records—brought in, he says, to correct "the laughingstock" of "The Man Can't Bust Our Music," but seeing himself as a fifth-columnist for the Revolution.

Fouratt became a life-in-the-fast-lane "house freak" in touch with executives, musicians, and "the community." "CBS," he says, "advertised in every paper I told them to. It was a lot of money, and when they did it, other companies did." Subsequent CBS ads told an amorous longhaired couple, then a joint-passing circle of hippies, a black, and a headdressed Indian, to "Know who your friends are. And look and see and touch and be together. Then listen"—to Blood, Sweat and Tears, the Chambers Brothers, and other acts. CBS even printed *Keep Your Ear to the Ground,* an "underground" paper for FM stations and head shops.

"We really believed that the music was coming out of a community," Fouratt recalls, "and if that community was expanded because they got our major-label distribution, the message was going to be clear and we were going to take over the world. Capitalism does not work that way. The money cut the artists off from the community."

For Clive Davis, this was no surprise. The Monterey Pop Festival, the current president of Arista Records recalls, had shown him a "very idealistic, very innocent and beautiful philosophy of life" and "a dramatic change in pop-music group playing that I would bet on." He had, and won, signing Joplin, Chicago, Santana, and others. "The business was run no differently after Monterey," he says. "The artists felt that it would look phony and be unrepresentative to their followers if there was any hint of interest in money or acquisition or competition. Some groups, the Dead being one, were noneconomically motivated. But I think the rap was real phony for most."

All the musicians might have started out practicing chords in the same garage, but now some were limousine liberals in a billion-dollar industry. And this split between artist and audience was intensified by the politicization of life in post-Chicago America. "Rock is out, dynamite is coming in," Sandy Darlington, who cared enough to be a rock columnist, noted somberly in the *Express Times.* "Let's see what Madison Avenue does with that."

The papers continued to push for community control of the music. Which led to conflict with commercial concert promoters, most notably Bill Graham.

Graham was no rookie. His first concert promotion in 1965 had been a benefit for the San Francisco Mime Troupe, which he'd managed. He'd fought overcommercialization at Monterey Pop, personally managed his halls, and shone by comparison with some of the greedheads who followed him into the business.

But Graham was older, a hip capitalist who'd succeeded at his Fillmore Auditorium while the more egalitarian Family Dog and the band-sponsored Carousel had flopped. And while Graham could be charming, he also did a great wild-boar imitation when angry. At one community meeting, Stephen Gaskin, a Haight street-guru who later led a large hip-fundamentalist community in Tennessee, would tell Graham: "When you started, you had to make a choice between love and money. You've got our money, so you can't have our love."

Graham's reply: "Fuck you, you stupid prick! Do you know what emotions are? Stand up and have emotions. Get up and work."

Graham's tenure at New York's Fillmore East, the rock hall he opened in 1968, led to major rows with the underground press. Initially, *Rat* and *EVO* had welcomed the hall as a home for great rock and community benefits. But differences emerged when Jeff Shero interviewed Graham for a *Rat* whose musical content ran from Jimi Hendrix to Vietnamese poems:

Shero: "People say that rock music is maybe a revolutionary expression of a new generation. . . . Do you think that this is a correct description?"

Graham: "No, it's good music. . . . It's an art form."

Soon New York underground writers were denouncing Graham as a capitalist carpetbagger from California who favored wimpy SF bands over such hardcore local outfits as the Velvet Underground. "He took a lot more shit than I would have," Shero says, recalling one meeting between Graham and various East Village street figures. "Then we went and denounced him some more for ripping off the culture even though we still took all the free tickets."

Graham's main adversaries were the Motherfuckers, the bikerlike, proto-punk apocalyptics who, every layout night, rolled into the *Rat* like angry tumbleweed to lay out a page of graphics. In one, an Indian-like figure proclaimed the tribe's musical view:

> We are a new music . . .
> A Free Music . . . not reflected
> by recording sales
> or promotion schemes . . .
> but by a new people
> expressing a new reality.

Shero liked the energy in their art; the rest of the staff was warier. The gang had tried to dictate an *EVO* story on crashpads, then denounced the whole *EVO* staff as "a bunch of counterrevolutionary two-bit capitalist assholes" after the writer publicized their tactics. Their slogan was "Armed Love"; so much for the flower folk.

That fall, the Motherfuckers led the charge for what *Rat* called the "cultural claim to the Fillmore East." Graham was caught in a pincers: some community representatives wielded chains, his insurance company threatened to lift his coverage if he let "the community" run his hall.

The nights went on, then drifted away. But Graham and the underground press would lock horns again.

SEVEN HUNDRED MILES to the west, a rambling building on fraternity row in Ann Arbor, Michigan, had become the beachhead for "a total assault on the culture." Poet-activist John Sinclair, an exploding-haired giant panda in wire-rimmed glasses, had moved the Artists' Workshop out of Detroit after pulling back a curtain during the 1967 riot and seeing a tank turret swivel toward the motion. Now he was trying to unite rock and revolution within a White Panther Party, an attempt to fuse hip energy and political militance. A color-phased version of the Black Panther Ten-Point Program called for free prisoners, media, soldiers, schools, time, and space—"everything free."

"Our culture, our art, the music, newspapers, books, posters, our clothing, our homes, the way we walk and talk, the way our hair grows, the way we smoke dope and fuck and eat and sleep—it is all one message, and the message is FREEDOM."

"Hill Street" filled with fringed-leather post-adolescents incandescing from acid, anarchy, and the certitude that, as Sinclair put it, "you don't need to get rid of all the honkies, you just rob them of their replacements and let the breed atrophy and die out." There were mimeo machines and marijuana, sex and shotguns, an infusion of Malcolm X and Jimi Hendrix, the outer-space Arkestra of Sun Ra and the Black Pantherism of Bobby Seale. It was the politics of no boundaries, as celebrated in the postpsychedelic posters of resident artist Gary Grimshaw, and in the pages of the Warren-Forest and Ann Arbor *Sun*s, and later the Ann Arbor *Argus*.

"MUSIC IS REVOLUTION," Sinclair exclaimed in a year-end piece called "Rock and Roll Dope," "because it is immediate, total, fast-changing and on-going. . . . At its best the music works to free people on all levels, and a rock-and-roll band is a working model of postrevolutionary life."

Among those bands, the Up may have been the skinniest in rock history, a three-chord anorexia nervosa. The MC-5 was another story, a pre–Sex Pistols fusion of white noise and white politics. They were the only out-of-town rock group to (try to) play during the Democratic Convention, and their concerts and debut album raised money and teen-aged expectations while dividing critics.

"Musical guerillas—an exploding theatre formed by a fusion of avant garde jazz and primitive rock," *EVO* rock writers Bob Rudnick and Dennis Frawley wrote. "A joke," critic Greil Marcus recalls. Others saw poseurs in symbolic blackface. Nor did Elektra president Jac Holzman share the Five's White Panther ideology. "I want to make it clear that Elektra is not the tool of anyone's revolution. We feel that the 'revolution' will be won by poetics and not by politics." When the Five played the Fillmore East, *EVO* denounced the band after a spokesman tried to finesse the argument over community nights—and a kicked-in drum—by saying, "We came here to play music, not politics."

But the most telling criticism came from an unexpected source. "Music ain't revolution," said William Leach, a Black Panther Party writer for *Inner City Voice* and the *South End,* two well-integrated newspapers around Detroit's Wayne State University. "Black folks have been singing, dancing, and blowing instruments, and we still ain't free."

Sinclair claimed that White Panther rules were "the same" as the Black Panthers', but in reality, the principles "Leaders suck" and "We are LSD-driven total maniacs in the universe" were not equivalent to "Obey orders in all your actions" and "Don't use drugs while on duty." White radicals, Leach felt, were anarchists who often acted as if oppression no longer existed. They were, he continued, either militant but relatively inactive (Young Socialist Alliance), undisciplined (SDS), or "silly" Yippies and White Panthers who "make a joke out of the revolution . . . literally perverting the Movement."

Leach similarly critiqued the underground press, exempting only the *Militant,* the *Guardian, Inner City Voices,* and other serious journals. "A revolutionary paper doesn't deal with sex, etc.," he wrote, "but with political issues." Leach was too quick to write off sixties counterculture, as Sinclair replied, but it was Sinclair, after all, who noted that one of the MC-5's greatest accomplishments was its campaign against underwear, and who also pioneered that intergender salute, the "titshake."

Rock and sex did go together, though, and in February, 1969, *Rolling Stone* published a lengthy story on groupies, the available backstage partners of male rockers. The article was heavily promoted, to establish *Rolling Stone* in mainstream circles, and to prevent *Time*'s catch-up story from stealing its thunder. Right there in the New York *Times,* a girl with Little Orphan Annie hair and come-hither eyes stared out of a $7,000 full-page ad. "When we tell you what a Groupie is, will you really understand?" a headline asked. "This is the story only *Rolling Stone* can tell, because we are the musicians, we are the music, we are writing about ourselves." Besides music, there were "the films, the politics, the literature and the visual arts of our generation."

The article and ad won interviews in *Time* and *Newsweek* for editor Jann Wenner. And though it didn't mention underground papers, it would be widely taken as a challenge over who represented the youth readership. But *Rolling Stone* also faced a challenge. On April Fool's Day, the number of United States troops in Vietnam peaked at 543,400. Two days later, the American death count there surpassed the total for the Korean War. On the cover of the latest *Rolling Stone,* a cop pinned a kid to the ground. Inside, Free Speech Movement veteran Michael Rossman wrote the lead story for this "American Revolution" issue; Wenner's editorial mirrored the extent to which even reluctant elements of youth culture had become politicized:

"Like it or not, we have reached a point in the social, cultural, intellectual and artistic history of the United States where we are all going to be affected by politics. We can no longer ignore it. It *threatens* [emphasis mine] our daily lives and our daily happinesses."

As that issue appeared, the now-weekly *Rat* ran posters of both the new, laid-back Bob Dylan of *Nashville Skyline* and contemporary folk singer Phil Ochs as a New American Revolutionary, complete with flag and rifle. But Ochs, who'd combine telling protest songs ("Here's to the State of Mississippi"), evocative artistry ("Pleasures of the Harbor"), and continued political involvement (civil rights, the Yippies, supporting the democratic socialist government in Chile), refused to denounce Dylan as a gone-to-the-country sell-out.

The Movement remained "the only hope left in America," Ochs said in an interview. But, he added in words similar to those used by the underground cartoonists, the artist's "responsibility is to write great things. And if he chooses to renounce his former works, that's OK. . . . I don't like the idea of a movement judging creators."

But the Movement did—especially, continuously, the Beatles. John Lennon and a writer named John Hoyland had one of the more interesting dialogues in *Black Dwarf,* a political English undergrounder.

The enemy, Hoyland said in an open letter that referred to Lennon's pot bust the previous October, wasn't mean individuals, psychological distress, or spiritual malaise, but "a repressive, vicious, authoritarian sys-TEM." Why, Hoyland wanted to know, had Lennon told people in "Revolution" to free their minds *"instead?* . . . What makes you so sure that a lot of us haven't changed our heads in something like the way you recommend—and then found out IT WASN'T ENOUGH?. . . . Why couldn't you have said 'as well'?" The way to improve the world was to destroy its evil, an act which, Hoyland wrote, was "one of the most passionate forms of love."

Lennon replied, unfazed, "Until you/we change your/our heads—there's no chance. Tell me of one successful revolution. Who fucked up communism—christianity—capitalism—buddhism, etc.? Sick heads and nothing else. . . . You seem to think it's just class war." Lennon's P.S.: "You smash it—and I'll build around it."

Lennon reiterated that message when an uncharacteristically giddy group of LNSers visited Montreal during his and Yoko's May "bed-in" for peace, just after the suppression of Berkeley's People's Park: "You're playing the establishment's game," he said. "And if you play their game they'll win. They know how."

Lennon would become more political in the early seventies, waging a campaign on behalf of John Sinclair, imprisoned in August, 1969, for giving two joints to an undercover policeman. And Lennon's own pot bust would be used by the FBI as a pretext to try to deport him.

By then, though, the MC-5 would no longer be a factor. Their live album had been too rough for those who hadn't seen the shows; subsequent LPs were more polished, but the edges were what counted. The lure of professionalism, and of money, distanced the band from Sinclair while he was in jail. Living on the edge took its toll.

"They were the best band any of us had seen," says rock writer Dave Marsh, then an editor for *Creem*, the Detroit music magazine that had begun publishing in March. "When they didn't conquer the world, it was very confusing."

IN APRIL, 1969, the contradictory practice of establishment firms advertising in radical journals began to unravel. *Rat* sounded the alarm with the claim that "CBS President Frank Stanton (who fired the Smothers Brothers) passed down the word to Columbia Records to stop advertising in the dirty little underground papers. At about the same time, Columbia mailed out a general press release boasting about the success of its phony 'Revolutionaries' hype. . . . For shame, too, on the underground press which feels it necessary to emulate the straight press by selling their editorial columns to such advertisements."

UPS editors talked about jointly boycotting Columbia acts, then decided that the musicians were pawns in the corporate game even as they hoped that the revenue-yielding ads would return. Instead, ABC, then other companies, also pulled out. Why?

Researcher Angus Mackenzie charges that something more than marketing was at work. Mackenzie has unearthed FBI and CIA memos concerning rock and the underground press. Late in 1968, for example, a CIA analyst attached to the antidissent Project Resistance had reported his shock over "the vast growth" of the underground press, and said that "the apparent freedom and ease in which this filth, slanderous and libelous statements, and what appear to be almost treasonous anti-establishment propaganda is allowed to circulate is difficult to rationalize."

This was "not a quality press," the CIA critic had continued. "Eight out of ten would fail if a few phonograph record companies stopped advertising in them."

In January, 1969, an FBI memo sent from San Francisco to Washington had claimed that Columbia Records' financial "assistance . . . appears to be giving active aid and comfort to enemies of the United States." The San Francisco office, Mackenzie says, "suggested that the FBI should use its contacts to persuade Columbia Records to stop advertising in the underground press."

In April, the ads began to disappear.

At CBS, Jim Fouratt was arguing against the newest ad campaign, which proclaimed that "The Revolutionaries" were on CBS. "I said, 'You can't do that—there are people dying and they are revolutionaries, and you talk about Paul Revere.' " Soon after losing that debate, Fouratt walked into his office and was stunned. "There must have been five thousand pieces of mail in there, with all the clippings of all the underground newspapers where there was an ad," he recalls. "Some of them asked, 'How can you advertise in papers that promote the overthrow of the government, or promotes free sex?' " Fouratt remains convinced that they were part of an orchestrated Right-wing campaign. Another account has Stanton ordering the ads dropped after *Evergreen* magazine ran a full-page photo of interracial lesbian sex next to a Columbia ad.

CBS executives were not without government and intelligence-community ties. Stanton headed a committee charged with reviewing the CIA-funded United States Information Agency and had chaired the board of the Rand Corporation think-tank. CBS board chairman William S. Paley had let the CIA use his personal foundation to help fund a research scholarship during the early 1950s; until 1961, the CIA had occasionally screened CBS News film and radio broadcasts and debriefed correspondents. Paley and a CIA representative had met in the past to discuss arranging press credentials for a field agent.

Still, nobody has produced a memo showing CBS directly responding to FBI pressure to cancel underground advertising, and Stanton denies a role by either himself or the FBI. "I was not involved in or consulted about Columbia's media selections during that period," he's written me. "Moreover, I know nothing about any approach to Columbia or CBS officials by the FBI concerning any matter involving Columbia or CBS Records." (Paley did not answer a similar letter requesting clarification.)

Underground ads were cheap, but Clive Davis says that they didn't pay anyway. "Just because the readership is young, if it is mainly political it doesn't make sense to advertise in that paper." That hadn't applied to *Rolling Stone,* to which CBS and other companies would advance ad revenue and offer management advice during a 1970 slump. "I didn't analogize *Rolling Stone* to those other papers that were more political," Davis says. "We were offered others. I wasn't interested."

When I slid a photocopy of Mackenzie's writing from *UnAmerican Activities* across Davis's desk, his brow furrowed. "I don't know anything about any of it. I never was approached by anybody," he said.

Whether because of repression, taste, or dollars and cents, the ads fell off. The papers shed cooptive advertising, but lost revenue intensified the stresses caused by reluctant printers and burnt-out editors, denied second-class postal permits and FBI harassment. Papers missed issues, and slowed their payments to LNS just as the service was trying to cover more international events.

Then came rock's watershed.

IN 1967, San Francisco's Human Be-In had drawn a then-amazing ten thousand people into Golden Gate Park. That same year, the Monterey Pop Festival had certified the West Coast music scene by attracting fifty thousand fans and freaks. Now there were three hundred thousand stories in a naked city called Woodstock, located on a farm outside Bethel, a town ninety miles north of New York. From August 15 to 17, a gathering celebrated the high-water mark of rock and the hip lifestyle—and certified the split between the now-militant radicals and rock's dominant musicians.

For me, Woodstock began in Lawrence, Kansas, where I'd headed after covering the splintering of SDS into arcane and adventurist shards, concerts in stadia from Detroit to Atlanta, and my own fraying. There Mary Sunshine and I cooled out in our friend Kay's rented farmhouse and worked in her hippie-jewelry factory. I picketed a military base, and wrote about pot-pickers on a Boy Scout reservation. (Later I learned that the FBI's Kansas City office had been charged with finding out what I was doing on my summer vacation.)

Soon the underground papers Kay sold began talking about an "Aquarian Exposition—3 Days of Peace & Music." Hendrix! The Dead! The Airplane! Kay simply closed up shop, and we drove off in her red VW bug. In Chicago, we scooped up Richard, a political-science major turned truckdriver and rock-band manager, and Straight Albert, an ex-sergeant turned transcendental meditator.

The underground did more than advertise Woodstock. LNS headlined its piece, "Rock Imperialists Make Plans for Woodstock," compared music consumers to Guatemalan˙peasants picking bananas for United Fruit, and rhetoricized that "the revolutionary energy of rock and roll is a response to oppression." *Rat*'s Jeff Shero, Abbie Hoffman, and others threatened demonstrations until the promoters kicked in $10,000 for food, a hospital, and a Movement City from which radicals could sally forth to organize the crowd.

But driving toward counterculture Mecca was a revelation; the HoJos of I-80 yielded an ever-thickening migration of longhaired refugees from the world's most affluent society slouching toward Bethel. The next morning we crushed the fences and christened ourselves a nation.

Speaker-tower technology was juxtaposed to skinny-dipping and backpacks. The bands' playing was often as chaotic as the scene around them, but the music became a soundtrack for tribal neighborhoods—freaks, bikers, college towns of mud, blankets, and tents. The Politics of Free appeared with a vengeance, as Motherfuckers and others distributed wares looted from concessions and drug dealers.

Covering Woodstock meant submerging in its human ocean; when photographer Skeets Millard stood up a thousand yards from the stage to snap the crowd for the *Seed,* somebody yelled "Down in front!" But when he and I made our way to Movement City, it turned out to be a desperate Leftist island amid the rock 'n' roll rabble, full of sterile meetings on how "we" could organize "them." I cranked out a flier, then headed off to talk hips down from bad trips in the tent hospital staffed by Yippies, doctors of the Medical Committee for Human Rights, and members of the Hog Farm, the affable hip commune that had been chastised for collaborating with the promoters even as it dealt with people rather than rhetoric.

Woodstock showed the gap between the sectarian Left and the freaks. "The cultural wing of the Movement could relate, adapt, do things," Jeff Shero recalls, "while all the Marxist types sat around and complained, 'These cats don't have the right consciousness.' I said, 'Those people are totally irrelevant,' and had no interest in them afterward." Nor did the hippie hordes, who'd never cared all that much about the Left in the first place.

"Nightmare in the Catskills," the New York *Times* headlined its fearful editorial. "Lemmings" marching "to their deaths in the sea . . . ended in a nightmare of mud and stagnation. . . . What kind of culture is it that can produce so colossal a mess?"

But even from ninety miles away, the *Times* sensed good vibrations too. "The great bulk of the freakish-looking intruders behaved astonishingly well," the editorial continued. "They showed that there is real good under their fantastic exteriors."

That acceptance was exactly the problem at the *Guardian,* too. Irwin Silber was sympathetic to a gathering where, "having nothing to lose but their inhibitions . . . they shed for a few days those hard protective shells which most Americans have created for themselves . . . to . . . survive the predatory jungle into which they have been born." But he remained committed to class-based change; Woodstock, he wrote, was "a 'revolution' the American ruling class could live with."

Most underground editorialists were more confident. It was "Free City in Sullivan County," I wrote in the *Seed. Rat* excerpted the New York *Times*'s version, then countered with several articles, including a fiery poem called "The Hip Fantasy":

> . . . I danced in the mud and the blood and the beer, baby
> we were in one cosmic entity, our unity was our power. we
>   were the armies
> of the mojo-mutated rebels, choogling down the line to zap and be
>   zapped by ourselves and our music . . .
> we arrived like refugees seeking our places in the final
>   armageddon . . .
> boogying to canned heat
> and creedence magic music was in the hearts and minds and bodies
>   of a million warriors of the rainbow . . .
> yeah, baby, my dope was free, and my food was free, and my
>   clothes were free, and my shelter was free . . .
> and honey, I was free, and that's what we're
> all about . . . we saw our revolution, and
> we built it, and we made it, baby, and I dug it so much that I'd kill
>   to make it happen forever . . .

Even during the celebration, the scene's fragility peeked through the rhetoric and the dreams. Seated on our island of blankets, Straight Albert determinedly quartermastered our tuna, beans, and water jugs. Sometimes he shared with strangers, sometimes he lied to those who asked for spare food, spare anything. "It's the Chicago syndrome," he thought. "We take care of our friends. It's cronyism, connections."

The *Times* did have a point: Woodstock was El Dorado, shimmering, illusory. Had helicopters not airlifted food and doctors, had water purifiers not been hastily installed, had the locals not caught the sharing spirit, Woodstock would have become *Lord of the Flies.* We were the largest love community on the planet—and one of its larger welfare states. "Woodstock. Woodstock," another *Rat* writer began. "The largest gathering of youth in the nation's history. A hip capitalist fiasco (so far). A religious experience. A glimpse of communism. The pinnacle of passive consumerism. First free dope territory in Amerika. 'Three days of music and peace.' And mud, and acid, and hunger, and freedom, and thirst, and community, and boredom. Containment—revolution."

Many Woodstockers carried away tastes of egalitarianism and authenticity, a real triumph of peace-and-love values. But Woodstock also provided a metaphoric denial of the underground's attempt to fuse politics and music. As the Who played "Pinball Wizard," Abbie Hoffman took the stage and asked the newly united crowd to free the just-imprisoned John Sinclair. Instead, guitarist Pete Townshend bumped him with his Gibson. An accident, Abbie says; Townshend later said that the brief encounter was "the most political thing I ever did."

Either way, the honeymoon was over between the rock elite and the politicized counterculture. Woodstock was "the birth of the Woodstock Nation and the death of the American dinosaur," Abbie would write in his clever *Woodstock Nation.* But the promoters would make their million selling the rights for a movie that deliberately excised signs of radical politics. The Who—and many of their listeners—would move from the optimistic rebellion of "My Generation" to the cynicism of "Won't Get Fooled Again."

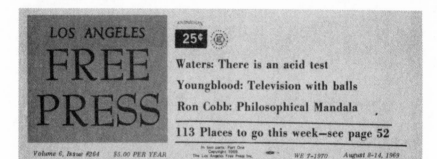

LOS ANGELES
FREE PRESS

25¢

Waters: There is an acid test

Youngblood: Television with balls

Ron Cobb: Philosophical Mandala

113 Places to go this week—see page 52

Volume 6, Issue #264 $5.00 PER YEAR   In two parts: Part One. Copyright 1969. The Los Angeles Free Press Inc.   WE 7-1970   August 8-14, 1969

NARCOTIC AGENTS LISTED
There should be no secret police

The people should know the men who are policing their communities. Even the Black Panthers do not propose simply abolishing police departments. Even they recognize the need for peace officers-but their program for community control of police demands that the policeman openly lives in the community in which he works so abusive exercise of power can be controlled.

Secret police forces are a threat to democratic government. History demonstrates that the secret policeman invariably uses his anonymity to become unaccountable to the people over whom power is exercised.

Recently there have been published stories of abuses of power involving narcotics officers. Several officers of many years standing have even been discharged for faking evidence.

Many, if not most, narcotics cases are thrown out of court because the officers have violated the constitutional rights of the suspect in conducting illegal searches and seizure.

But the public at large does not ordinarily hear of the violations of law committed by these secret policemen who are attempting to enforce laws as unwise and unenforceable as the now-banished prohibition of liquor.

There should be no secret police! In this spirit we are publishing in this issue on page 5 the official personnel roster of agents in the California State Bureau of Narcotics for the cities of Los Angeles, San Francisco, Santa Ana, and San Diego. The list is current as of June 1969. Know your local narc!

Know your local Nark

See Page 5

12

UNDER FIRE

ANN ARBOR, MICHIGAN—JULY 10–13, 1969: "The All-American City" had become a college town with a bombed ROTC building and a suburbia-in-revolt freak scene. Now, on a nearby farm, a shotgun-toting White Panther set the tone as three hundred editors and writers from forty underground papers unrolled sleeping bags, cooked over pits, danced to the music of local bands. The Revolutionary Media Conference was about to start.

Five hundred or so papers now distributed anywhere from 2 million copies (*Newsweek*'s estimate) to 4.5 million copies (UPS) to radicals, hippies, racial minorities, soldiers, and curiosity-seekers. Since the mid-sixties, the L.A. *Free Press*'s circulation had grown from 5,000 to 95,000, the *Barb*'s from 1,200 to 85,000. In four years, *EVO* had risen from 5,000 to 65,000, two-thirds of what it had taken the *Village Voice* almost fourteen years to amass. The *Seed* had gone from nothing to 23,000, and had merged with the more political Chicago *Kaleidoscope*. *Dock of the Bay* was San Francisco's new New Left entry. *Space City* was aloft in Houston, *Quicksilver Times* flowed in Washington, D.C. And in "hard low-down dirty straight-on Chicago," veterans of SDS's attempt to form an interracial movement of the poor were publishing *Rising Up Angry* to build "an organization, a giant tribe, a people's army" of young, white, working-class, street-fighting "greasers." There was even a paper to host the conference, the White Panther–allied

Ann Arbor *Argus,* edited by an energetic teen named Ken Kelley.

Just two days before the conference, "Vietnamization" of the war had led to the first U.S. troop reduction. Most of us weren't impressed: "Richard Nixon," I wrote for the *Seed,* "thinks he is good enough to hypnotize everyone into believing that sending a few thousand GIs back from Nam is the same as ending the war, or celestial enough to bring dead Americans and South Vietnamese and NLF troops and civilians back to life." SDS was on the ropes, and record advertising was waning, but the mood remained confident. "A daily underground paper in every city, and a weekly in every town," Tom Forcade predicted.

Then again, the papers would increasingly face questions about ownership, about whether they should reflect or organize their audiences, and about whether they would win or be crushed in the revolution nearly all of them had declared.

The White Panthers' letter of welcome to the conference participants intensified the claim that underground media were moving from resistance to revolution: "This is the year—1969—that the revolutionary youth media will reach beyond the hip, artistic and political enclaves in Amerika out into the bowels of this society—to all our young brothers out there in television land, in the suburbs, the school-jails, the factories and pool halls . . . inside this capitalistic, imperialistic, fascist state."

But the release also alluded to a continuing problem: "The shit is coming down too hard on all of us and our brothers and sisters throughout the world to spend our time arguing with each other."

"All of the preceding news conferences have had gripes associated with them," I'd written earlier that summer in a letter to propose a meeting, sent to UPS editors on behalf of a steering committee consisting of myself, *Rat*'s Jeff Shero, the *Freep*'s Art Kunkin, and *Other Scenes'* John Wilcock. "San Francisco to Iowa City—not enough structure, not enough politics. Madison—too boring, dominated by Newsreel." To minimize contretemps this time around, the opening sessions would offer nuts-and-bolts advice on production, advertising, etc., as well as "fun-filled evening(s) under the stars." Day three would discuss radical organizations and ideology. LNS, increasingly regarded as a junior-league Tass cut off from its readers' daily lives and inner visions, would state its case, after which the entire group would "describe its needs, differences of opinions, criticisms" and "feelings of ecstasy." UPS would undergo similar scrutiny.

Survivors of these disputes, I continued, could then talk about that favorite bugaboo, "The paper as art vs. the paper as radical medium." "Everyone can scream at each other, call each other 'revisionists,' 'flower

kids,' 'P.L.ers,' 'hippies,' 'left liberals,' 'spaced-out freaks,' 'bourgeois in-
dividualists' and other choice epithets."

Even as people arrived, a cloud hovered over the conference. Just before
the inauguration of Richard Nixon, the Washington *Free Press* had been
burglarized—by army intelligence, it was later learned. *Nola Express,* the
New Orleans paper, was under extensive FBI surveillance. So was *Rat*
in New York. During 1969 and 1970, the editor of Miami's *Daily Planet*
would be arrested twenty-nine times. He'd win twenty-eight acquittals,
but need $93,000 in bond. The civil war between the Black Panthers and
the authorities would lead a federal grand jury (reversed on appeal) to
order *Black Panther* editors to disclose management information, and the
FBI would not only convince a shipper to overcharge the Panthers, but
concoct a plan to stink-bomb bundles of papers.

At the conference, it was hard to sort out reality from paranoia—until
it came charging over the hill. When a carload of delegates was stopped
for possession of out-of-state plates and long hair, a passenger tried to
swallow some joints. She and the others were taken to the police station,
then told to return the next day. Nobody did, and no charges were filed
—but a flurry of "Urgent" messages were dispatched from the Detroit
office of the FBI to Washington and major field offices. Even as underground-press delegates discussed the impending trial of eight activists
indicted for conspiring with intent to riot during the 1968 Democratic
convention, squads of shotgun-toting, bulletproof-vested Washtenaw
County deputies and Ann Arbor police surrounded the clearing in search
of the missing miscreant.

"We better sing 'We Shall Overcome' or stand up," Abbie Hoffman
said. Police safeties clicked. Trigger fingers trembled. Art Kunkin and
some vegetarians from Santa Cruz split after seeing White Panthers go
for guns. As the women present were lined up and searched, a *Rat* writer
saw "visions of the St. Valentine's Day Massacre." Doors were kicked
in, papers taken—and then the police left. "Like a cold-water reality
shower," the *Rat* post-mortem read, "everyone realized how vulnerable
we are."

And yet, raids cut both ways. Sixty miles east of the conference, the
South End had replaced the *Daily Collegian* as the campus paper at Wayne
State University, a large, mostly commuter college. Under the energetic
radical editorship of Art Johnson, who'd later write for various Bay Area
papers, the *South End* redefined its readership as the poor community
around the University while mixing in a dose of White Panther–style
freak politics. The equally forceful John Watson had moved the paper
toward Marxism, the Black Panthers, and the radical automobile unions

DRUM and ELRUM, and been similarly active with the *Inner City Voice.*

Despite efforts by some Michigan legislators, the *South End* continued to receive university funding even as it joined UPS. But in July, 1969, university officials banned an issue celebrating freak culture, reputedly because of four-letter words in a John Sinclair article. "I am convinced that its publication would do serious damage to Wayne State University and to the future of student journalism here," the school's president said.

Cheryl McCall disagreed. The nineteen-year-old summer editor had run away from life as a Rotary Club Merit Award Winner in a Pennsylvania steel town to become what the Detroit *Free Press* would call a "fiery girl editor." Instead of accepting the ban, McCall, other *South End*ers, and some of the undergrounders caucusing in Ann Arbor took a midnight ride to the Wayne State campus.

"We drove back with guns, and ropes to tie up the guards," McCall recalls. "Thank God the guard was on a lunch break or something. If he had been there I'd be in jail now, but you know how crazed you got in those days. I was holding the gun, the real revolutionary—I wasn't; I was just being used by the men, and I was crazy enough that I would have probably shot him. I was so angry; freedom of the press—all those issues —came to bear." The need to unite journalism with radical social change and to make it relevant "was all part of it, thinking that my life had a meaning, and my work had a meaning."

The raiders reconstructed the *South End*'s copy out of the wastebaskets, set new type on the *Argus* machines, and found a printer. The resulting issue appeared, dedicated to "all the kids," denouncing the "senile, gray-haired men who run our schools and government."

At the conference, Tom Forcade became UPS director. A former business administration major and hot-rodder, Forcade had reinvented himself as a slow-talking freak who favored black clothing and a black Cadillac "staff car" with a Plexiglas-bubble top and stubby wings. Forcade's business acumen seems to have extended to the marijuana trade; in any event, he'd published *Orpheus*, the UPS anthology, and commissioned Bell and Howell to microfilm underground papers. He'd also retained the hipper Concert Hill Publications of Pennsylvania to serve successfully as UPS's national advertising agency. Now, declining record advertising and profit-oriented rock festivals were targeted for action, though Big Man of the *Black Panther* cautioned "Don't be taking these fuckin' capitalist ads." *Rolling Stone* was chastised for "cooptation" of the underground press; there were discussions about a "Revolutionary Press Movement" to produce special issues during crises.

"Virtually all of the editors," John Wilcock's post-mortem read, "agreed that the press should be an organizing tool for 'the revolution' rather than merely a vehicle for information (which, in the case of the straight press, is distorted information serving the ruling class)." But where was the line? When LNS was challenged for being rigid, one staff member simply responded that the service was an organ of propaganda, not news.

"If a split between the papers eventually develops . . . this is where it will come," Wilcock said. Still, he remained confident. "Are we going to be journalists or revolutionaries? Surely the answer is both."

IF JOURNALISTS were revolutionaries, then what form should their papers take? Art Kunkin's Los Angeles *Free Press* offered one answer.

The *Free Press* ran lucid news, commentary, and calls to action; Ron Cobb's editorial cartoons; a Living Arts section in which Harlan Ellison and Gene Youngblood were important critics of television and film. Circulation approached a hundred thousand on good weeks. A printing plant, and bookstores in Fairfax, Westwood, and Pasadena, made for a $2-million-a-year, 150-employee corporation.

By now, the typical underground staff collectively decided what articles ran in its paper. Most staffers wrote the stories; many did production and sold papers to stores and on the street. Advertising sales and bookkeeping (such as it was) were the most clearly defined positions. Money was pooled. Everybody—or nobody—owned the paper.

Kunkin preferred traditional management and ownership. "I wasn't really concerned with making the paper a representative of the new society," he says now. "What I was concerned with was making it into as strong an influence as possible. My own attitude was that there was nobody else's name on the line. From one year to the next, there were entirely different people involved. You can think that it was wrong, or bad, but I had a sense where the paper should go, and I didn't see a political maturity on the part of the staff."

There were protests over a time clock—installed at the behest of the National Labor Relations Board—and key staffers left after an incident of editorial sexual harassment (not by Kunkin). But Kunkin also welcomed a New Age union, and *Free Press* staffers could be nearly as well paid as mainstream ad reps and editors.

Kunkin also was less than convinced about new activism's own collectivity. "What in effect happened was that a few enterprising people would get together and set themselves up as the Movement, so I didn't feel at all bad about the question of individual ownership. My attitude was more of stewardship." In fact, he saw the *Free Press* as Los Angeles' strongest radical organization, which aided groups from San Francisco's *Express Times* to the Black Panthers.

In Berkeley, though, radicals were asking a new question: if deeded land could be turned into the People's Park, then why couldn't the *Barb* be turned into a people's newspaper?

The struggle had begun in June, when the Berkeley *Fascist,* a satirical paper edited by a local anthropology professor named Allan Coult, ran an exposé that put the *Barb*'s gross profits at about $5,000 a week, with editor-owner Max Scherr netting fully half of that. Regular writers were getting 25¢ per column inch and top editors $1.65 per hour—high by underground standards—but the scoop that Scherr outearned the entire staff was not well received. The Red Mountain Tribe—forty or so staffers who liked a cheap wine well enough to name themselves for it—argued that they were exploited labor, and, in the spirit of an emerging movement called women's liberation, complained that the *Barb*'s personal ads were sexist. Scherr reminded anyone in earshot that the *Barb*'s first darkroom had been in his pantry, its office in his front room, and its identity firmly opposed to censorship. Nobody was ripping off his baby.

One of those Scherr bitched to was Tim Leary. America's leading LSD exponent was running for office in California—"LUV FOR GUV" was the *Barb*'s headline. He wrote regularly for *EVO,* and one of his stories ranked underground publishers with rock musicians and drug dealers as cultural avatars. The papers reciprocated; "the prestigious" *Barb* and the "influential" *Free Press* endorsed his campaign.

Leary's rhetoric could be lighter than air, but now he offered Scherr some telling advice. "Look, Max," he said, "they're like your children. You're a mean bastard and they're mean. You raised 'em that way."

The staff made demands: raises, editorial input, press passes, bail for reporters, donations to worthy causes. Scherr moved, but, in the words of writer Stew Albert, "Bob Cratchit did better with Scrooge." Scherr's eyes twinkled less and less behind his wire-rimmed glasses; he was fifty-three years old and tired. With competitor Coult and candidate Leary acting as mediators, Scherr made a new offer: for $140,000 plus interest, the staff could buy the *Barb*.

The photographers who'd owned the *Seed* had ceded it to the staff for a couple of thousand dollars in debt payment. But the *Barb* was more profitable, and Scherr, oddly, was both more politically radical and more money-oriented. And the offer wasn't as outrageous as it sounded: Scherr would accept $1,000 a week, which profits could cover; some *Barb* writers had wealthy backgrounds; the East Bay's underground economy could be counted on for funds.

The sale collapsed when Scherr insisted that payments continue if the police shut the paper, which, in the wake of People's Park, seemed all too possible. More charges flew, and then Scherr, following in Marshall Bloom's save-the-baby footsteps, heisted his own subscription lists, typewriters, and supplies.

Early in July, radical Berkeley went bananas. There on University Avenue, blond, lion-maned Stew Albert marched in front of the *Barb*'s storefront with a sign saying "MAX MISER." "MAX IS A PIG" another placard proclaimed. As the underground writers and editors met in Ann Arbor, a *Barb on Strike* appeared. Don Quixote and his pen-lance were gone from the masthead, replaced by Max, dollars floating behind him. "Capitalist pig Max Scherr," its lead article began.

The rebels soon formed their own paper, the Berkeley *Tribe*. Editors were elected, and everybody received $30 a week. "Max had a dream of something beautiful," Stew Albert wrote, "but his soul had a broken slave at its center telling him the dream was a lie."

Suddenly a pariah in the People's Republic of Berkeley, Scherr defended himself in a truncated *Barb*. Taking his first bylines since the *Barb*'s debut, he charged "blackmail," decried playing into the hands of "ultra-conservative right-wingers . . . like Ronnie-Baby [Reagan]." He was sad too. "And here we are, tragically hurtling forward . . . one of the bummest trips that anyone could have imagined." He signed a story "Max the Pig."

More surprises loomed. Scherr soon sold the *Barb* to none other than Allan Coult, whose muckraking had sparked the split. But Coult moved away from politics, and disputes arose over the contract. In December, Scherr took back the *Barb*. By then, though, the *Tribe* was the radical paper in town.

In March, 1970, Scherr suffered the first of several heart attacks. "That gave us great pause," recalls *Barb* veteran George Kauffman, who'd shifted papers along with almost everyone else. "That was a very sad period; the revolution devouring its own."

But in the summer of 1969, the *Tribe* was young and healthy. On its first cover, most of the staff stood naked and smiling, making a graphic argument that it—and the Movement—had nothing to hide.

MEANWHILE, in Los Angeles, a summertime exposé was putting the *Free Press* at risk.

With drugs the decade's big buzz, underground papers ran the latest nonnarcotic prices and pharmacology, and countered mainstream sensationalism with both valid information and messianic hyperbole. They also decried "the narcs"—the narcotics agents who had busted 340,000 people across the country for weeds and chemicals between the 1968 Democratic Convention and the Ann Arbor meeting.

Art Kunkin printed referrals for still-illegal abortions, but was less likely than other publishers to kamikaze over the moment's cause. Still, several violent raids against peaceful soft-drug users had occurred in the Los Angeles area, and on August 8 the *Free Press* responded with a front-page editorial. "NARCOTICS AGENTS LISTED: THERE SHOULD BE NO SECRET POLICE," the headline read. The text ran over a screen of that marijuana icon, the Zig-Zag man.

"History demonstrates that the secret policeman invariably uses his anonymity to become unaccountable to the people over whom power is exercised," it said. Many narcotics cases were unconstitutional attempts to "enforce laws as unwise and unenforceable as the now-banished prohibition of liquor."

Inside, the names, addresses, and phone numbers of eighty California State Bureau of Narcotics agents could be found.

The list had come to the *Free Press* via a mail clerk from the state attorney general's office, who'd previously alleged crimes by the UCLA campus police. The photocopied pamphlet wasn't the world's most confidential document—it was a Christmas-card mailing list of the office's employees. One *Free Press* staffer quit to protest its publication, but, aside from a surprisingly small amount of telephone harassment, nothing happened to the agents or their families.

That wasn't the case with Kunkin. He'd been advised that publication was not actionable, but rage, generational alarm, and potential illegality led to charges against him and reporter Jerry Applebaum of receiving stolen property (*printing* such a list was not then illegal). The state attorney general lodged a $10 million obstruction-of-justice suit against Kunkin, his corporation, and the staff. The agents asked $15 million for invasion of privacy.

The case hinged on whether the list was a public document, whether it had been stolen, and whether Kunkin and Applebaum had known if it was stolen. In July, 1970, the defendants would be convicted, Kunkin receiving a $1,000 fine and three years' probation, Applebaum $5,000 and three years' probation, and the corporation a suspended $500 fine. That December, the paper would settle the obstruction case with a compromise $10,000 payment; a larger deal was made with the agents.

The criminal verdicts were later overturned on appeal because it had not been demonstrated that the defendants had received property knowing it was stolen, and the narcs never received the money. But the legal furor chilled the *Freep* off Southern California presses and forced Kunkin to print as far away as the Bay Area. Trying to maintain his independence and solve a logistical nightmare, he purchased a new, expensive web press —which soon became a malfunctioning monster.

Meanwhile, the rip-off ethic was ravaging the *Free Press* bookstores, which eschewed the turnstiles and mirrors of straighter shops. One aide put the people's shoplifting rate at 40 percent, a figure California sales-tax officials would refuse to accept. "Everything started to go awry," she recalls.

"If you're running a radical newspaper, you expect counterblows," Kunkin says. "In retrospect, though, I might have handled [the list of agents] differently, from seeing all the legal consequences."

Instead, he was being forced down the not-so-primrose path toward his eventual ouster from the paper that had begun the underground press.

Kunkin's attempt to build an independent printing apparatus for the *Free Press* and other papers would misfire, but the attack on Port Publications, in Port Washington, Wisconsin, showed why it was worth a try.

A Sam Ervin lookalike in his midfifties, William Schanen, Jr., printed several of his own weeklies and the local VFW newsletter. But by mid-1969, his was the only print shop between Iowa City and Kalamazoo willing to handle underground papers. Driving twenty-five thousand *Seed*s back to Chicago from Wisconsin might involve van tires blowing out from the weight of the papers, or some thrill-packed fishtailing after lazily loading only the back half of a rent-a-truck. But Port's doors were open to us. As Schanen told *Life,* "I don't agree with a lot of it, but what are we supposed to do, get rid of everything we don't agree with?"

We paid Schanen, but Schanen, an antiwar Democrat in a Republican town, paid the price when a nearby factory owner with a picture of Senator Joseph McCarthy on his office wall began his own protest. The boycott soon gained the support of the American Legion post named for Schanen's brother Bob, a World War II hero. Even as Schanen's Ozaukee County *Press* won a National Newspaper Association award for general excellence, Lueptow's furniture store and Leider's drug store and the electric company were canceling $200,000 in advertising. Schanen the local boy was now denounced as a smut peddler, and the FBI visited the plant.

Printing *Kaleidoscope,* the *Seed,* and the others eventually cost Schanen his Cedarburg *Citizen* and Mequon *Squire.* But a line under the Ozaukee *Press*'s logo declared it "The Paper That Refuses to Die." In 1971, Schaenen himself would die of a heart attack; his son would carry on both his name and his tradition of printing dissident papers.

ON SEPTEMBER 24, 1969, eight of the Movement's most media-identified activists began the sixties' most celebrated trial. This duel between radicals and various governmental agencies soon tested both mainstream and underground journalism.

"The Chicago Eight" had been indicted in March under an ink-still-wet Anti-Riot Law—"The Rap Brown Act"—that Senator Strom Thurmond had successfully attached to the Civil Rights Act of 1968. These "modern ideological criminals," as the deputy attorney general called them, were charged with allegedly conspiring and crossing state lines with the intent to incite a riot at the 1968 Democratic National Convention.

The list of defendants indicated a "get the Movement" strategy: Black Panther Party Chairman Bobby Seale, Tom Hayden out of SDS, National Mobilization Committee to End the War cochairs Rennie Davis and Dave Dellinger (also the pacifist editor of *Liberation* magazine), Yippies Abbie Hoffman and Jerry Rubin, academic activists John Froines and Lee Weiner. Eight policemen had been indicted, but seven had been acquitted and one had had his case dismissed. And radical cries for indicting such "conspirators" as Lyndon Johnson, Richard Daley, J. Edgar Hoover, Selective Service Director General Lewis Hershey, and antidrug czar Harry Anslinger had gone unheeded.

Many radicals were worried: trials consumed time, energy, resources, leaders. But the span of this indictment also offered unity and direction to a divided, frustrated Movement. And the God of Synchronicity was back, in the form of Judge Julius J. Hoffman. Perched amid the neon starkness on the twenty-third floor of the Dirksen Federal Building, Hoffman—with his Mr. Magoo appearance, squeaky voice, and feisty willingness to lock horns with any perceived challenge to his authority —guaranteed a circus. Hoffman was a Central Casting opponent for the defendants: elderly, Republican, well off, probably the circuit's most progovernment judge. Even his German-Jewishness opposed Abbie Hoffman's earthier Russo-Jewish roots.

But what kind of defense would be waged? One possibility was to fight the case on the legalism of its charges. A second was to concentrate less on legal issues than on political ones such as the war, police misconduct, and free speech. Successful conspiracy defendant Frank Bardacke, a leader of the antidraft demonstration that produced the Oakland Seven, would sum up this approach in the *Realist:*

"Just remember, if you fight people who have power, you will surely do something illegal. But when you get into court you may discover that

you can convince the jury that people with power are evil and wrong
—and you are right. The jury will then try to find a legal excuse to let
you off."

Judge Hoffman would oppose both approaches. He refused to admit
politics into a case that tried defendants for their intentions. He also
denied motions, jailed lawyers, and, defense counsel would claim, violated his judicial neutrality via contact with the prosecution. In response,
the movements, and the papers, raised the ante, and their voices, in the
courtroom and in the media.

During the five-month legal battle, Arlo Guthrie sang, Allen Ginsberg
chanted. Jerry Rubin's convention-week bodyguard reappeared as an
undercover cop; Ramsey Clark, attorney general of the United States at
the time of the convention, testified for the defense. The conspirators tried
to discuss the killing of Illinois Black Panther Party Chairman Fred
Hampton; a juror seemingly sympathetic to the defense received a mysterious threatening letter signed "The Black Panthers," which led to her
removal from the panel. Opposing counsel snarled at each other; specta-
tors vocally supporting the defense were ejected. Richard J. Daley, the
mayor-king of Chicago, testified; Abbie Hoffman made him smile by
asking if the two of them could settle things outside of court.

Many daily journalists grimaced at the judge's unfairness, but balanced
it against the defendants' "boisterousness," even though a subsequent
study would show their interruptions bunched around a few specific
events during the trial. Mainstream reporters also usually dismissed as
radical paranoia the defense charges of intra-governmental contact. But
a later-disclosed FBI Airtel of October 7 reads, "Judge Hoffman has
indicated to USA [U.S. Attorney] Foran, and USA Foran is in full
agreement, that many of the statements made by the defendants, their
lawyers, and possibly others, such as the unindicted co-conspirators, may
well be in contempt of court. Judge Hoffman has indicated in strictest
confidence that following the trial he definitely plans to consider various
individuals for possible contempt of court."

Another FBI memo says that Chief U.S. District Court Judge William
J. Campbell, the Daley ally who'd empaneled the grand jury charged with
investigating convention "disorders," advised SAC [Special Agent in
Charge] Chicago "in strictest confidence" a month into the case about
his belief that Judge Hoffman "may call a mistrial and send all defendants
and their attorneys to jail for contempt for six months."

("Flatout untrue," U.S. Attorney Foran said. "I never talked to Judge
Hoffman except in open court." Hoffman offered a similar dismissal.

(In 1981, the Federal Court of Appeals—without ruling on the allegation that these and similar documents showed improper out-of-court conversations—rejected the contention that they proved an already disruptive trial to have been irrevocably tainted. The then-remaining contempt citations—only thirteen of the one hundred seventy-five handed down by Judge Hoffman—were allowed to stand. No jail time was mandated. See Chapter 14.)

The government used real and imaginary journalists to make and monitor its case. "The next time your organization schedules a demonstration, march, picket or office party, let us know in advance," the leaflet for the New York Press Service had read. "We'll cover it like a blanket and deliver a cost-free sample of our work to your office. . . . We will photograph any single individual during any type of demonstration or bash. . . . What better way to show you were with it, or in it, or whatever." No wonder that, when New York Press Service reporter Louis Salzberg testified for the prosecution in November as a paid FBI informant, Dave Dellinger, a constant target of Salzberg's attention, softly slapped his forehead.

One infiltrator was worth his weight in paranoia. "It is noted that . . . his appearance resulted in howls of anguish from the liberal and New Left press over FBI use of a 'journalist' as an informant," SAC New York noted to the FBI director about Salzberg's testimony. Authority was asked to "prepare and mail anonymously . . . a suggested letter designed to take advantage of the current atmosphere of confusion in the New Left movement over the extent of FBI infiltration into their ranks through the press media. It is aimed specifically at the Liberation News Service (LNS) in New York by casting suspicion at their activities."

The provocative letter from "Howie" did just that. As "one who has long been associated with the forces of peace in Nixon's Amerika," he attached a copy of a condemnation of Salzberg's testimony by the then-liberal New York *Post.* "Now, for the good of the movement, I must ask one question," he continued. "How has the Liberation News Service survived these many years? It has suffered internal splits time and time again. Its books are in the red. . . . Yet LNS continues to operate much like the New York Press Service, which leads me to the obvious conclusion that federal bread constitutes its main support. . . .

"I (and several others) am taking steps to expose this fraud for what it really is—a government-financed front."

On December 1, 1969, the FBI director's office granted New York authority to send the letter.

The trial also turned the FBI into media critics.

On October 31, 1969, an FBI Airtel from Chicago to Washington forwarded several Chicago *Sun-Times* stories on the Chicago Eight proceedings, and a critique of them: "It is obvious that they are, in effect, supporting to a great extent the individuals on trial." The Airtel, sent "Attn: Crime Records Investigative Division," also referred to then *Sun-Times* editor Jim Hoge and to Marshall Field V, who had just become publisher of the *Sun-Times* and the Chicago *Daily News.* "Under the direction of these two men it is our observation that the *Sun-Times* and also the *Daily News* are becoming more and more sensational in their reporting. . . . The enclosed articles appear very definitely slanted in favor of the 'new left.' " The FBI preferred the *Tribune,* which "continues to support law enforcement, the courts, and particularly Judge Hoffman."

In late December, the FBI investigated a claim that, after a speech by Rennie Davis at Northern Illinois University, a juror's daughter had remarked that her mother doubted the government's charges. "The presiding judge is aware of this alleged incident and concurs" that the FBI should investigate the matter, its memo said. "The Assistant U.S. Attorney who is handling the case" had, it said, learned about the incident "from an unidentified reporter from the *Sun-Times.* "

Nearly a decade later, after I had metamorphosed into a *Sun-Times* reporter myself, I showed this memo to Jim Hoge, by 1978 the paper's publisher (he now publishes the New York *Daily News*). An angry Hoge asked who had covered the speech; the available clips yielded no story connected to the report.

The underground press denounced the conspiracy law as a crime against thought and the trial as a stacked deck. Papers poked fun at the prosecution and its case, ran long excerpts from defense testimony, announced demonstrations. There was little chance of mistaking who the underground's good guys were.

Paul Krassner, as usual, found his own path, woozily testifying for an increasingly incensed defense while tripping on LSD. "There were some who considered it irresponsible," the then-Yippie and *Realist* editor concedes. But he had his reasons—"anarchy," "psychedelic macho," "enhancing the experience," and "wanting to commit perjury [because] they had already testified to certain dates and stuff." There was one more reason, a slogan for the decade: "Ultimately, the answer is that I felt like doing it."

As time went on, the level of underground press invective hampered explaining the case to uncommitted readers. But the events of October 29th provided sufficient reasons for rage.

Bobby Seale, the last national leader of the Black Panther Party not incarcerated or in exile, had been indicted for conspiring with people he hardly knew or didn't know at all. For five weeks of the trial, he'd demanded either the counsel of his choice (Charles Garry, who'd defended the Oakland Seven and numerous Panthers) or the chance to defend himself. Denied both, he came to protest the trial as "a railroad operation . . . from Nixon on down" and denounce the judge as a "racist," a "fascist," a "pig." For the same five weeks, Judge Hoffman had insisted that attorney William Kunstler, who'd filed an early motion to see Seale in jail, was Seale's counsel for the duration.

On October 29, worldviews collided. After Seale again demanded to choose his own counsel, Judge Hoffman ordered marshals, "Take that defendant into the room in there and deal with him as he should be dealt with in this circumstance." When Seale returned, he was bound, gagged, and in leg irons—a stunning, awful image. As Seale continued to try to represent himself, the arrangement of gags and restraints was reconfigured until he resembled a man seated in an electric chair.

On November 5, Judge Hoffman finally allowed Seale to speak on what he deemed a "special occasion"—Seale's severance from the trial, complete with a forty-eight-month sentence for sixteen counts of contempt of court. "Free Bobby! Free Bobby!" many in the gallery cried. (Seale would never be retried for conspiracy or serve time for contempt —see Chapter 14.)

"The trial of the Conspiracy must be stopped," I wrote in a *Seed* cover story that concentrated on the searing antebellum image of a gagged Seale. "The trial forfeits its claim to legal justification when the judge gags and chains a man for demanding the right to cross-examine witnesses. It must be hated when the sole basis for the trial is a vague law with no purpose other than repression. . . . We see a tyrant masquerading as a judge, and a man made to look like a slave."

I had a point. But, as separate conversations with Seale and two of his codefendants and Seale's writing show, there was more to the story, though what there was is a disputed issue.

"Bobby Seale wanted to be gagged," Jerry Rubin says categorically. "Bobby Seale was being railroaded, and the only way to stop the railroad was to make Julius Hoffman so outrageous that the whole country would say, 'Stop oppressing Bobby Seale.'

"We were saying, 'Bobby, the judge is right there on the edge with you, and all you have to do is keep being provocative and do something really outrageous.' We didn't know what it was, but whatever it was, it was going to be hot. . . . They had already gagged him, but it wasn't a mouth gag—it was a procedural gag. Finally, Bobby got up, and finally Julius played right into our hands by gagging him."

In a separate interview, Abbie Hoffman says that key Panthers and other advisors "wanted him [Seale] in a straitjacket—you know, tied up, gagged, whatever." Besides Seale's being denied the counsel of his choice, "there were political-theatrical reasons. He was a bit player in Chicago; how's he going to get to be center stage? I mean, the blacks are supposed to be leading the whites, and nobody talks about the Chairman of the Black Vanguard Party the whole trial. He's only in Chicago [during the convention] for a little time—it's just an airplane ticket and a speech. And also Bobby had to establish a certain presence because of the trial coming up in Connecticut [several Black Panthers had been charged with allegedly murdering a suspected informant].

"He was correct to move to that situation. He had a right to his own lawyer. He wasn't supposed to be on trial. Why didn't the Chicago *Tribune* have a headline: 'Bobby Seale Railroaded'?"

Seale, though, recalls things somewhat differently. "I've got to force Hoffman to gag me today," he wrote after an October 29 dateline in his autobiography *A Lonely Rage.* "I'm going to make Hoffman gag his own self in the eyes of the public," he told a nurse just before going to court. "I was ready, with a need to triumph. . . . Hoffman will either allow my right to defend myself or he will be forced to gag me."

In a recent conversation, Seale characterizes Judge Hoffman as "a racist, fascist, idiot pig, and I had to find out how chickenshit he was." But he repeatedly denies the existence of a long-term strategy. "It evolved. It wasn't a planned situation. There's certain crap you're just not gonna take.

"He had mentioned two-three days before in so many little clouded words that I could be gagged." But, again, "I didn't have any plan to have him play into my hands per se." Rubin's and Hoffman's views are "their opinions, not my words."

But what would they have thought if an underground writer had come up with a story about any desire to push for a gagging before it happened? In conversation, Seale finds the question irrelevant; Hoffman says.

"It would have been a good news story, but it would have been kind of destructive for the strategy. If you're playing in the best of all possible worlds, of course the truth is the truth. But the answer wasn't, during that period, to have a page in the underground newspapers where everyone's dirty linen, in a sense, is being washed in public. Don't forget, the real underground press operating in that time is in the FBI memos."

Jerry Rubin: "Had they said, 'Julius Hoffman's overreacting played into Bobby Seale's hands because it enabled Bobby Seale to dramatize the plight of blacks in court by being a national image of a bound and gagged man'—I would have cut the article out and saved it for a couple of years, and said, 'This is a smart guy.'

"If it was saying, 'How outrageous!' then I would have said, 'This is a sell-out article.' It depends on where you lay responsibility, and I think responsibility had to be laid totally with the national administration, Daley, and Judge Hoffman."

"THE WAR was driving us nuts," Todd Gitlin recalls. "The Movement was out on a limb. Having committed itself to revolutionism in a situation that was not revolutionary, what were the choices? It was to go off the deep end, or to acquire some prepackaged theory of revolution, or to convert revolution into lifestyle, or to go into complete hippie withdrawal, go to the country and develop some crackpot theory about the origins of civilization."

By fall, the Weathermen were emerging from the ashes of SDS. The name came from the Bob Dylan line about not needing a weatherman to know which way the wind blows—an ironic choice, since the Protest Bob of "Subterranean Homesick Blues" had become the countrified romantic of "Nashville Skyline." Weatherman's superheated politics depicted home-front warriors allied with millions of soon-to-be-victorious Third World anti-imperialists. The Weathermen were mostly former middle- and upper-class students who saw themselves as John Browns on behalf of the National Liberation Front.

Inspired by the group criticism/self-criticism of China's Cultural Revolution, the Weathermen tried to transform themselves into new men and women by purging themselves of white-skin privilege, of possessions, hierarchy, monogamy, and, sometimes, heterosexuality. They also picked up the Cultural Revolution's cult of purity. When their "jailbreak" raids at schools and beaches were resisted by the kids they'd come to liberate, they showed their willingness to fight the (American) people rather than serve them. Often they lost.

From October 8 to 11, SDS's factions held their National Actions in Chicago. Three thousand marchers, most of them collegiate types, joined nonviolent demonstrations at jails, factories, and housing projects. But the thousands of street fighters that the Weatherman rhetoric machine had predicted would "tear up pig city" during their Days of Rage had shrunk to just a few hundred. Standing in Lincoln Park before a night trashing of the Gold Coast, the chilled, helmeted group psyched itself up with bonfires, NLF flags, chants. Watching them dogtrot away from the site of the Yippies' abortive Festival of Life, I felt not rage, but amazement that some of our best and brightest were stretched so thin. The Weathermen loathed anybody's pity. Soon a window-smashing Loop riot pitted "Ho, Ho, Ho Chi Minh," clubs, and bricks against batons and blackjacks. Overall, 287 Weathermen and women were jailed; 50 police and more demonstrators were hospitalized; Assistant City Corporation Counsel Richard Elrod (now Cook County Sheriff) was paralyzed while tackling a street fighter. "Sick little swine," the daily *Chicago Today* editorialized, recasting Movement pig-rhetoric while noting that "what they have accomplished is to bring about the end of Students for a Democratic Society." More irony—the Chicago dailies now reported that in 1968 the police had attacked the protesters at the Democratic Convention.

Underground papers had run advance statements from both SDS rumps; now they covered both the shock of the riots and the issues underlying them. Most papers criticized the Days of Rage as irrelevant or suicidal, and, as the clashes ebbed, writers met at the *Seed* for a forum that would be widely reprinted. "A white army ran through the streets of Chicago," a Weatherman exulted. Others (including myself, back from New York's *Rat* to cover the conspiracy trial) disagreed. "Few people want to join a kamikaze corps," Skeets Millard, SDSer turned *Seed*ling wrote. "Their polarizing tactic has succeeded—in uniting nearly everyone against them."

In the Berkeley *Tribe,* Eldridge Cleaver applauded whites fighting "the pigs." In the *Seed,* a reader's letter expressed concern for "the people" who'd been shopping downtown when all hell broke loose.

As broken windows, even broken heads, were only the lightest echoes of Vietnam's violence, so the Weathermen were a shard rather than the bellwether of antiwar protest. On October 15, the liberal Vietnam Moratorium protest attracted a million people across the country. The November 15 New Mobilization to End the War in Vietnam demonstration was the largest single protest in American history. The streets of Washington filled with hundreds of thousands of marchers, some of them returning their Vietnam campaign medals. At the "Injustice Department," the air filled with cries of "Smash the State" and with teargas; a friend of mine suffered eye damage when a canister hit her square in the face. I thought I saw Attorney General John Mitchell standing at a window; his wife Martha later said that the scene recalled the Russian Revolution.

Some of us had spent a fair chunk of our lives during wartime, and we were frustrated that it raged on. "Washington is a pretty city," I wrote in the *Seed.* "A lot of us saw it in 1963 when we went there to end racism.

A lot of us saw it in 1967 when we went there to protest the power of the Pentagon. A lot of us saw it this year when we went there to protest the war in Vietnam. Some of us may see it again if the Moratorium calls a peace march in 1984 to bring the boys home from Burma. "A half-million people came to Washington in November. A half-million people are about five hundred thirty miles tall if they stand on each other's heads. Richard Nixon is five feet, nine inches tall. Richard Nixon is eleven feet, ten inches tall if he stands on [Vice-President] Spiro Agnew's head. How come he looks down on us?"

Actually, what Henry Kissinger called "the hammer of antiwar protest" was restraining prowar zeal. Though Nixon had announced on September 26 that "under no circumstances will I be affected whatever by" protest, fifty thousand American troops recently had been withdrawn from Vietnam, air strikes were beginning to be limited, and Nixon had, at least for now, made "a decision to end offensive operations." But despite their impact, the Mobilization and the Moratorium were almost the last of the giant demonstrations. Radicals saw no light at the end of the tunnel, and even victories risked cooptation. "Many of the new antiwar speakers came from the ranks of the very men who helped formulate and defend the Vietnam policy," *Rat* opined, offering a pro-NLF view. "The guerillas' success on the battlefield converted these guys into doves."

Then, on December 1, the draft lottery began. Many of those who'd protested because the war wasn't worth *their* lives now held numbers keyed to their birthdates that were high enough to keep them civilians, and many now said goodbye to the Movement. Those who remained in it were tempted to become more extreme.

MEANWHILE, the Nixon administration was paying tribute to the effects of protest via its own media offensive. "North Vietnam cannot defeat or humiliate the United States," Richard Nixon said on November 3. "Only Americans can do that." Ten days later, in a speech from Des Moines broadcast over all three television networks, Spiro Agnew attacked the concentration of media power "in the hands of a tiny, enclosed fraternity of privileged men elected by no one and enjoying a monopoly sanctioned and issued by government." Most undergrounders agreed with the words, but not their source. Or their consequences. CBS had televised a half-hour report on the liberal Moratorium; there was no corresponding coverage of the more radical Mobilization. "We were thinking thrice," John Chancellor has recalled.

Radical broadcasters were more directly affected. At San Francisco's

KSAN, the Metromedia-owned radio station that was the country's best-known "progressive rock" FMer, announcer Roland Young would be fired after passing on a listener's suggestion that those who supported Black Panther David Hilliard's right to have made a "We will kill Richard Nixon" speech at the local mobilization should send telegrams to the president. Newsman Wes "Scoop" Nisker resigned after being told that his excellent audio collages were no longer welcomed.

On the day of Agnew's blast, an ex-AP reporter named Seymour Hersh broke the story of how Vietnamese civilians had been massacred by American soldiers in a village called My Lai (the death toll eventually passed three hundred). Running in mainstream dailies around the world, the stories confirmed charges that the Movement had been making for years. Moreover, LNS had just told its readers about Operation Phoenix, an assassination campaign that would kill numerous NLF cadre and others, and the service would soon report on "a defoliant used in massive amounts by the United States in Viet Nam [that] may cause birth defects, according to a report issued by the World Health Organization"—Agent Orange. These terror tactics, it correctly predicted, would "suffer the same fate as 'strategic hamlets' and 'provincial reconnaissance.' "

Subsequent observers would see Hersh's My Lai work as "the closing of a circle begun years earlier with Wilfred Burchett's reports from behind the lines in the *National Guardian* and [Green Beret] Donald Duncan's tale of murder and mayhem in *Ramparts.*" But Dispatch News Service, the Saigon- and Washington-based organization that syndicated Hersh's stories, merged the skills of disgruntled professional writers and syndicator David Obst. "The underground had much less influence on My Lai than my own reporting," Hersh writes. He'd worked independently of it, and says that he would not have gone to it had the dailies shunned his story. Hersh's evocative, documented work raised public disgust over the war. It also stole some of the protest papers' thunder.

There was another death to report. In Massachusetts, as October became November, Marshall Bloom had shut the door to the garage that had once held an LNS press, started Green Power, his rusting Triumph sports car, and waited for sweet release. He was twenty-five.

"SUICIDE PUZZLES FRIENDS OF FOUNDER OF RADICAL NEWS SERVICE," the New York *Times* headlined. Later there were explanations. "He wanted the world to be full of love, because the world was too harsh, too rough," Harvey Wasserman, a Woodrow Wilson Fellow turned LNSer, says. "And he never really recovered from the vicious assault on him after the

LNS split. In some ways, his suicide was a political act. He was saying, 'Listen, you must love each other more deeply.' "

In New York, though, a vivacious woman named Jane Alpert had fallen into armed love. Twenty-two-year-old Alpert, a recent Swarthmore grad, had joined the *Rat* in June, at a time when the Black Panthers were declaring that fascism had come to America and that being a revolutionary meant implementing both political rhetoric and personal transformation. Though she began as a (female) secretary despite previous publishing-house experience, she found something at the paper and on the edge of the Movement. "I think it was a need to wrap all the answers in one big answer," she says now. "I wanted the personal and political all to be contained in one. I wanted apocalypse, Utopia."

The *Rat* Alpert joined radiated casual violence. Few staffers had weapons, but when one cover fell through, Shero ran a Pop Art strip of smoking guns captioned, "Ooh, That Felt Good." "For some of the more politically sophisticated people it was a joke," Alpert recalls. "But some of us took it very seriously, partly out of youth, and partly out of a real attraction to violence."

Alpert's first story for the *Rat* described how to hijack an airplane—which she knew something about, since she and her lover, ex-*Guardian* staffer Sam Melville, had aided two French-Canadian air pirates associated with the Quebec separatist movement. Jeff Shero asked for a rewrite, feeling that the piece's advocacy would get the paper busted. Alpert had a different thought: "Oh wow, I've out-ratted the *Rat* editor."

Rat's Woodstock issue carried a communiqué from those who'd bombed the Marine Midland bank on August 20. The twenty injuries were an accident, the statement said, but the act was a political escalation: "nor will the longed-for ending of the war in Vietnam even begin to end the war in the U.S." *Rat*'s Days of Rage issue reported that police had invaded its office in search of communiqués connected with a mid-September bombing of the Federal Building in lower Manhattan. The paper reprinted the message as "our revolutionary duty to make public the truths about the Movement's progress that the State and the mass news media are in collusion to suppress."

For Jeff Shero, that progress seemed increasingly illusory. Woodstock had convinced him that an aging New Left was hopelessly out of touch. Unlike the Weathermen, he thought whites worth organizing, armed struggle not the only way to be revolutionary. Though more militant than the *EVO* folk, he increasingly shared Allan Katzman's opinion that the underground press was being taken over by "noncreative second-raters . . . the radicals who believe in what they say, and woe to anyone who does not believe accordingly."

One night, while walking down boisterous, dirty Saint Mark's Place toward an apartment proudly sublet from the poet W.H. Auden, Jeff came upon two winos arguing over a bottle of Thunderbird. "The streets belong to the people," everyone said, but at that moment he had an unlikely revelation: "I hate this street. I'm going to jail, or I'm gonna get shot, and I don't wanna get shot over things that I don't believe in."

On November 12, Alpert, Melville, and two others did go to jail, charged with conspiring to bomb eight corporate and federal offices, the United Fruit Pier, and four army trucks. One of them, George Demmerle, had been busted with Melville while on a bombing run, but soon surfaced as an FBI informant. Demmerle, who favored a Trojan helmet with big purple bristles, high-collar Nehru shirts, and bizarrely colored pants, had led the Crazies, a group that lived up to its name. He'd readily proposed violent acts; that he was a "leader" testified to revolutionary values and vulnerabilities—especially since *EVO* had all but accused him of being a fink.

The *Rat* defended Alpert. "She's done long articles about abortion, Women's Lib, and organizing highschoolers, she's very bright, open, articulate, and she's committed," it editorialized. "That she could be involved in the bombings, however, seems hard to believe. The government's case seems to be designed to soothe the public uproar and implicate the movement on the basis of purely circumstantial evidence." But not only had Alpert been involved; she'd slipped the Marine Midland communiqué under the *Rat*'s door. "I was a great stooge," artist-writer Paul Simon recalls. "Every time they'd blow up something, we'd go, 'far out.'"

By their own logic, the bombers did real damage only to the hated Whitehall draft-induction center. A score of innocents were hurt at Marine Midland, which, Alpert says, Melville had attacked on his own. United Fruit's pier, targeted because of that corporation's business in the "banana republics" of Central America, had been sublet to another company.

The bombings hardened attitudes against the Movement as much as they built support. They also were, Alpert now feels, "an ethical mistake," one she associates with deflecting personal difficulties onto "the system." But she also sees them in a political context. "The Nixon administration's intransigence in the face of peaceful protest made us feel justified in turning to more extreme measures." Some activists, fueled by the cold logic of extremism, would keep playing with fire, with harsher effects on themselves and others.

The bombings also greatly affected Alpert's status at the *Rat*. "If to the straight world I appeared a nice young girl drawn tragically into crime, to the movement I was a fearless Amazon," she'd write in her biography. "On my first day back at the *Rat* office my fellow staffers greeted me with cheers as though I'd been elected to office, not released on bail." Jeff Shero, who'd gone to Mississippi to write a book on the New South, returned and ran her jailhouse thoughts as a main piece. She wrote another cover story on the Panther Twenty-one, who'd been arrested in April for an alleged plot to bomb everything from department stores to the New York Botanical Gardens. "I soon discovered I could do no wrong," she'd write. "I no longer had to sweep and type. I didn't even have to come to the office. The telephone rang for me twenty times a day—reporters, old friends, Movement stars from other cities hoping to meet me—and the *Rat* staff dutifully took all the messages and never once complained."

Jane Alpert would become disillusioned—but that explosion concerned sexism as well as dynamite.

25¢
35¢ out of NYC

Womens LibeRATion

CHANGING A TIRE

You need

A car jack

Lug Remover

New or used tire on hub.

Most cars have complete tire changing gear in their trunk.

1) Put car in neutral with emergency brake on.

2) For Safety—Put bricks or support behind wheel that is diagonally opposite the tire you're about to change.

3) Assemble jack. Place underneath fender somewhat closer to side of flat tire. (If in front, don't put it on the parking light!!!). Hook the lift far back onto the fender so that it fits snugly. Turn switch to UP position. Insert handle and press it as far down as it will go. Each press raises lift one notch on rack. The jack will automatically raise the car once the lift is at a height where it rests on the bumper. Jack car at thei point only slightly up so that the flat tire is still resting on ground. This makes it easier to loosen the lugs.

LIFT SUPPORT under CAR

UP DOWN ← SWITCH

handle.

← JACK

Lug remover

4) Remove handle from jack and pry off hub cap.

5) Reverse handle to lug remover side and begin to loosen lugs. Make sure handle is onto lug securely. Lugs turn LEFT, counter clockwise, to loosen. Press or pull on furthest end of handle for best leverage. For really tight lugs "Liquid Wrench", sold in can or spray help loosen them. Leave lugs loosened and on.

6) Jack car up so that tire is completely off the ground—but not more than necessary.

There are also other kinds of jacks and lug removers . . . .

7) Remove lugs completely and put them in a safe place. Take tire off.

8) Put on new tire. Put it on so that studs come through holes on hub.

9) Replace lugs, turning them onto studs with threaded side facing in. Leave hand tightened.

10) Jack car down (adjust SWITCH) until tie tire is resting on ground.

11) Tighten lugs with jack handle . . . but not so tight that you can't remove them again.

hub cap remover

4 different fittings for lugs

12) Jack car completely down. Remove jack.

13) Replace hub cap making sure air nozzle comes through hole on cap.

← STAND

SCISSOR JACK (fits under chassis)

platform support

← base

cranking handle

13

THE RAT WOMEN AND THE STONEWALL

ANN ARBOR, MICHIGAN—JULY, 1969: Before the police raided the UPS media conference and searched the women attending it, a series of resolutions had been adopted. Male supremacy was to be eliminated from the papers. Women's bodies weren't to be used to sell products or papers. Articles on women's issues and staffs fully integrated by gender were to be encouraged.

Nevertheless, the next year would see the underground press split by schisms over a quest for gender equality that dated back through the century.

Women won the right to vote in 1920, and by the 1960s, education, Rosie the Riveter, birth control, social mobility, and economic imperatives were setting the stage for a new wave of feminism. Yet the image of Dagwood the breadwinner and Blondie the housewife was alive and well. Women earned three-fifths of what men did, faced discrimination at the jobs they had, couldn't enter some careers. In 1968, a Barnard College student was disciplined for lying about living "illicitly" with her boyfriend. One million illegal abortions a year were being performed; only a handful of states had even the mildest reform laws.

In radical circles, financial discrimination usually wasn't a factor; hardly anyone had money. And loving thy neighbor was a fringe benefit of sit-ins, be-ins, and demonstrations. "The more I make love, the more I make revolution."

Or so the saying went. Around the Movement and the alternative communities, women often were second-class comrades.

• In 1963, the great dream Martin Luther King told of during the civil rights march on Washington had called for unity between "the sons" of former slaves and "the sons" of former slaveowners.
• From 1964 to 1966, women in SNCC and SDS had questioned gender roles in the Movement; they were shouted down, even pelted with tomatoes.
• "The only position for women in SNCC," Stokely Carmichael had said in 1966, "is prone." "Pussy power!" a Black Panther leader had proclaimed at SDS's 1969 convention, thinking he'd paid a compliment until the shouts began to come.
• "Fuck your woman till she can't stand up," White Panther leader John Sinclair had declared, forgetting that not all Panthers had penises, or enjoyed being pounded into submission.

The situation in journalism was similar.

Few women worked in the dailies' city rooms, or as correspondents, editors, or publishers. The want ads were segregated by gender—and by salary. In 1964, the Civil Rights Bill had included protection against sex discrimination as an octogenarian representative's joke. That same year, reporter Lindsy Van Gelder was turned down at the New York *World-Telegram & Sun* "because I was a female and would no doubt run off and get married my first day on the job." After an editor at a second paper told her a similar story, she headed off to the State Human Rights Commission.

The underground press offered more potential, and for radical women was all the more disappointing because its promise was unfulfilled. After the Underground Press Syndicate's first conference in 1967, editors and writers had been invited to retreat to bucolic Big Sur—three people per paper, plus "women prepared to cook." The Summer of Love had loosened Movement attitudes and politicized hippies, but in 1969 Max Scherr gave an article on Berkeley's emerging women's movement the headline "The Women Are Revolting." Only a few underground papers had women making waves, or policy; nearly all automatically assumed male power and viewed the world through male eyes. "It left a lot to be desired in terms of women's full participation," NACLA's Alice Embree, who also worked at the *Rag* and the *Rat,* recalls.

Radical women were getting tired of fighting for everyone's freedom except their own.

Founded in 1966 by Betty Friedan and others, the National Organization for Women (NOW) sought full civil rights in the mainstream. Its members—mainly middle-class women (and a few men) would campaign for reforms in employment, education, and voting and abortion rights. But NOW was not radical, and after a 1967 women's march on the Pentagon, radical women broke away to build their own liberation movement. In the months that followed, they developed their own ideas and built on Movement and black-power assumptions. Personal situations often had political roots and consequences, and individuals had to organize collectively. Prejudice was ingrained in society, not simply due to mean individuals. Protest was good, and it paid. Empowering the oppressed was more important than pleasing established power. Separatism might accomplish equality, even superiority. Victory was inevitable, but patience wasn't a virtue. And those who became "women's liberationists" added a key theoretical point: "capitalism, imperialism, and racism are *symptoms* of male supremacy—sexism," Robin Morgan would write in *Sisterhood Is Powerful,* her anthology of women's thought.

In September, 1968, two hundred or so radical women demonstrated in Atlantic City against the Miss America Pageant's role assumptions and racism. Sexism, consumerism, the family were attacked. Undergarments were tossed (the burned bras were a mass-media myth). A movement hit the map, bumpily. "I remember long, large fights with Jerry Rubin and others," recalls Morgan, who'd gone from being a child TV star (Dagmar on *I Remember Mama*) through SNCC, CORE, various antiwar groups, and the Yippies. "They were saying, 'You must be crazy, going to demonstrate against something so irrelevant as the Miss America Pageant. The revolution is going to take place in Chicago!'"

The protest was widely derided in mainstream media, and a network cameraman, Morgan claimed, was told he'd be fired if he focused on the liberation banner unfurled in the balcony. But Morgan's postdemonstration *Rat* report gave an activist's-eye view, arguing that "men will not be free until women are free," then exhorting women: "And sisters, join us. We're a motley crew, not free . . . but trying to learn the motions, however awkward, of being ourselves, of respecting and loving each other, of refusing to prostitute ourselves before our own degradation."

Underground-press women were covering new subjects: extended families; lesbianism; abortion; self-defense; the politics of employment, housework, welfare, sex; the hundreds of Pink Stereotypes women faced. Articles, manifestos, conversations, and coffee-table, office, and bedroom revelations—all appeared. In the best tradition of the papers, people in a community thought out loud with each other, then acted.

Increasingly, the radical assumptions of just months earlier were targeted for censure. "The free sexual revolution," one feminist had told the *Guardian*'s Margie Stamberg early in 1969, "has only served to oppress women and especially radical women. If she doesn't want to sleep with men, a woman is 'hung up.' If she does, she's known as someone's wife or girl friend." Men still saw sexually active women as "bad." "The reverse, of course, is not true."

As many blacks had done, some women were declaring themselves independent, separate, even superior at a time when Movement men already felt beseiged. And though women's liberation might liberate all people, many Movement men sensed that the short run would cost them privilege. It was one thing for naked students to surround a *Playboy* representative at Iowa's Grinnell College and denounce sexual commercialization; the call to the Miss America demonstration had announced that "only newswomen will be recognized."

Reaction came.

" 'Women's Liberation Front' sounded like a joke, then like a lesbian conspiracy, and finally . . . like a Trotskyist splinter group," Marvin Garson, the talented *Express Times* editor, had bristled late in 1968. Each sex was oppressed, both needed liberation, he'd written—before adding that, "for obvious reasons, it is the men who do most of the talking." After *Rat* reprinted the story, a letter—from a man—had suggested that Garson substitute "nigger" for "woman" in his article and see how it read.

"I found it much harder to work there once I got involved in the women's movement," writer Claudia Dreifus said about life at the *East Village Other*. "People were just hateful and impossible and horrible to me. I lived easily in the world of men. My friends were men, and my mentors were men. My initial reaction to the women's movement was, 'This is another good thing that is happening,' and I was quite shocked that they did not think so, my brothers and my buddies.

"I didn't spend my time saying, 'Up against the wall, fuckers.' I felt none of that hatred. But where they had been laissez-faire about me before, they started sabotaging what I was doing."

The tension was aggravated by a new kind of alternative paper. "Like Sweden, the Underground has no prostitutes, and like Denmark, it has abolished pornography," *Oz* editor Richard Neville proudly stated in his aptly named *Play Power*. Then Al Goldstein rolled onto the scene.

Goldstein was a different kind of rebel. The alternative papers he'd edited were *Hush, Hush* and *Confidential*. After deciding that his industrial spying on the United Auto Workers would make a good radical story, he found *EVO* frivolous, *Rat* politically simplistic. He also noticed how many people bought *EVO* for the sex ads. As he says, "I am the guy in the raincoat."

In November, 1968, Goldstein and Jim Buckley, the managing editor of a second-generation undergrounder called the New York *Free Press,* unleashed a paper for the raincoat crowd. Immediately, progressives and radicals denounced its obsessional, sordid approach. "Dildo journalism . . . about as pro-sex as the clap," *Village Voice* cartoonist Jules Feiffer said. By issue two, Goldstein, who'd come of age listening to WBAI and was antiwar, was lashing out at a Left "as fucked up as the right when it comes to sex."

Protected by the decisions in *Roth v. United States* (1957) and *Memoirs v. Massachusetts* (1966), which defined prurient appeal, community standards, *and* utter lack of redeeming social value as the necessary standard for legal obscenity, *Screw* had survived arrests over insinuations about J. Edgar Hoover's sexuality and visual puns about "Tricky Dick" Nixon. Fueled by "Peter Meter" movie reviews and oodles of sex ads, it had taken off toward a peak circulation of 150,000. Which created problems for underground papers, especially in New York.

The first Los Angeles *Free Press* personal ad had been placed by a waitress looking for a roommate; reportedly, she later married a respondent. By 1969, though, "Tomcats, Alleycats and Pussycats," "The Swinging Headhunter," and other sections full of hardcore behavioral weirdness had gone from titillation and social service to dwarfing their papers' news stories. Some women and a smaller number of men staffers complained. A few papers, including the *Seed,* where the ads were never that weird (or profitable), dumped the nastier ones. At the *Barb,* Max Scherr cited his hatred of censorship while cashing the checks. Art Kunkin was candid: "Show me alternative revenue and I'll stamp 'em out," he told irate feminists even as the record ads began disappearing. But some weeks he did turn away a thousand or two thousand dollars' worth of ads. "We set a policy—no sadomasochism."

Screw and the ad sections were, *Life*'s Barry Farrell wrote, "bad smut" driving out the underground's "good smut—the kind meant to dissolve fear, not exploit it." *Screw*'s fixations pulled readers away from the political papers, presenting the underground with "the irony of being stomped out from below."

Faced with declining advertising *and* circulation revenues, *EVO* had launched *Kiss* in April. The debut editorial cited eroticism, sexual repression, and constitutional rights as reasons for publishing—"and mainly to make a bundle." "I want to call it *Kiss,* " one editor told *EVO* libertine Bob Rudnick, "because it's so beautiful, and sensual, and it's not going to be tawdry." "Of course," Rudnick recalls, "it was the cheapest, ugliest porno publication." *The New York Review of Sex* went arty—and out of business. *Pleasure,* published independently by *Rat*'s business manager, prospered as "the newspaper you can read with one hand."

The rush to revolution, the desire for liberation and power, the long-ings and distortions of sexuality were building toward critical mass.

Early in 1969, Marge Piercy, Movement veteran, writer, and feminist, had fired off a watershed piece called "The Grand Coolie Damn" in the Movement journal *Leviathan*. Why were women in a "human liberation" movement no better off than women in the mainstream? she'd asked. "Repression brings hardening," she wrote. But insensitivity and dishonesty did not produce "a more efficient revolutionary, but only a more efficient son of a bitch. We are growing some dandy men of steel nowadays."

Her somewhat reluctant but determined conclusion: "Sisters, what we do, we have to do together, and we will see about them."

This controversial choice intensified the argument between Left-firsters and women-firsters. "The enemy is not identified as man," London's *Black Dwarf* editorialized. "The ally is not the woman who supports and benefits capitalism. It is all people who are being crushed and twisted, who want space and air and time to sit in the sun." The radical feminist Redstockings disagreed. "In fighting for our liberation we will always take the side of women against their oppressors," the group's manifesto proclaimed in July. "We will not ask what is 'revolutionary' or 'reform-ist,' only what is good for women."

That month, charges of sexism hit the underground press during the *Barb-Tribe* split. "Max was very much a maker of the counterculture," writer Judy "Gumbo" Albert recalls, "but his attitude toward women was patriarchal, domineering, oppressive."

But the papers' Great Feminist Revolt would happen in New York, at the *Rat*.

JANE ALPERT, Ms. *Rat* of underground and mass media, was en route to Chelsea's Elgin Theater, where a benefit was being held for her bombing-trial defense fund. Outside, a male staffer was selling the latest *Rat*. Jane looked, and hated it. A court picture showed her lover and codefendant nudging her breast with his elbow. An S. Clay Wilson cartoon contained brutal amputations. Was "Clit Flit Big Hit" an apt headline for a story on clitoral orgasm? In Jeff Shero's absence, was the (mostly male) staff so low on ideas that a "Sex and Porn" special issue seemed like a good idea? If so, what did that say about the *Rat*'s future?

Redstockings, Weatherwomen, and guerilla-theater WITCHes com-plained that the issue was *Screw* revisited, and, at an angry meeting, won the right to produce their own issue of the *Rat*. At first, it seemed to have the usual rhetoric, including a piece advocating the guerilla violence men were being denounced for espousing. But Robin Morgan's article was the shot heard round the Left.

Increasingly drawn toward a utopian genderless society, Morgan had helped to gather women for the *Rat* issue. During a brainstorming session, somebody had asked her to write a piece on women and the Left. She did, in one sitting of rage and fear. Arguments flared when she handed it into the nascent collective, but "Goodbye to All That" was set in type and pasted up.

"*Rat* must be taken over permanently by women—or *Rat* must be destroyed," Morgan wrote. She then proceeded to take no prisoners. "We have met the enemy and he's our friend . . . and that's what I want to write about—the friends, brothers, lovers in the counterfeit male-dominated Left."

And so, she wrote, it was goodbye to a Movement dominated by the same white men "responsible for the destruction of human life and environment on the planet today." To the "Stanley Kowalski Weather-*men*." To "Hip Culture and the so-called Sexual Revolution, which has functioned toward women's freedom as did the Reconstruction toward former slaves." To Hugh Hefner *and* Abbie Hoffman. To Trashman's cartoon macho and the Young *Lords*. To old Yippie pal Jerry Rubin, whose press releases had been carried up these very *Rat* stairs by Nancy Kurshan, "the power behind the clown." To ten-years-for-two-joints John Sinclair: "Not one breath of my support for the new counterfeit Christ. Just one less to worry about for ten years.

"Women are the real Left," Morgan wrote. "We are rising, powerful in our unclean bodies; bright glowing mad in our inferior brains; wild hair flying; wild eyes staring, wild voices keening, undaunted by blood we who hemmorhage every twenty-eight days; laughing at our own beauty we who have lost our sense of humor; mourning for all each precious one of us might have been in this one living time-place had she not been born a woman; stuffing fingers into our mouths to stop the screams of fear and hate and pity for men we have loved and love still; tears in our eyes and bitterness in our mouths for children we couldn't have, or couldn't *not* have, or didn't want, or didn't want *yet,* or wanted and had in this place of horror. We are rising with a fury older and potentially greater than any force in history, and this time we will be free or no one will survive. Power to all the people or to none. All the way down this time."

"Goodbye to All That" then concluded with a list of twenty-five Movement women—including Morgan—to be freed.

Some activists saw the piece as a stab in the backs of increasingly besieged (male) Movement figures, including some who were on trial, and Morgan herself described an "amulet of madness" she said women had to rip from their necks to be free. Even without targeting the Panthers and the Puerto Rican revolutionary Young Lords ("at this point this was like going up to God himself and saying, 'You're a bad person' "), "Goodbye to All That" became a cause célèbre or a scandal, depending on who was doing the viewing.

Then the proposed cover for the next issue surfaced. "The Old Rat Is Back," said a headline as the trademark cartoon rat unzipped his fly. "It meant, 'The boys are back,' " artist Paul Simon recalls. "I didn't take that to be such a big deal."

That was the problem, the coalition of women decided after caucusing. They'd suffered a thousand insults, had had their work and movement slighted, and now the men were back to their old tricks. The women announced that they were retaining editorial control of the paper.

Now the men went through the roof. They'd built the paper, run Robin Morgan's piece on the Miss America demonstration even after they'd been told that men couldn't cover it, been raided for communiqués connected to the bombing conspiracy to which Jane Alpert belonged. If feminists wanted to avoid the hard work of starting their own paper, why didn't they take over *Screw?*

The women had the stronger hand. Some of the men rued the cheesier stuff they'd run. Paul Simon envisioned nightmare headlines in the *Daily News:* "*Rat* Men Evict Women." "*Rat* Men Call Cops." And what about the possibility of "Street-Fighting Women Beat Up Mousy *Rat* Men"?

In what was becoming an underground ritual, the brothers filched the subscription list. But when the next *Rat* came out, the trademark rodent on page three had breasts. Her message: "Up Against the Wall, *Rat.*"

Jeff Shero, veterans of both factions agree, might have kept the paper sexually integrated on relatively enlightened terms. Instead, he wound up feeding the takeover's fire—and incinerating his personal life.

He and Alice Embree had been a storybook Movement couple, meeting at a sit-in, teaming up to "liberate" documents at Columbia University. But at the *Rag* in Austin, he'd been the honcho; she'd run the Multilith. She'd written a few research-oriented pieces for the *Rat;* he owned it. Later, she'd criticize him for not sharing his knowledge; he'd already been exhausted by the tasks at hand.

When Jeff heard about the coup, he was in Mississippi researching his book on Southern whites. After a phone conversation with a male editor, he made a decision: "Let 'em have it." That made a visiting Alice happy. She was a feminist, knew some of the new staff, was one of the women Morgan had cited as needing to be freed. "I wasn't there when the women took over," she recalls. "I think it would have been an emotionally wrenching experience, because of my personal connection with Jeff."

But when Jeff told an old SNCC buddy about his decision, he ran into a buzzsaw. "That's bullshit," Jeff recalls his pal saying as they drove toward Greenville. "They're a bunch of rich bitches, dilettantes. They're destroying your friends, and they're going to denounce you." Moved by the argument, Jeff phoned his editor, a formerly working-class guy who'd driven cattle trucks in the summer to raise money for school. "This is a class fight," Jeff said. "Don't give in. Argue class against feminism."

The next voice he heard was a quiet one near his phone. "Where's the bus station?"

Alice was seething. In that moment, she saw Jeff embodying all the snubs conscious women could experience in late-sixties America and in the Movement. He was, she felt, betraying both her and her sisters. "She exploded like I'd only seen black people go hysterical in the South," Jeff says. "I pounded him," Alice agrees. Alice, a good woman, left Jeff, and became involved in women's music and printing. Jeff, a good man, faltered, feeling that everything he'd done was bad because women remained oppressed.

It was only one of hundreds of house-to-house battles taking place around the Movement.

In New York, the feminist *Rat* denounced its predecessor as an apolitical "pornzine," a statement given at least some teeth when it was busted for the previously published Wilson cartoon. But for an issue or two, the *Rat* remained on a cusp about gender. "We want to work it out," an editorial said. A male staffer's critique of the Women's Issue was easy-going or condescending, depending on who read it. Letters cried "Power to the Sisters" or snarled "Fuck you bitches, Go back to the kitchen." Before too long, the men were eased out. Last to go was rock writer Vince Aletti.

"I was really hurt," says Aletti, whose open gayness may have brought him closer to the liberationists. "It had to be done, but at the same time, I thought, 'Where do I fit in? I don't want to go back to those guys. They didn't even attempt to do something interesting on their own.'

"The women had pointed out things about the old *Rat* that alienated me from it. And they did take the spirit of the *Rat* with them—it was rightfully theirs."

The feminist *Rat* wasn't alone. That January, *It Ain't Me Babe* began publishing in Berkeley. In February, the first issue of the Washington, D.C.–based *off our backs* editorialized for the revival of International Women's Day (March 8), which dated back to 1910 German socialist Clara Zetkin. Iowa City's *Ain't I a Woman* offered radical-feminist ideas and tips for living them. The dual-gender underground press published Women's Issues, shared power more regularly, rooted out a core discrimination. Talented women found a home. "Most of the time my political comrades viewed my writing . . . as self-indulgent," Marge Piercy has recalled. "The big change for me came in the strong importance the women's movement placed and places now on cultural work."

Now women such as "a Venice sister" wrote honestly about real lives: "Then one night he said a bunch of people were getting together to make a woodwind tape for the light show and would I help out? He took me home afterward but couldn't stay because he had to go back and put out a mailing. After it sank in, this blew my mind: he asked me to help with the music, although my technique was clumsy, because he liked my musical ideas, and he didn't ask me to help with the mailing, women's work if there ever was."

Later, they became intimate.

"So I ground myself against his leg like he and all the other guys rubbed their penises against my belly—why should they get all the stimulation and not I, just because my belly happens to be right in front of their cock and their belly doesn't happen to be handy to my clitoris? . . . Hooh!" (Few papers, though, ran similar pieces about lesbians or gays.)

Others encountered less-ebullient but decidedly dedicated women:

"What I found were about fifteen women, terribly ideological but not necessarily wise in the ways of newspapers," writer Rita Mae Brown recalls about the *Rat,* which she joined after quitting NY-NOW because it had ignored lesbians. "These women were white and almost exclusively from the middle or upper middle classes . . . who have a disastrous tendency to be self-righteous. . . . Hell, it was easier being gay than being Southern among that group of reverse racists.

"Yet I came to like these grim, sincere women. They truly wanted to change our political/sexual system and this newspaper was their chance to speak to their own generation. . . . They began to connect the plight of non-American, cheap female labor to American profits. That was a revelation in those days, and the *Rat* women did try, I believe, to create an awareness of international politics concurrent with sexual politics."

But the explosion that was women's liberation split as well as healed. Men walked on eggshells, were criticized for not sharing abilities we weren't sure we had in the first place, wondered where we'd live in an

Amazon Nation or some other exclusionary land. And the question of whether women were on the Left or involved in women's liberation intensified. Weatherwomen at the *Rat* wanted to "Make Pigs Pay"; some feminists wanted to write favorably about women suing to get onto the police force.

As time went on, many women who stressed gender equality dropped out of the by-now not-so-New Left. "I left *Rat* with no recriminations," Rita Mae Brown recalls. "I felt they romanticized the groups they wished to align themselves with—fill in the blanks with chic oppressed non-American women. They wanted 'our' side to be good and the other side to be all bad, and kept taking 'gut checks' on one another. I went on to groups whose feminist sense was better formed and who decided—wisely, I believe—to concentrate on America as opposed to the entire world."

Robin Morgan's parting was more shocking. The God of Synchronicity had it begin in the *Rat* office, when a Weatherwoman saw her breastfeeding her son, a baby whose blanket sometimes was the "actively colored" red, blue, and yellow NLF flag.

"You have no right to have that pig [as in *white*] male baby," Morgan was told.

Stunned, Morgan looked down at "this funny, fat, sweet person who was sucking away at my breast."

"How can you say that?" she answered. "What should I do?"

"Put it in the garbage."

In a later, post-Weatherwomen, phase, *Rat* became *Women's Liberation*. By then, though, Morgan was off compiling *Sisterhood Is Powerful*. "I started calling myself a feminist," she recalls. "I was beginning to divorce myself from the idea of the Left as automatically good. That was a tremendous shock."

Feminism would be one of the sixties' lasting legacies, and hundreds of feminist institutions and newspapers would appear across the country. But in 1970, many highly energized women saw the changes at New Left and freak-oriented papers as tokenism, protection against charges of sexism, or a way to sell papers. "Because the Movement and underground press continues to treat us and our movement in the best male supremacist tradition, we must reexamine our relationships with it," Marilyn Salzman-Webb wrote in *off our backs* that April. "Many of us must leave the papers . . . and create new papers, magazines and radio programs that are solely to serve the women's movement." Many did, and their departure to a parallel but independent network weakened the multi-issue underground press.

THE PENTAGON MARCH had been planned. So had the Democratic Convention protests. Even Woodstock, that surprise breakfast in bed for three hundred thousand, built on a ballyhooed event.

By comparison, the birth of the gay-rights movement at the Stonewall Inn in Greenwich Village was an explosion looking for a place to detonate. By mid-1969, a critical mass of homosexual experience was primed for a chain reaction that would parallel feminism's relationship with the Movement and the underground press. As with the other movements, it had roots in the 1950s.

In 1951, the Mattachine Society began in Los Angeles, initially Leftist, attempting to secure within-the-system legal rights for homosexuals. Two years later, *One* magazine offered homosexual men something more serious than porn books or muscle magazines. In 1956, the *Ladder* appeared, published by lesbians affiliated with the recently formed Daughters of Bilitis.

Joe McCarthy's homophobic shadow was receding, and through the 1960s, alternative media helped gays inch out of the closet. In 1962, WBAI, the New York listener-sponsored FM radio station, broadcast a homosexual panel discussion. (The New York *Journal-American* christened the station "WSICK"; the *Realist* published the show's transcript; the then-liberal New York *Post* later exposed harassment of local homosexuals.) From its beginning, the *Barb* published gay personals and stories. Started in 1966, the *Advocate* lacked radical fervor, but its nonrhetorical news, lifestyle stories, and personals proved popular. The Summer-of-Love Haight had hosted the *Vanguard,* a peace-and-drugs gay monthly.

In 1967, the Oscar Wilde Memorial Book Store opened in Greenwich Village with a newsletter and the claim that it was "bringing Gay Power to New York." But in mid-1969, homosexuality remained illegal everywhere in America except Illinois.

On the full-moon Friday of June 27, 1969, men were twisting and trysting at the Stonewall when eight morals-squad policemen raided it for serving liquor without a license. Employees were arrested; ID-less patrons, and cross-dressers, were detained.

Standard procedure earned a surprising response. Previously, suit-and-tie-wearing gays had politely challenged liquor laws that forbade public drinking by overt homosexuals (instead of protecting them from both the Mafia and the police). But the clientele at this large, dark dance bar included dopers, transvestites, and other nonmainstreamers with less to lose than hide-and-seek businessmen. The angry eruption that followed marked the birth of a liberation movement.

But not for most Movement people, at least not right away. "I'll never forget calling up all my political friends and saying, 'There's a riot,' " says Jim Fouratt, Yippie and record-company executive turned sexual revolutionary. "At that time, when three people rioted anyplace, you could get a demonstration together. I could not get anyone to come, because it was gays."

Print coverage also missed the event's importance. The New York *Times* carried it as a crime story. In terms of its later espousal of gay causes, the *Village Voice*'s treatment was far more ironic. Lucian Truscott IV, a former West Pointer and the *Voice*'s Man Outside the Stonewall, wrote a well-crafted but bemused feature about how "the forces of faggotry" had traded "limp wrists" for beercans, bottles, and a parking meter turned battering ram. Howard Smith, the paper's Mr. Inside, recounted how he'd found himself trapped not with proud gays but with beseiged cops using a fire hose and their fists to avoid battery and immolation. Smith had baptized a wrench as his "scimitar"—for potential defense against gays, not cops.

Underground papers frequently attacked the *Times* for emphasizing violence in its stories on the Movement; now the *Rat* reveled in it. "The cops inside were scared shitless, dodging projectiles and flying glass. The orgy was taking place. Vengeance vented against the source of repression," said a story entitled "Queen Power: Fags Against Pigs in Stonewall Bust." *EVO* offered sterotypes. "The fags have had it with oppression. Revolution is being heard on Christopher Street, only instead of guttural MC-5 voices, we hear it coming from sopranos and altos."

Rat published the Gay Liberation Front's (GLF) statement of purpose, which condemned "this rotten, dirty, vile, fucked-up capitalist conspiracy" and linked gay rights with "all the oppressed: the Vietnamese struggle, the third world, the blacks, the workers." But most straight writers subsumed gay rights as a junior partner in the revolution, or no partner at all. The Young Socialist Alliance expelled a gay activist. Peaceniks tried to furl the GLF's banner at a demonstration. The GLF had held its first rally at the Women's House of Detention in Greenwich Village to support imprisoned Black Panthers, but Eldridge Cleaver wrote in his biography, *Soul on Ice,* that "Homosexuality is a sickness, just as are baby-rape or wanting to become the head of General Motors." Hips tended to be more accepting—yet Claudia Dreifus quit *EVO* after late-night layout gremlins luridly illustrated her story about an assaulted-in-jail draft resister. Openly gay staffers covering gay themes were few and far between.

In November, several Movement veterans "came out"—discussed their homosexuality—in *Win,* the magazine of the War Resisters League. Yet staff member David McReynolds did so with "a three-Miltown-a-day" pause. The League was a venerable peace group, *Win* a magazine with many older readers. "Do I have the right," he asked, "to threaten [its] public image . . . by a 'personal honesty' of this kind?

"My life must be all of a piece or it is shoddy," McReynolds decided —but with very mixed feelings.

"The black ghetto is alive, even if brutalized and repressed. Life flows from it. Children are conceived in it. The gay ghetto is a voluntary separation in which nothing lives, nothing is painful or dirty or gives birth.

". . . the cry for 'Gay Power' is, in a way, an effort to draw on the strength of the blacks, and in a way that is good. . . . I know faggot eyes too well, tragic cows seated on bar chairs . . . frightened, huddled together for strength. . . . If gay power can give any inner power to those eyes, those desperate eyes that I've seen in the bars of this nation, then okay, I'm for the slogan. But I'm not for the gay ghetto."

No wonder gays were publishing their own radical papers. The Gay Liberation Front's *Come Out!* appeared the same month as the *Win* issue, then turned independent of its founding organization. *Come Out!* was relatively short-lived, but, like the feminist *Rat* and other women's-liberation papers, it explored theories about living arrangements, gender, aggression, environment vs. heredity, and other emerging issues.

The staff of *Come Out!* saw itself as a group of Left revolutionaries, but soon this was not the only viewpoint in the gay movement, or the gay press. Founded in December, the Gay Activist Alliance (GAA) used its *Gay Activist* to discuss both gender politics and protective civil rights. The Bay Area's *Gay Sunshine* explored sexual liberation, celebrated gay achievements and the radical counterculture; the pamphlets of the Red Butterfly Cell were more Marxist-oriented. *Gay Power* and *Gay* were less-political papers from *EVO*'s and *Screw*'s publishers.

Through 1969 and 1970, gay publications ran position papers, personal views, news, and features that moved gay militance far beyond earlier petitions for acceptance. Reportorial and rhetorical excesses appeared, but the papers fostered personal legitimacy, community spirit, and political activism. Protesters zapped city-council meetings and trials, and criticized the New York *Post* for telling gays to keep a low profile at peace rallies. After *Harper's* printed an article that wanted to "wish homosexuality off the face of the earth," a score of activists occupied the magazine's office. Among them was Arthur Bell, who'd helped organized the GAA and come out in *Gay Power.* "I'm not sure it did the slightest good," a codemonstrator said after the action. "Yes it did," said Bell, who blended longhair softness with the righteous indignation of the gay-lib lambda he wore on his T-shirts. "It did a lot of good, for us." Demonstrators convinced the *Village Voice* to use "gay" in its classified pages. In June, 1970, when activists were arrested in New York for protesting Governor Rockefeller's policies, Bell wrote it up for the *Voice,* and stayed to become the paper's first openly gay staff writer.

Lesbians also were developing their politics in print.

In 1967, the *Ladder* had suggested that lesbians shared more with heterosexual women than with homosexual men; now, in May, 1970, Rita Mae Brown and several other Radicalesbians issued "The Woman-Identified Woman," a manifesto proclaiming their sexuality as the vanguard of women's liberation. "It is the primacy of women relating to women, of women creating a new consciousness of and with each other, which is at the heart of women's liberation, and the basis for the cultural revolution."

Not all women agreed, and lesbians began shifting their attention. "I don't believe the core *Rat* group ever . . . understood the connection between their perceptions of gay people and men's perception of them as young women," Brown writes. "They were busy discovering themselves as oppressed people and could not, at that time, take any responsibility for passing that oppression downward."

Rat did run Martha Shelley's "Gay Is Good" and other key pieces. But those Brown calls "well-intentioned lesbians" had a tough time working on underground papers. "If the gay woman wrote what the staff wanted (meaning 'forget about this gay shit') she was OK. Subconsciously, the straight women still wanted the approval of the men in their peer group.

"There was also the confusion over the Marxist puritanism of Soviet Russia and China, which states that gay people are a decadent by-product of capitalism."

Consequently, lesbians began espousing their politics at papers such as *It Ain't Me Babe* and Denver's *Big Mama Rag.*

Many gay men were moving on, too. "I wasn't really interested in the underground press," Arthur Bell, who was more militant than most, would tell me. "I was more interested in the *Voice,* in the *Times.* I have no reason to hate the world."

OUTLAWS OF AMERIKA

14

APOCALYPSE NOW

HICAGO, ILLINOIS—DECEMBER 4, 1969: It was an unlikely place for a press conference, a rundown railroad flat in the heart of Chicago's West Side ghetto. Yet the moderators had the rapt attention of the reporters they led past a bloodsoaked mattress in a room where the walls bore twenty-three bullet holes. Early that morning, Fred Hampton, the Black Panther Party's Illinois chairman, had been killed here. Peoria Defense Captain Mark Clark had died too, and four others in the apartment had been wounded. A police raid had brought the war home in a sudden, shocking way. It was the first of a series of events that would strain Movement dedication and underground writing, and climax horribly in May at Kent State University.

Fred Hampton had entered the civil rights movement through an NAACP youth group in Maywood, Illinois. Life in a suburb in the North's most segregated metropolitan area led him to join the Panthers, and with the white Young Patriots and the brown Young Lords, forge a Rainbow Coalition. Hampton implemented the Panthers' free Breakfast for Children program. He also placed a "pig" under citizen's arrest, and was himself convicted for some vague distribution of an ice-cream vendor's wares. His chapter's members were armed, but he denounced the Weathermen's Days of Rage as "Custeristic." Many—including the FBI—acknowledged his vibrant leadership.

Still, by late 1969, Chicago police and Panthers had died in unpremeditated shootouts, and the chapter was

223

hard-pressed by the power of its enemy, its militancy, and a lack of money and members. Then came the raid. When the smoke cleared, nearly a hundred shots had been fired by the police, one or two by the Panthers. "Chairman Fred," twenty-one, and Mark Clark, twenty-two, were dead.

In Chicago, that Bloody Thursday split the mass media. Accepting official reality, the *Tribune* misidentified nail holes in the apartment's door as Panther bullet holes, and reported a Panther-instigated "wild gun battle with police." Cook County State's Attorney Edward V. Hanrahan, who'd planned the raid in conjunction with the FBI, staged his version of events on local television. The Panthers did not get equal airtime.

Meanwhile, *Daily News* columnist Mike Royko questioned the state's attorney's story and knocked down the *Tribune*'s exclusive. But Royko also called the coaliton-building Panthers "racists . . . who hoard guns and preach violence." Reporter Brian Boyer quit the *Sun-Times,* claiming that his story highly critical of the police had been buried. In the black community and among radical whites, the word "assassination" was heard.

The *Seed* people shuttled between the house on West Monroe and our office, preparing a thirty-five-thousand-copy broadside that, among other things, extended our rhetoric into uncharted territory. That summer, Marshall Rosenthal, the paper's most pacifist writer, had worried that running a picture of a cop giving a photographer the finger would get the staff beaten up. Now he went beyond his horror to proclaim that "We're not going to be free until our brothers and sisters in the black community are free . . . through every means necessary." Skeets Millard, heir turned SDSer turned underground writer and photographer, stayed at Panther headquarters after the raid, to take pictures, and to provide a pale shield from more police bullets. "This is war, people," he wrote under the nom de guerre Armando. "If you haven't chosen, you must soon."

For me, it had been a long four months—Woodstock, the *Rat,* the Conspiracy trial. Now Fred Hampton's death brought me back to my *Seed* family. "When we left the house that blood built," I wrote about the Panthers' charnel house, "we knew that the road back had been sealed by the avalanche of what we had seen." But race, education, and a real dislike for guns made that an evocative untruth. And what did it mean to end the piece with the words "Bring the ghetto home?" Kill a cop? Kill me too? Would we have written about "murder" no matter what had happened, voicing politics rather than reporting?

Fred Hampton became more powerful in death than in life. The *Seed*'s scheduled issue denounced "the filthy lie" of a Panther attack on the police, linked the killings to other anti-Panther raids, noted that Panther leader David Hilliard had been arrested for threatening death while Fred Hampton's slayers remained at large. There were no murder indictments, and Hanrahan, police, and others connected with the raid were acquitted in 1972 of charges of conspiracy to obstruct justice. A $47.7 million suit by survivors and relatives in 1970 failed in 1977 after the longest civil trial in U.S. history.

But in 1972, State's Attorney Hanrahan was ousted by the coalition of blacks and white liberals that eleven years later elected Harold Washington the Mayor of Chicago. During the trials, evidence emerged of an FBI campaign against the Panthers, including details that the Chicago chapter's security chief was an informer who'd helped plan the raid. A reinstated suit was settled in 1982 for $1.85 million, and in 1983 Bobby Rush, once the local Panther Minister of Defense, was elected as a Chicago alderman. Brian Boyer became a mayoral speechwriter.

In late 1969, though, the *Seed* cover was a collage of Malcolm X, Ché Guevara, Lenny Bruce, Ho Chi Minh, Martin Luther King, Jr., jazz saxophonist John Coltrane, and a raised-fisted Fred Hampton.

All of them were dead.

EVEN AS Fred Hampton was being mourned by radicals in Chicago, three hundred thousand fans gathered on December 6 to take rock 'n' roll communion at the Altamont Speedway, a stockcar-racing track southeast of San Francisco. The bands were publicly held myths—the Airplane, Santana, and, above all, ladies and gentlemen, the Rolling Stones. The ideal was Woodstock revisited. Reality was grimmer. At Woodstock, off-duty cops had winked at pot-smoking. At Altamont, security was provided by Hell's Angels bikers, who soon proved themselves the true outlaws of America.

The Angels had peacefully guarded be-ins and concerts; here pool cues were wielded against anyone who "threatened" the stage, their bikes, their authority. Jefferson Airplane stalwart Marty Balin was beaten after protesting the violence. A flute-playing, wolf's-head-wearing Angel held center stage, defying the Stones and the world, celebrating the bikers' lupine ability to dominate a much larger number of sheep. "We had talked about solidarity, but they, not us, were willing to go down for each other in a showdown," Sol Stern later wrote in *Ramparts*.

It wasn't only the Angels who were shredding the Woodstock image.

"There was this big, fat guy in Bermuda shorts, real woozy," *Rolling Stone* writer Tim Cahill recalls. "He sat on a guy and grabbed his girl's tits. Nobody in this place where we were all mellow said anything—including, I'm afraid, me."

Then, as the Stones played "Under My Thumb," Angels pushed, grabbed, and beat a young black man named Meredith Hunter. He pulled a revolver; Angels stabbed, beat, and kicked him to death.

"STONES CREATE ANOTHER WOODSTOCK," *Variety* headlined as it and most of the daily papers rushed to celebrate the last story. Underground coverage, in contrast, discussed the down side of apocalypse. "The End of the Age of Aquarius," Todd Gitlin wrote in an LNS piece, was about "a generation . . . stripping itself naked" and "the star system; messiahs on the cheap. . . . If the Rolling Stones are part of the family," Gitlin asked, "why don't they turn back their profits into family enterprises?"

Gitlin centered on the stage. "Dots on the periphery of a large circle, with the music at the center. . . . Dots will not take responsibility for each other. Dots will crawl over each other to get a better piece of the real action—the center—the 'really heavy music.' . . . The question is whether the youth culture will leave anything behind but a market."

Gitlin was onto something; rock would continue to grow, but divide into performers and audience, sellers and consumers, "product" and "units," white and black music, art rock and heavy metal. In more ways than one, Mick Jagger had been prescient to wear an omega on his T-shirt. Something had snapped at Altamont.

It was a third reportorial force, *Rolling Stone,* that most acutely caught the shift from rock dreams to bitter awakening. Initially, writer Greil Marcus and managing editor John Burks wanted to quickly deal with a bad day at the racetrack; news of Hunter's slaying changed that. With Jann Wenner's focus and all-hands-on-deck files, *Rolling Stone's* "Let It Bleed" issue became an eighteen-page, fifty-photo attack on greed, carelessness, and violence.

The story had its shortfalls. "It tried too hard to say how exactly how many cars were parked on this side of the road at this hour," Marcus recalls. Wenner hired Jon Lombardi of the Philadelphia *Free Press* after the undergrounder knocked the premise that Altamont was "The Death of Rock Culture." But, Jann continues, it "ended certain notions about how groovy everything was, and how everything was going to take care of itself." Gitlin's story was apt commentary about a Movement in crisis; *Rolling Stone* outreported everyone, while forcing hips to examine their values. In 1971 the magazine won Columbia University's National Magazine Award for Specialized Journalism, earning mainstream respect even as it challenged the underground press's claim to the youth culture.

OVER THE first eight days of December, the week of death in Chicago and at Altamont, Charles Manson and his "family" of desert rats were indicted in Los Angeles for a series of murders that included the August slaughter of actress Sharon Tate and friends. The houseful of people had been stabbed, slashed, choked, and dismembered; Tate had been pregnant.

The underground press paused over the arrests. In the past, indictments had been challenged, though sometimes that had more to do with gut feeling, blind faith, or political prejudgment than real knowledge or investigative prowess. Most staffs had more police defendants than police reporters, and, as *Rolling Stone* would say, freaks in general were "hypersensitive to the relentless gloating of the cops who, after a five-year-search, finally found a longhaired devil you could love to hate." That included some big cops: "Manson Guilty, Nixon Declares," would be only one headline as the case moved along amid mass-press frenzy.

Those indicted were longhaired Haight-Ashbury vets who made music, took LSD, and lived communally (while trying to foment a civilization-ending race war). Some undergrounders defended freaks against what San Francisco's *Good Times,* the granola-esque successor to the *Express Times,* called "a public frenzy of hate and fear not only against Manson but also against communes and longhairs in general." Others went further, and paid in credibility. The L.A. *Free Press* gave Manson a column. *Tuesday's Child,* an allegedly hipper L.A. paper, ran a photo of him cut by a large diagonal proclaiming "Man of the Year: Charles Manson"; its next issue depicted him as a crucified hippie. Both papers ran free ads for Manson's record (though the *Free Press*'s bookstores refused to sell it). Even *Rolling Stone*'s substantial, more skeptical special report ballyhooed "The incredible story of the most dangerous man alive," while asking the underground's magic question: "Is Manson a hippie?"

Ed Sanders found his own grisly answer. The Fug, peace creep, and poet was writing *The Family,* the definitive freak's-eye reconstruction of Manson's "commune of hackers" that would hold its own next to prosecutor Vincent Bugliosi's *Helter Skelter.* In a series of stories for the *Free Press,* Sanders detailed how the penal system had helped mold Manson and argued that an entire lifestyle shouldn't be indicted along with a few werewolves. But one night, a source put a photograph on a bar that made Sanders nearly upchuck his vodka tonic. There was once-lovely Sharon Tate, eyes open, belly sliced, a rope around her neck.

"It was beyond the worst visual experience for me in my life," Sanders recalls. "I realized that anything that supported that type of behavior was something I was totally opposed to with all my moral being."

Others on the Left would be seduced. Here's Jerry Rubin describing his jailhouse visit to Manson:

"I fell in love with Charlie Manson the first time I saw his cherub face and sparkling eyes on national TV. . . .

"We met Gypsy and Squeaky, two of the Manson Family not in jail, and they were outasight. Squeaky is tiny with a squeaky voice, blond hair, blue eyes, and a face and smile you'd trust. She's supposed to have offed a couple of people but I don't believe it. Squeaky? No! . . .

"Charlie entered. I tried to shake hands or embrace. . . . His words and courage inspired [me] . . . and I felt great the rest of the day, overwhelmed by the depth of the experience of touching Manson's soul. . . .

"He said he was innocent of the Tate murders and was being persecuted by the pigs because of his lifestyle. . . ."

Was Manson innocent or guilty? "What is innocence and what is guilt?"

The Weathermen were asking a similar question.

By now, the SDS vanguard/remnant was intensifying every axiom of Left politics and freak lifestyle. If need be, they were prepared to kamikaze on behalf of Third World Liberation. Their antibourgeois morality had them, as one flyer put it, "moving, dancing, fucking, doing dope, knowing our bodies as part of our lives, becoming animals again after centuries of repression and uptightness." At the same time, they demanded Korrect Sexual Behavior of each other.

Three weeks after Manson's indictment, the Weathermen held their War Council in Flint, Michigan. A pantheon of red-and-black posters covered the walls of the Giant Ballroom: Bobby and Huey and Fidel, more of martyred Ché and Malcolm, a necro-wave of the just-murdered Fred (who, ironically, had denounced the Days of Rage). White dismissals of "honkies" and cries of "piece [as in *weapon*] now" rang out under a large papier-mâché machine gun. A karate lesson resembled a Saint Vitus Dance class. Some attendees sang entries from a forthcoming songbook:

> He's a real Weatherman
> Ripping up the motherland . . .
> Knows just what he's fighting for
> Victory for people's war
> Trashes, bombs
> Kills pigs and more—
> The Weatherman.

At one point, Weather-leader Bernardine Dohrn discussed the Manson Family's butchering of a white, middle-class couple named Leno and Rosemary LaBianca, which had come complete with a carving fork plunged into the dead man's stomach. Ignoring a slew of contradictions for radicals—Manson's racism, his treating women as sex objects and brood sows, general human decency—Dohrn saluted new partners in outrageousness: "Offing those rich pigs with their own forks and knives, and then eating a meal in the same room—far out!" Some attendees gave a new greeting: four fingers held up, slightly spread: a fork.

After the council, the group went underground, to bring the war home.

"Weatherman is a logical consequence of intellectual flabbiness and dishonesty on the Left as a whole," a then non-Marxist socialist named Hendrik Hertzberg (now editor of the *New Republic*) declared in a *Win* symposium. He offered examples: verbal overkill, a double standard that called the U.S. a police state while exempting the Soviet Union and the People's Republic of China, an acceptance of violence that lacked military meaning and outraged most Americans—trends also widely represented in the underground press.

In the *Seed,* Skeets disagreed for both political and visceral reasons. "A debate now rages within Weatherman as to whether killing white babies is correct," he wrote. "In perfectly logical terms, it is. Pleased to meet you, hope you guess my name. . . . There is Weatherman in nearly all of us. There is Altamont lame-out hippie in all of us, even the Weathermen. The Weatherman side of us is probably the better and stronger side, if only in that I'd rather have Weathermen on my side than lame-out passive hippies."

It was such a long way from the condolence card Marshall Rosenthal had sent Sharon Tate's husband, Roman Polanski.

BATTERED EQUIPMENT and a flood of paper littered the offices of the *Street Journal,* San Diego's Leftist underground newspaper. Two days after the break-in, the front page of the paper's January 16 issue catalogued a long train of abuses under the headline "WHEN WILL WE STOP THIS TERRORISM?"—a firebombed car, $4,000 in destroyed machinery, twenty-five hundred papers stolen, a raided fundraiser, busted staff and street vendors. Elsewhere in the community, a free school, local bookstores, and law offices bore bullet and bomb damage. "Where," the editorial asked, "will the fascist perverts strike next?"

Why was a paper with a circulation of eight thousand receiving all this attention? In 1967 and 1968, Herbert Marcuse, the radical professor who'd coined the idea of "repressive tolerance" to explain how democracies maintain their power, had been physically threatened by local Far Rightists and severely criticized by the San Diego dailies. Some of his graduate students had guarded him from the former, and then had decided to start a radical paper to counter the latter. Their *Free Press* soon became the *Street Journal,* an eclectic Leftist weekly that printed sections from the Black Panthers and the Brown Berets, a Chicano organization. Twenty-five or so *Press*ers established a People's Commune, which did everything from run a general store and a soup kitchen to produce military and feminist newspapers.

Unlike some of its counterparts, the *Street Journal* wanted to rake muck as well as rhetoric. In October, 1969, it had begun detailing the financial dealings of San Diego's power elite, among them leading banker and Nixon supporter C. Arnholt Smith. The *Wall Street Journal* had broken the story in June, but San Diego's mass media had largely sat on it. And the *Street Journal*'s politics were decidedly to the left of the other *Journal*'s.

The general response in San Diego was less than sympathetic to the *Street Journal.* "It was basically a southern military town," then-staffer Lowell Bergman recalls. "When I first got there in 1966, one cop threw me up against the wall for walking down the street and told me they'd run all the hippies out of town." Now there were warrantless searches of both the paper and the commune, and nuisance visits from fire inspectors. An undercover policeman infiltrated the staff. Vending machines were confiscated, a hundred twenty street-sellers arrested. A prospective landlord was persuaded, with a subsequently dropped murder charge, to break a lease.

Continuing to publish, the staff placed rifle-toting guards at each People's Commune house. There were night visits from the Secret Army Organization, successor to the Far Right Minutemen, and a near-clash with armed members of the black-nationalist US organization, which resented the paper's Black Panther ties. One day, two staffers visiting a right-wing gunstore they'd covered learned that it was stocking pistols called "Lowell-shooters."

The *Street Journal* situation was only one skirmish among many around the country. At the *Seed,* we were working late when a bullet shattered the front window. Two weeks later, it happened again. Finally, our assailants—we'd christened them "The Pistoleros"—presented themselves: two gun-toting, pizza-faced, leather-jacketed teens angry about "hippies" and "Commies." Hippies at heart, Marshall Rosenthal and I tried to talk them onto our side. After some back and forth, they left, returned to toss some rusty guns through our plate glass, then vanished. We were more holy fools than brave guys.

A few blocks away, *Second City* was under attack by vigilantes from the Far Right Legion of Justice organization, the putative parents of our Pistolero pests. After *Second City* reported attacks on Chicago-area offices of the Socialist Workers Party, Legion members invaded the Guild Bookstore, the paper's home, on two occasions. When a lone staffer pulled a legal gun, a dozen cops arrested him and pressed charges that cost time and money to beat.

Houston's *Space City* was bombed; Stoney Burns, the Dallas *Notes* editor who'd exposed a hit-and-run incident by subsequent underground-press enemy Congressman Joe Pool, was sentenced to ten years imprisonment on a minor drug charge that the American Civil Liberties Union called a conspiracy. Roger Priest, a Navy man who published the antiwar *Om,* was convicted of "promoting disloyalty and disaffection" after a surveillance campaign involving twenty-five undercover agents and his garbage. Papers lost printers and advertisers.

With a circulation of a hundred thousand, the *Black Panther* continued to attract special attention. Paper shipments were overbilled, or hosed down in transit. In June, the FBI's Newark office suggested that "an opportunity might arise to spray the [Panther] papers with a chemical known as Skatole (C_9H_9N). A very small amount of this chemical disburses a most offensive odor. . . . It is believed that this measure was previously considered as a move to affect distribution of the *Worker.*"

In *UnAmerican Activities: The Campaign Against the Underground Press,* the PEN American Center Report that details many of these actions, editor Geoffrey Rips and investigator Angus Mackenzie document that Far Right groups received money, tear gas, Mace, and surveillance equipment from military intelligence and local Red Squads. In 1975, Secret Army Organization leader Howard Berry Godfrey and American Civil Liberties Union lawyers would tell Congress that the FBI and San Diego police had recruited and trained SAO members to attack the *Street Journal* and other Leftists (the FBI denied the claim).

Late in 1984, C. Arnholt Smith would be sentenced to prison after being convicted in 1979 on charges of grand theft and tax fraud. But by August, 1970, the *Street Journal* was gone; a sectarian version would linger, then fold. Twenty-four-hour togetherness, gender battles, and the antimoney ethic had played their divisive roles. And, as Laurence Leamer would point out in his underground-press study *The Paper Revolutionaries,* "the harassment of underground papers pushes them relentlessly, inexorably away from the trust and openness that once was at the essence of the Movement."

FEBRUARY 18 saw the conclusion of the trial of the Chicago Seven (down from eight after Bobby Seale's severance from the case). The jury acquitted academics Lee Weiner and John Froines of all charges. All defendants were absolved of conspiracy. Abbie Hoffman, Jerry Rubin, Dave Dellinger, Tom Hayden, and Rennie Davis were individually convicted for crossing state lines to incite a riot. Judge Julius Hoffman then spent two days handing out 175 contempt citations worth nineteen years of prison time to the eight defendants and to lawyers William Kunstler and Leonard Weinglass. In Seale's and Kunstler's cases, the contempt sentences ranged as high as four years, though neither had been convicted under the original indictment.

The underground press reacted with the rage of partisans who'd watched friends and comrades bake for five months in "the neon oven." Papers reprinted the defendants' searing speeches, as well as curses against the judge and "the system." Covers showed a skull-faced Statue of Liberty. "Don't Bank on Amerika" articles praised the destruction of the Isla Vista, California, branch of the Bank of America in one of The Day After demonstrations that erupted over the verdicts.

(Two years later, underground-press claims that the government's case was a loser began prevailing when the U.S. Court of Appeals overturned the verdict and many of the contempt citations, stating that "the demeanor of the judge and the prosecutors would require reversal if other errors did not."

(In 1973, U.S. District Court Judge Edward T. Gignoux, Mr. Rogers to Judge Hoffman's Mr. Hyde, reversed all but thirteen of the remaining citations and voided outstanding jail time.

(Then, in 1976, Jerry Rubin wrote an infamous Chicago *Sun-Times* guest column that, among other things, questioned the underground press's key assumption around the trial: "We WANTED disruption. We PLANNED it. We WERE NOT innocent victims. . . . Guilty as hell. Guilty as charged."

("I told you so," Judge Hoffman pronounced. Peace activists, even codefendants, criticized Jerry for distorting their politics and speaking for them. Abbie Hoffman split the difference, saying that Jerry was guilty but he was innocent.

("It was a mistake to say 'we' and 'guilty,' Jerry says in the eighties. "What I was saying was that we"—ironic word—"wanted a confrontation. We were not innocent.

("If it were God and not Julius Hoffman, I would liked to have stood up and said, 'A country that is bombing Vietnam should have a riot in its center so that it can look at itself and make necessary changes, not ignore the reality that we are dropping bombs on people in Vietnam. The city officials are crazy enough that instead of figuring out how to co-opt us, they will do the same to us that they did to the Vietnamese, and use force.'

("But Julius said, 'This is not a political trial and your views of Vietnam are irrelevant here'—so my defense would not have been allowed. [Hoffman and Daley] were corrupt, and that we tried to come across as victims doesn't reduce their corruption. They were essentially more corrupt than we were because they were part of the violent system of Vietnam."

During the conspiracy trial, Jerry had a surprising reservation. "Around 1969, 1970," he says now, "I looked at the Movement meetings and said, 'I wouldn't trust these people with power.' " Others included Jerry in that reservation. At the *Seed,* Marshall Rosenthal panned Jerry's *Do It* for easy rhetoric, then broke with the generally increasing stress on violence. "Guns. I won't become a pig. . . . I do not want to perform anti-evolutionary acts, even at the price of being called counterrevolutionary. I will not eat the flesh of another animal; how can I think of rending the flesh of another human?"

The Movement had opposed the war; now politics, rage, repression, hate, adrenaline led its edge—its proclaimed leading edge—to war against a society seen as irredeemably racist, imperialist, sexist, fascist. The NLF, Mao, the Black Panthers were heroic, beyond criticism. Cops were "pigs." America became first a Kafka-esque "Amerika," then a Ku Klux Klan "Amerikkka." The *Seed's* "Spring Equinox Survival Supplement" excerpted both *The Whole Earth Catalog* and *Firearms and Self-Defense.* Even reaction could feed into the idea of an inevitable victory.

"People have asked me how I stood the beating and what I was thinking about," an arrested activist wrote in *Leviathan* about a post-demonstration police encounter. "What I did think about was Bobby Seale and Nguyen Van Troi, the VC fighter who was assasinated for attempting to kill [Defense Secretary Robert] McNamara when he visited Vietnam. . . . The name Bobby Seale was like armor I put on to shield the pigs' blows. Nguyen Van Troi is a light inside the heart.

"I'm sitting writing this in a room. All around the room are OSPA-AAL posters from Cuba, posters proclaiming Days of Solidarity with people all over the world struggling for National Liberation. . . . It's that feeling of solidarity with people fighting the pigs of the world I have."

The writer had been transported from one precinct to another with several demonstrators, among them "a beautiful hippie" who'd traded in peace-and-love for something stronger. "He had been beat on but was still going strong. He rapped with the cops about Tom Jefferson, communes, Senator Joseph McCarthy, the *Rat,* about Communism. . . . He would have taken on those pigs then and there if they had unhandcuffed him. My head was aching, my legs and arms were bruised, but inside, in my bones, this kid made me feel that the Revolution was coming. No mistake about it."

On March 6, the Berkeley *Tribe,* owned collectively and circulating fifty-three thousand after its split with Max Scherr, called for a People's Militia—"To defend ourselves against mounting pig terror, we must take up the gun." That day, Weathermen three thousand miles away were working on taking the offensive.

The organization had gone underground in February, a few guerillas moved by ties with Third World revolutionaries and a primal discontent with Amerika. Weathermen had firebombed the home of the presiding judge in the Panther Twenty-one trial (and were praised in the *Rat*), then, after prolonged argument, decided that the use of U.S. antipersonnel weapons in Vietnam justified using them at home. Now one of its guerilla cells was manufacturing a bomb in a Greenwich Village townhouse when it exploded prematurely. Ted Gold, Diana Oughton, and Terry Robbins died. Kathy Boudin fled, on a run that would end after gunshots erupted around an ambushed Brink's truck late in 1981.

Still, the edge extended. In the spring of 1968, there had been ten bombings on college campuses, including ROTC buildings, defense-industry labs, and the like. Over the 1969–70 school year, at least one hundred seventy-four such events would occur, along with seventy or more at offices, armories, and other likely installations.

On April 3, the *Tribe* ran an article called "Responsible Terrorism," which changed the argument from whether bombing was right to the ethics of targeting: "With several hundred successful bombings through-out the country in the last year, the movement rose from frustration to the pulse-quickening embrace of concerted revolutionary action." But "Good-hearted revolutionary fools" with sloppy plans were denounced. "The hip community has to make clear that only certain sabotage opera-tions serve the people, that carefully selected institutions which enslave people should be the targets, and that lives should be spared."

There was also irresponsible terrorism by "revolutionary fools." Over two issues, the *Rat* would print a Weatherman bombing leaflet, then warn about errors in it. "It is ridiculously foolish to think that reading an article in an underground paper is enough preparation to work with any dangerous chemicals," the item cautioned. "It was a serious political mistake for *Rat* to print this leaflet without a postscript explaining that the contents were not checked out by the staff and were not intended as a recipe for *Rat* readers."

On April 8 in Yosemite, California, Governor Ronald Wilson Reagan threw down the system's gauntlet. "If it takes a bloodbath, let's get it over with," he told the Council of California Growers. "No more appeasement."

"The freakout is almost complete," wrote Jaacov Kohn, *EVO*'s editor, in mid-April. "The nightmare is becoming more and more of a reality and the laugh is on those who refused to take their paranoia seriously." A back-cover poster for the "6th Spring Demonstration to End the War against Vietnam" was captioned, "If You Think We're Tired, Ask the Vietnamese How They Feel."

Like their movements, the papers were involved in a strange dialectic of growth and exhaustion. LNS had six hundred regular subscribers, and on April 5 the New York *Times* ran a story called "Underground Papers Are Thriving on Campuses and in Cities Across Nation."

Together, Movements and papers lashed out, and imploded:

• *April 12*—In New York, the *Guardian*'s Workers Collective, aided by supporters from *Rat, WIN,* the Gay Liberation Front, Newsreel, and Women's Liberation, occupied the pre-underground paper. Was the paper stressing traditional, class-based Marxism to the point of ignoring Third World liberation movements? Was power being equitably shared? "Confronting their oppressors wherever they find them," the rebels said. "Weatherman terror tactics," in-house editors replied. The staffs split into *Guardian* and *Liberated Guardian*—a paper for each faction.

• *April 15*—Moratorium demonstrations blanketed the country. There were battles over ROTC in Berkeley, firebombings at Penn State. On April 19, the Moratorium Committee, by now relatively moderate, dissolved. "There is little prospect of immediate change in the administration's policy in Vietnam," spokesmen announced.

• *Late April*—The New York office of the Committee to Defend the Panther Twenty-One was torched, as was a Movement coffeehouse in Los Angeles. Coffeehouse operators were jailed in Columbia, South Carolina; Legion of Justice members were acquitted in Chicago.

• *April 24 to May 1*—Yale University President Kingman Brewster and Vice-President Spiro Agnew clashed over whether black revolutionaries could receive fair trials in the U.S. As thousands converged on New Haven to protest the murder trial of Bobby Seale and other Black Panthers, papers echoed cries for freeing Seale "by any means necessary."

· *April 30*—The invasion of Cambodia was announced as a "protective response" against a never-to-be-found NLF headquarters.

· *May 1 and 2*—President Nixon railed against "these bums . . . blowing up the campuses" even as American troops were blowing up portions of Southeast Asia. ROTC buildings were firebombed at Hobart, Tulane, Oregon—and Kent State University, in Ohio. "When dissent turns to violence," Nixon said, "it invites tragedy."

· *May 4*—Members of Troop G of the 107th Armored Cavalry Regiment of the Ohio National Guard grouped atop "Blanket Hill" at Kent State. After demonstration, taunts, and a few rocks, thirteen seconds of sustained rifle fire from the guardsmen killed four unarmed "bums," wounded nine.

These were not the first students to die at the hands of the authorities. On February 8, 1968, three had been shot to death at South Carolina State, in Orangeburg. Many more had been slain in Mexico City during the summer of 1968.

But the four Kent State students were white Americans, and their deaths convulsed the country. No longer were Columbia and Berkeley the only hotbeds; within three days, students at 437 schools were on strike, among them Whittier, Smith, Amherst, and Finch, the Presidential family's colleges. ROTC buildings at Utah and Idaho were bombed. Nearly sixty firebombs exploded at the University of Wisconsin at Madison. A dozen people were wounded by police gunfire at the University of Buffalo; ten were bayonetted at the University of New Mexico.

A revived Moratorium Committee and seventy-five to a hundred thousand people marched on Washington. Nixon spent an hour at the Lincoln Memorial, telling demonstrators that the world's main problem was the search for "the meaning of life," then left—amazingly, without incident. Demonstrators massed in Paris, Berlin, London.

"The four victims did nothing that justifies their deaths" was the conclusion of the 1971 study by the mainstream Knight Newspaper/ American Newspaper Publishers Association Foundation, *Reporting the Kent State Incident.* The decision to invade Cambodia, not any SDS agitation, was "the prime and immediate cause of the trouble."

Moreover, the report continued, the media deck was stacked in favor of authority: "So we are left with an adversary proceeding, with the National Guard on one side and the students on the other. One side is allowed to speak through the media; the other is not. In a fair encounter, we are told, truth will ever emerge victorious. But when only one side enters the arena, what then?"

Still, the report dismissed the idea of each side telling its own story as a process that "would produce no truth and much chaos."

To be at *EVO,* the *Seed,* or the *Tribe* that week, though, was to engage in a People's Telethon. The phones never found their cradles, as activists and writers from other towns called in their angry street actions, or we called out. "March in Ann Arbor, with trashing at the ROTC building." "Dig this—LNS says Alaska Methodist University is on strike." And a hundred more.

There was rage—and near-perverse satisfaction that America, especially our near-peers of collegiate America, was learning what the underground had known for a while. "I was on acid when the news came over," the *Realist's* ever-oblique Paul Krassner recalls. "I remember Walter Cronkite saying, 'What has been feared has finally occurred.' And when he said it, I found myself saying, 'Good.' Good because it had already happened; there was nothing I could do about it. And, though I knew it was a terrible tragedy, I thought, 'Maybe this will wake more people up.'"

Undergrounders ran maps of struck colleges, recapitulations, reports, and editorials for a larger-than-usual audience. At the *Seed,* we color-printed a cover picture from the San Jose *Red Eye* of Mickey Mouse wearing a Richard Nixon watch and sold out thirty-eight thousand copies in two days, our highest press run ever. And the papers pronounced Kent State a victory of sorts. "The U.S. is seriously, inexorably, losing the war," Skeets editorialized. "They simply cannot continue to placate the antiwar sentiment at home and escape defeat abroad. Nixon, then, is the man who history has forced to preside over the dissolution of the Amerikan empire."

In April, *Rolling Stone* had produced a major takeout on the Chicago Conspiracy Trial. Two years after Jann Wenner's attack on the Yippies, Abbie Hoffman had graced the cover; inside, a long, well-crafted story by writer Gene Marine had denounced the conviction of a culture in Chicago. "Crazy judge," Wenner recalls; "a great story." The issue sold poorly.

In June, *Rolling Stone* published "On America 1970: A Pitiful Helpless Giant," its Kent State issue. The title inverted a Nixon pledge about what he would not allow America to become: the quarter-fold cover pictured demonstrators outside the White House. Stories covered Kent and Jackson State; antiwar rallies and the Wall Street hardhats; the trials of Bobby Seale and Roger Priest, the publisher of the Navy underground paper *Om.* There was an angry poem by Allen Ginsberg and an antiviolence ad from Elektra Records. The usual music news and dope page rounded out the issue.

It was a major effort from an alternative magazine with a larger circulation than any single undergrounder. It described a "barbaric" war and "slaughter" at Kent State. But its sole advocacy was a vague page-one admonition to "Read it, and then, in the words of the Universal Life Church, do what's right!"

Rolling Stone editors liked the magazine because it was journalistic and progressive and cultural, but was neither mainstream nor underground. "At the *Express Times,* I had complete freedom, and the editing was inspirational rather than direct," Greil Marcus recalls. "*Rolling Stone* was a much more professional operation, even in those days. Jann was a much better editor than Marvin [Garson], in conventional terms, and I liked not having to deal with people who were so stoned you couldn't have a coherent conversation. We were doing good stuff, taking chances. We didn't know yet what the definition of the magazine was."

But that spring, with Wenner away from the office, some editors had begun complaining that he was too bossy, too chummy with the subjects they covered and "the suits" who ran the record companies. He'd over-spent, they'd charged, on a British *Rolling Stone,* on insert "flyers" that challenged underground papers in several cities but folded after a year, on the new *Earth Times.*

Returning to face dissonant music, Wenner said his piece. He'd helped plan the Kent State issue, but parts of it had turned shallow, provocateur-ish. He stressed that music and reporting should come before rhetorical advocacy. "Jann's basic attitude," Greil Marcus says, "was that you wouldn't get anywhere with guns or with fighting in the streets. The establishment is too powerful; you're going to win by burrowing from within."

The sides soon found something to clash over: how to play Bob Dylan's receiving an honorary degree from Princeton. Wenner thought the story "fascinating"; several editors saw a Random Note, at best. And there was another problem—*Rolling Stone* was nearly broke. "During the next two weeks, while the sun still shines on brightly and the advertising is still slow, we'll be taking a little vacation break," Wenner wrote in the skimpy forty-page issue being prepared for August 6. It would take a $100,000 advance from the magazine's distributor and aid from several record companies to save the day. Wenner saw this help as fortunate, generous; some editors felt compromised.

Wenner refused to be the Max Scherr of 1970, an exile from his own publication, and a major editorial turnover followed. "Everybody got swell-headed, I mean everybody," he'd recall eighteen months later. "They thought they were something other than what they really were, and that we were something other than what we really were. It was a money crisis ... an overdue housecleaning." Managing editor John Burks, one of those who left just before the "On Vacation" issue went to bed, saw things differently: The magazine "was going to stick with the rock and roll trip, and not get into all this troublesome political shit."

These days, Wenner says that the "political shit" hadn't been worth the trouble. "America with a *k*—with three *k*'s—it was childish, it was disrespectful to our history, not all of which is bad. Smash the State— good luck! That immaturity was one of the things that turned me off. There was nothing realistic or possible happening on that side."

The mid-1970 underground press dismissed such statements as excuses for inaction, defenses of the status quo, counterrevolutionary sentiment. Kent State, Armando wrote in the *Seed,* would revive the Movement. "Antiwar and student protest has been slowly smothering in its own irrelevance and impotence since April of '68, two years ago. . . . The general public . . . accept this series of campus strikes, riots, seizures, etc., as absolutely natural. . . .

"As this is written, it looks like school is mostly over in Amerika this year. The next step is to shut it *all* down."

Skeets was right about the government being unable to sustain both the war and popular support for it, and Vietnam would represent a cresting of America as world policeman. And there was no telling how the war would have evolved without the protests at home. But the pendulum soon swung to the right:

• *May 8*—Hardhats declared class war on Wall Street, where they beat student demonstrators and were regaled with ticker tape.
• *May 13*—Person or persons unknown blew up the transmitter at KPFT, Houston's listener-sponsored radio station.
• *May 14*—Two black students were killed, eleven injured at Jackson State College, in Mississippi. There were few eruptions over this second slaughter —a tribute to exhaustion, to implicit racism, and to a perception of how far the ante had been raised.

In Washington, a thousand marshals from the Mobilization (which would soon split in two) had blocked militants from reaching the Justice Department building. Campus demonstrations enhanced student power, but radicals at Northwestern University, the University of Chicago, and elsewhere were isolated, especially if their tactics turned from protesting the deaths or the war to attacking their schools. A national *Newsweek* poll soon showed majority backing for the invasion of Cambodia; 58 percent of those responding blamed the students for events at Kent State, 11 percent the National Guard. A Gallup poll found more opposition to the Movement than to the war.

That fall, the Scranton Commission would decry "unnecessary, unwarranted and inexcusable" killings—and be denounced as "pabulum for permissiveness" by Agnew. In Ohio, demonstrators would be indicted, not guardsmen or their commanders. It would be 1979 before the state of Ohio paid the families of the dead $675,000, accepted responsibility, and publicly apologized. By then, a gym, not a memorial, would occupy the site of the metaphoric "end of the sixties."

Within the underground and alternative press, Kent State proved to be a cost-effective tightening of the noose knotted at People's Park, and cinched by Fred Hampton's murder. "I felt that it was time to go underground or get out," says Cheryl McCall, who the year before had packed a gun to keep the *South End* under radical control. "I thought that the war was just escalating, was never going to stop, that Nixon was absolutely crazed, that these people had taken over everything, that the Movement didn't have a chance. They had put up with us protesting, marching in the streets, but now they were just going to kill us. It was a lack of courage, it was disgust."

"It wasn't just that they finally got tough with us," *Crawdaddy* founder Paul Williams says. "The burnout level was already very high."

"The Movement went into shock," the *Guardian*'s Julius Lester says. "I never heard so many white people talk about nonviolence. And the alternative was the Weathermen."

The result was a cul de sac. "Smoke clears, war remains," the *Seed*'s post–Kent State issue ruefully declared.

RISING UP ANGRY

NOVEMBER 1969   25 cents   Vol. 1, No. 4

TO LOVE WE MUST FIGHT

gears, guns, grease

15

PRESSING ON, MOVING ON

PLAINFIELD, VERMONT—JUNE, 1970: The white heat of Kent State was still in the air as two thousand underground-press people, DJs, activists, and freaks representing three hundred papers gathered at funky Goddard College, turning the central-Vermont campus into the Alternate Media Conference. The largest countermedia meeting in underground-press history was trying to draw the movements and the papers together. It wouldn't be easy.

The papers represented at Goddard were themselves increasingly similar. Most believed that some sort of youth-minority revolution was possible, desirable. There was less talk about lifestyle and eros, more about Third World struggles and gender issues. Gender-mixed collectives had replaced most of the single strong (male) editors—Shero, Garson, Scherr, Bloom —with varying degrees of efficiency. Graphics of enraged demonstrators or nightmare visions of Nixon and Agnew had succeeded images of mellow lovers. Politics, energy, exhaustion, and shrillness vied for supremacy. Readers were told—often lectured on— the need to combat the ravages of authority.

One such media battle had occurred on May 13, 1970, when UPS's Tom Forcade had testified before the Commission on Obscenity and Pornography. He'd laced into the "ancient myths of sterile blue laws," then given example after example illustrating the politics behind underground-press obscenity arrests. He'd denounced "walking antiques . . . trying to stomp out *our* . . . working model of tomorrow's paleocybernetic culture, soul, life, manifesting love, force, anarchy, euphoria . . . flowing new-consciousness media on paper, coming from our lives in the streets. "So fuck off, and fuck censorship," he'd concluded, punctuating his remarks by tossing a pie at the panel.

Then again, Forcade would have his victory in just a few months.

The Goddard conference replaced pies with seminars and ideas: "Capitalism and Alternative Media," and the headier "The Spiritual Responsibility of the Alternative Media." A tape exchange for the "video freeks" emerging around the country was drawn up, as were semiparanoid plans for truly underground radio should fascism really come. New York's Media Project reiterated the political nature of media, and the need for radicals to attack oppressive institutions instead of "making culture a commodity." A Movement Center distributed all the papers, and analytical and technical packets from Newsreel, the Committee to Defend the Panther Twenty-One, Media Women, and other Left groups. Recent returnees from Hanoi and the first Venceremos Brigade (the volunteers who'd gone to Cuba in November, 1969, to cut cane in solidarity with that country's revolution) confirmed the Movement's increasing internationalism. People exchanged suggestions, made connections.

But Goddard also confirmed another side of the papers' collective behavior, one recalled by Chip Berlet of Colorado's *Chinook:* "You achieved your purpose by running naked pictures to outrage the straight people, calling for the overthrow of the government not from any political perspective, but because the government seemed so tedious that you might as well get rid of it. I think to a large degree, all people in the underground press wanted to do was just create such havoc that there would be change."

Berlet's appraisal seems overstated, but Goddard was a free-fire zone for purists and hedonists alike. Down past the pine trees, for example, the Hog Farm staffed a circus tent à la Woodstock, serving macrobiotic rice and lemonade laced with four hundred hits of LSD furnished by a record-company executive. As delegates turned bacchanalian, dueling revolutions ensued. "Flowers or guns? Confrontation or counterinstitutions? Politics or transcendence?" the *Atlantic*'s Richard Todd wrote in his conference recap.

Leftists charged elitism in rock; don't dictate to the artist, DJs retorted. Feminists prevented the filming of a "fuck-in," then chanted "Full of shit!" as a band played hard rock with sexist lyrics. Legs braced, mike in hand, the lead singer thought they were yelling "Take It Off."

Following that imagined advice proved to be a set-killing mistake.

Bob Fass, WBAI's founding alternative-radio father, played loud, distorted tapes to "spark group action by creating something that had to be overthrown." He succeeded—and was carried from his own panel. Jerry Rubin, who'd "expected that the people in power would turn to us out of desperation that they couldn't handle things," left to begin serving a jail sentence for protesting the war. Communists grumbled about the presence of the hip media execs who'd paid for the conference rooms and rent-a-cars. A workshop on "Free Enterprise and the Cultural Revolution" changed tone abruptly when a participant pulled a gun and opined, "This may turn into a workshop on killing people."

A last session, "Cartoons and the Mass Consciousness," drew two hundred people to the college library's basement, a high box of a room resembling a racquetball court. The Tower of Babel would have been more appropriate. Dope-smokers, babies, and dogs mingled. An acideater lurched about, screaming "I am the freak man!" As he was led away, a young woman told him, "I love you for doing your own thing."

Even as the others were talking about media, cartoonists Gilbert Shelton and Art Spiegelman had produced on-site comix. Their collaborator, and the key speaker, was Harvey Kurtzman, whose *Mad, Help,* and other 1950s work had inspired underground cartooning. But Kurtzman's inking of the spoof "Little Annie Fanny" for *Playboy* proved unpopular. "Mr. Kurtzman," a woman asked wryly, "why don't you have Annie Fanny and her friends take over the offices of *Playboy* and show them where it's at?"

"Did she ever turn against Daddy Warbucks?" Kurtzman responded good-naturedly. Then he turned sober: "I like to do my own secret political things, but I think it's the worst environment . . . when you have to conform to any kind of rules, messages, regulations."

There was applause, and then another woman spoke: "When the revolution comes, you're going to be crushed! And you write such funny comics, it's not fair."

"Sexist!" "Humorless!" "Counterrevolutionary!" Charges flew, and then a new sound was heard! "Thwack-thwack; thwack-thwack"—a man and woman were hunching on the carpet, "cooling out the vibes." As the crowd clapped in time, a second couple followed (un)suit. I watched from the balcony, a voyeur at the revolution.

"What was missing throughout," the *Guardian*'s Irwin Silber wrote almost surrealistically, "was any sense that the political relevance of alternative media was dependent, in the first place, on its indelible connection to movements based on mass struggle."

It was a typical underground-press convention, more valuable for getting together than for getting work done. It also showed the difficulty of projecting increasingly radical and diverse politics within increasingly factionalized, isolated, and incoherent movements.

TALENT, and who was served by it, now ranked as a contentious quality.

By now, some undergrounders had technical ability and an interest in bettering their skills. But wasn't craft merely a bourgeois concern when comrades were being killed? In an egalitarian culture, who decided what was "better" art, "better" politics? Who spoke for feminists, or gays, or other rising constituencies? What if people were jailed and nobody could replace their skills? Since when did the underground press require a resumé?

Many staff members felt pained by elitism, or victimized by shitwork. Men often were charged with sexism. "The rap," *Seed* writer and women's liberationist Flora Johnson recalls, "was that you men who had skills were hoarding them. It wasn't that you had three stories to write."

LNS exemplified the changes of the past few years. "We had a 'dictatorship of the talented,' at least for a while," recalls Ray Mungo about the hippie days in Washington, D.C. "There were definitely people who did nothing but sweep the floor, or do inept journalism that seldom got printed. They got a sense of belonging." LNS's collectivization had bothered him. "You had to sacrifice everything to the cause. The company was always right."

LNS rethought its collective several times after Marshall Bloom left New York. The printers declared themselves a proletariat exploited by bourgeois writers; "the women" formed a graphics caucus, and eventually became a defined two-thirds of the entire staff. Previously unrealized talent came forward, enriched the political mix, replaced dropouts and burnouts. "People were trying to learn how to live a good life under the circumstances," LNS's Sheila Ryan says.

But, she adds, "in the name of democracy some pretty terrible tyrannies were imposed." At LNS, she and George Cavalletto were berated for being married, another staffer for being in therapy instead of more into class struggle. Deadlines fell before endless meetings, or an emerging revolutionary hierarchy that seemed to place a Third World lesbian vegetarian with an AK-47 at its zenith, even if she couldn't write or draw.

The new movements began including limits as well as liberation.

"After 'Goodbye to All That' I wrote a number of pieces for *Rat*, with my byline on them," Robin Morgan recalls. "At a certain point I was told that too many letters were coming in about my pieces, and it was moving toward a star system, and so would I take my name off? Of course, like a good radical, I did.

"A few months later, there was another confrontation—'Your work is still identifiable! It's too passionate, it's too this, it's too that. What you should do is remain on the paper but not write for it.' And I thought, 'That's the best skill I have to give to the Movement. Why are we trying to out-oppress the oppressed?' "

UNDERGROUND PAPERS filled with reports on Movement actions and trials, accompanied by exhortations to "Free All Political Prisoners." SDS ideas about a worker-student alliance were reflected in stories such as the one that ran in Boston's *Old Mole* about a strike at a General Electric plant in Erie, Pennsylvania. At least some workers "respond with enthusiasm to magazines like *Liberation* and to underground newspapers," the *Mole* writers said, pleased and perhaps a bit surprised. These workers are people who "would like to talk to people from the student movement; who oppose the war and see connections between their oppression . . . and the U.S. government's goals in Vietnam; who understand the 'race problem' as the result of white racism."

But youth-culture radicals were less involved with workers than with the physical, separatist, politicized communities that Tom Hayden envisioned in a *Ramparts* piece that was reprinted elsewhere. A decadent culture of egoism, competition, aggression, racism, and sexism, Hayden said, would bow to communes, redefined work, women's and children's centers, free medical and legal services, noncommercial music and art, and consciousness-exploring drug use. He added a note of militance: these territories would confront "all imperialist institutions . . . the occupying police . . . tax, draft, and drug laws." Consequently, "training in physical self-defense and the use of weapons would become commonplace as fascism and vigilantism increase."

Others went further. In a piece called "It's Just a Shot Away," the women's-liberation *Rat* espoused sabotage "to aid in creating the power base out of which can come the army that can in fact stand and win against the vastness of Amerika." The *Tribe*'s call for a People's Militia in Berkley had been a collective editorial. "Guns and grass are united in the youth underground. . . . Freaks are revolutionaries and revolutionaries are freaks," a widely reprinted Weather Underground "Declaration of War" claimed.

The sentiment was less than unanimous. In the White Panther commune where many *Seed* staffers lived, the militants had prevailed over those of us who thought arming against "the pigs" was suicidal. When violence did come our way, it was as a rape attempt against a female housemate —and nobody remembered where the rifle was cached.

Now, during a meeting at the *Seed* office, the question was: "Will the paper advocate armed struggle?"

"Are you kidding me?" someone else answered—only to be interrupted by the appearance of the paper's very own Red Squad surveillance agent. His Mission Impossible consisted of finding the leader of what now called itself the Weather Underground: "None of you guys know where Bernardine Dohrn is, do you?" He exited red-faced as the staff looked in drawers and garbage cans, crying "Bernardine, Bernardine!"

Things didn't stay funny for long.

On July 17, Patrolman Anthony Rizzato and Sergeant James Severin, two white members of the Chicago Police Department, were walking through the Cabrini-Green housing project when shots rang from one of the tall buildings, killing them both. A massive, no-holds-barred manhunt ensued. Soon two young black men were charged with murder.

The cover of the previous *Seed* had featured cartoonist Skip Williamson's cartoon guerilla scaring the boots off a Chicago cop. Now it was my turn to write a piece called "Just a Shot Away."

The story described horrid housing projects that stacked an underclass atop itself, and analogized police to the army in Vietnam. Weaving quotes together—but not personally interviewing police or survivors— I caught the varying responses to the shootings. The police superintendent called the perpetrators "animals" but reined in his angry men, at least officially. The Illinois chapter of the Black Panther Party refused to "be sorry and mourn or cry because two armed members of the oppressor's forces got killed"; Fred Hampton's mother attended the wake for one of the policemen, whose mother said that "malice and violence should never come out of something like this." "Can you get behind the shootings?" I asked a freak in the park. "Yeah," he said derisively, "way behind." The same question to a young black—"All pigs are the enemy."

The piece captured the tension of the home-front war, and was balanced if one accepted the shootings as what the *Tribe* had called "responsible terrorism." Yellow and black people were dying in Vietnam and America; didn't being part of that revolution require violence here? Wasn't backing off just copping out to the accident of having been born white?

But I hadn't been in a fight since the army three years before, and nobody had said that these particular cops were brutal. My head understood revolutionary violence; my heart longed for peace-and-love; my gut was getting scared. My story—written at arm's length for a paper that demanded engagement—defined a Rubicon I would not cross, one of two that I'd look back on when I left the paper for good.

Rock music had never been more popular, nor the underground press more disenchanted with it. The musicians might want virtuosity, but fan-militants saw activism and accountability slipping into the mainstream even as the record ads faded away. In Oregon, the governor would stage a rock festival to siphon numbers from a demonstration.

Here too, violence became a factor influencing underground press coverage.

In New York, *EVO* covered a bombing at the Electric Circus, a local rock hall, and intimated that a similar fate might befall the Fillmore East, where music-for-the-people advocates had battled promoter Bill Graham, and where *EVO* traded advertising for office space. No shrinking violet, Graham rushed upstairs and confronted several *EVO* staffers.

Then-editor Jaacov Kohn, who like Graham had fled the Nazis, and was old enough to have fought in Israel's 1948 war for statehood, says "I always believed that every generation had its right to express itself. . . . If you're violent, what can I do?"

Wasn't that irresponsible?

"Of course it was," Kohn replies. "But what made it responsible to march down Fifth Avenue? There were demonstrations all over New York. Responsibility had nothing to do with it."

On July 24, this rock-politics tension crested in a rock-'n'-bottle concert in Chicago's Grant Park. Close by where police had beaten demonstrators in 1968, city officials were hosting a concert, this one starring the funky, innovative, integrated Sly and the Family Stone. Blonde Southwest Siders mingled with black South and paisley North Siders; grass was mixed with Ripple; thirty-five thousand people began boiling under the summer sun.

Sly was late, or had been told the wrong time. Restless fans climbed onto the stage; others tossed bottles at them that fell short. Bottle wars ensued, and then the police became targets of opportunity for kids who'd been hassled for long hair or dark skin or pot, or had simply been touched by the casual violence permeating the country. Initial restraint gave way as an officer tossed teargas. An occupied patrol car was trashed, a panicky cop fired his gun. Longhairs were dragged away, a police car was burned. Forced back, the cops formed a line and fired seventy-five or so shots, not all of them into the air. Seven hours after schedule, one year after Woodstock, seven months after Altamont, the casualties were posted:

three shot, one hundred sixty-five arrested, $50,000 in damage, twenty-six civilians and thirty cops treated for injuries—and a few underground writers feeling themselves being squeezed out the door.

"It was a riot, pure and simple. No willful intent, forethought or planning," Marshall Rosenthal wrote—for *Rolling Stone,* which had put him on $50-a-week retainer *just for writing* after he'd stopped by while in San Francisco, recuperating from work at the *Seed.* His style was different for *RS*—less personally evocative, but well crafted, full of quotes from demonstrators and cops, promoters, and performers. "I called the editor for some guidance," he recalls, "and he said, 'Well, write it as you saw it. Don't worry about length. And talk to the cops.'

"I said, 'Talk to who?' God Almighty! I found myself calling the Chicago Police Department. I identified myself as the reporter from *Rolling Stone,* and the spokesman answered all my questions. It was easy."

"It's war," Marshall had written in his reporter's notebook, "and for first time I feel the anger and fear of both sides. . . . Do *Seed* people take the rhetoric seriously? Why did no *Seed* person take part in offing the pig and intensifying the struggle? *Seed* folks are irresponsible producers."

Marshall offered the *Seed* his story—it was OK with *RS,* and, as his first national-magazine reporting, special to him. We rejected it. "We may not agree with your conclusions," I said, "but we can use some of your interviews."

Marshall cursed me silently. The underground press had represented many of the viewpoints within its communities; now there were one-and-only positions. When a staff meeting concluded that the system's violence was to be condemned, the people's praised, Marshall asked that his name be taken off the masthead.

Eliot Wald wrote the *Seed's* Sly article. Eliot, my East Village roommate who, after seeing an ebullient letter of his reprinted in the *Seed* early in 1968, had dropped a teaching assistantship in psychology at the State University of New York at Stony Brook and headed off to Chicago and another milepost on our magical mystery tour.

Now it was Korrectness time.

"The biggest problem had come from the crowd, and, frankly, I didn't feel the cops had started it," Eliot recalls. "I thought they overreacted by pulling their guns, but they had committed no great excesses, and had been attacked in some ways. The problem was figuring it out politically, because I knew what had happened.

"It was very, very hard to write, because I felt like I had a line I had to follow. I couldn't say the cops were right—they weren't really right.

But I couldn't say the people were wrong. It was like reviewing a movie by your best friend."

Written with eyes looking over his shoulder, "his" article recounted "an exhilarating day. . . . It's going to be hard to forget the sight of three thousand people refusing to be intimidated by . . . the violent enforcers of a rigged system, the symbol of the sort of repression that *creates* the ugly situations. . . . Now that we've fought on the same side, let's *stay* together and fight the real enemy."

"I remember feeling that I'd done a pretty good job with it," Eliot says. "But I didn't think I had told the entire story." When he quit the paper, he'd date his departure back to this story.

At *Rising Up Angry,* there were no such qualms. The organization, like its paper, was designed to attract the lumpen-proleteriat young of Chicago's ethnic streets of fire; some of the founding ex-SDSers had battled the cops during the Democratic Convention and the Days of Rage. Rising Up Angry, cofounder Michael James recalls, "developed groups of white working kids who would get hip to the revolution, cool it out on the women's stuff, not be prowar, not be as racist. If anything, [we tried] to neutralize 'em as well as win people over." Articles in the group's paper were eight-cylinder, fight-the-pigs polemics. "Later the organization changed," Mike recalls, "but at that time we tended to glorify youth hostility, in music, in a lot of ways."

One summer day, *Seed*lings and Angries were lounging outside the *Seed,* which let other community organizations use its light table, darkroom, photostat machine, and other production equipment. Someone had sliced up a watermelon, and as a Cadillac drove down Halsted Street, "Hamill," a wiry kid who'd been politicized out of a gang by Angry, lofted a rind at the "bougie car." It splattered the windshield, to Angry cheers.

Then the driver pulled over and charged out from behind the wheel. Hamill raced into an alley, but the swarthy, somewhat stocky man moved surprisingly fast, reaching down to his calf, coming back up with a snubnosed revolver, closing the distance, grabbing Hamill by the scruff of the neck as if he was putting out the cat. As we caught up, his gun was behind Hamill's head. One of the women from Angry talked about excitable boys and just-kiddings and you were young once too. Mike James's eyes flashed from cop to gun.

Finally, the cop cursed and pushed Hamill away.

Angry, though, argued that revolution depended on effecting a change from reactionary to revolutionary violence. Its report on the Sly concert was blunt. "Face it, pigs, the people are pissed off. They wanted an excuse to waste some pigs . . . We won't fight our beautiful people. We want pig's blood. We'll get it, too."

AS A SERIES of actions in August and September showed, the Movement's most militant edge was now committed to revolutionary violence. These acts "brought the war home"—to America, and to the underground press. On August 7, seventeen-year-old Jonathan Jackson yelled, "This is it!" pulled a gun, and tried to spirit several prisoners out of a courthouse in San Rafael, California. One of the escapees put a shotgun to a Superior Court judge's neck and yelled "Free the Soledad Brothers"—three other prisoners accused of killing a prison guard after another guard had shot three black inmates. The best-known Soledad Brother was George Jackson, Jonathan's natural brother, a charismatic figure drawing increasing Movement support.

Jonathan Jackson and the jailbreakers attempted to reach a getaway van. When the firing stopped, Jackson, two prisoners, and the judge were dead. Three other people were wounded.

In mass media, the prisoners were animals, or at best victims. Most underground papers called them heroic prisoners of war. "Colossal," Huey Newton said. Tom Hayden: "Where they fell we begin. If our rulers do not free our prisoners of war and cease their universal aggression, if they do not make peaceful change possible, then it is tragically clear that all of Amerikka will be taken hostage in the vast jailbreak ahead."

Two weeks later, though, underground writers divided over the slaying of Ronald Tsukamoto, a Berkeley cop who was by reputation a nice guy. "DON'T CHORTLE OVER DEAD COPS," a sober Max Scherr headlined. "Don't keep urging the blacks, the browns, the poor, the women, to go get guns," said the *Barb*'s article. The *Tribe* took the opposite tack, approving the slaying.

"Why Tsukamoto?" "Ariel" protested in a letter to the *Tribe* that praised Jackson's act for "causing panic to the power structure" responsible for "this corrupt, reprehensible system of justice" while denouncing Tsukamoto's shooting as "an act of gratuitous violence." "WHY NOT TSUKAMOTO?" the *Tribe* headlined the letter, which ran next to a box containing the names of five men blinded or killed by the Berkeley police or Alameda County sheriffs.

"Ariel," a young radical who'd exposed an undercover cop after warning him to leave a meeting, still didn't buy it. "Violence," he recalls, "had been completely separated from any political struggle. That was disastrous."

In Wisconsin, the issue of violence involved an advocacy reporter's protection of sources. Demonstrations in Madison ranked with cheese and beer as a major state product, and early on New Year's Day, a stolen plane had dropped three bombs on the Baraboo Ordnance Plant north of the city. The bombs were duds; the action, the bombardiers told *Kaleidoscope,* was a small but imaginative payback for what B-52s were doing in Vietnam. But early on August 24, an explosion shook the darkness at the University of Wisconsin, killing Robert Fassnacht, a civilian research assistant at the oft-picketed Army Mathematics Research Center.

Despite arrests, a bombing and shooting, and the boycott of printer William Schanen, *Kaleidoscope* had established branches in several midwestern cities and sold as many as forty thousand copies a week. In January, it had published the names and photos of three Madison-area undercover agents. Now a supporters' leaflet sought to explain the military uses of the mathematics center's research, "the story the news media never covered." But killing a peripheral civilian, even accidentally, was not so easily explained, and *Kaleidoscope* soon ran a communiqué from the New Year's Gang—named for the munitions-plant bombing—that expressed "great sorrow" over the researcher's death, but cited the war and said, "If it had to be done again and again, we would do it again and again." The gang promised further actions unless several Black Panthers were freed from jail and ROTC was abolished at Madison.

Almost immediately, Mark Knops, Milwaukee *Kaleidoscope*'s twenty-seven-year-old editor, was subpoenaed to divulge his sources. The Wisconsin Supreme Court accepted the principle of journalistic immunity—but not where a crime had been committed. Knops eventually served four months for contempt, the longest such sentence in American history, before a federal court released him.

Pun Plamondon, the White Panther minister of defense suspected in the bombing of a CIA office, had been captured after tossing a beer can out of a car. But Huey Newton had just been freed from jail after his manslaughter conviction was overturned on appeal, and Bobby Seale had widespread support in his Connecticut murder trial. Many underground writers attended the Black Panther–led Revolutionary People's Constitutional Convention held in Philadelphia from September 4 through 7, which called for political, economic, and sexual equality, an end to imperialism and repression, and consciousness exploration. The once-hippie *Seed* discussed something called "ecology"—and denounced the "total domination" of Puerto Rico, applauded the urban-guerilla Tupamaros of Uruguay, and ran a Venceremos Brigade sister's exultance over a country "living in an era in which a socialist society is being created, and all forms of discrimination are being swept away."

After the Popular Front for the Liberation of Palestine staged a largely successful multiple hijacking on September 6, the reports from Jordan by LNS's Sheila Ryan and George Cavalletto compared the plight of the passengers with that of the huddled masses living in nearby Palestinian refugee camps for more than two decades. But in New York, Allen Young, both a Marxist and a Jew, felt "really clobbered with clubs by George and Sheila on the Middle East. They did bring back a certain amount of information about the history of the Middle East and the complexity of it from the Palestinian point of view." But he, at least, heard glee in descriptions of guerillas cradling Kalashnikov rifles. "They were so firm on pushing a line through at LNS—we should support the Palestinians, and Israel had no business being there.

"I pretty much caved in. I remember LNS getting material from another point of view, and we dismissed it out of hand. There were certain pacifist articles about Vietnam that were not adequately pro-NLF that we didn't run. LNS became very concerned with this whole correct-line business. I was certainly as much to blame for promoting that as everyone else."

On September 12, a jailbreak in California sought to unite hippies and politicos, including those in the underground press.

Since 1966, Timothy Leary had been repeatedly arrested in connection with his soft-drug messianism. Imprisoned early in 1970, he faced up to twenty years behind bars. Now he'd escaped from the California Men's Colony West, near San Luis Obispo. His getaway was aided by the Weather Underground, financed by acid dealers collectively known as the Brotherhood.

In 1966, Leary had proclaimed the Politics of Ecstasy. Four years later, the post-escape manifesto he sent to *EVO* caught the shift from Let It Be to Let It Bleed. "I declare that World War III is now being waged by short-haired robots whose deliberate aim is to destroy the complex web of free and wild life by mechanical order. . . . To shoot a genocidal robot policeman in the defense of life is a sacred act. . . . WARNING," the letter ended, "I am armed and should be considered dangerous to anyone who threatens my life or my freedom."

Leary's former Harvard LSD researcher Richard Alpert, whose own long, strange trip would transform him into guru Baba Ram Dass, raised a common reservation when he said that "one thing we do not need is one more nut with a gun." Then came an even more surprising report:

Leary had been given shelter in the Black Panther Party's Algerian embassy-in-exile.

In a widely distributed article, Berkeley *Tribe* writer-militant Stew Albert conveyed Leary's "love and best wishes for a violent revolution," and quoted Eldridge Cleaver as saying, "The same pigs who wanted to ice me are after Leary. They hate him because he made their children rebel." "We used to quote the *I Ching* a lot," Leary's wife Rosemary said, "but now it's going to be Kim Il Sung and the thoughts of Chairman Mao."

"Our revolution has taken an inevitable turn," Stew Albert enthused. "In Algeria, the gun protects the flower. In Algeria, the flower becomes the gun."

THE *Old Mole* had begun in Cambridge just after the 1968 Democratic Convention. Since then it had spent more time on power analysis than on personal adventures. Which made the biweekly's "An Article About Ourselves" a telling tale of radical limits.

The Mole people were veterans of Columbia and Chicago, of harvesting sugar cane with the Venceremos Brigade in Cuba, of who knows how many protests. They supported working-class and Third World peoples, comrades in the revolution to come. But they were guilt-ridden about being white, educated, verbal, eccentric, defensive, stuck up—and about engaging in liberal guilt trips.

"Sometimes it seems like we all gave up what made us most human when we went into the Movement," the article mused. "One of us feels she mustn't paint; it's bourgeois and not contributing directly to the process of making a revolution. . . . Others, who got into the movement younger, have never even found out what they would really love to do . . . How can we make a human revolution by torturing ourselves, by giving up all we care for in our past?"

The *Mole* applauded eclecticism instead of calling for a simplistic correct line. "Instead of perceiving and accepting the situation we have at this time—not one movement but many separate movements . . . we tend to view it as a situation of competing strategies." As writers, they felt crippled by rhetoric. "Unless every sentence they say has either the word 'imperialist' or the word 'capitalism' in it, they are afraid they will be accused of insufficient zeal."

"We were swept up," LNS's Sheila Ryan explains. "You have to remember that we were still emerging from the Cold War. When I was a child, the discussions of Communism engendered nightmares of North

Korean soldiers coming up the stairs to tear the rosary beads from under my pillow. So you go to a place and see that in fact these people are human, that they are wiping out parasites and giving milk to children and trying to abolish alienation in labor. It's a revelation.

"We were leaving out many of the difficulties in making any kind of social transformation. And we didn't know enough at the time, I think, to discuss in a really serious and substantial way what those programs were. People had a sense that this just sprang out of nowhere. If you feel you are a continuation of some kind of historical [revolutionary] struggle, you don't have to reinvent the wheel."

Too much ideology, or too little, or the wrong one? In any event, most Americans loathed the bombings, the dope, the loose sex and loose talk. The hostility was mutual—underground papers casually labeled tens of millions of Americans "pigs."

The *Mole* sensed the isolation. "As long as we are caught in the competitive cycle of being 'more left than thou,' we will keep getting further out and more unable to communicate with most Americans."

Other activists engaged in more surprising reconsiderations. On December 6, the Weathermen closed out 1970 with their "New Morning, Changing Weather" statement. Nine months and two dozen blasts after the one that killed three of their number, the group that had led the white charge toward guerilla actions dismissed the "tendency to consider only bombings or picking up the gun as revolutionary, with the glorification of the heavier the better" as "the military error. . . . Only acting openly, denouncing Nixon, Agnew, and Mitchell, and sharing our numbers and wisdom together with young sisters and brothers will blow away the fear of the students at Kent State, the smack of the Lower East Side, and the national silence after the bombings of North Vietnam."

The *Mole*'s statement had allowed for side-by-side movements. But at LNS, Allen Young was being stretched by dividing loyalties.

In 1969, Young, an ardent supporter of Fidel Castro's revolution, had made the first of several trips to Cuba. His reports had accentuated the positive, but he'd returned with a newfound wariness about a state-run society. And, as a gay, Young was especially disturbed that Cuba's new man seemed to be homophobic.

Still "a closet case" at LNS, Young had joined the Gay Liberation Front early in 1970 to try to fuse gay and Movement radicalism. "Some homosexuals denounce the Movement because they feel that it has not sufficiently embraced the homosexual cause," GLF activists had noted in *Come Out!* after attending the Black Panther Party–sponsored United Front Against Fascism rally. "However, in order for our goals to become part of the Movement, we must define our cause and ourselves, thereby creating a radical homosexual consciousness. Then we can begin to educate our radical sisters and brothers to our oppression and our needs."

But as Young's gay involvement increased, he confronted a situation he recalls in his recent book, *Gays Under the Cuban Revolution:* "As long as my involvement with gay liberation meant confronting the atrocities gay people suffer under the capitalist government of the United States, I was not jeopardizing too much of my privilege and status in the movement; but in confronting Cuban homophobia, and challenging the policies of the Cuban government, I was going beyond an acceptable boundary."

Young also was finding the LNS collective increasingly rigid. Straight friends asked Young to stay with LNS "for the good of the Movement." Gay friends urged him to leave for the good of Allen. In September, 1970, he went. "I had always assumed that my community was the Left, and I realized that there was another community that was really where I belonged."

He was not the only gay activist facing dueling loyalties. Gays, with Huey Newton's explicit support, had openly attended the Revolutionary People's Constitutional Convention that September. But lesbians had accused them of ego-tripping, and when gay men had protested sexual name-calling by some black delegates, they were in turn denounced by Third World gays. Now underground papers began reporting splits between the GLF, the less Movement-oriented Gay Activist Alliance, various Third World gay organizations, and lesbian groups.

As 1970 ended, the LSD-Black Panther alliance in Algeria began to unravel.

"Naturally, I will totally accept the discipline of the Black Panther Party," Tim Leary had told the *Tribe*'s Stew Albert. Now there was trouble in paradise. Leary's dual loves—for LSD and media attention—bothered both Algeria's Marxist government and the Black Panthers who'd shot and hijacked their way into exile. The Panthers demanded $10,000 for Leary's upkeep. Reputedly, Cleaver eyed Rosemary Leary. Tim Leary fell under twenty-four-hour surveillance.

Then, on January 9, 1971, fugitive Panther Eldridge Cleaver hit acid-head jailbreaker Tim Leary with a "revolutionary bust." When the story broke early the next month, it featured Cleaver denouncing Leary as a drug-addled racist and calling the whole drug scene into question:

"It was very useful some years ago when people rebelled against the straitjacket rules and regulations of Babylonian society . . . by shattering to smithereens those values, by getting high, freaking out, whatever term you want to apply. . . . It is no longer useful to our struggle and it has to be stopped. . . . We want people to gather their wits, to sober up and get down to the serious business of destroying the Babylonian empire."

So much for the fragile alliance between politicized freaks and militant radicals seeking to mobilize the counterculture. And the freakier papers responded in kind. "At a time when the Movement as a whole and the Black Panther Party in particular are in serious internal disarray, Cleaver's substance and timing are to be questioned," *EVO* editorialized. "When you get right down to it, all busts look alike. Revolutionary or otherwise, THEY STINK."

If Leary's life was in disarray, so was the Panthers' organization. Minister of Defense turned Supreme Commander Huey Newton expelled eleven of the thirteen remaining Panther Twenty-One bomb conspiracy defendants for denouncing the Weatherman New Morning statement as unmilitant, for criticizing a "self-proclaimed vanguard" within the organization, and, in some cases, for jumping bail. The entire Algerian outpost was doubly exiled by Newton after Cleaver despaired over the "total collapse" of the party. One group followed Newton's imperium; a New York cell moved toward the underground Black Liberation Army.

The Berkeley *Tribe,* whose staff was as close to both factions as any other, called on the Panthers to drop their "swagger-stick image" and stop portraying Newton's thoughts as "invincible." Instead, the March 6 *Black Panther* accused Cleaver of murdering an alleged lover of his wife, among other things. In Algiers, the Cleavers denounced the story; in New York, one of their supporters was killed after fighting with people selling the paper. The March 20 *Black Panther* called for Cleaver's death. Meanwhile, the predominantly white underground press, which had revered the Panthers' politics, bravery, blackness, and martyrdom, had lost one of its few remaining rudders.

MOVEMENT POLITICS had taken on an edge of violence and frustration. Talented underground staffers chafed under collectivity. Music, sweet rock music, was slipping away from political ties that had been amorphous even at their peak. Underground-press staffers felt beseiged. Various alliances—acidheads and Panthers, gays and socialists—were forming, then blowing apart. The Panthers—the very vanguard party—had finally suffered a split caused by ideology, ego, the isolation of their militant position, and ceaseless government repression. And the underground press itself was bogging down in formula, violence, negativity, cant, uncritical reporting, and a sometimes repressive collectivity.

Now another, "alternative," press was bidding to represent youth communities that were growing older—some said growing up.

New community papers that stressed reportage, electoral politics, and consumer-oriented fun over rhetoric, radical politics, and antimaterialism dated back to 1966 on both coasts. The entertainment-oriented *Boston After Dark* had started as a supplement to the Harvard Business School newspaper. In San Francisco, the more muckraking *Bay Guardian* had begun as an antiwar but reformist tortoise to the *Barb*'s flamboyant hare, then unearthed the real estate speculation around the Bay Area Rapid Transit System and attacked the "Manhattanization" of San Francisco. "I was glad the underground papers were there," *Bay Guardian* founder and former mainstream reporter Bruce Brugmann recalls, "because I never wanted to use their formula. If they hadn't been there, I would've had continual pressure to become radical, and do the things that I had some problems with."

Brugmann saw strengths in such underground papers as the *Barb*. "Max Scherr didn't go to journalism school and study objectivity, like a couple of people in Nixon's White House. He was very honest about what he was doing, and in his time he did it pretty effectively."

Yet a new audience was forming: baby-boomers looking to get on with life in America rather than destroy the place. "Max was a break-through artist," Brugmann continues, "because he would do things that the straight press wouldn't. But in many ways, he was just an inversion of the old Hearst formula of sex, drugs, and violent politics."

In Chicago, the 1968 Democratic Convention, with its beaten newsmen and printed-without-comment mayoral White Paper, had spawned the *Chicago Journalism Review*. Now several young reporters were starting a weekly to fill a gap between the dailies and the *Seed*. Initially, we welcomed the *Free Press* as another nonmainstream medium; disillusion-ment set in when the paper proved more trendy than trenchant. Then a battle erupted between the underground and the alternative presses.

The first half of 1970 had seen feminist writing enter the underground press, first in supplements, then in women's articles, finally throughout the paper. During the summer and fall of 1970, the *Seed* ran a series of pieces by "Jane," a pseudonymous "problem pregnancy" service that off-ered women without money or connections an abortion alternative to back-alley butchers. The Movement was about living one's politics, and soon women were moving between safe houses, performing or assisting in many of the several thousand abortions Jane would do before the procedure was legalized.

"Connie" and I had met the year before at the Chicago Eight defense office, where she was a graduate student taking sociology out of the classroom. She was smart, pretty, aware, and we'd begun living together. Now she was writing for the *Seed,* working with the Chicago Women's Liberation Union, working with Jane.

Always on call, she responded grittily. Once I and my near-my-age nephew escorted her out to Chicago's West Side ghetto, where she had to staunch a hemorrhage. While the Brave Men napped, she and the girl's mother battled rats lured by the blood.

Police came and went around Jane. Detectives investigated the service, but left well enough alone.

Then a female writer at the *Free Press* did an undercover story on the service, and journalistic worlds collided.

The story would deprive women of a needed service, folks at Jane, Rising Up Angry, and the *Seed* charged; enterprise journalism, the *Free Press* staff answered. Another story about gangs would increase racial tensions, several Angry members had told *Free Press* editors before publication. Prior censorship, the editors had responded.

On Friday the thirteenth of November, several Angry women invaded the *Free Press* office. They sprayed the word "pig" on a wall six times, painted office machines, scuffled with a large male staffer, then issued a snarling statement: "They [the *Free Press*] acted as total pigs, and the sisters went down to deal with them as pigs."

The raid sparked another lengthy *Seed* meeting. Angry would trash us if we ever deviated from their version of revolution, some staffers said. Being against censorship meant just that, others felt. Everyone agreed that the *Free Press* article had been opportunistic, damaging.

In the *Seed*'s follow-up story, I allowed that the street gang the *Free Press* had described weren't saints, and that some activists had charged the Angry women with "fascism" and seconded the *Free Press*'s labeling of the action as "childish and disappointing." But the article reiterated the value of women taking care of other women's problems even if what they did was illegal. It accused *Press* editors of having been "in the ozone" about their stories' effects, and quoted Angry's charge that the paper "doesn't see us—see Revolution—as legitimate."

My story didn't mention the *Seed*'s, or my, closeness to the service. But a coda noted that *Free Press* editors had asked me to write a piece on communes. "Unless some heavy changes happen," I replied in print, "my answer is painted on your wall. Take a stand for radical change and I'll show up with an article—and a paintscraper."

During the 1968 Democratic Convention, I'd kept editing after a bullet whined through the *Seed* window. Early in 1969, the American Civil Liberties Union had helped me and others fend off a selective indictment for obscenity. In February, 1970, Marshall Rosenthal and I had nonviolently stood our ground across from armed right-wing kids who'd shot out another *Seed* plate-glass window. Police spies had been in my life for two and a half years. In September, the underground press had largely won its battle for free speech when a Southern judge threw out a case against a *Nola Express* masturbatory spoof of *Playboy* on the grounds that mere offensiveness was not the same as constitutional obscenity. As I wrote, listener-sponsored Houston radio station KPFK had just been bombed off the air for the second time, and the government in Saigon had closed daily newspapers.

My *Seed* piece backed the Revolution. But after it ran, I left the staff —this time for good.

In Washington, most of the commissioners of the Federal Communications Commission attacked drug-oriented lyrics on FM radio, and Senator Thomas Dodd (D-Conn.) proposed outlawing papers that *talked* about overthrowing the government. And the Movement was eating its own. Paul Krassner, whose *Realist* had been the underground's iconoclastic grandfather, was now picketed as a sexist pig. David Fenton left LNS after he was told not to put his name on his book of photos and was passed over for a trip to Vietnam in favor of a far less experienced woman. Robin Morgan, Krassner's denouncer during the feminist takeover at the *Rat,* was herself confronted. "Leftist women were buying the line that the only good use for a typewriter or a mimeograph machine was to drop it out of a window and have it land on someone's head. That got to me as a writer."

Around this time, Jeff Shero, the now ex-*Rat* editor who'd been active since the civil rights struggle, ran into a rising mainstream magazine writer.

"I used to envy your freedom," the writer told him. "Now I have more freedom than you. You can't offend blacks, women, hippies, anyone except upper-middle-class white men."

Jeff shrugged. "You're right."

Psychedelic dreams also were dissolving. "We were infiltrated by the culture itself, which started turning violent," recalls *EVO*'s Allen Katzman. "Our enthusiasm got the best of us. We were telling everyone, 'Drop acid, smoke marijuana, try drugs, it's a turn-on.' Then we turned around and said, 'Oh, wait a minute, let's start warning people, "This stuff is no good, that stuff is OK."' It turned into such a snowball that we were trying to report the news as it happened tomorrow."

In San Francisco, where the Haight-Ashbury was descending from utopia to slum, *Good Times*'s Sandy Darlington, rock writer turned cynic, punctured the balloon of a psychedelic utopia:

"I had hoped and thought that when people tripped out and dropped out, they would see that a new world had to be built. [But] middle-class values are deeper than acid.

"Now there's a large mass of people we can call the Alternative Culture. But what does that mean? It includes *Rolling Stone, Rags,* all communes, all longhairs, rock music, underground papers, all heads, a large part of the young white radicals, hip capitalists, all the people who are acting under the slogan of 'move to the country,' plus the new organic gardening types, yoga types and health-food types. Mostly a vast horde of spaced-out children stumbling around Amerika like lost robots.

"Our prevailing ethos is still a plea to Big Daddy. Give us welfare, give us food stamps, and we'll go off by ourselves and smoke dope, drop acid, roam around in nature. . . . our wants are simple. You can buy us off for next to nothing. . . .

"We've painted ourselves into a corner," Darlington said. His only hope was that it was spring again.

Others saw no hope in that. "This hippie nonsense about the virtues of poverty has had it as a trend," Warhol figure Paul Morrissey told *EVO* early in 1971, "Money will be the next big youth kick, with cash, clothes, and jewelry replacing peace, love, and poverty."

At the *Seed* that spring, a piece on city communes radiated difficulty. Another—from Skeets Millard and Lester Doré and other ex-staffers who'd moved to a Wisconsin farm—beamed. "We've each become healthier, more optimistic, more relaxed. Together we've been working on eliminating the evils of individualism and competitive hassles, petty game-playing, male chauvinism/sexism. Learning to work together, learning to use our hands minds bodies. Men learning to cook clean sew, women learning to split wood fix cars do carpentry." Their letter reiterated the direction LNS/Mass had taken, trading radicalism for a more tangible but less ideological lifestyle. "It didn't take long," wrote the farmers, "for the 'hip' bombings, the 'hip' newspapers, as well as cities and TVs, to seem very alien to us."

Underground papers had been balms for alienations; now many were themselves alienated, alienating institutions. "We started fighting with our audience," recalls Eliot Wald, who'd struggled with writing the *Seed*'s Sly concert-riot article. "It became the Movement and not the readers. There was a tremendous amount of pressure to be pure and right, and I always felt that I wasn't quite adequate because I didn't want to take up the gun and didn't analyze everything in terms of the Revolution. I was just too loose for a Revolution that was real, real tight."

That spring, a half-dozen staffers and freelancers left the *Seed* for good.

They were tired of missed issues, endless harangues, Movement gutchecks, the sheer inertia of the war, having a commune-mate borrow "our car" only to return with a damaged vehicle and word that *"your* car has a problem, man." Most began "Radio Free Chicago," an eclectic, under-staffed, underfinanced rock-and-politics program that proved as taxing as the *Seed.* I did the news, then I stayed home, trying to catch a literal second wind.

Connie and I lived in a three-flat building on Chicago's North Side. On the first floor, some Rising Up Angries handloaded bullets; on the second, a young working-class guy beat his wife. One day our cat ran out the door; chasing her down the stairs, I nearly crashed into "Pod-herek," an Angry who, shotgun cradled, was stalking the Siamese in a greaser version of "Peter and the Wolf."

Connie was weary, and our conversations drifted to the conundrum that abortion might be both desirable and murder. Ironically, I envied her for having a reason to believe—sisterhood, though difficult, was power-ful. But I had another, literally more pressing problem: I seemed to be dying. My asthma had worsened. Crawling across the floor one morning, I barely gasped out my dilemma to the 911 operator before collapsing. The System probably saved my life.

"Many of us are burned out," a new *Seed* collective admitted just three issues after taking the helm, in the paper's umpteenth call for unity between freaks and radicals. But the new staff found energy in gender issues, alternative community, and the impending May Day 1971 antiwar, antisystem demonstration in Washington. Article after article explained targets and the politics hiding behind them. In Washington, the armies of the night rallied themselves for one more campaign. By mid-May, there were twenty thousand veterans, twelve thousand of them with police records from a truly mass arrest.

Key reports were written by David Moberg, a University of Chicago graduate student active with the New University Conference, an organi-zation of grad students and faculty whose democratic socialist politics approximated those of an earlier SDS. "Writing for the *Seed* was an extension of organizing," he recalls. "It seemed that *Seed* readers would be more likely to participate in militant actions." It also gave him a way to experience the alternative culture. "Partly because it was a literary enterprise, I felt more at home than I might have. I wasn't deeply into the music, and I certainly wasn't a dope dealer."

May Day didn't match its own rhetoric, a *Seed* editorial admitted— the war machine rolled on, and far more people had attended a rock concert than the political events. Yet the staff was happy. "Why smile?"

the *Seed* asked. "Because for the first time ever, we made the mass movement into a personal movement." Most of these writers hadn't been at Selma with Doctor King, or at Berkeley with Mario Savio, or in Chicago with Abbie, Jerry, and Tom. May Day would be the last large Vietnam-era demonstration, but the first-person accounts were fresh, alive, full of talk about love for brothers and sisters. These writers still wanted to say something, still had some things to say about movements for change. A baton had been passed.

But not to me, or Connie. Once youth and trips, moral force and political victories and dancing in the streets had made us feel immortal. Now we were leaving Amerika before it came crashing through our door.

SunDance

November–December 1972 / 75¢

Nixon & the Mafia

Plus:
Sex
Jazz
Yoko
Vets

16

THE HOWLING

OYSTER RIVER, COLORADO—SUMMER, 1971: The cabin was high in the mountains, up by the Continental Divide. The gathering was called the Oyster River Massacre, after an Indian victory against some bygone cavalry. And the guests had victories of their own to crow about. Bobby Seale and Ericka Huggins were free of murder charges connected with the death of a Connecticut Black Panther named Alex Rackley, and the judge had ruled that Movement protest made it impossible to empanel a new jury. The remaining thirteen of twenty-one New York Panthers charged with conspiracy to bomb various local targets had been acquitted in May, a development *EVO* had detailed more thoroughly than any other New York paper.

Nobody knew how many papers were publishing now: eight hundred with ten million U.S. readers was one estimate, four hundred with twenty million was another. But this gathering was smaller than usual, representing the news services that fed or tried to organize the papers, and that often competed instead of cooperated. Among them, LNS had sent reporters to Africa, Latin America, and the Middle East. The College Press Service had radicalized a bit. Dispatch News Service was pursuing investigative journalism in the wake of its Seymour Hersh/My Lai revelations; so was the Pacific News Service. The Underground Press Syndicate had lost $5,000 or so to some "helpers," but was regaining strength in New York under the aegis of the always-mysterious Tom Forcade.

The twenty-two writers and editors on hand talked seriously about reporting—and list maintenance, addressographing, and other nonideological concerns. And they buried hatchets as old as as Marshall Bloom's founding of LNS back in 1967 after his ouster from the United States Student Press Association. "This is madness," someone said. "There's not enough of us around to have this feud." The heat was on. "You're going to have to identify . . . some sort of base that the straight press can't coopt," Tom Forcade added. "Either sex, drugs, or politics." In 1974, Forcade would start *High Times,* the druggie's *Playboy,* out of the UPS office. By then, UPS wouldn't need the space.

Newfound harmony and continued readership aside, the dissident press faced real problems. On a mundane but practical level, the loose change of the Great Society was drying up. The papers had grown by being in synch with "outsider" products desired by a coherent, self-identified audience: rock records, rolling papers, hip clothing, incense, sex ads, and Movement, hip, and occult books. Now even daily newspaper critics spread the musical word to a wider audience without automatically denouncing corporations that talked about "product" instead of songs. The Fillmores, the Kinetic Playground, the Electric Circus had closed— taking their ads with them. Many headshops were turning into trendy boutiques, while the papers' core readership remained in jeans and army jackets. Undergrounders were dropping sexist ads (though some, such as the *Barb,* were drowning in them). Drawers filled with phony IDs left by vendors as collateral for papers advanced them. Staffers worked seventy hours a week, and were broke. Papers owed back taxes to the government they advocated dismantling.

There was also political criticism.

Norman Fruchter was a Newsreel veteran who'd brought U.S. prisoners of war back from Hanoi. The idea of propaganda—as in *propagation* —didn't bother him. The Movement's substitution of propaganda for political action greatly upset him, though, and just before Oyster River he'd written the lengthy "Games in the Arena: Movement Propaganda and the Culture of the Spectacle" for *Liberation.* It threatened to be an underground press obituary.

The Movement, Fruchter wrote, had become fixated on media, to the point where the Yippies had defined the mass press as their constituency, and working in the underground press *replaced* building a movement. Newspapers were task-oriented, absorbing, a learning process, a way a few media workers could order the world into Us and Them even while avoiding the people with whom political organizing had to be done.

Often reflexive, argumentative, rigid, the papers substituted verbal ferocity for really exploring political validity and how to comprehensibly communicate it. Even their structure could be both substitute and placebo, Fruchter warned, since "the *products* of that work have been so devoid of vital and politicizing content" that they were isolating both the collectives that created them and the larger Movement."

Some countercultural and Movement victories just hadn't been as clearcut as the papers made them out to be. Fleeing both American and Black Panther jails, Tim Leary had found refuge in Switzerland, birthplace of LSD—only to be arrested on June 30. In Connecticut, several Black Panthers had been convicted of torturing and killing an alleged informant, and Ericka Huggins and Bobby Seale's jury had deadlocked, not declared them innocent.

Julius Lester, who'd once hailed urban guerilla warfare, had clashed with editors at *Liberation* over a midtrial piece in which he aired the Panthers' dirty linen even while lambasting young whites for the "revolutionary and sexual fantasies" that had, he said, made them active participants in the party's destruction. "We have gone from the Port Huron Statement to the mess that is around us today. And, we've scarely paused to see what we have done to ourselves . . . ; we've simply flung out the rhetoric, even more banal and empty and always louder. . . . May 'the people' in whose name we claim to speak be spared our ascendency to power."

"If the Movement has to start lying to people, then there's something wrong with the Movement," Lester says now. "I'm an absolutist on that. If intellectuals align themselves within an ideology, they have sold out their birthrights as intellectuals. You have to be able to live with a certain kind of not being accepted, not being trusted to do the job you're supposed to do as a writer."

The story was among Lester's last Movement pieces. "I stopped because it was very clear to me that the Movement was over," he recalls, "that the Movement had become irrelevant, and that I had nothing more to say."

Acting out a journalistic dialectic, the papers moved toward the margins even as some of their key issues went mainstream. On June 13, 1971, the New York *Times* began excerpting the Pentagon Papers, a 7,100-page chronicle of U.S. decision-making in Vietnam from 1946 to 1968. The compendium had come from Daniel Ellsberg, a Marine intelligence officer turned dove. Ellsberg had given the volumes to Senator William Fulbright late in 1969, but the invasions of Cambodia and Laos persuaded him to wait no longer for Congress to publicize them. "I had the feeling that America was eating its young, was destroying some of its most dedicated, most patriotic, most concerned citizens," he'd tell writer Michael Maclear.

Ellsberg and his friend Anthony Russo were charged with theft and contempt respectively; reporters were subpoenaed; the United States Supreme Court upheld the press's right to publish; President Nixon's White House troops came to include those who'd burgle the office of Ellsberg's psychiatrist—an act that set the glacier of Watergate slowly adrift.

Like Seymour Hersh before him and Bob Woodward and Carl Bernstein to come, Ellsberg had launched a blockbuster story. Yet undergrounders simply dismissed the documents. "They haven't told us a thing we didn't know and rave about ever since this paper existed," *EVO*'s Jaacov Kohn intoned. That was largely true, but it missed the Pentagon Papers' credibility, the newsmaking power of the *Times,* and the consequences of its accepting the volumes. Unlike Hersh, Ellsberg had considered publishing in the underground, specifically in the L.A. *Free Press.* But not after the *Times* had greenlighted him. "It was top or bottom," he says. "The *Times* would make much more of an impression."

EVEN AS the Pentagon Papers were appearing, readers of *Liberation* and other journals were examining pages of documents proving all those rumors about repression against the underground press. These were FBI records taken from the agency's office in Media (!), Pennsylvania, on March 8, 1971, by the anonymous Citizens' Commission to Investigate the FBI. "As long as a great economic and political power remains concentrated in the hands of small cliques not subject to democratic control and scrutiny," they said, "then repression, intimidation, and entrapment are to be expected."

The Media files proved that the underground press had been the target of a coordinated campaign of often-unconstitutional interference with reporting, printing, advertising, and distribution. And the files were the first step on a path that in 1976 would provide the far more massive disclosures of the Senate Select Committee to Study Governmental Operations with Respect to Intelligence Activities. Underground papers had been or were being hounded out of existence—Dallas's *Notes,* Mississippi's *Kudzu,* San Diego's *Street Journal.* Others were crippled, or hampered. "The paranoia itself added to the ennui and the burnout syndrome," says repression investigator Chip Berlet, then with the College Press Service and Denver's *Straight Creek Journal.* "Sometimes the

FBI made it so obvious that they were watching you that it affected your ability to function. And there are FBI documents that say, let us encourage this idea that there is an agent behind every tree."

At the College Press Service, a writer named Sal Ferrera had shown up just after the May Day demonstrations, chockablock with radical credentials. "We thought that was great," Berlet recalls. "I mean, here we have this collapsing service—we were bundling it up in a truck and taking it from Washington to Denver to escape the creditors—and here's this guy who says he wants to be our Paris correspondent." Berlet was less thrilled after Ferrera was accused by radicals of helping to stick renegade ex-CIA agent Philip Agee with a bugged typewriter and of infiltrating the offices of the Provisional Revolutionary Government of Vietnam. "I saw that as a real blot on my record," Berlet says ruefully. (The New York *Times* subsequently reiterated some of the charges; Ferrera has denied ties to the CIA in an interview with investigative reporter Angus Mackenzie.)

Agents were not the government's only means of intervention. Since 1967, conspiracy indictments had failed in Oakland, Boston, Chicago, and New Haven. But the doings of the Weather Underground and the bombing of a bathroom in the Capitol (a blow to the seat of government?) had sent the administration off on a national grand-jury fishing expedition that netted, among others, Tom Miller, a Tucson-based free-lancer close to radical sources.

Miller's motion to quash the subpoena cited the case of Earl Caldwell, a New York *Times* reporter who'd successfully resisted a San Francisco grand jury's call for his Black Panther sources. On September 1, 1971, a U.S. District Court judge gave Miller the benefit of the doubt. "He appears to be a member of the group [the Movement] about which he reports rather than an objective reporter. He enjoys a dual capacity." But the judge upheld Miller's need for reportorial "trust and confidence" unless the government met the Caldwell case's test for "compelling need." The government appealed, but as with Caldwell, the grand jury's term elapsed before a decision was reached. (In 1972, *Branzburg v. Hayes* would severely limit such privilege.)

As Berlet again points out, such forays were expected even as they were fought. "The government was at war with us, and many of us saw ourselves as having almost established a beachhead in America. Many thought it was a fight to the finish. We went up and trained with guns in the mountains, and took all that seriously. A lot of underground journalists knew how to handle arms of all sorts—not because they were gun nuts but because they really thought that at some point they and the political movement as a whole were just going to push one step beyond, and the government was just going to drop the anvil on their heads. I mean, we had our contingency plans for hiding the press and disbursing the collective and regrouping, and stuff like that."

At least one new constituency was already fighting that war.

At twenty-nine, George Jackson had spent more than ten years in jail for a $70 robbery. It was his third offense, and in San Quentin he'd headed a black gang, but he and the underground papers stressed his transformation into a field marshal of the Black Panther Party. An indictment of him and two other inmates for allegedly killing a guard in January, 1970, the papers argued, was either a frameup or revenge for the slaying by guards of three inmates. *Soledad Brother,* his autobiography, was a gripping indictment of racism and the penal system. His seventeen-year-old brother, Jonathan, had been killed the previous August while trying to free prisoners (see Chapter 15). In the underground press, George Jackson was a man of carbon steel.

On August 21, 1971, he made his move. There may have been aborted plans for an assault on the prison by Black Panthers and an armed white group called the August 7th Movement, but it was Jackson who produced a 9mm automatic and told other prisoners, "The Black Dragon has come to free you." Two white convicts and three guards had their throats slashed by razor blades. Then Jackson sprinted toward a twenty-five-foot wall, gun blazing. Two returning shots later, his body lay in the prison yard.

A final bloody crime to add to his record, authorities said. "Murderous lying," a prison supplement in the *Seed* proclaimed, questioning the circumstances of Jackson's death, hyperbolizing that "once a black man is in prison, it is doubtful that he will come out again, except in a wooden box," promulgating the consolation that Jackson's death had sped Revolution and drawn attention "to the most repressed, enslaved segment of our population." Quieter moments found many Movement and underground-press people, in the words of former *Ramparts* writers Peter Collier and David Horowitz, "bewildered by the nature of these events as well as by their velocity."

From September 9 to 13, more than a thousand inmates at New York's Attica state prison rebelled. The facility's courtyard became a tent city, a prisoners' Woodstock. Negotiations ensued: twenty-eight of thirty demands were tentatively accepted, while the inmates dropped a pie-in-the-sky call for transportation to anti-imperialist countries. But there was a deadlock over full amnesty and replacement of the warden—and over the death of a guard under uncertain circumstances. Then Attica became a penal Kent State as seventeen hundred police and national guardsmen crushed the uprising. Thirty prisoners and nine more guard-hostages died. "Attica is all of us!" extensive underground coverage said, linking the prisoners' revolt to struggles from Vietnam to Wall Street. "Amerika," the *Seed* declared in its Jackson-Attica supplement, was one big jail, Attica was My Lai, convicts were the most likely rebels. The prisoners, LNS concluded, had not died in vain "because the uprising at Attica did not start here nor will it end here."

Nor did it. Other prisons flared up, and in November, 1983, the same New York *Times* that had erroneously denounced the prisoners for killing the hostages would report a New York State Appeals Court finding that the government had "intentionally used excessive force." Meanwhile, revolutionary politics tossed the entire concept of crime into the ashcan of bourgeois behavior. "The masses" had a broader definition of who the victims of crime were. The result left the Movement further isolated than ever.

VIOLENCE wasn't the only pressure on the papers. At *Chinook,* the Colorado paper that had cohosted the Oyster River meeting, lifestyle politics took a new turn as a group of staffers simultaneously became followers of the boy guru Mahara Ji.

"They came in with these glowing smiles; it was as if someone had just dropped enormous downers into their soup," *Chinook*er Chip Berlet recalls. "One week, they're running around like maniacs putting the paper together, the next they come in and saying, 'It's OK if the paper's going to be late,' and everybody else is running around saying, 'My God, what about all the advertisers who've prepaid?' "

Chinook survived by merging with the *Straight Creek Journal.* WPAX was less fortunate.

The call-letters signified a plan by Abbie Hoffman and others to air rock-'n'-peace broadcasts over Radio Hanoi. But the collective of freaky Tokyo Roses collapsed amid arguments, ripoffs—and, Abbie has charged, U.S. governmental pressure on Aeroflot, the Soviet airline, not to transport tapes to Hanoi.

At LNS, continuing gender issues precipitated the most serious rift in the news service since Marshall Bloom's self-theft of 1968.

In January, 1971, Allen Young had again visited Cuba. The Cubans accepted that he was gay, but had chilled after he began distributing gay-lib literature. "We invited you because you're an anti-imperialist journalist," he recalls being told. Soon he was openly criticizing the Castro regime—and much of the American Left's merely pro forma acceptance of gay rights. But his fervor could be a correct line of its own: "It may be utopian to think that all people who now define themselves as straight will become gay. But it is not utopian to ask people who call themselves revolutionaries to struggle against sexism by working toward establishing a gay identity."

Now Young was editing a newsletter called *Gay Flames* when he received what became known as a "Letter from Cuban Gay People to the North American Gay Liberation Movement":

"Sisters and brothers," it began, and proceeded to chronicle how, "since its beginning—first in veiled ways, later without scruples or rationalizations—the Cuban revolutionary government has persecuted homosexuals." Subject to punishments from beatings and prison farms to "psychological repression [and] social isolation," the letter charged, Cuban gays lived in fear.

The letter called on both of Young's divided loyalties. "I didn't know what to do with it," he recalls. "I was still trying to sit on the fence, being pro-Cuban and being a gay activist. And I felt on a gut level that [the letter] was authentic."

Young knew about the negative remarks gay members of the Venceremos Brigades had encountered during their cane-cutting expeditions to Cuba, and that in April, 1971, the First [Cuban] National Conference on Education and Culture had defined homosexuality as "social pathology" and called for a purge of "notorious" homosexuals. He would learn that that was only the latest of several purges.

About to leave a New York gay movement "beset by increasingly dogmatic preoccupations," Young did what he saw as politically correct and gave the letter to two Hispanic members of the Gay Liberation Front. Soon a translated version appeared in the gay press. By then Young had moved upstate, away from a gay movement "beset by increasingly unpleasant encounters over dogmatic preoccupations" for a rural life he now found "more relevant—politically and culturally." But other gay activists demanded that LNS distribute the letter. And at LNS, factions immediately debated contradictory credos of radical journalism.

Since forming in 1967, LNS had supported self-determination for Third World countries. "How much did LNS really know about the Cuban historical experience?" one group asked. "And are we sure this anonymous letter is authentic?" After all, the staff had been victimized by the distribution of a bogus packet of antisemitic articles.

"What about the rights and self-determination of gay people?" the other group countered. "If gay Cubans are saying this is happening there, we should be prepared to write about it just as much as we would here in the United States."

Was Cuba homophobic? Was the Left? After all, East Germany, a Communist society, had stricken its sodomy laws in 1968; maybe Cuba would follow suit. Perhaps it had only stumbled en route to neutralizing the effects of centuries of machismo and Mafia imperialism. Perhaps, it would be suggested, the CIA had organized a gay fifth column. And if push come to shove, weren't land and bread more important than being open about sexual preference?

Or were Young's new instincts correct, and Cuban homophobia a sign of a flaw in Marxism-Leninism itself?

LNS distributed the letter—with deletions of some criticism of the Left. "I agreed that was censorship," says Alan Howard, who'd taken the internationalist point of view. "Most papers carry on censorship according to what their politics are." The rift deepened after an LNSer returned from Havana and communicated Cuban criticism that publishing the letter had aired the Movement's dirty laundry. It split wide open with a Cuban attempt to select LNS's representation to a conference celebrating the Cuban revolution. In October, Howard and another LNSer were expelled from the collective.

In January, they distributed an eighty-one-page critique called "Liberation News Service: Bourgeois or Revolutionary Journalism?" "I'm not sure how much of it I would defend with my life today," Howard notes now, "but as Uncle Walter would say, 'That's the way it was.' "

The manifesto excoriated "political confusion and journalistic incompetence" at LNS—as revealed in part by the "slanderous" Cuban-gay letter. LNS packets, they charged, were filled with lifts from "the bourgeois press" seasoned with stock right-on phrases. In fact, the thinly staffed collective had become so dependent on mainstream papers and its own clients that, despite sending out nearly forty pages of coverage on the Attica rising, LNS had taken ten weeks to send a reporter upstate.

The purgees' indictment continued. LNS's stories failed to link specific events to larger movements. The collective even distrusted its own sources: Howard charged that his on-the-scene story of CIA manipulation of Chilean copper prices had been held until the New York *Times* confirmed the story. The *Times,* he and the others complained, "continues to be considered a more reliable source of news at LNS about the war in Indochina than the news agency of the National Liberation Front of South Vietnam or the DRV [Democratic Republic of Vietnam], if we are to judge by the amount of material taken from these respective publications for use in LNS."

That argument ignored such questions as the DRV's own media agenda, or its denial that Hanoi troops were fighting below the Seventeenth Parallel. But the united writers remained politically confident. "It is fashionable these days to speculate about the movement being dead," they admitted. "But such speculation is only wishful thinking on the part of the bourgeoisie and a momentary lapse of historical consciousnessness on the part of some comrades. . . . Revolutionary journalists also understand that in addition to their honesty . . . they also have the weapon of a science of revolution known as Marxism-Leninism, the theoretical validity of which has been proven under a wide variety of historical conditions." The present collective, the writers charged, felt that "this science has no central relevance to their work of producing propaganda for our movement."

The dissidents had their points. But if their appendixed survey of subscribers proved that little LNS copy was being used, it also showed that lifestyle or "celebrity" pieces were about all that the subscriber papers were running. Even at the height of SDS, many editors had opposed LNS's attempts to "organize" them. Now there was even less mandate for LNS using lumpy rhetoric to set the correct line.

FROM ITS BEGINNING in November, 1967, *Rolling Stone* had stressed rock over politics, reform over revolution, peace over violence, professionalism over psychedelic innovation, ownership over collectivity. The approach had paid off. Its financial crisis weathered, *RS*'s biweekly circulation now approached a quarter-million. A new writer named Hunter Thompson was saying the damnedest things about something called "Fear and Loathing in Las Vegas," and was about to explore similar conditions on the campaign trail. For Jann Wenner in November, 1971, the magazine's fourth anniversary, the Movement was a bum steer rather than a great helmsman. Spurred by a dispute over whether or not Abbie Hoffman had stolen parts of *Steal This Book* (which Hoffman vigorously denied), Wenner said his own goodbye to all that.

The "Woodstock Nation" was a fantasy, he wrote. "As long as there are printing bills to pay, writers who want to earn a living by their craft, people who pay for their groceries, want to raise children and have their own homes, *Rolling Stone* will be a capitalist operation." Violent rhetoric was "the weapon of Spiro Agnew," talk of armed struggle "insane fantasy." And, again, rock 'n' roll would not jump through radical hoops.

Counterculture utopians disagreed. The Rock Liberation Front, a street-hardened, scruffy group of writers, musicians, and freaks, raided *RS*'s New York office, carrying off memos they believed projected the magazine's view that it was the best home that record advertising could have. Other critics put their objections into print. *Rolling Stone,* Berkeley radical Craig Pyes wrote, "leads the way in branding 'politicos' as austere, lifeless, tight-assed straights, who only want to kill and repress, and not have a good time." It "was designed to channel the energies and imagination of youth culture . . . into dependence on American business, while using its influence to quiet *real* dissent."

Wenner denied such overt motives, but Pyes's denunciation was more interesting than most; now he was coeditor of *SunDance,* a magazine designed to be both radical and readable. And now he had John Lennon on his side.

SunDance's prospectus saw beginnings, not ends. "America has just gone through the first part of a political/cultural renaissance, the seed of which was embodied in the counterculture, rock music, and the whole underground media, permeated by New Left–wing politics and a new aesthetic." Nobody, said Pyes and coeditor Ken Kelley (late of the Ann Arbor *Argus*) was reaching the audience touched by those forces. The daily press offered "dry-as-dust, exclusionist journalism." Existing Left publications were "academic . . . and ideological." *Rolling Stone* was "an organ of the music industry . . . lax and cynical in its news coverage." And Pyes and Kelley identified an area of inadequacy not often subjected to a radical critique: the underground press, "parochial, rhetorical, and crude . . . often uneven and sophomoric."

"The *Tribe* had degenerated into a Southeast Asian publication," Pyes recalls. "The *Barb* was doing great sales where people would take it home to find a 'well-hung black stud.' The underground press was dying, and there was a huge readership projected."

SunDance, Pyes and Kelley fervently believed, could reach it. Committed writers included some of the best and brightest radicals and progressives—Robert Scheer, Kate Coleman, Todd Gitlin, Jeff Gerth, Allen Young, Frank Bardacke, Paul Krassner. Stringers had familiar bylines too: Tom Miller, Harvey Wasserman, Claudia Dreifus, Abe Peck —and John and Yoko. Lennon, the man who'd denounced Movement "minds that hate" in 1968's "Revolution," now wanted to join up.

Lennon had cooled toward *Rolling Stone* after Wenner surprised him by reprinting his vivid, lengthy "Lennon Remembers" interview in book form. But the change also was Jerry Rubin's coup. Lifted from his own depression by "Working Class Hero" and "Hold on John," Jerry had called Apple Records and arranged a successful rendezvous. In November, Lennon played an Apollo Theater benefit for the Attica prisoners. The next month, he helped realize the Yippie dream-merger of music and politics.

That was quite a group onstage at Ann Arbor's Crisler Arena. Stevie

Wonder and Bobby Seale. Bob Seger and Dave Dellinger. Archie Shepp and Allen Ginsberg. All were there to Free John Sinclair, the White Panther leader serving ten years for giving two joints to an undercover agent. Way past the midnight hour, a new lineup appeared. John Lennon, a "Free John" button on his cap, sang "Attica State," "Sisters O Sisters," "Luck of the Irish," and "(It Ain't Fair), John Sinclair." Jerry Rubin shook his maracas and banged away on congas. The music was scattered, the performance fifteen minutes of anticlimax with the audience wishing for boogie more than for barricades. But it made for great political imagery—especially when Sinclair was released three days later, officially because of forthcoming changes in the state marijuana statutes.

What freed one John got another in trouble with a third one. Conservative Senator Strom Thurmond soon advised Attorney General John Mitchell that John Lennon had some new friends, and was planning to demonstrate at the 1972 Republican National Convention. "Constructive surveillance" ensued, and Lennon would have a four-year fight on his hands before defeating an attempt to deport him based on a minor 1968 British soft-drug conviction.

By then, Lennon would rue his radicalism, and his public statements would attribute the change less to government harassment than to an echo of World War I radical John Reed's statement about politics playing hell with your poetry. "It almost *ruined* it, in a way," he'd tell Pete Hamill —and *Rolling Stone*. "It became journalism and not poetry." But that was later, in 1975; back in 1972, he and Yoko Ono not only joined a roster of artists, poets, actors, and producers in fundraising for *SunDance,* but were columnists when the magazine debuted in April.

In the four-color, slick-covered, oversized tabloid bimonthly, Robert Scheer lent a critical eye to Nixon's startling February trip to China. Other stories discussed strip-mining, Attica, abortion, the youth vote. The writing was more to the Left than the alternative papers. But it was post-Movement reportage rather than revolutionary rhetoric. The words *socialism* and *communism* were hardly used.

The first issue sold most of a twenty-thousand-copy press run. There was talk about going monthly, maybe even weekly. Pyes and Kelley wondered whether they had the next *Ramparts* on their hands.

Certainly there were topics to write about. On April 15, tax dollars paid for the bombing of Hanoi and Haiphong. In May, J. Edgar Hoover died and George Wallace was shot. In June, several burglars were arrested at a Washington, D.C., apartment complex called the Watergate. As *Sun-Dance* had predicted, fewer underground-press stalwarts were around to cover the stories. The *Tribe* had gone under in May, choked by penury and incomprehensible diatribes aimed at turning Berkeley into North Korea. *EVO* and other papers again dismissed Nixonian corruption as something they'd been charging for years. They were right, but so much for expanding their audience—or holding it.

On August 22 and 23, twelve hundred demonstrators were arrested as Richard Nixon was nominated for reelection in Miami. Some protesters established a rapport with older residents, and antiwar, welfare-rights, and racial-justice groups made their points. The Yippie honchos now supported George McGovern; freaks known as Zippies lambasted them as old fogies while protesting with a zeal that often became obnoxious. "What a bunch of screaming assholes," thought Tom Miller, the Yippiephile reporter who'd outlasted a grand-jury subpoena for his sources, as he watched the chaos on television. "We really look bad to everybody. This is awful."

After the convention, Miller traveled to Texas, where he did a story for *SunDance* on the auctioning off of Jack Ruby's effects. Soon after, an editor from *Esquire* called to compliment him on the piece. "If you don't mind," he asked, "how much did *SunDance* pay you?"

"Well, if I ever get the check, it will be fifteen dollars."

"Gee, that's too bad," the editor said. "We would have paid you seven hundred fifty for the same thing. Keep us in mind." Miller was stunned. "Here are these magazines we've been calling the pig media, and one of them wants to pay me good bucks to do an article." Had he changed? Them? Both?

"SunDance just might replace *Life*," San Francisco's *Good Times* said in its review of the debut issue. That was hyperbole, but meaningful stories did appear. The third issue found Jeff Gerth writing about crime-syndicate types around the Nixon White House, Robert Scheer arguing that not backing George McGovern would leave "many of us on the Left . . . with a stain of complicity in genocide."

But the *Good Times* prediction proved only half correct; both *SunDance* and *Life* would fold. At *SunDance,* money ran low, some members of the collective proved more equal than others, and the third issue was the last.

If radicals were surprised, a new breed of alternative journalists wasn't. "*SunDance* had no editorial cohesiveness, no central editorial vision, and appeared as an amateurish, if lavish, indulgence of the underground sensibility," a University of Texas journalism student named Chet Flippo wrote in a master's thesis on *Rolling Stone,* where he would soon begin work.

By then, though, a successful hybrid magazine was gaining strength.

Ms. had begun independent publication in July, a demonstration of feminism's rapid (if belated) emergence into mass culture. A prototype had appeared in *New York* magazine the previous December, and Gloria Steinem, Pat Carbine, and other members of the *Ms.* collective had been able to raise $1 million for the magazine. *Ms.* merged pieces on matriarchy with stories on obtaining full access to mainstream jobs, and was of great value to a growing women's movement—and to readers who'd never previously been touched by women's liberation. Its first issue contained a petition for safe and legal abortion and a demand for the passage of an Equal Rights Amendment, a style of "responsible protest" it would maintain.

Harry Reasoner, then at ABC, gave *Ms.* five months before it ran out of material. In 1982, the magazine's tenth-anniversary issue would celebrate numerous victories (though not passage of the Equal Rights Amendment), a nonprofit magazine circulating nearly a half-million copies that had given away more than $1.5 million through its Foundation for Women. But articles on women mayors, salutes to male executives who'd helped women secure equal employment, and ads from Revlon, American Express, and Zales Diamonds were not what radical feminists had in mind in 1972.

Late in 1972, many activists remained hard at work. There were stark, angry comments, as when *Nola Express* headlined an article on Christmas air raids by the U.S. Air Force "Enemy Bombs Hanoi." And there was more patient organizing: at *Rising Up Angry,* writers and photographers staffed a health clinic and other serve-the-people organizations.

But the press of criticism still could be highly uncritical, as Danny Schechter, the LNS and *Old Mole* writer who'd become "the news dissector" of Boston's WBCN radio, found out when he went to Havana for a gathering of the more Left media:

"There were people from the *Great Speckled Bird* [Atlanta], the *Guardian* [New York] and WBAI [the New York listener-sponsored radio station]. And I raised some questions about the gay movement's criticisms, and questions about why the Cuban press seemed so tame and unwilling to play any kind of critical role. There were problems ordinary people talked about; Fidel made a speech about why the sugar-cane harvest didn't work. Where was the press investigating all this stuff?

"I got chided for being a counterrevolutionary—not by the Cubans, but by the other people in the alternative media. I was struck by the unwillingness of these people in the underground press to raise these questions even when they felt them."

By now, the underground press also had its own generation gap; papers purporting to represent youth culture were not attracting new young people, because of changing priorities or more attractive alternatives.

As a high school kid with a rock 'n' roll heart, Cameron Crowe thought that the hippie-oriented San Diego *Door*, which had outlasted the more politically radical *Street Journal*, was "the coolest thing I'd ever seen." But the more Crowe wrote for it, the less enthusiastic he became. "I was made to feel that I was doing scrap work for the Movement," he recalls. "Plus someone in the collective was stealing the best records."

At one issue post-mortem, Crowe saw that one of his articles had been butchered. He waited patiently while heavier matters were discussed, then asked for a chance to speak. "I like the issue," he said, "but this Carole King review has a bad mistake in the headline."

Crowe had a point: "Cosol Kirg" wasn't exactly correct. But he didn't exactly get satisfaction. "They were like, 'Oh, dude, c'mon. It's *just* a record review,' " Crowe recalls.

Maybe, but not for him. After meeting a *Rolling Stone* editor at the Rolling Stones benefit for the victims of the December, 1972, earthquake in Nicaragua, Crowe began writing a string of articles that would include numerous cover stories. *"Rolling Stone* was a grown-up version of the *Door,"* he says, *"the Door* refined in a commercial direction, but still with the communal spirit. *Rolling Stone* started getting even more slick, and a couple of [*Door*] writers got disdainful. I didn't hear from them for a while—and then they wanted to write for *Rolling Stone."*

The *Door* would close in 1974. But by then, several record execs had solved a mystery for Crowe—how the *Door* had managed to hold onto its music ads while so many others had lost theirs. "Isn't that the paper," they'd asked, "with the guy who sold us the great weed?"

CONNIE AND I left the country in the summer of 1971 to salvage our nerves, our perspective, my health, our relationship. In London and Paris, we stayed at communes associated with underground papers. In Crete, we camped on a beach under a night sky so clear that patrol planes shone for hours like stars on short orbits.

But as we traveled, an unexpected issue began to surface.

In Berlin, we visited with a family whose son had stayed with Connie's as part of a church exchange program. After dinner, the *frau* broke into a fleshy, hippolike smile. "Juden?" she asked, looking my way. Connie's "What did you do in the war" diatribe produced a lame rash of "We didn't know" disclaimers.

In Egypt, we clambered over the Great Pyramid, explored temples at Karnak and Luxor, and learned that the first cataract of the Nile was an

Arab-to-Nubian changing neighborhood. As a whole, Egyptians are extremely friendly, and we hooked up with what was probably the country's only rock 'n' roll band, setting up house in the guitar player's empty apartment, nearly starting a riot by doing the Woodstock stomp during the group's "concert" at the university in Alexandria.

But en route to Aswan in these pre–Camp David days, a young Italian woman asked if I was Jewish, then said I was crazy to be traveling past a MiG-laden air base.

Back in Cairo, staying closer to the din of Ramses Square than the touristy insulation of the Nile Hilton, I said "Christian" when asked my religion. But the fib bored like an earwig into my sense of self and my friendships with Hassan, Moenas, and the others. My perspective brightened when Hassan took us home for dinner and spoke about peace between Egypt and "the other place." But though I'd supported the idea of a binational Palestine-Israel, and after the skyjackings of 1970 had put together a Third World Airways travel poster for the *Seed,* I was chilled as Hassan's sister screamed, "Into the sea, into the sea." It was a disillusionment that the murders of the Israeli Olympians at Munich would accelerate.

"The other place" also had its difficulties. Praying for my father at the Wailing Wall in Jerusalem moved me, and I sensed the diaspora's coat-of-many-colors homecoming. But the country's garrison-state sensibility and a refugee camp outside of Hebron darkened my stay. As we headed toward Istanbul and our return to the States, I'd become a Jewish cynic about the Middle East.

Winter was approaching, and two other issues were now in play. By now, Connie and I had fought our way across three continents; the end was nigh for us. But returning home meant Doing Something. The *Seed* also was over for me. What was next?

We get by with the help of our friends, I thought as I sent letters off to Chicago and New York. I was, I wrote, now ready to take a job— with flexible hours, social validity, and a sense of fun. And at the American Express office in Athens, I found an answer. It was from Marshall Rosenthal, the *Seed*ling with whom I'd shared so many ups and downs, and who was now writing for the Panorama section of the Chicago *Daily News,* the thinking person's arts section at the town's thinking-person's paper. My man!

Marshall had thought hard about my request, he wrote, and finally come up with something flexible and rewarding and fun and noncoopted that paid a bit of money. "The season is almost upon us, and if you hurry back, you may be able to get a post as a department store Santa Claus."

It was a Zen knock on the head; this transition was not going to be easy.

Back in Chicago, Connie and I didn't last long; pretty soon, only the kitty-cats were living at home. But I began to write again, reviewing books about the Left and counterculture for the *Daily News.* And I and some other former *Seed*lings began hatching a plan for a successor to the *Seed.*

September 21, 1972. Location: Lincoln Avenue, Chicago. Page 145716, Chicago police intelligence files:

"Information has been received that the subject is in Chicago attempting to raise money to publish a Magazine. The Magazine will be concerned with political editorials and articles. It is understood that the SUBJECT already has $10,000 to begin work on the Magazine."

People had suggested to Eliot Wald and Flora Johnson and artist Peter Solt and I that we reposition the *Seed* as a post-underground paper. That was impossible; the *Seed* belonged to a particular community, a Movement, a time. It wasn't ours to change, and any change would be rightfully resisted by those who were now the *Seed.* Instead, we began a monthly magazine called *Chicago 606* (as in the zip code). It had some good reading, a good calendar, a good look. But it substituted a wary rotating editorship and self-conscious hipness for a timely editorial vision, collective or individual. Chicago's major local distributor wanted to take *606* on, but its offer belatedly showed that printing costs alone would soon bankrupt us. Five issues in, we pulled the plug.

The winner of the replace-the-*Seed* derby was the *Reader,* begun on October 1, 1971, by, among others, a burly University of Chicago political-philosophy student named Bob Roth, whose models were *Boston After Dark* and *New York.* "I wasn't into it," he'd say of the sixties scene. "College and grad school were both rigorous places, where there was emphasis on quality, and critical abilities were almost a fetish."

Starting with little advertising, giving the paper away, the weekly almost went broke printing fifty-six thousand copies. But the *Reader* approach began to attract support. There were personal yet reportorial features as opposed to hard news or radical rhetoric. Listings, personals, and reviews reached "hip consumers" (a by-now transcended contradiction in terms). Instead of strident advocacy, the *Reader* offered the early ideal of the Los Angeles *Free Press*—a community forum—with the radical political purpose removed. "We don't call it 'editorial schizophrenia,' Roth would say. "We call it 'unpredictability' and 'freshness.' " And there was another difference from the underground press—"We hoped to make money." The *Reader*'s cash flow would turn positive in the third year of publication. By then, the *Seed* would be gone, buried in back taxes and old business.

On April 26, 1973, the Central Intelligence Agency joined the media critics with its previously cited "Situation Information Report: The Underground Press." Smarmy and reductionist, the document also accurately read a trend—one it had helped create:

"The underground press . . . was the product of a changing national consciousness reflected most visibly by young people. Although lacking a clear analysis . . . many made motions to Marxism but actually leaned heavily toward anarchism.

"The underground press is now in decline," the document continued. "It would appear that the vitality of the 'alternative' press was directly proportional to the health of the radical movement in general. The underground press arose from the ferment of the times, and the abatement of that ferment has undercut its strength and need."

THE UNDERGROUND PRESS REVUE

July / August 1973

Published by the Underground Press Syndicate, Box 26, Village Station, New York, N.Y. 10014; (212) 242-3888.   Vol. 8 No. 5

It is time, we believe, for a name change. The consciousness of our particular media community, founded in 1966, has undergone a definite change. Then, there were five papers. The ideas and lifestyle they espoused were shared only by small pockets of people on Haight Street, Telegraph Avenue, Topanga Canyon, the East Village. The five papers formed the Underground Press Syndicate. It was definitely underground. Then.

Now, the UPS list shows over two hundred members around the world, from St. Louis to Bombay. The underground ideas and lifestyle have emerged into the mainstream of thought everywhere, in books, plays, films, advertising. Even the established press has adopted our new journalistic style and our role as questioners of authority. The rock press has co-opted our youthful orientation. The sex press has given unhealthy implications to the word "underground." Meanwhile, increased acceptance, public visibility, and a general shift in editorial content away from shocking the public towards "serving the people" has made "underground" a misnomer.

At the Boulder Conference in June, the trend of thinking was very clear. Most papers prefer the designation "alternative" and even find the word "underground" an obstacle to reaching more readers. In the UPS office, too, we find that researchers, the media, Madison Avenue, and interested individuals are distracted by the term before they have time to see what we are really about. Though we are the only press uniquely equipped to go underground at a moment's notice, what we are really about is viable, social alternatives.

Therefore, we hereby submit the following proposal for a vote to the entire membership in all parts of the world. Resolved: that the name of the Underground Press Syndicate shall be changed to Alternative Press Syndicate.

Please fill out the coupon as soon as possible and send it in to be counted. Any other suggestions for names will be considered, and if necessary, resubmitted for another vote.

Resolved: that the name of the Underground Press Syndicate shall be changed to Alternative Press Syndicate.

( ) Yes. We vote for the change.
( ) No. We vote against the change.
( ) We want a change, but not to APS. Here is our suggestion:

Name of Paper _____
Address _____
City, State, Zip _____

Signed by Staff Member _____

Return to: Box 26, Village Station, New York, N.Y. 10014.

17

AMERICA DRINKS UP
AND GOES HOME

BOULDER, COLORADO—JUNE 8-10, 1973: People swirled through rooms at the Community Free School. The underground's first national conference in three years had attracted a hundred fifty people from fifty-three papers and news services. Instead of the guns and guards of 1970, this meeting was about more subtle survival—and whether it was time for the underground to level with itself.

Through summers of love and winters of discontent, the papers—"colorful shots of freaky glee," writers Thorne Dreyer and Victoria Smith called them—mirrored their movements, represented "the positive and the negative, the vision of a better way and the need to destroy the old, the loving and the burning." But dreams of creating a new society in the shell of the old, or even of seizing state power, were proving illusory. It was shocking to those of us who had believed in impending change, but "the People" had rejected "the Revolution."

As our enclaves shriveled or adapted to less intense times, community-based, multi-issue underground papers began adapting or dying. Audiences had been alienated by condescension, rhetoric, error, irregularity, ugliness, Movement violence, more state violence—and by the serious demands radical social change entailed. Even success had its price—antiimperialist, antiracist, antisexist politics, rock, sex, and environmentalism were filtering into more palatable publications. Many papers could no longer count on raising press-run money from ads that couldn't appear elsewhere; cynics said that rising welfare payments had dried up the supply of street vendors. In January, Hanoi and Washington had signed the Paris Peace Accords, and though it would be twenty-seven months before the war really ended, American involvement in Vietnam—and the dreaded draft —were winding down.

Many of the first-generation, culture-based papers hadn't made it to Boulder. The *Oracle's* paisley pages lay buried amid the rubble of the Haight-Ashbury, its ex-readers tripping more quietly, living in the country, or busy proving *Good Times* writer Sandy Darlington's plaint that middle-class values were stronger than acid. The *Fifth Estate* hung on in Detroit, but *EVO's* ledgers had turned murky, then terminal. The *Barb* was drowning in sex ads; London's bright, playful *Oz* was about to fold. The L.A. *Free Press* still had a ninety-thousand circulation, and the conviction against editor Arthur Kunkin and reporter Jerry Appelbaum for publishing the list of narcotics agents had just been reversed on the grounds that the accused lacked sufficient reason to know it was stolen. But Kunkin, now an employee after being bankrupted by the malfunctioning presses he'd bought to preserve his freedom to publish, soon was told by the *Freep's* new owners not to bother with a story about something called Watergate, and to pull the *Freep* out of UPS. A month after Boulder, he would be fired from the paper he had begun—the paper that had begun the underground press.

Many second-generation papers—those that had sought to merge the New Left with youth lifestyle—hadn't made it either. The *Rat* had become *Women's Liberation,* then incandesced in Weatherwoman frenzy. The *Tribe* had choked on the Kim Il Sung style book. The GI-socialist *Bond* was folding with the withdrawal of U.S. troops from Vietnam. The *Ladder* and the *Furies,* two generations of lesbian papers, were giving way to other journals. *Kaleidoscope, Good Times, Helix*—gone.

On one near flank, *Rolling Stone* was two months away from declaring itself "a general interest magazine, covering modern American culture, politics and arts, with a special interest in music." On the other, an actual underground press was abuilding, its Weatherman publications to be called *Prairie Fire* and *Osawatomie*—too feeble, violent, and gibberish-laden to matter.

At Boulder, the sponsoring paper was Denver's *Straight Creek Journal,* which hadn't existed during the 1960s. And at Boulder, at least, the heroes were changing—from Tim Leary and Huey Newton to I.F. Stone, the wizard of the anti-establishment yet verifiable story, whose *Weekly* pre-dated the underground press.

"What I call the third generation," Chip Berlet, then with *Straight Creek,* says, "was when there was a shaking out and you saw the under-ground papers begin to do investigative articles—begin to take journal-ism more seriously, frankly." *Straight Creek's* big story, after all, was not about some apocalyptic demonstration but a link between a Winter Olympics committee and ski manufacturers that, when unearthed, led voters to nix the entire event. "What's left in 1973," Berlet continues, "is, more than anything else, alternative journalists looking for an audi-ence. And you have people coming up from *New Times* in Arizona, and they say, 'Hey folks, there is a third way. There is hope for a journalism in America that continues to be antagonistic towards the status quo, but more in the way it approaches stories than either in jargon or style. And what that needs is a firm advertising base.'

"And that was the basic premise of Boulder."

There were Marxists at Boulder—and Jesus people. Denver's *Big Mama Rag* was the only women's paper represented, and, after a survey showed the dearth of female decision-makers on hand, a quick protest added a workshop on feminism to the agenda. Some women were bitter; weren't the white men leaving now that they no longer held center stage?

At one session, Art Kunkin spoke about how the papers filled the vacuum created by the lack of a mass political party. Other speakers talked about Attica; the clash between Indian activists and the FBI agents at Wounded Knee, South Dakota; Chicano rights; grand juries. There also was what the *New Yorker's* Calvin Trillin would recall as "philosophical arguments pitting people committed to keeping their bodies free of all chemicals against people who had too many chemicals in their bodies to put up much of an argument."

But many in attendance had come for the controlled-circulation work-shop, or to discuss a national advertising agency and a graphics service. Some felt like mammals among dinosaurs, and Trillin saw them trying to become "journalists rather than revolutionaries or harbingers of the New Zonked-Out Millennium."

Tom Miller, he of the grand-jury source hunt, was less thrilled. "The conference was, if anything, the final plunge in the long dive from political flamboyance to economic stability," he'd write in the *Barb* just after the event. "Some of the more outrageous aggressiveness has been sacrificed for something called 'credibility.'

"Four years ago a conference calling itself 'alternative press' might have attracted the *Nation, Rolling Stone,* the *Texas Observer,* and a few other periodicals," Miller would continue. But on the meeting's third day, Chip Berlet took the microphone. "The underground press is dead," he bellowed. "Long live the alternative press!" Unable to let an era end without at least a whimper, Miller posted a note announcing a new organization called OFUP—the Old Farts of the Underground Press. One acronym addict signed up.

It fell to Stephen Foehr, editor of the *Straight Creek Journal,* to propose what amounted to an obituary: "The underground press was rhetorical, radical, psychedelic in its layout, not business-oriented and had very low credibility." Foehr advocated trying for a "more stable footing by dropping this rhetoric and getting involved in their communities at the neighborhood level."

"It is time, we believe, for a name change," the *Underground Press Review* told UPS members in its July-August cover story. "Increased acceptance, public visibility, and a general shift in editorial content away from shocking the public towards 'serving the people' has made 'underground' a misnomer.... Though we are the only press uniquely equipped to go underground at a moment's notice, what we are really about is viable social alternatives.

"Therefore, we hereby submit the following proposal for a vote to the entire membership in all parts of the world. Resolved: that the name of the Underground Press Syndicate shall be changed to Alternative Press Syndicate."

The story included a ballot.

The vote ran 20 to 1 in favor of change.

ON A CRISP, cool Chelsea morning, I walk down a block on Manhattan's West Side, past the art galleries and apartments of the new hip-oisie. Entering a faceless warehouse near the Hudson River, I tell the watchman, *"High Times* sent me." Recognizing the name of the magazine of obsessional recreational drug use, he rises from behind a steel-gray desk and leads me toward what I've come to see.

Into a freight elevator, then out. Down a ramp, past rows of walk-in lockers, through a tunnel. Wire mesh and dust are everywhere; imaginary rats scurry just beyond the mind's eye. Then the watchman digs for his keys. We are at the last stash of Tom Forcade, the former Underground Press Syndicate head who'd started *High Times* out of the old UPS office. The magazine had prospered, but despite its success, Forcade shot himself in 1978.

In the storage cage, stacks of brown cardboard boxes contain hundreds of underground papers. There are images of war, racism, community; women's-liberation symbols and gay-lib lambdas; Spaceship Earth and the werewolf moon over the houses trashed by Charles Manson and William (My Lai) Calley. There are Huey Newton and Huey helicopters; the Beatles, Bob Dylan, and Kent State—new heroes, new mornings, new martyrs.

The images are Icarus-like. The Haight-Ashbury, the Amazon Nation, the People's Republics of Berkeley, Vietnam, China, Cuba—every underground utopia had failed to materialize or proved to have problems more severe than we'd written about. Downward mobility and a fun subculture hadn't been substitutes for an economic base and a sustaining mass theory. The boat people, Kampuchean horror, cocaine abuse, heroin chic, babies making babies, hardcore porn, ERA's defeat, Solidarity's suppression and sabotage against the Sandinistas, Ronald Reagan's ascendency, a black underclass, rampant consumerism and individualism, a new cold war—stories of mistakes and backlash most of the papers had not survived long enough to report.

Now, in Tom Forcade's locker, a water leak has faded the rainbows of protest.

But turning the pages suggests another set of legacies. From December, 1972, to April, 1975, alone, DDT was banned, abortions were legalized, the draft ended, U.S. troops finally left Vietnam, the American Psychiatric Association "de-diseased" homosexuality, and draconian sentences for smoking plants were reduced. The safe-energy movement began when an activist chopped down a reactor-connected weather tower on Washington's birthday in Montague, Massachusetts, where Marshall Bloom had relocated his LNS flock. Richard Nixon resigned. The war ended, with an outcome the underground press had supported.

Whether revolutionary, radical, or alternative, the underground press questioned, altered, sought to radically change that status quo. It helped topple one warrior president and challenged another who said he was not a crook. Early on, it saw that there was no light—or a Red light—at the end of the tunnel. In life during wartime, the papers had to shout over bullets to be heard, and a generation of writers eschewed the more patient tools of sourcing and checking to get the message out *now*. By the end, some papers deserved to die. But if havoc hadn't been the best way to build a Movement, the howling did help pull the boys home.

Underground papers could be arrogant, shrill, unskilled, adventuristic. Many also possessed the movements' strengths: dedication, cooperation, experimentation, playfulness. Radical in the best sense of the word, they examined the roots of society, acted on their findings, helped shape—at least for a while—a flowering of idealism and hope. Herpes and AIDS would be called social diseases; so, the underground press said, were sexism, racism, and militarism, the war against the poor and the environment. "If the entire experience of the alternative press serves to do nothing more than produce a cadre of media-aware workers with more or less nonhierarchical and nonsexist views about personal and job relationships," a 1973 *Nation* article opined, "I would say that the alternative [read *underground*] press has earned a large and well-deserved niche in this country's history."

The papers changed minds, and lives, and showed people that they could fight city hall. They ran the news that didn't fit when nobody else would. They provided an alternate history for a decade, and beyond.

While I was writing this book, one front page of the Chicago *Tribune* (now the more liberal daily in town!) covered the ERA, the European peace movement, and a gathering of eighty thousand antiwar folks at the Rose Bowl. The stories didn't advocate those causes, but were fairer and more balanced than what might have appeared fifteen years ago. In general, the mass press seems less slavish toward official sources—in part based on journalistic experience during the sixties, or due to the influx of reporters who grew up then.

But contrary to hallucinatory predictions, the New York *Times* did not merge with New York's *East Village Other*. Reporters write with more stylistic latitude—but this owes at least as much to the New Journalism of the cultural neoconservative Tom Wolfe and other professionals and the challenge of television's often-phony warmth as to the wild and wooly underground. Former underground-press people do good work *within* the mainstream.

Editorial gatekeepers pronounce "objectivity" even as they swing in accord with their own "news judgment." Once-taboo subjects—gay rights, Palestinian rights, covering the rebels in Central America—now appear, but are filtered through a mainstream agenda. The Sandinistas have shortcomings, but are judged through harsher mass-media microscopes than were focused on Anastasio Somoza's oligarchy. Papers owned by large corporations contain advertising-heavy business sections, but no labor sections. In the recent election, unions became Mondale's special-interest cross to bear, while Reagan's plutocrats ran free. Minority journalists remain relatively scarce; women at some dailies have had to sue for equal rights. Few in either group are in positions of publishing power. Beyond San Francisco, is there an out-of-the-closet gay daily reporter writing on gay themes?

The ideology of mass media, Hodding Carter III has written, "moves from roughly A to E, with A being anchored to the right and E barely making it to center left. . . . For better or worse, and I think for worse, we have a press that does not so much question the national consensus as reflect it." Ted Koppel's *Nightline* is one of the few mass-media forums combining an expanded array of viewpoints with a bright, honestly subjective sensibility. The *Nation*'s Alexander Cockburn's monthly foray into the *Wall Street Journal* is the exception that proves the rule about Leftist columnists appearing in a press that often stresses demographics over democracy. As Duke University political scientists David Paletz and Robert Entman have written, "The press thrives on people robbing banks, not banks robbing people."

Surprisingly, there may be as many dissident papers now as there were during the sixties, though the diffusion, ebbing, and absorption of the movements discussed here have led to single-issue focus and smaller circulations. Too many lack the spark that comes with thinking your ideas actually are changing the world; many sit in the shadows of alternative weeklies that too often match inert politics with rampant consumerism —or conservative journals fueled by the subsidies the Right always accused the underground press of having.

But community papers, women's papers, lesbian papers, gay papers, consciousness papers, environmental papers, rock-politics papers have continued or appeared. The *Nation*, the *Village Voice*, the *Progressive* (for which I've reviewed), and the *Guardian* have endured, joined by *In These Times* and *Mother Jones*. Stories from problem Pintos to DES damage to the public availability of alleged H-bomb secrets have begun with them. They continue to provide counter-explanations for hundreds of other events, both spectacular and everyday.

I'm not rooting for it, and I can't predict my reaction to it, but polarization is in the air. Whether defending gains or pushing the pendulum back in the other direction, counter-media will have their role. As the *New Yorker*'s A.J. Liebling said, freedom of the press belongs to those who own one. And as Wes "Scoop" Nisker, the sixties newsman known for his bright sonic collages at KSAN-FM, once said, "If you don't like the news, go out and make some of your own."

"If you think you are the same person you were a decade ago," San Francisco *Chronicle* columnist Herb Caen wrote in 1975, "you are deluding yourself, or you are a fool." But the unflexing of the Movement's fist has made it harder to sift the gold from the iron pyrite today. Socialist radicals and gay-liberationists argue about whether Cuba is progressive or reactionary. Some see Russia in Afghanistan as a people's victory, or a blow for women's liberation; others (such as I) see imperialism. Punks rejected hippie lore as mindless optimism. The nuclear family no longer rules, but support systems are often shaky, poverty often feminized. In a single morning, I read reports from China denouncing its 1960s Cultural Revolution (and implicitly Mao Tse-tung) and watched Bobby Seale, former chairman of the Black Panther Party for Self-Defense, plug a book about—barbecuing. Two interviewees for this book and three Woodstock companions are dead: two from cancer, and one each from diabetes, a car accident, and flying in over the Gulf of Mexico with engine trouble and who knows what in the cargo bay.

Values combine oddly. "When my daughter came to live with me for a year, I started shoplifting more," Paul Krassner notes. "You've got to be responsible." And are these words from a 1972 FBI memo about a certain heroic guerilla a compliment or an embarrassment? "Peck was interviewed by various other police officials during his association with the *Seed* and although never disclosing information of great value, was always friendly and congenial."

While with the Student Nonviolent Coordinating Committee, Stokely Carmichael said that personal politics are determined by what you see when you look out the window. As I write, Carmichael sees Africa from self-imposed exile; I look out a high-rise window toward an old *Seed* office. I am older, and, wiser or not, play it safer. I also have a loving family, better health, rewarding work, creature comforts, a life that, for now at least, is personally free of authoritarianism posing as either friendly government or liberated behavior. I am something I thought I'd rejected—an American.

Still, the God of Synchronicity keeps things interesting. Seven years after my writing about snipers killing two cops began my departure from the *Seed*, I married the daughter of the judge in the case. During the 1968 Democratic Convention, I'd watched police riot on Chicago's Michigan Avenue; in the eighties, I stroll down that broad boulevard as part of a nuclear-freeze parade marching with a police escort. Ego and principle vie when a South African literary agent asks to buy reprint rights to an article; the money goes to Amnesty International. I attend a speech by an ambassador from Nicaragua, and find myself being picketed by demonstrators from the Right—and then get angry when somebody tries to prevent a conservative protester from speaking.

These days, I see myself in Cornell University professor Theodore J. Lowi's characterization of sixties activists as "extreme reformists": "They used radical action to gain attention, but their demands and hopes were for the present society to live by its own ideals. . . . And the Sixties movement succeeded to a large extent. Universities reorganized themselves; there is more public access to agencies; there have been civil rights advances; there is more pacifism. Success is one reason for the decline of the movement."

And yet, doubts nag. About compromise, about Left mistakes then and tilts to starboard now, about not having the Answers. Romanticism lingers about the dangers we faced until it confronts paralyzed vets—and a bomb-cratered Vietnam. But former *Resist* editor David Harris is right: dreams die hard—including those of a world without paralyzed vets and bomb-cratered countries.

AFTER THE REVOLUTION: WHO ARE THEY NOW?

OF THE almost one hundred writers, editors, and activists sought out for this book, some ceased to write after the Movement ebbed; others continue at radical journals. I, like many of us, followed a centripetal path toward mass media.

If the underground press was about commitment, it also was a street-corner journalism school, even, as ex-*Seed* writer Eliot Wald puts it, "a place to be bad" while practicing how to be better.

The second-tier "skin mags" and their outsider stance welcomed many writers without established credentials. I edited and did celebrity interviews at one incarnation of *Gallery,* earning while I learned, while staying away from the girlie copy.

I'd applauded *Rolling Stone*'s music coverage, and been less critical than some of its politics and competitiveness; editing there from 1975 to 1977, I began professionalizing a craft in creative though sometimes volatile company. When the tanks rolled from the North into Saigon, many radical veterans celebrated a liberation. I was mainly glad that the war was over.

As the freelance music columnist for the Associated Press, I traded the heart of rock 'n' roll for learning how to make anyone in America understand Z. Z. Top in six hundred short-sentenced words.

Writing and editing at the Chicago *Daily News* and the Chicago *Sun-Times* during the late 1970s taught me the value of such "bourgeois" concepts as fairness, accuracy, and balance, and that stories could vary because of idiosyncrasies and competition as well as belief systems. I felt the pulse of a city and a metropolitan daily, wrote articles that might otherwise have not appeared, touched some people, got taken on a story or two, won a couple of awards.

Editing a youth supplement called *Sidetracks* proved that what we christened "an alternative section in a daily newspaper" remained a contradiction in terms. By the time it, and the *Daily News,* folded in the spring of 1978, though, I felt more comfortable with the paper's implicit centrist assumptions, even the mass-press tendency to dismiss stories defined as marginal, trivial, overly avant-garde, or radical.

I was asked only once to back off a story; it concerned a judge who, FBI documents indicated, had discussed the Chicago Eight trial with the FBI. And the paper backed me against criticism in other media after I toured the city with a then-fugitive Abbie Hoffman. But in 1980, I applied for a leave from the *Sun-Times* that became a resignation. Editors said otherwise, but I felt caught up in the feed-the-machine nature of too much daily journalism, and had come to chafe at the instances where I'd substituted the paper's values for my own. Worst of all, I wasn't quite sure what I felt.

I began teaching at Northwestern University's Medill School of Journalism, initially to support this book, then because I liked it. My courses —magazine writing and production, arts criticism—allow for multiple points of view and tend toward collective organization. My office overlooks a street that students blocked after Kent State; at a dinner, a university official told me that all save one sixties demand by black and white students are now university policy (maybe it's good they rejected letting students hire faculty). A recent class broke into a locked school building—to do homework on a prototype magazine. And, of course, j-school's a good place to stand and pick on media.

For all its arguing, the sixties were also a time of pluralism. So are the eighties. As the voices that follow mine show, underground alums have limped off, stayed right on, moved on to careers and compromise, to nostaglia and alienation, or to being just fine, thank you. They offer surprising candor, agree with or are philosophical about revisionism such as mine, build verbal bridges over having believed one thing then and its opposite now. Still others, feeling the Big Chill, even the paranoia about Red Dawn, ask to bypass their long-ago communism, or drug deal, or—shades of self-inflicted McCarthyism—a former membership in SDS!

What follows are last words about the underground press and its legacy from many of the people interviewed for this book. Initially, we met from

1981 to mid-1984, and biographies were updated prior to the original publication in 1985. Where names had changed, the entries were alphabetized by how they were known during the 1960s. These original bios and comments are found below, intact, in normal type.

During the summer of 1990, I contacted this alternative alumni association to update their deeds and words. The idea was to provide a collective timeline of their reconsiderations or reinforcements "after the revolution."

The subsequent bios and comments of those who could be located, and who then responded, appear below, in italic type.

(Note: Responses were solicited prior to the war in the Persian Gulf. Thanks to Medill School of Journalism grad students Elise Bittner, Chris Dinsmore, and Kim Delaney for helping to locate as many people as we did.)

JUDY CLAVIR ALBERT (*Barb, Tribe*) has taught at Mills College and is a feminist who moved from Berkeley to Portland, Oregon. She coauthored *The Sixties Papers*, an anthology of major movement speeches and documents.

"The papers organized huge numbers of people and they projected a culture. They gave information to people and brought them out of the isolation that people were living in. They couldn't survive without the Movement....

"Because we've sort of tasted what it could be like to work and live and exist in a nonalienating environment, we are estranged from the traditional work world we live in. We have that sense of sort of being strangers in your own land....

"I don't have a sense of politics for these times. What we have maintained and rediscovered a lot are the old connections that we had in the sixties. Despite people's different politics, or whatever, we have a kind of very broad family."

Albert is currently executive director of a statewide hotline for people seeking a way out of drug and alcohol addiction.

"I'm no longer estranged from the traditional work world; in fact, I feel as if I've come home. I use all the skills I learned in the sixties in this job. And also the analysis: I used to fight for free legal abortion on demand; now I'm looking for free, community-based [drug] treatment on demand. We understood a lot about drugs in the sixties, but we also missed something—addiction. We saw drugs as leading to freedom but we didn't understand the slavery of having drugs or alcohol control your own life, or the lives of your family. A lot of recovery work is based on sixties principles of empowerment, spirituality, and personal freedom.

"Politics for these times? I'm on the Board of our local Names Project (AIDS Quilt), and I'm very involved in working on electoral campaigns of outstanding women candidates—for governor, state assembly, city council. Inside the system—a

position I had a lot of disdain for 20 years ago. But what I bring to these women is the sixties network of skills, people, and progressive values. And that feels good. What do I miss? Risk-taking and being where the action is."

STEW ALBERT *(Barb, Tribe)* worked as a private detective in the Bay Area. He coauthored *The Sixties Papers,* and lives in Portland, Oregon.

"There's something that anybody who reflects on that period should remember. Most of what we've talked about in my own life covers the period between twenty-five and thirty. I was still a young guy, and most of the people in the *Tribe* were younger than me, as young as seventeen or eighteen. Weaknesses that are in retrospect obviously discernable were the kinds of weaknesses that young people get into. . . .

"I am against everything that I was against in the sixties—anti-imperialist, antiracist, antisexist. Looking at America under Reagan, there's no way were wrong about the country. If it just happens to be that America is somehow greater than Sweden and France and Cuba, it would just simply be saying, 'Well, what circle of hell isn't as bad as the others?' There's still something very wrong with the American system, and if some kind of rebellion starts developing in the United States, that'll stir a lot of creative thinking again. The Movement invented our ideas."

Albert is currently involved in desktop publishing, edits several newsletters, and is editor of Portland Agenda, *the monthly journal of the Portland Chapter of New Jewish Agenda, a progressive Jewish organization.*

"I still agree with my old comments about America and the Movement. I would also say that in the past seven years greed has become the national religion and that people try to make you feel guilty about not being out for yourself; they certainly try to make you feel like a schmuck. I think the greed theology is breaking up. There is a hint of populist rebellion in the air. The S&L fiasco might be the last straw. But will the populism be rightwing or leftwing? I don't know. I'm still trying to make my contribution for the Left. Despite the death of my friend Abbie Hoffman, I'm still hoping for a happy ending.

"I'm getting more Jewish, both culturally and religiously. I'm feeling a need for a spiritual family and tradition. I'm trying to express my politics through a Jewish context, a Jewish liberation theology."

VINCE ALETTI *(Rat)* has been a recording executive in New York, where he writes about popular music for the *Village Voice* and other publications. He is dance-record buyer for Tower Records.

"The *Rat* really spoiled me, dealing with people who printed pretty much whatever I wrote, and if they didn't I would leave. The *Rat* was really good to me and easy for me, but it certainly didn't prepare me for dealing with any kind of editor at *Esquire,* and I didn't.

"The only time since Woodstock that I had any feelings about unity was going to the 'ten minutes of silence' for John Lennon in Central Park. It may have been totally fake, but there was a real sense of, yeah, there still are people who feel like I do, or are part of what used to be the Movement and still is here [as] people's spirit together."

Aletti continues to write about dance-oriented music.

JANE ALPERT (*Rat*) spent four-and-a-half years as a fugitive after pleading guilty to conspiring to destroy government property. While at large, she wrote "Mother Right," which rejected the Left of the time in favor of feminism. Surrendering in November, 1974, she served two years in prison. *Growing Up Underground,* her autobiography, set her radical actions within a context of sexual domination by Sam Melville, her lover, who was killed during the 1971 Attica uprising.

"The women's movement has been more successful in accomplishing the goals that we had in 1970 than anybody ever dreamed. Women have been more integrated into the established structure, [but] I don't think we made much of a dent on the bottom levels of society. The gap has gotten worse, and it is also true that among the poor, the majority are women....

"I don't know that any revolution would be an improvement over what we've got—although I don't like what we've got. I think I'm capable of more satisfaction in producing some limited degree of change than I used to be. I'm less nihilistic than I was ten years ago....

"I think the underground press was a symptom of the times rather than a cause of them."

An active feminist in New York, Alpert now has a free-lance business consulting and writing for nonprofit organizations and universities. Growing Up Underground *was recently reissued by Citadel Underground.*

MICK ARCHER (*Rising Up Angry*) was asked to leave the Rising Up Angry organization in 1975 (the paper ceased publication in 1975; the group dissolved in 1976). He plays and teaches music in Chicago, and publishes a youth-oriented quarterly in a working-class neighborhood.

"I'm not a Communist now; I'm an anti-Communist.... I have a poster I did: 'Solidarity with the Cambodian revolution.' I look at this poster now and say, 'How horrible.'... I get pathetic letters from Lithuania, from my relatives—'Would you send us some food?' I don't even have a fucking country anymore, you know....

"After I burnt out totally on sixties radicalism, I started reading about thirties radicalism. After the Hitler-Stalin pact, what do all these people who have all these emotions do? They get into art. They say, 'Let's free the imagination.'... Communists are afraid of the imagination. Look at fucking Russia, at what they do to their avant-garde artists.

"I feel like I was wrong on Communism, but at the same time America really fucked over its youth. A lot of rhetoric I said then I could still say now. We sent our people over there [Vietnam] to die for a really shoddy cause. There are beautiful things about the sixties I still talk about: love and imagination and art. And what was this formed by? By reading those papers and listening to the music.... The *Seed* just set the whole thing in my mind about being a writer, and now I've got my own paper."

Archer's paper folded after eight issues, but he went on to teach English as a second language for the City Colleges of Chicago and with the Spanish Coalition for Jobs. He became involved with the American Federation of Municipal and County Employees.

He has been a songwriter, arranger, and professional piano player, recording as Mick Archer and the Factory Boys. Currently he is a manager of a large nightclub.

"I'm making more than three times what I did as a teacher. And, since I pass for 25 though I'm nearly 37, I get to date girls that were in diapers when I was picketing the Federal Building during he Chicago Eight trial.

"When the Berlin Wall went down, I felt a huge desire to say 'I told you so' to all of the doctrinaire Marxists that I had long ago abandoned. But no gesture of acquiescence to a huge historical blunder came forth from any of the few hardcore lefties and their publications. I felt vindicated, ahead of my time, but strangely abandoned in this new, frightening world of nonideological stalemate. My heroes— Milan Kundera, Gunter Grass, Saul Bellow—seem to...fall into space that I do not want to be in, land that is within the grasp of what I instinctively feel is enemy territory.

"There is much more I would like to say, but I must get back to the piano, which is the one true thing I have found in this world...."

FRANK BARDACKE (*Express Times*, others) has written for various radical and union papers. He lives in Watsonville, California.

"We helped set limits on the ability of the ruling class to wage war in Vietnam. We helped create a space for the black movement. We reshaped higher education in the U.S. And we ended a period of nonpolitical participation. Those four things were crucial victories.

"What happened was that we had revolutionary hopes in a nonrevolutionary situation, so it came to an end."

"I can't say it any clearer than that."

DANA BEAL (*Yipster Times*) has edited *Yipster Times* and its successor, *Overthrow.* He coauthored *The Secret History of the Seventies,* and lives in the Yippies' New York loft.

"We created Nixon, and then we destroyed him. It was like playing with a little Frankenstein doll.... Watergate was the one national catharsis. It was like a little Greek drama, and when it was over, like a Greek drama, everybody was drained...."

"The fact is these hardcore people are more disposed towards revolution in this country than they ever were before. And that is a long-term plus, because we're gonna need it. Hurry!"

Beal has been active with Rock Against Racism. He is developing "a breakthrough cure for [drug] addiction, ibogaine."

ARTHUR BELL (*Village Voice*) wrote 179 stories and a regular column for the *Voice* before dying of diabetes in June, 1984.

"We were anything but passive in those days, but our feelings, our instincts, were primarily those of the love children—for gays. When the establishment gays got in, it got a little bit lousy."

KARIN BERG (*Changes, EVO*) is an A&R executive for Warner Brothers Records in New York.

"I think what the papers accomplished is almost like what goes on in very good music, improvised music. It's not on record, but it's made such an impact on the people who've heard it, and extends beyond the people who have heard it.

"What was wrong with some of the underground press was that it didn't have the same standards as the mainstream press. You still have to use the same discipline, the same research. It has to be rigorous."

Berg is currently vice-president East Coast A&R for Warner Brothers Records in New York.

"I think as the years go by, we miss the underground more sharply—that is, we as a nation, since young people seem to have lost their voice. They now leave the idea-making to rock bands, TV, and the movies. They have become more passive and accepting of all political leaders and not active, choosing their own leaders. The underground press of the past voiced young dissent, young ideas. I look forward to whatever form this voice will take in the future, because if the young don't take charge of their destinies, others will take charge of it for them."

LOWELL BERGMAN (*San Diego Street Journal*) is a producer with *60 Minutes*.

"During the period of repression, the attitude was that all cops were pigs. But we learned while trying to do real reporting that there were honest cops who want to apply the law equally, and were stopped by the same power structure that exists today. Some of those people became our sources, and some of them are sources now."

"I'm just returning to 60 Minutes [10/90] after a six-month leave of absence. Completed an hour for PBS on the international waste trade, and I am more convinced than ever that we are entering a time of continuing positive change. Like the sixties, the ideology current in the U.S. is not functional, with savings and loans, the bill for deregulation coming due, and the Middle East. So I am looking forward to a brisk traffic in stories with meaning.

"I for one am realizing my entry into 'maturity' as this latest crop of teenagers goes off more focused, more traditional (college, European study) than their older brethren (tree trimming and horticulture).

"And traditional politics is less and less relevant to real people and power."

CHIP BERLET (*College Press Service, Chinook, Straight Creek Journal*) edits *Public Eye* and works at Midwest Research, Inc., which examines governmental spying and Far Right political activity. He has a printing press in the basement of his Chicago home.

"To this day, when I hear governmental officials say something, my immediate assumption is that they are at the very least guilty until proven innocent. But I criticize the political Movement too. I think that it was an error not to criticize the political Left, because it led to people repeating mistakes....

"We tied our own hands. You should be constructive in your criticism, but to fail to criticize is to condemn any political movement into being a closed feedback loop of failure."

Midwest Research turned into Political Research Associates in Cambridge, Massachusetts, which continues to "monitor the organization, individuals, and activities of the American political Right wing." Berlet contributes investigative stories to many periodicals and National Public Radio's "All Things Considered," and has been secretary of the National Lawyers Guild Civil Liberties Committee. He is married, has a child and "a house with a mortgage."

"*The printing press was sold and replaced with a large office-style 11" × 17" photocopier and a DOS-based desktop publishing system. The basement is also home to AMNET, the American Information Network computer bulletin board with complete files on how to file a Freedom of Information Act request. 617-221-5815. 300-2400 bps, 24 hours 8 bit word length, No Parity setting, 1 stop bit (8,N,1).*

MARSHALL BLOOM (LNS) committed suicide on his communal farm in Montague, Michigan, in November 1969. Some friends say they've since heard from him.

WALTER BOWART (*EVO*) moved to Arizona in 1969. After living in a teepee, he started Omen, a book publishing house. He has taught journalism, worked at the *Aspen Daily News,* and is the author of *Operation Mind Control,* a look at the CIA use of psychoactive drugs. He published the Port Townshend [Washington] *Daily News* and now edits *Palm Springs Life.*

"The real freedom of the press replaces the rumor circuit with the printed word."

Bowart was asked to leave Palm Springs Life after, among other things, characterizing the magazine as "a Sears catalog for the congenitally rich." He now lives in a "remote mountain wilderness," where he is completing The Other Crusade, *his memoir of the sixites.*

"One of the most positive effects of electronic technology is the collapse of secrecy and the totalitarian states. Like [Marshall] McLuhan said, 'When information travels at the speed of light, there can be no secrecy. . . .'

"I see the 'Me Generation' and the Yuppie lifestyle as a disease, a materialistic cancer, a rot in the collective mind which was fed by a fear of change. . . . The impressions I get from my kids, who are 17 and 19, is that we're emerging from that fearful, self-centered time. These kids . . . are concerned about our environment and are taking it very personally, planning permacultural (renewable, ecologically sound) ways of living for their future. . . .

"I'm very close to my kids, all four of them. They make me feel positive about the future. Despite all our setbacks and failures as a generation, we (the sixties generation) dreamed big. I think the seeds of that dream are sprouting in the minds of the young today.

"As my daughter recently told me, 'The future belongs to the young, Dad. But the eternally young, like you, are welcome to come along with us.'"

RITA MAE BROWN (*Rat, the Furies*) has written *Songs to a Handsome Woman, The Hand That Cradles the Rock, Rubyfruit Jungle, In Her Day, Six of One, Southern Discomfort,* and *Sudden Death.* She lives in Virginia.

"I miss those papers. I miss the energy, the concern, the lively (and sometimes sleazy) debate. I do not miss the arrogance, the lack of credible research (money, again), and cutting copy according to ideology instead of sticking to the facts. Yes, the *Times,* the *Post,* the *Constitution* have their hidden, ideological agendas, but there is still a half-assed commitment to the story. We wanted the *story* told our way.

"Personally, I learned a great deal about journalism. I learned about people, too, and I learned to fear the excess of ideology. . . .

"I am proud of us . . . ; for all our faults we *cared.* We worked. We spoke out. We marched. Some of us died—and far too many of us died in the rice paddies. I wouldn't trade one minute of those years. I don't want to go back, but as I go forward I carry that information and pride with me. The time may well come again when we must band together and resist our government, or force constructive change—our years in the sixties and seventies should serve as well—and I hope we have all matured to the point where we don't need some of the histrionics or harsh tactics of the past. We're not perfect. We'll make mistakes. But I hope we've got the stomach left for a good fight."

Brown has since written High Hearts; Poems, *a collected edition of two poetry works;* Starting From Scratch, *a nonfiction book about writing;* Bingo, *a sequel to* Six of One; *and* Wish You Were Here, *first in a series of kitty crime mysteries coauthored with Sneaky Pie Brown. A historical novel,* Dolley Madison, *will be*

published in 1991. She is president of American Artists, Inc., which options novels for television and film.
"If we have to, I'm still willing to fight."

BRUCE BRUGMANN (*Bay Guardian*) publishes his San Francisco weekly.
"I was first and foremost a journalist. I think that's one of the reasons the *Guardian* has survived while the underground papers haven't."
Continuing as publisher, Brugmann is backing a bill in Congress to abolish the Joint Operating Agreement under which many newspapers are published under one management.
"The Bay Guardian *and the alternative press represent the force of independent journalism....From the beginning, we sought to create the kind of independent newspaper that could successfully compete with the Big Chain monopolies in the one-newspaper cities that now dominate California and the United States....*
"After 24 years, we like to think the Bay Guardian *and its form of independent, competitive journalism has become a model for dozens of other alternative weeklies competing effectively with local monopoly dailies; six in the Bay Area alone, 17 or so in California, 69 or so throughout the U.S. and Canada.*
"In short, we like to position ourselves as the small (growing), locally owned, competitive, non-monopoly, unsubsidized, community-based newsweekly up against the government-licensed JOA...."

TIM CAHILL (*Rolling Stone*) is a featured writer for *Outside* magazine and contributing editor of *Rolling Stone*. He lives in Montana and is completing a book about mass murderer John Wayne Gacy.
"There's no honor in death. If the Berkeley *Barb* and the San Francisco *Oracle* are gone, you have no stake in society. It's not crass to say that you have to succeed to say something."
"My book on Gacy, Buried Dreams, *was a best-seller. Two outdoor-oriented books,* Jaguars Ripped My Flesh *and* A Wolverine Is Eating My Leg, *was followed in January 1991 by* Road Fever *[a book about driving from the bottom of South America to the top of North America]."*

GEORGE CAVALLETTO (LNS) lives in New York and belongs to the Palestine Solidarity Committee.
"The best writing wasn't journalism. It was something thicker than journalism....
"I just went back to Columbia, [even though] I tried to make it so I couldn't go back when I went into the Movement. We stayed as Movement people much longer than anybody else. The Left has shrunk in its ambition tremendously."
Cavalletto continues graduate work at Columbia University's Teacher College, "meanwhile and more importantly raising five kids with my wife Sheila.

"When I said those embittered words almost ten years ago, I thought the Movement was something from which one escapes. Now, having finally gone back to graduate school for real, unexpectedly I have discovered that our experiences in the Movement had unalterably marked us. We had witnessed the world of value and trust collapse, and we had been agents in that destruction. Forever after, we find ourselves marked with a moral seriousness which repeatedly questions any institution or endeavor about what is really at stake. There is no way for us to unlearn our historical lesson; that the given relations conceal hidden interests, and that what is at stake ultimately is the authenticity of one's own being and of one's own action."

ALLEN COHEN (*Oracle*) spent time in a Mendocino community designed "to develop an intimate life using the methodology of so-called primitive peoples... and consensus opinion making." He published *Childbirth in Ecstasy*, and writes poetry in San Francisco.

"I still think LSD and marijuana are very good medicines for the soul, and marijuana for the body too. If I had to take some sort of personal responsibility for some person's bad trip, I'd also take responsibility for all those good trips. I'm neither that proud nor that guilty."

Cohen has just published The San Francisco Oracle Facsimile Edition *through Regent Press in Oakland, California. He is married, lives in Walnut Creek, and is doing childcare for 12 children in his home.*

"What happened in the sixties resulted in so much change in world culture. During the Czechoslovakian revolution, a folksinger sang John Lennon's 'Imagine' to 200,000 people in a public square. The New Age Movement was born in the sixties. The creativity of the underground press launched many of our writers and artists. And we are still dealing with the national puritanical ambiguity of the attitude toward our use of drugs—prescribed, legal, and illegal."

CAMERON CROWE (*San Diego Door*) has written for *Rolling Stone, Playboy,* and other magazines. The author of *Fast Times at Ridgemont High,* the screenwriter of *Ridgemont* and *The Wild Life,* he lives in Los Angeles.

"The feeling was that the government was trying to kill people at the *Door.* I remember thinking it was paranoia, but they weren't too far off."

Crowe has written the screenplay for Say Anything *and other films.*

ROBERT CRUMB (*Zap, Fritz the Cat,* etc.) draws comics in his Northern California farmhouse.

"You just can't quite become a company robot again after that. Can't buy the whole industrial civilization thing quite as much, that horrible phonus-balonus programmed trip. Everyone who went through the sixties and seventies thing is still somewhat more independent in spirit.

"There was a lot of burnout. It's taken me a long time to get rolling again. I never really got back to that original strong feeling I had in '67 or '68. Buy

anything experimental, there are going to be a lot of failures. Some of the mutations make it, some don't."
Crumb has recently been drawing in France.

STEVE DIAMOND (LNS) is engaged in "the mass marketing of spiritual consciousness" in Ojai, California. He has written *Panama Red*, a novel, and describes himself as a "romantic realist."

"LNS was sloppy. It was kids who didn't know what they were doin'. But the papers were a joyous expression of American freedom, and because they were done in that spirit, they had clout and made things happen. The 'weaklies' around the country today, they're makin' money and selling ads and talking about furniture, and they're not allowing for a joy factor."

Diamond lives in Santa Barbara and is very involved in the New Age Movement. In 1987, he helped organized the area's Harmonic Convergence activities, and he is active in a weekly meditation group for world peace. In civilian life, he works as a rehab counselor, finding jobs for injured workers.

"I believe that a major shift occurred during the Harmonic Convergence, when millions of people around the world focused on thoughts of peace at the same time. Within two months after the convergence, Gorbachev announced a pullout from Afghanistan and Reagan announced that he would meet Gorbachev in Washington. Since then, the Berlin Wall has fallen, and the two greatest enemies—the U.S. and U.S.S.R.—have moved dramatically closer together. Thoughts have wings."

LESTER DORE (*Oracle, Seed*) spends most of his time on a rural homestead in Wisconsin. In Chicago, he has designed, illustrated, and written for the *Heartland Journal*, a Chicago paper about "health, sport, culture, and change."

"Sometimes I think of the *Heartland Journal* as the *Seed* grown up. More responsible. A lot of things we said and did in the *Seed* were not responsible. Now I see that everything you do has a consequence.

"The emphasis has shifted from gettin' high to getting healthy. Gettin' high too much was not good for my health. I want to live a long time now."

Dore currently lives in Madison with his 11-year-old son and works three part-time jobs: associate art director of The Progressive; *graphic designer for the Environmental Awareness Center, an institution focused on environmentally conscious regional design; and illustrator for the Wisconsin Department of Natural Resources. He is working on an educational slide show on "Inland Waters of Wisconsin," is in the final year of work on an MFA from the UW-Madison with an emphasis in graphics, and free-lances out of his home for the* Heartland Journal.

"Seven years after I commented on what I said and did over 20 years ago, dumpster-diving at the Wisconsin State Historical Society for collage materials, I

found a roll of microfilm. I held it up to the light and saw that it was microfilm of the Seed, circa 1970. My own copies are beginning to disintegrate due to the high acid content of newsprint.

"What has happened to the revolutionary content of sex and drugs and rock 'n' roll? Drugs have become a plague in the inner city. Casual sex has contributed to the epidemics of STDs, and practitioners of 'free love' have been exposed as calculating abusers of power. Thankfully, rock 'n' roll does still have some progressive practitioners, and my son listens to them and absorbs the content of those songs.

"The potential for an end to the nuclear arms race has never been greater, and not a moment too soon. But many of the other issues we struggled with in the sixties are still with us. The Middle Eastern conflict, continuing problems in this county with racism, environmental degradation.

"One thing that's different is that our children are more aware of these wrongs at an earlier age than we were. And that's partly the result of an information revolution that we helped to instigate in the sixties. We may have been wrong about an unlimited potential for transformation through drugs and sex and rock 'n' roll, but we were exercising 20/20 vision when we saw that the emperor had no clothes.

"One thing that's still the same—I still have hope for the future—that if we can get enough information to the people, past the censorship of the government and the establishment media, that the people will see the injustices and act to correct them."

CLAUDIA DREIFUS (*EVO*) lives in New York and is the author of *Radical Lifestyles, Women's Fate,* and *Seizing Our Bodies.*

"We didn't build institutions and connections the way earlier radical generations did. We built nothing. Nothing! And I think that's a real, sad loss. As a generation we've been very ahistorical.... The people in my past are like an undigested meal....

"*EVO* had a fantastic reputation as a major avant-garde paper. People read it to see what was new and exciting, and what people thought. It was a rival to the *Voice,* and in some ways more exciting. As a writer, it gave me the freedom to just play around. I never then worried about making a fool of myself. I'm a much better writer now, but there was a tremendous freedom then, a playfulness and experimentalness."

Dreifus has "a kind of human-rights and special issues beat" for Playboy, Ms., Mother Jones, McCalls, Glamour, The Progressive, and The Nation. Her book-in-progress, Nancy Klein's Right to Life, *covers a recent abortion-rights case in New York and will be published during 1991.*

"If I look out at my peers in magazine journalism today, I think it's significant that there's almost no one else who came out of this huge, enveloping, era-defining experience. It was, 'You didn't get the revolution or are embarrassed by something you said, so let's not fight for social justice and participate in civic life anymore.' The unwillingness to compromise was the fatal flaw of a generation."

ALICE EMBREE (NACLA, *Rat*) is an Austin-based feminist, union organizer, and graduate student in planning.

"I guess I'm just a frustrated revolutionary.... The underground press was able to give people the feeling that they were part of something bigger, and that all of the issues were connected, and that we were part of an international struggle.

"I remember how we used to say in NACLA that the next Vietnam would be in Latin America. Truer than ever before."

Embree works in the research and planning section of the Texas Child Support and Enforcement Division. She is active in her union, the PTA, and childcare advocacy. She's also part of a community organizing effort to relocate Austin's inner-city airport. She lives with her artist husband and two children in the neighborhood she grew up in, "which must be unique.

"*The underground press was the connective tissue for a nationwide movement. It was gutsy and inspirational. It was also flawed with youthful arrogance and sexism. We need to rebuild the connections and rekindle hope. I think the Jackson campaign helped break down barriers of race, gender, and age. Nelson Mandela walking out of prison and Chile's return to democracy are also inspirational—and reminders that change doesn't happen instantaneously.*

"*I've been more focused on domestic issues than I was in the late sixties, especially our nation's family policy—or, rather, the lack of one. Our domestic neglect mirrors our arrogance in the international arena. It's shameful that a land so full of possibility has such a poor record in literacy, infant mortality, and healthcare. For our children's sake, we can't afford to succumb to cynicism. They deserve the future we dreamed about.*"

BOB FASS (WBAI-FM) lives in New York and recently returned to WBAI.

"Abbie [Hoffman] was on my show and said that the sixties will never happen again. What did happen was an alliance, collision, interaction, friendship of avant-garde arts and politics. It's happening in Germany with the Greens, it may take other forms in America. It has to keep happening, trying to improve and defend the way people live....

"If there's another underground press, it'll be fascist because [now] there is no money for anything like that—unless the technology suddenly opens up."

Fass does two programs a week on WBAI. As part of The Living Theatre collective, he cowrote and is acting in "The Body of God," which incorporates the lives of homeless people into an attempt to humanize the problem of "rooflessness." He is collecting the tapes of counterculture radio and video programs "to keep alive the time when people said, 'Hey, it doesn't have to be this way.'

"*It may sound superficial or glib to discuss a decade in a moment or two on the phone, but the sixties was a surge of something that happens every so often in human history, when people say, 'Yes, we are sexually polymorphous. Yes, good feelings are good. Yes, incorporate more ideas and expand your consciousness.' Now it's fundamentalists saying, 'If you can't get high on Jesus, don't get high at all.'*

"At the same time, nostalgia is a sickness. It's necessary to be here now. You need to be an activist in the nineties. There are the people who deny humanity, the reality of the ecosphere, the interrelatedness of life, whose terrified greed wants to turn the earth into a concrete mall floating in space. And there are the people who are fighting a holding battle against that."

DAVID FENTON (LNS) was publisher of the Ann Arbor *Sun,* publicity director at *Rolling Stone,* and coproducer of the MUSE antinuclear concert at Madison Square Garden in 1979. He is head of Fenton Communications, Inc., whose clients have included Rodale Press, the Greek and Nicaraguan governments, and the National Nuclear Freeze Campaign.

"The [political] alternative press has very little audience, and I think the natural heirs to what we did then are probably the people who are entering the traditional press....

"I would say I'm kind of a modified socialist now, where I was much further Left back then in many ways.... And another way I've changed: I think this is clearly one of the best and freest countries in the world. But while I have that perspective, that doesn't make me any less rigorous in my desire to keep changing and improving this society.

"I wasn't concerned about making a living back then. I was concerned about digging bomb craters on the University of Michigan campus to protest the war. Being concerned about money is a big change, but I try to keep it in perspective, and I continue my political work. When I decided to go into public relations, my main concern was, would I be able to do it with clients I had some affinity for? And so far I've been able to. If at any point that doesn't work out, I'll really have to question what I'm doing."

Fenton now operates his company out of Washington, D.C., where he lives with his wife, writer Beth Bogart, and their sons.

"So far, it's still worked out. Fenton Communications only represents progressive clients whose politics we essentially agree with. Our most recent exploits of note include organizing the campaign against the chemical alar in apples for the Natural Resources Defense Council, and organizing the PR work for the visit of Nelson Mandela to the United States. Our other work is for a socially responsible, ethically screened mutual fund, for publishers when their books are about progressive topics, for the governments of Angola and Jamaica (under Michael Manley), a project on the media and the death penalty, and other such topics. We are very fortunate that we are keeping the sixties alive here in the nineties while making a living too.

"These days, it appears the alternative press is once again growing in influence—

witness Utne Reader *and other such efforts, and this is a good sign. As Huey P. Newton once said, 'People can only act on the information made available to them.' Of course, our slogan is, 'If you don't like the news, go out and make your own.' "*

TOM FORCADE (*Underground Press Syndicate, Orpheus*) began publishing *High Times*, the *Playboy* of pot, in 1974 out of the former UPS loft. The magazine prospered, but Forcade shot himself in November, 1978.

JIM FOURATT (Communications Company, *Come Out*) is active in the New York music scene.

"People continuously tried to mythologize the heroes rather than talking about the contradictions that make them much more heroic. And that was very destructive to young kids who tried to emulate them and could never be those myths. The underground press played a significant role in creating those myths. We created the underground press, and anyone who didn't agree with us we got rid of, or we made look like assholes or fools....

"I think drugs were one of the things that really destroyed everything. They were romanticized, and made people into monsters."

Fouratt has managed several major New York clubs.

ALLEN GINSBERG writes poetry and meditates at the Naropa Institute in Colorado. His files were instrumental in the compilation of *UnAmerican Activities: The Campaign Against the Underground Press*, prepared by the PEN American Center.

"The problem is that the problems to be attacked are insoluble, the world situation is 'hopeless.' There is no way out by negative protest.... The right action is patience, generosity, observation, not to be afraid of death, not to be afraid of the Apocalypse... and see how you can alter your own body politic before pointing the finger at others."

Ginsberg's most recent works include White Shroud *and* Collected Poems 1947-1980.

TODD GITLIN (*Express-Times*) is associate professor of sociology and director of the mass communications program at the University of California, Berkeley. He has written for the *Nation, democracy,* and mainstream newspapers. His books include *Uptown: Poor Whites in Chicago* (coauthor), *Busy Being Born* (poetry), *The Whole World Is Watching: Mass Media in the Making and Unmaking of the New Left,* and *Inside Prime Time*. He wrote about the underground press in *UnAmerican Activities*.

"One—it was fun; no small thing. Two—at their best, the papers really were thinking out loud, abandoning the assumption that journalism is a message from the external world which is complete, closed, final, fixed. They took responsibility. They were first-person. They were full of question marks. And that broke the whole, really suffocating sense that the world is out there only to be mastered by the pros—professionals, pros with bad prose—and that if you're an outsider you really have no choice except to accept or reject what the Delphic oracles are saying.

"At its best, we were skeptical even about our own saints, analytical about what was going on the Left. It was an arena for debate, a place where the Left had something to say about what was going on its demonstrations at a time when that was given short shrift by the establishment.

"There was a lot of good writing. It really was a workshop for serious writers—otherwise, where the hell would we have gotten the chance?

"Weaknesses? Politically shallow, often uncritical of the heroes of the moment, whether Huey Newton or Fidel Castro or Ho Chi Minh. Politically wrong often enough, because uneducated. Uncritically druggy; I don't think that drugs were simply a gift from the gods for human emancipation. In general, our papers were not skilled at dealing with the dark side. Nobody was.

"I think we got carried away with the notion of this all-possible youth revolt. The war was driving us nuts, and nobody really acquitted themselves that well in terms of political lucidity in the late sixties. I just wish we had all been better. But we weren't so bad. We could have been worse....

"In some ways, the mainstream press has improved. They have a generation of reporters—John Kifner, Ray Bonner [since departed from *The New York Times*], Cindy Gorney—who are more sensitive to the concerns we always raised. I think there is also somewhat more sensitivity to overt racism. There are a few more blacks around. Otherwise, I don't think there's been a change. The system is absorptive, so it's always taking account of where the push is....

"I wouldn't be satisfied to hire the staff of *In These Times* and fire *The New York Times*' people and think I'm getting better journalism. My leftwing friends think I'm a liberal waffler, but I'd like to see a number of points represented, rather than have everything smothered in grayness."

Recently Gitlin became a full professor at Berkeley and is a contributing editor of Tikkun *and* Dissent. *He has married and written* The Sixties: Years of Hope, Days of Rage, *and edited* Watching Television.

"I'm glad to say that I'm not going to be much of a revisionist of my own revision. Obviously it took hundreds of pages of my Sixties *to play variations on themes you tape-recorded from me early in the last decade. Today I would still say that the mainstream press has improved from the sixties, though not from '81 or whenever we did that interview. The press enlisted in the Panama invasion, which was not a pretty picture. It enlisted at first in the drug war, though later pulled back. It shrank from the money-grubbing scandals of Reagan's Gilded Age, belatedly playing catch-up thanks to the conspicuous labors of Neil Bush. Television, of course, continues to speed up and dumb down.*

"But credit where credit is due: the establishment press did a good job in 1989 whaling away on Bush for failing to take up Gorbachev's initiatives; there is a bit more space for opinion and, horror or horrors, a disciplined subjectivity. At the same time, general magazines continue to be buried beneath heaps of coated stock and glossy prose. As a result, who isn't tempted to tube out when faced with 'information' glut?"

AL GOLDSTEIN (*Screw*) continues to publish in New York.

"The Left resents me because I took what they had just a glimmer of [sex] and I made it a single-purpose focus. I expected support from the Left; I forgot all the political ideology I'd have to overcome. They're so involved in their own rhetoric and their coterie of eight friends that they don't care about communicating to a large mass of people. They really feel superior. They're no different, frankly, from the Moral Majority that presumes to know what's better for us. I really loathe the Left much more than the Jerry Falwells of the world."

Goldstein's current projects also include the Midnight Blue *cable-tv show and* Gadget, *the "Newsletter for Grown-Up Kids." He is contributing editor and X-rated video reviewer for* Penthouse, *a monthly columnist for* Forum, *and has appeared in* Film Comment, Harper's *and the* New York Times.

"The poisonous sense of déjà vu I feel when I read my words of almost a decade previous makes me want to vomit all over the Left once again. Just recently, leased-access cable television was almost forced off the air in New York City. This blatant act of censorship was done not by the religious bigots, but by the left-wing intelligensia which controls the political apparatus here. The 'underground' has moved on to other media, and my leased-access cable show, Midnight Blue, *penetrated a lot further into the public consciousness than* Screw *ever did.* Screw *continues merrily on—the issues keep coming like spittle from a stutterer's mouth— but video and cable is where it's at right now."*

DAVID HARRIS (*Resist*) spent twenty months in jail for draft resistance. He has written *I Shoulda Been Home Yesterday, The Last Scam,* and *Dreams Die Hard.* He lives in the San Francisco area and writes frequently for the *New York Times Magazine.*

"After the Paris Peace Talks, I felt liberated. By then, I'd been a Movement organizer for eight or nine years. I was tired. I had covered a lot of distance, gone through a marriage, come out of the joint. I knew I did not want to be a political organizer all my life. I wanted the war to be over. I wanted to get on."

Harris has written The League.

ADAM HOCHSCHILD (*Ramparts*) helped found *Mother Jones* magazine, for which he writes. He lives in California.

"We try not to be propagandists. We try not to use a lot of jargon. We're not supporters of any particular political group. We've had favorable articles about various kinds of efforts, but we try to have critical articles about countries, movements, whatever, that are generally speaking on our side. Above all, we're constantly trying to use every possible technique of the straight word—direct mail, promotional advertising, newsstand sales, radio spinoffs, authors appearing on TV talk shows—to reach the largest possible audience. I really think other magazines on the Left don't see that as a goal. They might say they would like to have a larger audience, but they really don't."

"Although I still occasionally write for Mother Jones, *I've spent most of my time in the last few years writing books:* Half the Way Home: A Memoir of Father and Son *and* The Mirror at Midnight: A South African Journey.

"How do I feel about the world? I'm somewhat less certain of solutions than I used to be, but I feel the problems we became aware of in the 1960s are still very much with us, some more so than ever: the growing gap between rich and poor, both at home and abroad; the pollution of the environment; and the vast inequalities of opportunity in the world, where your chances for a good life depend so much on what race, class, gender, and country you are born into. A passion for doing something about social injustice was definitely out of fashion in the 1980s, but I hope that the nineties will see the rebirth of that passion—the best and most enduring legacy of the sixties, which will long outlive the decade's craziness—once again."

ABBIE HOFFMAN (*Yippie*) wrote *Revolution for the Hell of It, Woodstock Nation, Steal This Book, Vote!* (with Jerry Rubin and Ed Sanders), *To America with Love* (with Anita Hoffman), *Soon to Be a Major Motion Picture,* and *Square Dancing in the Ice Age.* Starting in 1974, he spent nearly seven years as a fugitive after being charged in a cocaine case; as "Barry Freed," he was honored for helping to organize the Save the [Saint Lawrence] River campaign in New York. He subsequently served a year in combined community service and jail. He lives in New York City and in the upstate town where he was once incognito. As I write, he has just returned from Nicaragua. He and Jerry Rubin are engaged in a series of Yippie vs. Yuppie debates that mix vaudeville, meaning, and a way to pay the rent.

"There's a sense of guilt, of having walked away from the cause. You feel like you lost, because your work is never done. And there's a lot of revisionism. But people tried the hardest they could possibly try, and did the best they could.

"If you could count up the body count, it's a relatively cheap revolution. I think people back there who were in a sense marked are quite surprised they made it through without being killed."

A speaker on many college campuses, Hoffman also coauthored Steal This Urine Test *(with Jonathan Silvers). In April, 1989, a year after a bad car accident, he died from an overdose of phenobarbital in Bucks County, Pennsylvania. His writings have been anthologized in* The Best of Abbie Hoffman.

ALAN HOWARD (LNS) does public relations for a New York union, and is at work on a novel.

"I think that the illusion of objectivity is very important for getting your views across. That's why *The New York Times* is so effective—and effective propaganda. Today the Left really does need organs that people think are fair and in which various views are offered, that would be propaganda for the working class of this country and for other oppressed sectors."

"It's nice that I was able to provide Abe with a quote here so splendidly evocative of the 'lumpy rhetoric' that supposedly nobody cared about back then and surely not today. I probably did use a formula like this in the course of our lengthy interview, but I don't like the way it was extracted to make the tone subvert the substance. (I can almost see Abe, with his fine ear for the language, silently pouncing on those two sentences as we spoke, hardly believing his good fortune at having finally found a subject who talked like a Bolshevik.) But anyone inclined to snicker at terms like 'propaganda' applied to the New York Times, *or 'oppressed' to people like the $17,000-a-year clerks and hospital workers in the union I still work for, should read a few books by folks like Noam Chomsky and grow up a little.*

"It would do wonders for our political discourse in America."

MICHAEL JAMES (*Rising Up Angry*) co-owns the Heartland, a healthy-food restaurant-and-general-store complex in Chicago. He is publisher of the *Heartland Journal.*

"I'm interested in culture, music, sports, ecology, politics. *Angry* tried to do some of that, but the environment of the Left at that time was to be more and more politically sectarian until no one would read it. I'm always trying to tone things down now.

"I'm still trying to turn people on to engaging in both personal and social change. I don't really have an organization, I have a business with organizational tendencies. But honestly, I'm trying to make that more like a business. I'm not sure what the format is for our work in the community."

James continues to work at the restaurant and on the newspaper. He has toured Nicaragua and the Soviet Union in conjunction with Athletes United for Peace.

FLORA JOHNSON SKELLY (*Seed,* Radio Free Chicago) spent a year sleeping sixteen hours a day in what she recalls as a "collapse—nothing made sense anymore." Since then, she has written and edited for *Chicago 606,* the *Chicagoan, Chicago,* and the Chicago *Daily News.* She also has written for the Chicago *Reader* and the *Chicago Lawyer/Chicago Journalism Review.*

"Everything the women's-liberation movement said about me was true.

At the same time I was making a revolution, I was building a résumé. With hindsight, I'd say that I was trying to turn myself into an adult, through experience. At this point, I'm pretty fond of myself. When I was nineteen, I was insecure, naive, inexperienced."

Skelly is currently special projects editor at American Medical News *and was editor of* Chicago Times. *She published a newsletter and taught a college-level course on the brain. She notes, however, that summarizing someone's life in terms of jobs they've held is "strikingly out of step with 'sixties sensibilities,'" and that she has spent most of her life as a free-lancer. "My 'career'—not a word I like to use with my life—has been a series of circles and spirals, diversions and digressions, not in any sense a straight line.*

"Though I've no doubt I said something like what's said in the previous quote, the lines that were chosen don't reflect what I had hoped at the time to express. To add to them now would only compound the error by seeming to affirm it."

ALLEN KATZMAN (*EVO*) lives in New York. When we spoke, he hoped to start a magazine of New Age consciousness.

"I think that people just overloaded. You had to come down, come to a state of rest, and start to absorb all the changes. And those who didn't got completely wiped out."

Katzman died in a car accident in the mid-eighties.

JAACOV KOHN (*EVO*) lives in New York.

"The underground press made me a raving patriot. Nowhere in the world could I have done what I did in the sixties and seventies."

Kohn died in the mid-eighties after a series of strokes.

PAUL KRASSNER (*Realist*) stopped publishing his monthly in 1974. After a controversial tenure as editor of *Hustler,* he resumed work as a stand-up comedic commentator. He lived in San Francisco, where he wrote an "unauthorized autobiography" and published an anthology of the *Realist.*

"We inspired people and reassured them and stimulated them and were the catalyst for a lot of people changing their lifestyles and values."

Krassner received two awards for his one-person comedy show, and in 1985, he started up the Realist *again, as a satirical newsletter. He provided on-air commentary for the Fox Network's "Wilton North Report" and is a writer on HBO's "Night-Rap." His "unauthorized autobiography" is scheduled for publication in 1991.*

"Just as the sixties counterculture exploded out of the blandness and repression of the Eisenhower years, I see a counterculture exploding in the nineties out of the blandness and repression of the Reagan years, only this time with a loss of innocence. My optimism may be due to chromosome damage."

ARTHUR KUNKIN (*Los Angeles Free Press*) edited the Los Angeles *Weekly News* and the Hollywood *Daily News,* wrote *Behind Organized Crime,* taught journalism, and studied various metaphysical pursuits, in part to explore the possibility of training leadership. He is at work on the biography of *Hustler's* Larry Flynt.

"When I lost the paper [after going bankrupt and being fired by its new owners], it wasn't a big personal blow. Because when I started the paper with some sense of what radical journalism is all about, I didn't really know if it was going to last a couple of weeks. The fact that it lasted 10 years, and that I was making money off it and had 150 people working for me in various enterprises—that was totally gravy....

"This may sound like an old-line analysis, but these forces with legitimate grievances weren't connected with the essential [economic] mechanisms of society."

Kunkin currently edits The Whole Life Times, The Immortalist Papers, *and* Journal of the Senses, *and teaches classes in Los Angeles "using powerful methods to train people to think clearly, be emotionally balanced and possess great compassion... spiritual aspects of life radicals unfortunately have not previously emphasized in leadership training." He is "actively involved in raising the millions necessary to publish a new national news magazine competitive with* Time *and* Newsweek.

"During the sixties, the alternative press performed many communicational and organizational functions of a political party because of the absence of a significant third party in the United States. That vacuum still exists and inevitably will be filled again, at first by new publications, then by new organizations.

"Because I want to live many more years and be functional as the new movements develop, I now also own a large laboratory where I scientifically research ancient alchemical and herbal methods for life extension."

JULIUS LESTER (the *Guardian*) teaches in the Afro-American Studies and Judaic Studies departments at the University of Massachusetts, Amherst. His latest novel is *Do Lord Remember Me.*

"I think the Panthers were one of the biggest mistakes that happened. They had a rhetoric of violence which got a lot of young black people killed and put in jail. And I don't see that they produced that much to justify it. I think that Lenin's phrase about leftwing adventurism—they fit it to a T."

Lester continues to teach in the Judaic Studies Department at Amherst. His last book is Failing Pieces of the Broken Sky.

"I find myself bored by the sixties now."

JAY LYNCH (*Bijou Funnies*) has continued publishing *Bijou Funnies,* and writes "Phoebe and the Pigeon People" for the Chicago *Reader.*

"I am for something that promotes the free exchange of ideas. When a

Left group wishes to censor, it's just as bad as when a Right group wishes to censor."

"What I said above—which was quoted from a tape recording and reads kind of clumsily in its unedited state—still applies. I heard that Andrew Dice Clay's concert movie will not be released by the film studio that made it due directly to pressure from [women's groups]. I can't defend Clay—or the content of his stage act—but I do think less of the studio for submitting to this pressure. This serves as a timely example of the gist of my quote above. [A 20th Century Fox spokesperson said that censorship was not the reason for killing the film.]

"Today we can say only that I am a packaging and product development consultant to the advertising premium industry."

GREIL MARCUS (San Francisco *Express Times, Rolling Stone*) has written *Mystery Train: Images of America in Rock 'n' Roll Music* and edited *Stranded*.

"Things don't have to last forever to work. The papers that were good did work. They told people about [events] that they couldn't find in other ways. They helped people think about things they wouldn't have otherwise thought about. They were entertaining. They made all aspects of what was going on more real. They were a network of communication, they were a grapevine. They did what they were supposed to do.

"By '71 or '72, *Rolling Stone's* coverage of politics was far more serious and effective than it had ever been during the so-called political period. That magazine was at its absolute best in '72, '73, '74. That's when I think it became the really progressive journal that Jann [Wenner] wanted it to be."

Marcus still lives in Berkeley. He edited Psychotic Reactions & Carburetor Dung, *the work of late rock writer Lester Bangs, and recently wrote* Lipstick Traces: A Secret History of the 20th Century. *He writes a book column for* California *magazine, and a music column for the* Village Voice, *and has written for* Raw *and* The New Yorker. *He is working on a book about Elvis Presley since his death.*

"Reading Robert Draper's Rolling Stone Magazine: The Uncensored History *and watching 'Between the Lines' again the other night made me think the current alternative weeklies could do with a little careerism. All too many writers, myself not the least of them, sometimes seem to have settled very comfortably into a self-made ghetto of pure self-referentiality. The fact that such people/we live in a world where the letters 'PC' are used not as a joke but as a password makes me ill, but the places where careerism might take a writer today—classier publications or the movies—are even more smug.*

"The way out might be a kind of anticareerism, writing in newly invented, really hermetic, places—or books too long, convoluted, subjective, and extreme to be easily accepted or dismissed. Any way you cut it, what I read today in the legatees of the unofficial press of 20, 25 years ago is the sort of frustration that hides satisfaction, and nothing else."

DAVE MARSH (*Creem*) became a music critic at *Newsday* and a writer for the *Real Paper* and *Rolling Stone*. He has written *Born to Run: The Bruce Springsteen Story, The Book of Rock Lists, The Rolling Stone Record Guide, Elvis*, and *Before I Get Old: The Story of the Who*. He lives in New York and publishes *Rock and Roll Confidential*, a monthly muckraking newspaper.

"The one tragedy to me was that we lost our grip on the whole race issue, and either got into a very sick hero worship with people like the Panthers or just gave up on that and decided it wasn't a relevant issue.

"I came out of poverty, and the last thing I really every wanted to do was end up a Yippie on the Lower East Side. I knew what it was to miss a meal."

Marsh's more recent books include Glory Days: Bruce Springsteen in the 1980s *and* The Heart of Rock & Soul: The 1001 Greatest Singles Ever Made. *He also helped edit* Pastures of Plenty: Woody Guthrie.

"*Well, I was certainly right about the sick hero worship, though I must say that the lionization of Eldridge Cleaver did not really prepare me for the lionization of Reagan, Trump, et al. And in the wake of the ideological assumptions of once 'alternative press' writers like (New York's) Joe Klein and once 'countercultural' publications like Rolling Stone, losing our grip on the race issue seems a far too polite way to put it.*

"*In the current climate of censorship and fear, it's hard to know whether it's more shameful to be a journalist or a citizen of this big bullying nation. I continue to hold my head up only so far as I've got the guts to spit in the eye of either and both.*"

ANDY MARX (LNS) left in 1972, then returned in 1977 and stayed until the service folded in October, 1981. He lives in Brooklyn.

"I think it played a really valuable role building an antiwar movement. I'm convinced it played a major role in getting the U.S. out of Indochina. There's an incredible diversification through commercial media....

"The underground press suffered a great deal from what the entire Left suffered from—a real impatience with things. A lot of papers established a readership and then decided the readership wasn't where it was at, and moved onto something else.

"I was a dissident on folding it. I thought Ronnie [Reagan] was going to create a situation where something like LNS could revive and grow. What made it a pipe dream was that we couldn't find people who could operate on hope rather than make money to live on."

CHERYL McCALL (*South End*) won an Overseas Press Club award while at *People* for a story on child exportation from Bangladesh. She works at *Life*, is producing a documentary on runaway and abandoned children, and lives in New York.

"It's terribly embarrassing to read some of the things I wrote when I was nineteen, but I've forgiven myself. It's the style [or lack thereof] more than the content that I find so juvenile.... [But] there was a lot of information in those papers that you couldn't get from the straight media. More importantly, they built a sense of community among the Left in each town or city. Any newspaper is a vital organ for the community. Those were vital organs....

"What changed me was working in the city room at the *Detroit News*. I thought everybody was my enemy. Finally, I started to make friends with some of the older reporters, and covered three murders a night, City Council meetings, fires, all sorts of sob stories. That made me realize that there was good in people even though their politics was totally opposite mine....

"'Rock 'n' roll, dope, and fucking in the streets'—that's silly now. At the time it seemed avant-garde, outrageous, revolutionary, and scared our parents, which is what they were trying to do. What worries me is that in some way we may be responsible for the thousands of younger kids today who are either members of cults or into total nihilism. I shudder every time I see a Moonie or Krishna or whatever, and wonder how they could choose such a regimented, controlled, and apparently joyless life when we risked so much in the name of 'freedom' and 'alternatives' in the sixties. Maybe it's such a frightening concept that we scared them into these cults....

"Many of us who were in the underground media or the Movement are now working in the very bowels of the establishment, and I believe that our attitudes can't help but infiltrate into our coverage. *Time, Newsweek* and *The New York Times* are demonstrably more liberal now than they were in 1969, and the major networks are as well....

"I'm not nostalgic for the sixties. I'm not living in the past, and I have no regrets. I acted upon the information I had at the time, and upon what I believed in. Since then, in the course of my journalistic career, I have been to Northern Ireland, China, Bangladesh, India, Nepal, Haiti, and South America, and all over Europe. I've learned that a revolution couldn't have happened here, that other countries are far more oppressive and unfair, that China wasn't and isn't the utopia we all imagined when studying Chairman Mao (that was the biggest shock, I think). I'm still intolerant of any injustice, racism, sexism, or infringement of anyone's rights, but I think that makes me more of a knee-jerk liberal than a knee-jerk radical....

"The papers were legitimate reactions to the time. I really feel that there was substance to them, not just form. I don't think you can say that Richard Nixon was right, or J. Edgar Hoover. Time has not vindicated them. It has vindicated us."

"McCall left Life *in 1986. Since then, she has won several major journalism awards, and served on the Board of Governors of the Overseas Press Club, where*

most of her work attempted to free imprisoned journalists. She co-authored a book on the recording of "We Are the World," for which all profits went to famine relief in Ethiopia.

Streetwise, a documentary on runaways for which she was producer-writer, was nominated for an Academy Award and won several other prizes. She also has written for television.

McCall has earned a Master's in Law from Yale and a Juris Doctor from UC Berkeley. While a student, she worked in legal clinics for the homeless and for battered women.

She is a staff writer for Life and Entertainment Weekly, but works from her home in Northern California, where she is "a single mother by choice" of a year-old daughter.

"I found those sixties experience and the deep distrust of power and the Establishment served me very well in law school. I brought a more critical eye and a different perspective to discussions about power and the law in classrooms filled with 23-year-olds. It was a shock to return to a university environment and find such a different, apolitical, and more self-obsessed student body than we were. But almost two decades have passed, and wreaked their changes.

"What I said about China proved to be prophetic, I guess, but was based on my own observations in 1980 while doing a story there. I've lived long enough now and certainly seen enough in my world travels that nothing should shock me. But I can't help but feel disappointed when ideals are crushed under the jackboot of fascism."

SKEETS MILLARD (*Chicago Kaleidoscope, Seed*) helped establish Karma Farm, a commune in rural Wisconsin, and became road manager for Sky Farmer, a country-rock band. He died in 1974 in a traffic accident involving the band bus.

TOM MILLER (free-lance) lives in Tucson and has written *The Assassination Please Almanac* and *On the Border.* He also has written for *Esquire,* the *Village Voice, The New York Times,* and other publications, and has continued working on more books about Latin America.

"Stories I would have done for the underground press I'm now doing for the daily papers. So either I'm slowing down or they're catching up."

"I'd like to see the underground press again. The alternative papers [now] have justified margins—politically as well as typographically."

More recently, Miller has edited Arizona: The Land and the People, *and co-authored* The Panama Hat Trail. *In the fall of 1990, he arrived in Cuba to work on a book about that country. He also has compiled "The Best of La Bamba" for Rhino Records.*

"I have recently gone through a couple dozen moldering cardboard boxes full of underground papers, handouts, strike announcements, rock 'n' roll rags, and other *surviving print propaganda from 1967–74. In mentioning this hippie trove to others, I'm struck by two responses reflecting its value: (1) Sell it off piece by piece, it's a seller's market in the bazaar of lefty lit; (2) Donate it to a research library— scholars, authors, and journalists can mine it for treasures revealing the strength of diverging movements (not to mention the tax break an appraised donation like this could yield). This tells me that a wider, more dispassionate audience is taking us seriously now. Certainly we're less dangerous, and maybe we're more interesting.*

"(PS—What am I bid for Rolling Stone, *Vol. 1, #1, very gd. cond.?)"*

DAVID MOBERG is senior editor at *In These Times,* a nationally circulated democratic socialist weekly. He writes regularly for the Chicago *Reader* and other publications.

"The underground press was probably one of the most exciting and healthy contributions of the time. There was so much local creativity. People just said, 'We can start a newspaper.'"

"There was also incredible sloppiness, and an unwillingness to take the responsibility for good journalism. But there was a real community that sustained it just like any other community newspaper. When the community vanished, the underground press lost its place."

"I have the same mixture of feelings of affection and embarrassment, nostalgia, and reproach, for both the times and the publications. There was passion without much discipline, but at least it wasn't mass-produced, sanitized infotainment. Both the sins and virtues of the underground press were those of amateurism."

ROBIN MORGAN (*Rat*) lives in New York and is a freelance writer and contributing editor at *Ms.* She edited *Sisterhood Is Powerful* and wrote *The Anatomy of Freedom: Feminism, Physics and Global Politics.* Her poetry collections include *Monster, Lady of the Beasts,* and *Depth Perception.* She appeared in the documentary "Not a Love Story," and edited *Sisterhood Is Global: The International Women's Movement Anthology.*

"I look at a lot of people whose lives were destroyed or damaged. I think of those who dropped out of school because there was such an anti-intellectual line, and now, in the last five or six years, find themselves in their mid- or late thirties, still in fringe employment and wanting to start all over again. There was a lot of destructiveness in terms of personal lives.

"But there was an idealism before it soured that was remarkable, that was markedly different than the old Left....

"There's no movement looking over my shoulder anymore. I'm an equal opportunity offender."

More recently Morgan has written a novel, Dry Your Smile, *another book of feminist theory,* The Dream Lover: On the Sexuality of Terrorism, *and* Upstairs in the Garden: Selected and New Poems 1968-1988. *Her thirteenth book, another novel,* The Mer-Child, *will be published in 1991. Now 49, she is editor-in-chief of the new (ad-free)* Ms. *and still an activist in the International Women's Movement.*

"More feminist than ever. More radical each day. Still crazy after all these years—or, as Elizabeth Cady Stanton said, 'I shall not grow conservative with age.'"

JOHN MRVOS (*Seed*) went from bylining his stories "Walrus" to being program manager of WXRT-FM in Chicago. He is now an A&R man at Arista Records in New York.

"That foundation helped me form my job skills and, most importantly, it made me a team player. To me, there is no greater joy than that of shared labor that is gratifying and rewarding."

Mrvos is vice president of A&R for the Warner Brothers-distributed label Giant Records in New York City.

"If there is one thing I hang onto, it is the refusal to become cynical, that the essence of ideals we fought for in the sixties are still a major part of my life in the nineties. I still don't believe that our government is a caring one, or peace-loving. Drug addiction, homelessness, and an ever-widening gulf between the rich and the poor are issues that need to be addressed with perhaps the same vehemence that we used during the Vietnam War.

"On a personal basis, I'm still committed to change, growth, and spiritual discovery, all-the-while working in one of the most corrupt and debauched businesses."

RAY MUNGO (LNS) has written *Famous Long Ago, Total Loss Farm, Return to Sender,* and *Confessions From Left Field: A Baseball Pilgrimage.* He has operated the Pacific Book Exchange, which sells American titles to Japanese outlets, and published *Creative States,* a contemporary but not underground magazine.

"They were not intended to be institutions; they were messages thrown in bottles. They definitely served a purpose, and the purpose was resolved, so they had to go....

"Most people are in favor of choice [for abortions]. People don't want to go to war with anybody. People will now be polite to someone who's gay; in the past, they might have been horrified....

"I went through hard times in coming to the regrettable conclusion that our society was not turning into some perfect utopia. That in fact I had to make money to pay for Pampers. I was no longer allowed to be broke. I still think of myself as very idealistic. I don't buy no neutron bomb no way. But I also feel very small. In the sixties, I think we felt larger than we were. Because we were really united....

"I definitely built a cocoon around myself in the early-to-mid-seventies.

Probably because I felt there was no longer that society of brothers and sisters to sustain me. But in the early eighties it changed again. Now I'm back in touch with hundreds of people I knew in the sixties. The cocoon has blasted open....

"We're entering the Age of Aquarius. When you say that, people say, 'This guy's got cotton candy for brains.' But I honestly believe the only thing that will help us survive is just that kind of trust, cooperation, sanity prevailing.

"If we don't take over the serious media in the next ten to fifteen years, we will have, I think, reneged on our responsibility."

Mungo has recently written Lit Biz 101: How to Get Successfully Published *and* Beyond the Revolution: My Life and Times Since Famous Long Ago. *He founded and produced the Writers' Jamboree on the Monterey Peninsula, is special projects editor at* Palm Springs Life, *and is currently working on* Palm Springs Babylon. *His first three books,* Famous Long Ago, Total Loss Farm, *and* Return to Sender, *have recently been reissued in one volume called* Famous Long Ago *by Citadel Underground.*

"We've taken over the serious media. Now, watch out."

P. J. O'ROURKE (*Harry, EVO*) edited at the *National Lampoon*. He has written for *Rolling Stone, Harper's,* and other magazines, and has scripted several films.

"I think that they just took the natural course of a naive and useful phenomenon. They were instruments of a general mindset that began in teenagers around the end of the fifties. It's remarkable that people forget how much better the United States is now than 20 years ago. We did amazing things. The world that John F. Kennedy was elected into was an insular, a provincial, a strict and mean and violent place....

"I moved into fairly conservative politics without any feeling of conflict. I think that the 'get the fuck out of my face' political principle was the main thing at work all along. Now, as a taxpaying adult, I don't want the government too much involved in my life. I agree that a young man who is not a radical has no heart, an old man who is not a conservative has no brain. I'm politically conservative because I believe now, as I believed then, that the government is not your mother."

O'Rourke is now the Foreign Affairs Desk Chief at Rolling Stone. *He is the author of four books:* Modern Matters, The Bachelor Home Companion, Republican Party Reptile, *and* Holidays in Hell, *and is currently working on a book about American government. He lives in Sharon, New Hampshire, and Washington, D.C.*

"I still think some beneficial changes were made in America during the 1960s. But many of these changes turned out to be less enduring (in the case of race relations) or more dangerous (in the case of sexual mores) than I thought they were half a dozen

years ago. Looking back on it, the bohemian minority of 25 years ago, to which I wholeheartedly belonged, made no contribution to the nation. Any progress we've seen in this country has been the result of the efforts and sacrifices of the 'squares' we despised.

"The underground press (though, as I recall, Harry was perfectly legal and on the first floor) was full of young talent. None of it matured. Veterans of the underground press who achieved later success had to start over and learn an adult trade."

CRAIG PYES (*Tribe, SunDance*) worked at the Albuquerque *Journal*, where he did an extensive series on death squads in El Salvador. He writes out of the Center for Investigative Reporting, in Washington, D.C.

"A lot of what we did in the underground press was interesting and experimental. It's like little kids who tear things apart to see what's inside them. But that culture's dead. There are little enclaves, but it isn't important today....

"I'm more professional. I have more technical expertise. I don't feel so messianic. I find myself personally more in favor of straighter journalism. There's a whole code of ethics in journalism that I have accepted....

"I'm glad I supported the NLF. I would support the NLF in the same circumstances—an indigenous, national force. What they did afterward is a different set of questions....

"The underground press was ahistorical. It grew out of the intractability of publishers and editors who would not let certain material into their newspapers. And the underground press expanded the boundaries so greatly that editors and publishers today read a lot of the material that was in it."

Pyes remains a reporter and writer.

GEOFFREY RIPS (*Space City*) edited *UnAmerican Activities: The Campaign Against the Underground Press.* He is editor of the *Texas Observer*, in Austin.

"The publishing industry is becoming more and more ossified. It almost demands some independent presses. It encourages, if not underground newspapers, then underground magazines."

Rips is policy coordinator for populist Texas Agriculture Commissioner Jim Hightower.

"The failures of our democracy are not simply a function of the failures of our candidates and the interests they represent. To a large degree, the constriction of democratic debate in this country is a result of the increasing concentration in ownership and control of the news media. Alternative voices and venues are crucial to our maintaining a democratic dialogue—now, more than ever, as Tricky Dick's partisans used to say."

TOM ROBBINS (*Helix*) is the author of *Another Roadside Attraction, Even Cowgirls Get the Blues, Still Life With Woodpecker,* and *Jitterbug Perfume*. He lives in Washington state.

"I had sort of ambivalent feelings about the *Helix*. As a practicing psychedelic revolutionary, I deeply identified with its attitudes, audience, and aims. But having worked for metropolitan dailies in Richmond and Seattle, I was put off by the amateurism of the underground press, always felt a little bit ashamed by the lack of journalistic standards. I wanted to turn on the world, but, by God, I wanted to do it professionally.

"I doubt sincerely if I did much to raise the professional standards of the paper. My best *Helix* effort was an account of a late-night telephone call that I made to Pablo Picasso from a Seattle bar. I also contributed in other ways, such as stealing photos from the library at the *Post-Intelligencer* (where I was employed part-time on the copy desk), leaking information gleaned at the *P-I*, setting up interviews, etc. However, I had my own radio show (1966–68) on a noncommercial, listener-supported station, and that was my psychedelic pulpit. I had control of my self-expression, and didn't have to worry about the typos. Moreover, I was working on my first novel and wasn't too interested in writing much beyond that. Besides, I've never been attracted to group activities.

"The *Helix* created quite a stir when it first appeared, but it was soon assimilated—at least, right-wing, pro-war types quit trying to bomb its offices and beat up its hawkers. I think it was a healthy influence, and I'm happy that it was there when we needed it. Next time, I think we'll do it better."

Robbins' latest book is Skinny Legs and All.

"One of the more irritating and dishonest shortcomings of the sixties revisionism currently in vogue is its downplaying or outright denial of the important ways in which drugs shaped the era. Without psychedelic drugs, there would have been no underground press. There would have been no underground. There would have been no sixties."

MARSHALL ROSENTHAL (*Seed*) became *Rolling Stone's* Chicago stringer, and then a staff arts writer at the Chicago *Daily News*, an editor at the *Chicagoan* magazine, and a writer at WBBM-TV, Chicago. He is a writer/producer at WMAQ-TV, Chicago.

"I fell into the *Seed* from being a self-styled poet. Everything that came later, I kept falling into. From the *Seed*, I fell into *Rolling Stone*, and that was really good. And from *Rolling Stone*, I fell into the *Daily News*. A great editor said, 'Write whatever you want to write; we want to have your voice.' Then I realized a lifelong dream was to write in a Chicago daily newspaper. Golly!

"I no longer write my impressions. I manage part of what goes on television every day. So, there's no comparison. I don't do that kind of writing I did in *Seed* anymore....

"I don't think the underground press was the start of the new journalism. But it continued the kind of thing that the *Village Voice* was doing before— observing and reporting on its own community, with all the strengths and weaknesses of that....

"I met a Green Beret. I told him what I was doing at the *Seed* when he was in Special Forces. And he just said, 'Well, what a time that was.' We both nodded in an unspoken, knowing way—what a time that was."

"I'm reminded of what one of Abe Peck's college students said when Paul McCartney's name came up in class.

"'McCartney?' said the student. 'Didn't he used to be with Wings?'"

MICHAEL ROSSMAN (*Barb*, others) has written *The Wedding Within the War* and *New Age Blues: On the Politics of Consciousness*. He lives in Berkeley.

"Even with all the criticisms, I think the papers are tremendously important. They brought that breadth of openness, of legitimation, to millions and millions of people. It wasn't simply a matter of style, but a whole range of attitudes other than the normative. You look around the country now. So many of those ideas formed the compost that fertilized various things.... People in America now know that you can make a paper. The legacy of the papers is part of the free press. It's easier because it's demystified....

"The war was a real tragedy for us. You never would have had that terrible debacle of the attempted resurgence of ideology in the late sixties were it not for the pressure of the war....

"Sexual roles have not re-coalesced. The state of America and the Empire has not gotten redefined. [But] there are more signals of death on the horizon, rather than less....

"I didn't run for shelter inside an institution. And I don't think I found a noninstitutional working group that was dense enough to support work, in both the fiscal and moral sense. I think I'm suffering from that."

Rossman teaches science in the Bay Area, and spoke energetically about the times and their lessons in the PBS documentary "Making Sense of the Sixties."

JERRY RUBIN wrote *We Are Everywhere, Growing (Up) at 37*, and *Do It!* and coauthored *Vote* and *The War Between the Sheets*. He worked as a security analyst, is president of the 500 Club, a business network based in New York, and is the Yuppie to Abbie Hoffman's Yippie.

"The underground press was an organizing tool, a way to mobilize people.... It was also a way for me as an organizer to reach people with a message.... Part of the underground press' role was to freak out bourgeois society and, secondly, to define an alternative community and give it voice and consciousness and an identity. Those things it did pretty well....

"There were tons of things the underground press didn't do because it was lazy and because it had all the defects of the movement itself—sloganeering, quick solution, eulogy of foreign countries....

"So many of the myths of the sixties proved out to be bullshit—they really did. Vietnam is not a healthy society and China became a capitalist society and Cuba has got a lot of problems. There's no socialist Shangri-La out there that we're all groping for.... We ran out of ideas, 'cause too many ideas were rooted in Marx, or rooted in Vietnam, or rooted in Cuba, or in something that was outside of our own experience.

"I'm not putting down the sixties—I think there was a lot of beauty there. The good part was we were the carriers of an excitement and [sense of] adventure about life, and a vision of an alternative. The vision was not clear, and the vision has a lot of mishmash to it, but we still woke the country up.... The good outweighed the bad. The major thing of the sixties was to curb military aggression in Southeast Asia, and that was done.... Also, the sixties shook up the class system—it's a mellower class system... We didn't have a real alternative to the class system so we ended up being liberals, really. We ended up being reformers....

"If a [new] alternative movement is simply, 'Into the streets and tear everything down,' I will oppose it.... A lot of the things that I said as Yippie statements were misunderstood.... I had a lot of stupid ideas like the cult of rebellion, the cult of dirt, the cult of shock, and all that.... that was unfortunate....

"There was a time in the seventies when I felt that my life was over, that the sixties was the greatest period of my life. I don't think that any-more.... I think five years from now I'll be heading a conglomerate that will have thirty wings to it.... The world is off my shoulders, thank you. I'm passing the world on. You want to put it on your shoulders? Here it is—take it."

Along with wife Mimi, Rubin is a distributor with Omnitrition, which markets nutritional snacks and drinks. They live in New York and operate Jerry Rubin Network Marketing, Inc. They are setting up training centers across the USA "using both video and the telephone to teach people how to go into business for themselves and then teach others the same.

"I am 52 years old with two infant children. . . . My parents died when I was in my early 20's of cancer and heart attack. I am a great believer in nutrition and in taking personal responsibility for one's own health. . . . I believe in life extension. . . . The 1980s were about nutritional awareness, but what the 1990s will be about is bringing nutrition to the people. Because of the aging of the baby-boomers, longevity and life extension will be the most popular health themes of the 1990s.

"I believe that I am at the beginning of a movement in the 1990s that will be, in its own way, as significant as the 1960s—the movement to save the American economy by turning America into one big school for entrepreneurs. . . . Only the people can stop the trend toward centralization and sameness and provide a self-directed business opportunity for all Americans.

"I am building the largest organization in the history of direct sales and Network Marketing. . . . I have not felt so involved since the 1960s. I am alive, on a mission. We invite all the old soldiers from the 1960s: Come join us as we create the movement of the 1990s—mass entrepreneurship! We need you!"

P2sheila ryan (LNS) is active with the Palestine Solidarity Committee.

"The Movement was just organized around the war, so when the war disappeared as an issue affecting people's lives, the Movement kind of fell apart too. And analytically, there wasn't very much to it. The whole thing had sprung out of nowhere. There wasn't a lot of clarity. . . .

"It's very hard to accept a change for the worse in the political climate, but it happened. There's been a terrible swing to the right, and paralysis in whatever's left in the progressive movement. People don't see that they can do anything now that will improve the situation. . . .

"At times I could've done things more wisely. But I don't regret my whole participation in the Movement. It was the right thing to do."

Until recently, Ryan was director of the Middle East Peace Network. She lives in New York with her husband George Cavalletto and their five children.

"In the spring of 1990, in an instance of hope, I decided to pursue Master's degrees in public health and social work in order to prepare to help spend the peace dividend. Days after my tuition deposit was sent in, U.S. troops were deployed in Saudi Arabia. As I combine graduate work and speaking out against impending war, I am reminded how much the experience of the sixties was one of bouncing back and forth between hope and fear."

TERRY SEBELA SAMPSON (*Seed*) works for a California utility.

"I've often thought that if I had the opportunity to go back to any period of my life, that two years would be it. People from completely opposite corners came together to get something done every two weeks. And it did get done, and we has a lot of fun doing it. . .

"I was talking to a friend and I made some comment about welfare cheaters. He said, 'Wow, back then you would take every advantage you could to work around the system.' Back then I was crazier. I didn't own anything, so that affects your politics. Everything I owned fit in the Bug. Now I have bills, a house, animals to support. Although not lavish, there's a certain comfort that I can't really see myself giving up, and that changes you."

"As I listen to an old S&G album, it seems the old songs still appeal to me more

than what is put out today, although Gloria Estefan probably would have fit in pretty well back there.

Back there, back there....in many ways I'm still searching for those projects and opportunities which bring people together, where all the energy and creativity is directed toward one end. I miss all that so much.

Today I'm involved with horses and polo and attempting to cope with the thought that there may never be a 'significant other' in my life."

ED SANDERS (the Fugs, *L.A. Free Press*, others) left New York City after his wife was mugged on New Year's Day, 1974. He has written *Shards of God, The Family: The Story of Charles Manson's Dune Buggy Attack Battalion,* and *Fame and Love in New York*, and recently reconstituted the Fugs. He lives in Woodstock, N.Y., and periodically publishes the *Sanders Report*, a muckraking newsletter about New York State's public utilities.

"Chicago—I decided to paint it rosy. It was a tactical error in terms of my career. I could have written a great first-person account of a classic American street riot, with political and national overtones—and I quailed in the abyss....

"I moved because I just wanted my daughter brought up like a regular American, and be a radical or vegetarian or whatever she wants to be. She's science-oriented, plus she's been exposed. You know, once Allen Ginsberg dances around your kitchen nude a few times....

It's an easy thing to say you're burned out and that your shoulder hurts from shoving at this horrible wheel, and that therefore you're going to work on your tennis elbow. But I think there's still a lot of people out there, and a new, wonderful, tough, quiet generation of people that are pretty radical. They're just not rolling around screaming."

Sanders has been active in progressive politics, toured as a one-man poet-band, and published the award-winning Thirsting for Peace in a Raging Century: The Poetry of Edward Sanders, 1961-85. *His epic of the Lower East Side,* Tales of Beatnik Glory, *was recently published by Citadel Underground.*

DANNY SCHECHTER (*Ramparts, Africa Research Group*, the *Old Mole*, WBCN-FM) has done investigative reporting for the Cable News Network and ABC television. He lives in New York.

"Consistently, the underground press championed oppressed people and provided an outlet for them. We turned people against the war, and we desanctified institutions. There was a period of nonviolence that the underground press transmitted, but the political movement changed and the press maybe became more strident than it should have. But again, this was the work of people seventeen through twenty-five. I don't know if you want to sit back ten years later in a trendy Japanese restaurant on Columbus

Avenue and say, 'What a bunch of assholes!' I think you have to evaluate people in the context of their times....

"We did often confuse advocacy with sloganeering, assuming that people supported our viewpoint without evidence and substantiation. There wouldn't be that much emphasis on what is considered to be journalistic fair play....

"I think there was a tendency not to subject the people we supported to the same standards of critical scrutiny as people we didn't.....I went to Vietnam. I wrote about Vietnam. But I had certain questions and impressions about Vietnam—and I was in the North and the South—certain doubts that I wanted to raise....I don't think any of us were prepared for just how difficult things would turn out. We all expected that the Vietnamese would win and the Americans would lose. But the difficulties of building a society, and the boat people, certainly cannot be denied....

"People who have strong passions and real beliefs—you don't see them on television very much. Everything is contained and controlled by the structure and format of presentation....But the Right has been very effective in organizing groups like Accuracy in Media, and has the money to buy commercial time. People on the left side of the spectrum have been deficient in trying to communicate."

Schechter cofounded Globalvision, a New York-based television production company with the goal of "doing well and doing good." His first series, "South Africa Now," has been on the air for two-and-a-half-years on PBS stations nationwide, and is carried overseas. He is producing a documentary of Nelson Mandela's tour of America.

"In some ways, my career has made a U-turn back to the values that animated the underground press—but hopefully with more professionalism and sophistication.

"'South Africa Now' was started to fill a void in TV coverage from South Africa created by media censorship there and network indifference here. The show has demonstrated that the story can be done—often in the voice of the people most affected, black South Africans. Predictably, the show has come under attack...

"I think what I am doing now is consistent with what I told you over sushi a few years back. At that point, I was nervous about being quoted about my feelings about working inside a network. I was frustrated by what I saw as the trivialization of news and information. Finally, I decided to quit, following the spirit of the dictum of an old friend of mine [Scoop Nisker], who used to end his radio newscasts by saying, 'If you don't like the news, go out and make some of your own.'

"That's what I am trying to do now, with 20 years of broadcasting experience, most of it in commercial television, under my belt. My partner and I have been heroes of 'downward mobility' because of our plunge into independent work—but it has been gratifying. Even though I have been banned from going to South Africa, I have been able to cover a historic story in an ongoing, committed manner....

"Right now, I can't say if our company will be successful or not in the long run. But we are making a shot at it. We are all dead in the long run anyway."

MAX SCHERR (*Barb*) proclaimed in August, 1973, that "cocks and cunts are still not matters of shame in these pages," but promised to drop sexist advertising because "no man is a cock and no woman is a cunt." The ads stayed until 1978, when they were split off into the *Spectator*. Scherr officially sold the *Barb* in October, 1973, but stayed on as editor emeritus until 1978. On July 4, 1980, *Barb* number 735 showed Don Quixote slumped over a horse, his lance in his back. "Barb Bows Out," the headline read.

On Halloween, 1981, Max himself bowed out from cancer. "We were a lot of well-meaning fools," he said while still in the hospital, bitter over his ostracism in Berkeley and the pain in his body. "All of us were tainted by the environment we were brought up in. We had no revolutionary base, no real class consciousness. Along with the good, we developed a large rip-off philosophy."

But he still had a vision of what was possible. "We broke down a lot of barriers to honest though and opened up a whole visionary realm to the future, which has to be worked on."

JEFF SHERO (*Rag, SDS Bulletin, Rat*) became Jeff Nightbyrd in 1972. In 1974, he founded the Austin *Sun* alternative paper. Subsequently, he edited at *Hustler* before becoming "the only guy you know who quit a job paying $40,000 a year for looking at dirty pictures." He is a director of Low Power Technology, Inc., a community television company located in Boulder and Austin.

"We created a multiracial society that lived up to the constitutional guarantee that all men are created equal. People don't even believe it in my old hometown, Austin, when I say 'I remember segregated water fountains.' That was fundamentally important.

"We posed the question, 'Are the institutions that govern the country working?' Our answer was, 'Absolutely not.' Education was not educating, justice was not just, the military was not keeping peace or safeguarding the country.

"We were antimaterialistic: people have to think of other values besides how much crap you can own. I think we're entering a new era—decent, small is beautiful, letting people decide. . . . I think it was the beginning of the death of nationalism.

"In all, we had many pluses, and I feel good about it.

"Minuses—much too extreme and absolutist. It damaged a lot of people and institution that shouldn't have been damaged. It's probably what went on in the cultural revolution in China: professors in universities were made to feel horrible when all they really wanted to do was study Keats' poetry.... I think many people thought they were on the central committee after the revolution; that's elitist-pig stuff....

"At one time I supported the Cuban revolution. I don't support them now because I have pretty good accounts that it is a one-party state with a hierarchy, no free speech, none of the basic civil liberties....

"Our historical failure was that we didn't build anything that lasted. We built sand castles."

Nightbyrd is founder of Byrd Laboratories in Austin, Texas, "purveyor of fine urine products. Our motto: Test your government, not your urine." He has spoken out nationally against the administration's drug policy and sold products to combat urine drug tests. His desktop publishing pamphlet, Conquering the Urine Tests, *is going into its seventh printing. "I've made more money writing a urine pamphlet than from any other writing in my career." He is currently organizing speak-outs and teach-ins against war in the Middle East.*

"To build a good society, people need to avoid cliches and correct lines. Think originally. I'm struck by the Buddhist notion of human foolishness: If you can't laugh while you organize, the outcome may be as grim as you are."

IRWIN SILBER (*Guardian*) wrote *The Cultural Revolution: A Marxist Analysis.* He wrote and edited for *Line of March,* a Marxist-Leninist theoretical journal, and *Frontline,* a national newspaper. "It is only natural, I suppose, that the messengers of what is, when all is said and done, merely a mild alteration in our value system should imagine themselves to be the bearers of revolutionary tidings. Now that this cultural eruption has settled down into the appropriately harmless vocation of providing an illusory oasis of freedom in the midst of fundamentally unchanged oppressive social relations, we can perhaps better appreciate it for what it was....

"At its best, the underground press was the needed voice of white, petit-bourgeois iconoclasm at a time when the system's traditional political institutions could not extricate themselves from the morass of a morally stultifying and politically unwinnable war in Southeast Asia. For that brief moment, the underground press and the larger counterculture of which it was a part intersected with a profound shift in the world balance of forces away from imperialism and toward socialism and national liberation. That it should return to its more natural habitat where the privileged anxieties of its constituencies are mistaken for a revolutionary vision of the future was probably inevitable. Never mind. It had its moment of glory."

Silber has recently written a series of historical studies on popular songs at significant junctures of U.S. history—the American Revolution, the Civil War, opening of the West, etc. He is also the author of two pamphlets analyzing recent developments in the Soviet Union, and currently serves as an editor and analyst for Crossroads, *a national magazine.*

PAUL SIMON ZMIEWSKI (*Seed, Rat*) is an acupuncturist in Taiwan.

"Its weakness was its naivete, its refusal to acknowledge the sea in which it swam—which was American business—and perhaps most significantly, the lack of understanding of the ulterior motives and acting-out of its participants."

Zmiewski is now a Ph.D. and chairman of the Department of Chinese Language and Civilization at the New England School of Acupuncture in Watertown, Ma., and Director of Acupuncture Detoxification at Dimock Community Health Center in Roxbury, Ma.

"I still feel we were very naive, more so than ever, but I've come to respect and cherish that naivete. We had beliefs, we had ideals, we had passions. Silly as some of them may seem today, at least we had them. For the generations that have followed, there is nothing really new anymore, nothing worth having strong beliefs about. The passion is gone. We were called hippies, but it's the Reagan and post-Reagan kids who are really hip in the truest sense of the word: uninvolved, cynical, unwilling, or incapable of having any strong beliefs about anything. All they have left is making a buck and buying more stuff. I feel sorry for them."

ANDY STAPP (American Servicemen's Union, the *Bond*) writes for *Workers World*, the New York-based paper of a Marxist party that supports all socialist countries and national liberation movements.

"I don't think those were socialist papers. They were progressive, antiwar, antiracist.... The war was generated on the need for U.S. capitalism to expand or die; I don't think that was entirely understood. Vietnam was not such a big deal as far as investment goes, but they've got to draw the line somewhere....

"They had to concede the war, and we had to concede the antiwar movement. I'd trade 'em any day. People wonder where the Movement went. Well, we won the war. The Vietnamese won the war.....

"You can't be a summer soldier. It's easy to be for the Movement when it's riding high, not so easy to be for it when it's on its face. I've always been modest in my life. I've always known I had the potential to turn tail and run away from socialism. I never thought I was better than all those people who quit.... I can learn from what happened to them. There will come the winter of my discontent, and I will not crack because I know I'm capable. When I have anticommunist thoughts, I think, 'That's an anticommunist thought.' I don't think, 'That's the new reality.'"

ELIOT WALD (*Seed*, Radio Free Chicago) produced "Soundstage" and "Sneak Previews" for public television and documentaries at WBBM-TV in Chicago. He was a feature writer and TV columnist for the Chicago *Daily News*, and Chicago *Sun-Times*. He now lives in New York and is a writer and production executive for *Saturday Night Live*.

"I was young and fairly neurotic, and this was a culture that was young and tolerated a lot of deviance and allowed you to act out. But if you lined up all my *Seed* articles in front of me and I suspect that, not from the point of view of professionalism, but writing, there would only be five or six that I would say, 'Oh God, this is wacky, I'd rather this didn't have my name on it.'

"In general, I think that the effect of the *Seed* was to spring people, and it worked. We were never newspapermen. We were polemicists doing rallying cries debunking the myths that you read in the other press. We tried to cast doubt on the straight press, and now, we're reaping the legacy of that, in that I'm not particularly happy people don't believe what they read in the papers. The straight press is a limiting force, and it doesn't respond well, and in some ways it reinforces the traditional view of corporate America. But I think it is a real block that prevents us from flying off in another direction."

Wald currently lives in New York and writes comedy screenplays, including 1989's See No Evil, Hear No Evil.

"The above was, I believe, taken from an audiotaped interview. As I reread it, it seems as incoherent and garbled now as it probably seemed acute back when I said it.

"On reopening this book, I was struck by a quote in the last chapter: "The press thrives on people robbing banks, not banks robbing people." How ironic (and unprophetic) in light of the massive coverage of the recent S&L scandal, the Keating Five and the trials [of various sorts] of Boesky, Milken, and Neil Bush.

"It seems to me that we are currently drowning in 'news'—Donald Trump, the Fall of Communism, Al Sharpton, AIDS, Malcolm Forbes, Shi'ite Moslems, Christian Brando—an avalanche of information that aggrandizes the trivial and trivializes the significant. As the sixties (and my twenties) dwindle to a speck in the rearview mirror, I sometimes find myself wishing I had a towel to throw over the bird cage."

DAVID WALLEY (*EVO*) has written *No Commercial Potential: The Saga of Frank Zappa and the Mothers of Invention* and *The Ernie Kovacs File.* He lives in New York state, writes television scripts, and free-lances for *Alternative Media* magazine.

"It gave me a chance to write out my Pope, my Swift, my Dryden, and my Boswell. It gave me a chance to become a better writer, to see things I ordinarily wouldn't see, and, as a rock 'n' roll journalist, to live a lifestyle I could not afford....

"People got too freaked out. They saw too much in the sixties. So we have all these -ologies, and the touchie-feelie brigade, and the macrobiotic-munchie brigade.... The weight of media horseshit makes me think that it was all a dream. And I know damn well it wasn't. The country has swung to the right. But it's coming back."

HARVEY WASSERMAN (LNS) helped form the Clamshell Alliance, the New England antinuclear organization. He is author of *Harvey Wasserman's History of the United States* and *America Born & Reborn*, and coauthor of *Killing Our Own: T he Disaster of America's Experience with Atomic Radiation.* "I think we learned during the Vietnam antiwar movement that we can make a difference. We saw our underground press spread from nothing, with no money and just a lot of chutzpah, to an immensely powerful cultural and political force.

"The underground press, the LNS in its best moments, embodied a certain quality in the human spirit of loving, open-minded, zestful, thirst for life. But in a purely organic, individual sense, I think at this stage of evolution our nervous systems can take only so much. It was the cultural, political, social revolution all wrapped up in one.

"I think a good deal of the message got through. I don't think the underground press was a failure just because it didn't survive. If anything, I'm sorry it didn't go further.

"[The mass press] is constipated, and corporate-dominated, and dangerous in many ways. They presume to tell the whole truth and they don't. Look at nuclear power. You never heard a word about nuclear power in the major media until Three Mile Island. Where were they all those years? Why did people have to burn draft cards and go out and get arrested before anybody would pay attention to the war?"

Wasserman is currently senior adviser to the Greenpeace Nuclear Campaign. "The focus of our campaign is stopping the new generation of commercial atomic power plants. We have stalemated the industry at just about 120 (in 1974 Nixon promised 1,000 in the U.S. by the year 2000, so we can take credit for knocking off about 880 of the beasts). In 1989, three licensed reactors were shut down by political protest (Rancho Seco, California; Ft. St. Vrain, Colorado; Shoreham, Long Island).

"But after ramming Seabrook through (just Unit One; we did stop Unit Two), the industry is pushing a new generation of "safe" plants. Aside from the fact that they aren't demonstrably any safer than the last horrendous batch, the industry can't bring them on line for at least three or four years.

"In the meantime, we need to finally show the public (and the media) that solar power is the viable alternative we've always known it to be. The Luz generating facility in Southern California is cheaper to build and operate than nukes, as are thousand of windmills now operating around the U.S.

"The question is: can we get mass-scale solar into the breech before they come at us with these new reactors? The answer: Hell yes, we have no choice."

JANN WENNER (*Rolling Stone*) publishes and edits that biweekly, which circulated more than 800,000 copies per issue as of mid-1984.

"They [the underground press] never had a correct notion and theory of what society was about, and how society worked. Nor did they have a sound grounding in their own profession. . . .

"Part of the postwar baby boom is the rock 'n' roll culture that *Rolling Stone* spoke for. *Rolling Stone* really does represent the mainstream of the group. . . . In the end, the more authentic thing *was* finding a slightly more hip, legitimized style from the beginning. All those other explanations are explanations for failure."

Wenner lives in New York, is married, and has three chlidren. Rolling Stone's rate base was 1,200,000 as of August 1990. Wenner owns and is editor-in-chief of the 1,000,000-circulation biweekly Us, *and is planning a men's magazine that may appear in late 1991.*

JOHN WILCOCK (*Other Scenes*) wrote several more *$5 a Day* books. He hosts a public-access talk show on New York cable TV.

"It is no longer economically feasible to do an underground paper, to go for a broad audience. You can only go for a small, special audience in a limited area. . . .

"They were interesting and valuable times, but I personally have never managed to recover financially from getting so involved in the underground press. I've been scratching for a living ever since. . . . I'm not bitter. I followed what I believed in, and I still believe in it. I'd probably still do it again."

Wilcock wrote travel stories for the alternative press in Los Angeles, and is reportedly on the road again.

ALLEN YOUNG (LNS, *Gay Flames*) coedited *Out of the Closet: Voices of Gay Liberation* and wrote *Gays Under the Cuban Revolution*. He reported for a small daily in New England, and operated the Millers River Publishing Company, a regional press.

"Whenever anyone would find out something bad about the Soviet Union, old Leftists would say, 'Let the capitalist press do that.' The same thing happened more recently with Cuba. If your journalism is designed to inform and to communicate truths, you cheat your readers when you hide things. You don't give them credit. . . .

"There is a generation of liberal journalists working in the straight media that were so heavily influenced by the underground press that they are creating a vision of America that's somewhat out of touch.

"The underground press' role in originally publicizing the gay liberation movement is very important. For all the criticism I have about the Left, the papers did provide the space. . . .

"I may not be so crazy about having waved an NLF flag, or I may not be so crazy about having glorified revolutionary violence, and so on. But as far as interrupting the normal course of my life to speak out vociferously and journalistically against the American involvement in Vietnam, I continue to have very positive feelings."

Young became assistant editor of the Athol Daily News. *He currently lives in Royalston, Mass., and is director of public relations of a 50-bed community hospital. His effort at book publishing resulted in a dozen local-interest books, but the enterprise has been shelved. He lives in a handmade octagonal house on wooded land off a gravel road and is a member of the board of directors of a community land trust.*

"What I meant is that too many journalists today are enthralled with the idea of uncovering evil, challenging authority, and stirring up shit—and especially with putting down America. The collapse of Eastern European 'communism' is a good antidote.

"But I hope we never see the jingoism of the early 20th century or the ignorance and fear of the 1950s and early 1960s again."

NOTES

Note: Complete bibliographical information for the books cited below can be found in the Bibliography.

PREFACE

*1964 to 1973 as years of study—Chip Berlet, "How the Muckrakers Saved America," *Alternate Media,* vol. 1, no. 1, pp. 5–7.

*Happy amateurs—Todd Gitlin, "The Underground Press and Its Cave-In," in Geoffrey Rips, ed., *UnAmerican Activities: The Campaign Against the Underground Press,* p. 21.

Chapter 1: THE PROTO-UNDERGROUND

Interviews for this chapter—Allen Ginsberg, Paul Krassner, Ed Sanders.

*Protestant ethic—Stanley Rothman and S. Robert Lichter, *Roots of Radicalism,* p. 397.

*Conform or Die—Jack Newfield spotted this slogan in the offices of the Hunter College *Arrow* in 1956. Jack Newfield, *A Prophetic Minority,* p. 40.

*"Sick nik"—*Time,* July 13, 1959, p. 42, as quoted in Marty Jezer, *The Dark Ages: Life in the United States, 1945–60,* p. 287.

*Several books contain valuable material on American radicalism and previous protest papers while, I believe, overestimating the effect of prior movements on sixties rebellion and the underground press: David Armstrong, *A Trumpet to Arms: Alternative Media in America;* Jezer, *The Dark Ages;* Laurence Leamer, *The Paper Revolutionaries: the Rise of the Underground Press;* Harvey Wasserman's History of the United States; and Howard Zinn, *A People's History of the United States.*

*John Reed's quote—Wasserman, *History,* p. 203.

*One magazine—Toby Marotta, *The Politics of Homosexuality,* p. 10.

*Paul Sweezy quote—Alexander Cockburn, *Nation,* June 9, 1984.

*Dien Bien Phu and *Brown v. Board of Education*—Zinn, *People's History,* p. 463 and p. 441 respectively.

*Progressive profitability in 1954—Erwin Knoll to author, May, 1984.

*"Tract for Our Times"—*Liberation,* March, 1956, pp. 3–6.

*Politics magazine—Jezer, *Dark Ages,* pp. 294–95.

*Television outsiders—Mel Tolkin in "Playing Comedy Is No Laughing Matter," New York *Times,* November 14, 1982, p. B 22.

*Village Voice—Kevin McAuliffe, *The Great American Newspaper:* Village scene, pp. 6–7; Dan Wolf on journalism, p. 13; not liberals, p. 4; not Leftists, p. 114; Norman Mailer and the *Voice,* pp. 22, 40–41.

*Mailer on Henry Miller—Norman Mailer, *Pieces and Pontifications,* p. 93.

*Hip vs. square—Jezer, *Dark Ages,* p. 255.

*Youth as new race—Albert Goldman, *Elvis,* p. 205.

*Al Feldstein on *Mad*—Marie Winn, "What Became of Childhood Innocence?" *New York Times Magazine,* January 25, 1981, p. 17.

*Robert Crumb, Patti Smith, and Paul Krassner on *Mad*—Tony Hiss and Jeff Lewis, "The Mad Generation," *New York Times Magazine,* July 31, 1977, p. 14ff. Krassner's other remarks are from author's interview of August, 1981.

*George Lincoln Rockwell disclaimer—*Realist,* November, 1962, p. 14.

*Michael McClure—"Nights in North Beach," in Lynda Rosen Obst, ed., *The Sixties,* pp. 26–28.

*Ginsberg reading "Howl"—see Jack Kerouac's *Dharma Bums,* as quoted in Jezer, *Dark Ages,* p. 269.

*"Howl"—Allen Ginsberg, *Howl and Other Poems,* pp. 9–22.

*Jack Kerouac, *On the Road,* p. 8.

*Newsweek on Kerouac—cited in Chicago *Tribune,* August 9, 1982.

*"America"—Ginsberg, *Howl and Other Poems,* pp. 31–34.

*Big Table—Bruce Cook, *The Beat Generation,* p. 146.

*Gregory Corso's "subjective revolution"—"Variations on a Generation," *Gemini,* vol. 2, no. 6 (Spring 1959), pp. 47–51, as reprinted from Thomas Parkinson, ed. *A Casebook on the Beat.*

*Corso on hippies—Cook, *Beat Generation.*

*"The Port Huron Statement"—from Steve Wasserman, "A Manifesto Lost in Time," *Progressive,* December, 1982, pp. 32–36.

*Tuli Kupferberg and the East Village poetry scene—Steve Kraus, "Don't Perish: Publish (It Yourself!)" *Alternate Media,* Spring 1982, pp. 10–12.

*Tom Robbins—letter to the author, October, 1982.

Chapter 2: THE FIRST WAVE

Interviews—Arthur Kunkin, Max Scherr, Adam Hochschild, Frank Bardacke, Greil Marcus, Stew Albert, Michael Rossman, Jerry Rubin, Walter Bowart, John Wilcock, Allan Katzman, Allen Cohen, Lester Doré.

*James Baldwin—"Letter to America," *Peace News,* date unknown, as quoted in *Orpheus,* vol. 2, no. 2, p. 6.

*"I Have a Dream" speech—as quoted by Ralph Abernathy in "Martin Luther King's Dream," Obst, *The Sixties,* p. 94.

*Farce on Washington—*The Autobiography of Malcolm X* (New York: Ballantine Books, 1964), pp. 280, 301.

*Additional information on Kunkin and the *Free Press*—Lionel Rolfe, with Dennis Koran, "Freeping Out," *Reader* (Los Angeles), June 19, 1981.

*Free Press as first underground paper—Tom Forcade, ed., *Underground Press Anthology,* p. 1.

*Role of revolutionary paper—V.I. Lenin, *What Is to Be Done? Burning Questions of Our Movement,* pp. 41, 52.

*John Bryan—as quoted in Steve Long, "Underground Writers' Reunion," *Alternate Media,* vol. 9, no. 5 (January–February, 1977).

*Jack Newfield on "rhetoric of objectivity"—"Journalism: Old, New and Corporate—The Reporter as Artist: A Look at the New Journalism" in Michael Schudson, *Discovering the News: A Social History of American Newspapers,* p. 184.

*Core values of news—Herbert Gans, *Deciding What's News,* p. 61.

*James Deakin on White House reporting—as quoted in *Newsweek,* March 5, 1984, p. 83B.

*Estimates of reporters working with the C.I.A.—400 is from Carl Bernstein, *Rolling Stone,* October 20, 1977; 50 to 100 is from the New York *Times,* December 27, 1977.

*News as pacifier—Gaye Tuchman, *Making News: A Study in the Construction of Reality,* p. 214.

*Mass-media coverage of SDS—Newfield, *A Prophetic Minority,* p. 35.

*Coverage of SDS march—Todd Gitlin, *The Whole World Is Watching,* pp. 46–53.

*Watts—see the Los Angeles *Times,* August 17, 1965; the L.A. *Free Press,* August 20, 1965; Zinn, *People's History,* p. 450; Milton Viorst, *Fire in the Streets: America in the 1960s,* pp. 311, 329–30.

*Time on Watts—July 29, 1966, p. 57.

*Clark Kerr's quote—Abe Peck, "Cracks in the Crystal Ball," *Oui* magazine, 1975.

*FSM, Mario Savio, interconnectedness of movements—see Viorst, *Fire in the Streets,* pp. 281–300.

*Need for alternative vision—Frank Bardacke, "Steps," no. 1, December, 1966, as quoted in Mitchell Goodman, ed., *The Movement Toward a New America,* p. 380.

*Tonkin Gulf incidents—Michael Maclear, *The Ten Thousand Day War: Vietnam 1945–1975,* pp. 111–15.

*John Bryan's papers—Steve Long, "Underground Writers' Reunion," and Glessing, *The Underground Press in America,* pp. 18–19.

*Max Scherr's pre-founding conversation—Berkeley *Barb,* 10th anniversary issue, August, 1975, as reprinted in the Max Scherr memorial *Barb,* December 11, 1981.

*Readers feeling it—*Time,* July 29, 1966.

*Editorial content—*Barb,* August 13, 1965.

*Little movements—*Time,* July 29, 1966.

*Hefner of the underground—Michael Lydon, "The Word Gets Out," *Esquire,* September, 1967, p. 106.

*Effect of activist papers—Leamer, *The Paper Revolutionaries,* p. 32.

*General background—Abraham Leshkol, "The EVO Eye Is Watching You," in "New York," *World-Journal-Tribune,* November 27, 1966, pp. 10–13.

*First-issue editorial—*East Village Other,* October, 1965, and October, 1970.

*John Wilcock's background—author interview and McAuliffe, *Great American Newspaper,* pp. 21, 68.

*The freaks' *National Enquirer—*Thorne Dreyer and Victoria Smith, "The Movement and the New Media," *Orpheus,* vol 2, no. 2, p. 13.

*Personals—*East Village Other,* May 13, 1967.

*Life as art—Tuli Kupferberg, Berkeley *Barb,* August 4, 1967, as excerpted in Jesse Kornbluth, ed., *Notes from the New Underground: An Anthology.*

*Rise of LSD—Albert Hofmann, *LSD: My Problem Child,* Jonathan Ott, trans., pp. 55–58.

*East Village Other art—Charlie Frick, "Tripping the Lightbox Fantastic: Psychedelic Design Made Easy," *Alternate Media,* vol. 11, no. 1, 1979.

*New morality—Aldo Guinta, *East Village Other,* October, 1966, as quoted in Kornbluth, *Notes from the New Underground,* pp. 231–33.

*Katzman as existential newspaperman—*East Village Other,* August, 1966, as quoted in Jerry Hopkins, ed., *The Hippie Papers,* pp. 90–92.

*Time and Barb headlines—Charles Perry, *The Haight-Ashbury: A History,* p. 25 of galley proofs.

*The *Fifth Estate*—vol. 1, no. 1, November 19–December 2, 1965.

*The *Paper*—vol. 1, no. 1., December 3, 1965. Kindman's quote on "the bureaucratic mind" comes from *Time,* July 29, 1966.

*Haight background—Hunter S. Thompson, "The 'Hashbury' Is the Capital of the Hippies," *New York Times Magazine,* May 14, 1967, p. 20.

Oracle's color—Ethel Romm, *Editor and Publisher,* November 11, 1967, as quoted in Glessing, *Underground Press,* p. 40.

*Cohen on why people read the *Oracle*—author interview and Lydon, "Word Gets Out," *Esquire,* September, 1967.

*Alan Watts—*Oracle,* February, 1967.

*Timothy Leary, *Oracle,* as quoted in Forcade, *Underground Press: An Anthology,* p. 56.

*Anti-intellectuality—Newfield, *Prophetic Minority,* pp. 120–21.

*Katzman on UPS—*East Village Other,* June 15, 1966.

*"Fuck censorship" press—John Wilcock to Steve Long, "Underground Writers' Reunion."

Chapter 3: THE SUMMER OF LOVE

Interviews—Allen Cohen, John Wilcock, Greil Marcus, Paul (Simon) Zmiewski, Robert Crumb, Lester Doré, Ken Emerson.

*Ron Thelin's letter—encore edition of *Other Scenes* printed for the July, 1969, UPS conference in Ann Arbor, Michigan. The reprint, Dreyer's and Smith's "The Movement and the New Media," helped re-create the Stinson meeting.

*Human Be-In—Steve Levine, *Oracle,* January, 1967; various magazines; Charles Perry, "The Gathering of the Tribes," Obst, *The Sixties,* pp. 188–92.

*Gathering of the Gurus—*Oracle,* February, 1967.

*Max Scherr's Be-In critique—John Wilcock, as published in *International Times,* February 13, 1967.

*UPS planks—Richard Neville, *Play Power: Exploring the International Underground,* pp. 196–97.

*Media blitz—Michael Rossman, *The Wedding Within the War,* p. 209.

*Beaded writers—Kornbluth, *Notes from the New Underground,* p. 284.

*Mainstream language—"The Hippies," *Time,* July 7, 1967, pp. 18–22.

*Journalists and drugs—Thompson, "The 'Hashbury' Is the Capital of the Hippies," *New York Times Magazine,* May 14, 1967, p. 124.

*Don't come story—San Francisco *Chronicle,* March 24, 1967.

*The Haight as hip Rome—Walter Bowart, *East Village Other,* April 1, 1967.

*The commercialization of Haight Street—*Barb,* May 5, 1967.

*Chester Anderson's remarks—various Com/Co fliers.

*"Serious adolescence"—Dave Marsh, reviewing the Doors in Dave Marsh and John Swenson, *The New Rolling Stone Record Guide,* p. 149.

*First Chicago Be-In—*Seed,* vol. 1, no. 2.

*Michael McClure, "Poisoned Wheat," *Oracle,* August, 1967.

*Ed Sanders, *The Family: The Story of Charles Manson's Dune Buggy Attack Battalion,* pp. 39–40.

*Drug-related deaths and the *Oracle's* reaction—"End of the Dance," *Time,* August 18, 1967, p. 22–23.

*Gray line spiel—Horace Sutton, "Summer Days in Psychedelphia," *Saturday Review,* August 19, 1967, p. 36.

*Changes in *Oracle* graphics—slide presentation and interview with Allen Cohen.

*Death of Hip coverage—Don McNeill, *Village Voice,* November 30, 1967, as quoted in Don McNeill, *Moving Through Here,* pp. 290–300; "hungry consent"—quoted in Kornbluth, *Notes from the New Underground,* pp. 284–86; Earl Shorris, "Love Is Dead," *New York Times Magazine,* October 29, 1967, p. 114ff; "Hippies: Death on a Sunny Afternoon," *Rolling Stone,* November 9, 1967.

*"To All Who Would Know" appeared in the *Avatar,* June 9, 1967. Follow-up description. David Felton, "The Lyman Family's Holy Siege of America," *Mindfuckers,* pp. 176–78.

Chapter 4: THE SUMMER OF DETROIT AND VIETNAM

Interviews—Jeff (Shero) Nightbyrd, Chip Berlet, David Harris, Paul Krassner, Art Kunkin.

*See Jerry Farber, "The Student As Nigger," as reprinted in Goodman, *Movement Toward a New America*, pp. 303–304.

*Lyndon Johnson's fear of being lynched—David Halberstam, *The Best and the Brightest*, in Todd Gitlin, "Seizing History," *Mother Jones*, November, 1983.

*Prairie power—Kirkpatrick Sale, *SDS*, p. 206.

*Rag—Dreyer and Smith, "Movement and the New Media," *Orpheus*, vol. 2, no. 2, p. 13.

*Mass press on April 15, 1967, peace rally—the New York *Times*, April 16, 1967.

*Ed Sanders on LBJ—Lydon, "The Word Gets Out" *Esquire*, September, 1967.

*No leaders—*Barb*, April 21, 1967.

*Resistance statement and critique of organization—Staughton Lynd, "The Movement: A New Beginning," *Liberation*, May, 1969, as reprinted in Goodman, *Movement Toward a New America*, pp. 488–97.

*Need for militance—John Kelsey, "Is Love Obscene?" *Canadian Free Press*, May 26, 1967, as quoted in Kornbluth, *Notes from the New Underground*, p. 269; Jack Newfield, "One Cheer for the Hippies," *Nation*, June 26, 1967, pp. 608–610.

*Kennedy satire—Paul Krassner, "The Parts They Left Out of the Kennedy Book," *Realist*, May, 1967; reaction in "The Case History of the Manchester Caper," *Realist*, June, 1967.

*Stokely Carmichael—Viorst, *Fire in the Streets*, pp. 343–81.

*Detroit riot—Frank Joyce, "Death of Liberalism," *Center Magazine*, March, 1968, as cited in Goodman, *Movement Toward a New America*, pp. 176–78; Harvey Ovshinsky, *Fifth Estate*, as reprinted in the Berkeley *Barb*, August 4, 1967.

*Rap Brown speech—*Open City*, August 17, 1967, as reprinted in Hopkins, *The Hippie Papers*, pp. 183–90.

*Knowing Panther coverage—Sol Stern, "Call It the Black Panthers," *New York Times Magazine*, August 6, 1967, pp. 10–11ff.

*Television coverage—*Movement*, July, 1967, as reprinted in the *Black Panther*, July 20, 1967.

*National Conference for New Politics—Cynthia Edelman, *Seed*, vol. 1, no. 8.

*Conservative coverage—Chicago *Tribune*, August 3 and September 2, 1967.

Chapter 5: THE FALL OF THE PENTAGON

Interviews—Ray Mungo, Frank Bardacke, Walter Bowart, Bob Rudnick, Andy Stapp.

*Meeting—Ray Mungo, *Famous Long Ago: My Life and Hard Times with Liberation News Service*, pp. 17–19; interview with author.

*Caravan of death—*East Village Other*, as quoted in *Time*, August 6, 1967.

*Oakland demonstration—Frank Bardacke, "Stop-the-Draft Week," *Free University* (Berkeley), December, 1967, as reprinted in Goodman, *Movement Toward a New America*, pp. 476–79.

*Bowart speech—LNS, September 26, 1967.

*LNS roots and beginnings—"Former *Student* Chairman Bloom Heads Underground News Service," Amherst *Student*, April 8, 1968; News Media Project, September 26, 1967; Mungo, *Famous Long Ago* (on Marshall Bloom, pp. 7–9, 24–26; Ray Mungo, pp. 3–5, 7; Mungo and work, p. 10; uneasy coalition, p. 19); Jim Foudy, "The Case of the Angry Young Man from Boston," *Collegiate Journalist*, Spring, 1967, pp. 4–5.

*Bloom's Pentagon preview—*Seed*, vol. 1, no 9.

*The New York *Times*'s Pentagon coverage—various stories, October 21–23, 1967.

*Editorial malaise—*Newsweek,* October 27, 1967, p. 57.

*James Reston's analysis—"Everyone Is a Loser," New York *Times,* October 23, 1967, p. 1.

*LNS's Pentagon coverage—LNS, October 23 to early November, 1967.

*Thorne Dreyer's analysis—LNS, as reprinted in the *Seed,* vol. 1, no. 10.

*Revolution has not yet arrived—*Movement,* November, 1967.

*Oakland shootout—LNS, December 15, 1967.

*LNS's alternative journalism—LNS, October 23, 1967.

*LNS coverage—LNS, October, 1967–February, 1968.

*Revolution not yet here—*Movement,* November, 1967.

*Contents of LNS packets—LNS, October, 1967, to February, 1968.

*Washington house—Mungo, *Famous Long Ago,* pp. 23–31.

*Accuracy—ibid, pp. 67–68, and interview.

*GI papers—Andy Stapp, *Up Against the Brass;* Glessing, *Underground Press in America,* pp. 137–39.

*Tet—David Culbert, Chicago *Tribune,* January 30, 1983; Fox Butterfield, "The New Vietnam Scholarship," *New York Times Magazine,* February 13, 1983, pp. 26–31; William V. Kennedy, *Press Coverage of the Vietnam War;* Harry G. Summers, Jr., "Tet, Fifteen Years After," *New Republic,* February 7, 1983.

*Hanoi strategy—Kennedy, *Press Coverage,* p. A 6.

*Irrelevance of military victory—Butterfield, "New Vietnam Scholarship," p. 52.

*Barb articles—February 2 and 16, 1968.

Chapter 6: KING AND COLUMBIA

Interviews—John Wilcock, Greil Marcus, Todd Gitlin, Steve Diamond, Jeff (Shero) Nightbyrd, Alice Embree, Allen Young.

*USSPA meeting—LNS, February 7, 1968; Mungo, *Famous Long Ago,* pp. 71–76; Jerry Rubin, *Do It,* pp. 133–37.

*Underground circulation and readership; Katzman and Garson predictions—Thomas Pepper, "Growing Rich on the Hippie," *Nation,* April 29, 1968, pp. 569–72.

*Two views of civilization—Neville, *Play Power,* p. 18.

*Stokely Carmichael, "A Declaration of War," San Francisco *Express Times,* February 22, 1968.

*"The Red and the Black"—Marvin Garson, *Express Times,* February 29, 1968.

*Southern civil rights movement—*Great Speckled Bird,* vol. 1, no. 1 (March 15–28, 1968).

*Ghetto risings—*Report of the National Advisory Commission on Civil Disorder.*

*Defense of black trashing—*Seed,* vol. 1, no. 11.

*Black storm troopers—*Seed,* vol. 2, no. 3.

*King's and Hutton's deaths—*Seed,* vol. 2, no. 5; *Great Speckled Bird,* vol. 1, no. 3 (April 12–25, 1968); Stu Glauberman, Berkeley *Barb,* April 12–18, 1968.

*LNS packets—reviews, February 3, 1968; spoof on Rolling Stones, March 11, 1968; Columbia coverage, April 10, 1968.

*Subway ripoff—Anon., "How to Make It in the Jungle," *Rat,* March 18, 1968.

*Columbia—*Rat,* various articles, May 3–16, 1968, and subsequent issues.

*New York *Times* coverage of Columbia and radical response—Sale, *SDS,* p. 442.

**Times'*s management and Columbia—Gitlin, *Whole World Is Watching,* pp. 274–75.

*Class-based students—Allen Young, May 8, 1968.

*Mark Rudd—Meryl Levine and John Naisbitt, *Right On* (New York: Bantam Books, 1970), p. 70, as quoted in Rothman and Lichter, *Roots of Radicalism,* p. 35.

*Consciousness—Jeff Shero, *Rat,* May 3–16, 1968.

*Mirror-image coverage—Gitlin, *Whole World Is Watching,* p. 196.

Chapter 7: CHICAGO: HIPS, YIPS, AND POWER TRIPS

Interviews—Jerry Rubin, Abbie Hoffman, Paul Krassner, Paul Williams, Bob Fass, Michael Rossman, "Vito," Jann Wenner, Greil Marcus, Warren Hinckle, Ed Sanders, Eliot Wald, John Mrvos, Bob Rudnick, Todd Gitlin.

Daniel Walker's *Rights in Conflict* has been a valuable general source for this chapter.

*Stock exchange—New York *Times,* August 27, 1967.

*Abbie Hoffman background—Abbie Hoffman, *Soon to Be a Major Motion Picture,* pp. 72–83; and Hoffman interview with author.

*Jerry Rubin background—Viorst, *Fire in the Streets,* pp. 425–31; and Rubin interview with author.

*Yippie announcement—LNS, January 16, 1968.

*Rubin release—*Seed,* vol. 2, no. 3.

*Alan Watts, Jerry Rubin, Tim Leary—*East Village Other*s, February, 1968.

*Yippie as internationalist—*Seed,* vol. 2, no. 3.

*Stony Brook—New York *Post,* March 8 1968; *East Village Other,* March 1, 1968; *Newsweek,* undated clip from author's files; New York *Times,* February 28, 1968.

*Max Lerner—New York *Post,* undated clip.

*Yippie puff—New York *Post,* March 18, 1968.

*Absorption by media—Norman Fruchter, "Movement Propaganda and the Cult of the Spectacle," *Liberation,* May, 1971.

*Mutual manipulation—Jerry Rubin, *Growing (Up) at 37,* as quoted in Armstrong, *Trumpet to Arms,* p. 133.

*As media junkies—Paul Williams, *Pushing Upward,* pp. 211–13.

*Rossman critique of Yippies—letter to Jerry Rubin, March 16, 1968, as published in Rossman, *Wedding Within the War,* pp. 262–70.

Voice and Yip-In—Don McNeill, *Moving Through Here,* p. 230.

*Yippies vs. Mobe—Chicago *Sun-Times,* March 25, 1968.

*"Don't Take Your Guns to Town"—Jeff Jones and Mike Spiegel, *New Left Notes,* March 4, 1968.

*Yippie as effective—Julius Lester, *Guardian,* as reprinted in the *Seed,* vol. 2, no. 6.

*Raid on Yippies—Chicago *Tribune,* April 28, 1968.

*Open Letter to Daley—*Seed,* vol. 2, no. 7.

*Daley on Communists—*Newsweek,* September 9, 1968.

Sun-Times coverage of Peace March—*Chicago Journalism Review,* October, 1968.

*Shit pies—*Seed,* vol. 2, no. 8.

Rolling Stone on Yippies—*Rolling Stone,* May 11, 1968. (Several histories erroneously cite a March publication date for this article.)

*Abbie Hoffman on Jann Wenner—Hoffman, *Soon to Be a Major Motion Picture,* p. 124.

*Abbie Hoffman on RFK—*Realist,* September, 1968.

*Abbie Hoffman on "recount"—Jerry Rubin to Viorst, *Fire in the Streets,* p. 447.

*Sirhan Sirhan a Yippie—Rubin, *Do It,* p. 161.

*Jerry Rubin on politics—*Seed,* vol. 2, no. 10.

*"Psychedelic Bolsheviks"—Rubin, *Do It,* p. 82.

*"Don't come" letter—Abe Peck, *Seed,* vol. 2, no. 11.

*SDS position—*New Left Notes,* August 5, 1968.

*Upbeat festival—Abbie Hoffman, *Realist,* September, 1968.

*Peck/Hoffman debate—*Seed,* vol. 2, no. 12.

*Tom Hayden on Chicago—*Rat,* vol. 1, no. 4.

*Tuesday and Wednesday events—drawn from the author's experience; see also Abbe Peck, "The Other Convention in Chicago," in Obst, *The Sixties,* pp. 260–66.

*Right to demonstrate—*Ramparts Wall Poster,* August 27, 1968.

*Police welcome to newsmen—Walker, *Rights in Conflict,* p. 255.

*Hugh Downs on "pigs"—ibid, p. 293.

*Cronkite and Daley—*Newsweek,* September 16, 1968.

*Local coverage—*Chicago Journalism Review,* October, 1968.

*Reporters and police—Chicago *Tribune,* August 28, 1968.

*Police, peace movement—*Newsweek,* September 9, 1968.

*Rubin's expectation—*Other Scenes,* March, 1968.

*Walker findings—Walker, *Rights in Conflict.*

*Effective Movement institutions—*Movement,* October, 1968.

*Revolution has come—Allan Katzman, *East Village Other,* September 6, 1968.

*Doggerel—Bob Rudnick, ibid.

*Public support of police—*Newsweek,* September 9, 1968.

*Macho revolt—Gitlin, *Express Times,* September, 1968, as reprinted in Goodman, *Movement Toward a New America,* pp. 561–62.

*Author's violent rhetoric—Chicago's *American,* September 15, 1968.

*Pig cover—*Seed,* vol. 2, no. 13.

Chapter 8: REVOLUTION?

Interviews—Ray Mungo, George Cavalletto, Sheila Ryan, Steve Diamond, Allen Young, Harvey Wasserman, Paul Williams, Julius Lester.

The main books on the LNS split are Ray Mungo's *Famous Long Ago* and Steve Diamond's *What the Trees Said: Life on a New Age Farm,* both of which support the Virtuous Caucus. I also interviewed Mungo, Diamond, Young, Cavalletto, Ryan, and Harvey Wasserman for this section. Unless noted in the text or below, their quotes are from these interviews.

*Role of revolutionary paper—Lenin, *What Is to Be Done,* p. 166.

*Max Eastman on *Masses*— Eastman, *Enjoyment of Living,* p. 421, as cited in Daniel Aaron, *Writers on the Left: Episodes in American Literary Communism,* pp. 21–22.

*John Reed—Eastman, *Heroes I Have Known,* p. 223, as cited in Robert A. Rosenstone, *Romantic Revolutionary:* p. 347.

*Eastman on art and politics—"Clarifying the Light," *The Liberator,* vol. 4, June, 1921, pp. 5–7, as cited in Aaron, *Writers on the Left,* p. 54.

*Eastman's disillusionment—*Enjoyment of Living,* pp. 316–20. The remark on the "social misery" of the Soviet artist first appeared in Eastman's 1934 book, *Artists in Uniform.*

Express Times complaint—cited in LNS/Mass, no. 100, August 16, 1968.

*AP heist story—LNS/Mass, ibid.

*LNS/NY version—August 17, 1968.

*LNS/Mass version—ibid.

*Colin Pearlson's boat ad—*Seed,* vol. 2, no. 13.

Kudzu editorial statement—David, *Kudzu,* September 18, 1968.

Old Mole editorial statement—*Old Mole,* September 13, 1968.

*Open Letter—*Seed,* vol. 2, no. 13.

*"Here We Go Again"—*Seed,* vol. 3, no. 1.

*Frank Zappa on toilet seat—*Seed,* Vol. 3, No. 4.

*Gary Snyder—as quoted in Goodman, *Movement,* p. ix.

*John Kois description—Burks, *Rolling Stone,* October 4, 1969.

*New Chicago paper—Chicago *Kaleidoscope,* October, 1968.

*Chicago nonunderground dissident paper—*Second City,* November 23, 1968.

*LNS/NY packets—September–November, 1968.

*Beatles more influential than Movement—Ralph Gleason, LNS/NY, no. 111, October 16, 1968.

*Julius Lester—*Seed,* vol. 3, nos. 1–3; and interview.

*"Don't Vote for Shit"—*Express Times,* October 31, 1968.
*Pig covers—*Seed,* vol. 2, no. 13; vol. 3, no. 2.
*Whites uncritical of blacks—Richard Neville, *Play Power,* p. 154.
*Lester vs. Carmichael and Black Panthers—*Seed,* vol. 3, no. 5.
*Negative media effect on Panthers—Kathleen Cleaver, "How Television Wrecked the Black Panthers," *Channels of Communications,* December, 1982.
*Lester vs. Eldridge Cleaver—*Seed,* vol. 3, no. 5.
*Defense of Panthers—Karen Wald, *Seed,* vol. 3, no. 5.
*Election attacks on liberals—Chicago *Kaleidoscope,* vol. 1, no. 2 (November 22, 1968); *Other Scenes,* vol. 1, no. 8.
*Movement's lack of election success—LNS/NY, no. 116 (November 7, 1968).
*Ann Arbor bombing—LNS/NY, no. 111 (October 16, 1968).
*Lester's caution—*Seed,* vol. 3, no. 1.
*"Who Stole the Cookie Jar"—FBI memoranda 100-4496-98-34-32: September 9, 1968; October 7, 1968; November, 1968.

Chapter 9: PARANOIA STRIKES DEEP

Interviews—Geoffrey Rips, Allen Ginsberg, Chip Berlet.

The basic overview on domestic intelligence activities against the underground press in the 1960s remains the Final Report of the Senate Select Committee to Study Governmental Operations with Respect to Intelligence Activities, *Intelligence Activities and the Rights of Americans: Book II* (general history, pp. 21–65; COINTELPRO, pp. 65–88; Martin Luther King, p. 12; Committee conclusions, pp. 19, 99).

FBI memos secured by various investigators and the author continue to illustrate the extent of its campaign.

The best contemporary source on underground press repression is Geoffrey Rips, ed., *UnAmerican Activities: The Campaign Against the Underground Press,* which includes the research of Rips and Angus Mackenzie, and assessments by Allen Ginsberg, Todd Gitlin, and Aryeh Neier. David Armstrong's *A Trumpet to Arms* is also useful. Additional analysis occurred at a September, 1981, PEN America press conference held to publicize the publication of *UnAmerican Activities,* in which Ginsberg, Rips, Gitlin, Allen Katzman, Tuli Kupferberg, the author, and other underground-press veterans participated.

*Dallas *Notes*—"Stoney Burns: Alive and Living Well in Dallas," *Dallas Life,* Dallas *Morning News,* January 2, 1983, p 8ff.; Tom Forcade, "Underground Fuck," *Express Times,* December 11, 1968. The police officer who raided the *Dallas Notes* office is quoted by Forcade in Mel Howard and the Rev. Thomas King Forcade, eds., *The Underground Reader,* p. 170.
*Joe Pool incident—New York *Times,* July 15 and 16, 1967; "How 'They' Got Stoney Burns," *Iconoclast,* November 29–December 6, 1974; Rips, *UnAmerican Activities,* pp. 107–108.
*Meschbach graphic—*Seed,* vol. 3, no. 4.
*FBI at bank—SAC Chicago to Director FBI, file N 100-453454-1, April 14, 1969.
*FBI vs. LNS—Angus Mackenzie, "Sabotaging the Dissident Press," *Columbia Journalism Review,* March–April, 1981, pp. 57–63.
*Repression history—see introductory note.
*Hoover's "burrhead" remark—review of David J. Garrow's *The FBI and Martin Luther King* (New York: W. W. Norton, 1982) in *Progressive,* January, 1982, p. 49.
*Actions against Black Panther Party—Rips, *UnAmerican Activities,* p. 125.
*FBI vs. L.A. *Free Press*—Chip Berlet, "COINTELPRO: The FBI's Zany and Disruptive War Against the Alternative Press," *Alternate Media,* Fall 1978.
*FBI vs. *Ramparts*—Mackenzie in Rips, *UnAmerican Activities,* p. 160.
*FBI and *East Village Other'*s flower-airdrop ad—Washington *Star,* May 5, 1976.
*FBI squelching of unfavorable press—Senate Select Committee, *Intelligence Activities,* p. 16.
*FBI "friendly media" memo—reprinted in Rips, *UnAmerican Activities,* p. 70.

*Bob Woodward's remarks appear in Armstrong, *Trumpet to Arms,* p. 158.

*The FBI's "Twelve-Point Master Plan"—reprinted in Rips, "The Campaign Against the Underground Press," ibid, pp. 61–63.

*Repression of political involvement—Eldridge Cleaver, speech as run in *Ramparts,* December 28, 1968, and reprinted in Goodman, *Movement Toward a New America,* p. 192.

*Armageddon News—vol. 1, no. 2 (October 25, 1968); Director, FBI, to SAC, Indianapolis (105–5621); evaluated in Armstrong, *Trumpet to Arms,* p. 145.

*FBI-influenced news services are described by Mackenzie in Rips, *UnAmerican Activities,* pp. 167–68.

*FBI surveillance memo—Armstrong, *Trumpet to Arms,* p. 136.

*The Project Resistance memo—Mackenzie in Rips, *UnAmerican Activities,* p. 165.

*Selective arrests of radicals—Tom Forcade, *Underground Reader,* p. 170.

*No prison for FBI wrongdoers—Allen Ginsberg in Rips, *UnAmerican Activities,* p. 31.

*FBI's "greater good" justification—Select Committee, *Intelligence Activities,* p. 14.

*Underground press as wave of the future—Forcade, *Underground Reader,* p. 170.

Chapter 10: STREET-FIGHTING MEN?

Interviews—John Wilcock, Todd Gitlin, Julius Lester, David Fenton, Robert Crumb, Jay Lynch, Judy Clavir Albert, Allen Young, Art Kunkin, Allen Katzman, Frank Bardacke.

*Madison conference coverage—Thorne Dreyer, LNS/NY, December 5, 1968.

*Freak view of Madison—Lennox Raphael, *East Village Other,* December 27, 1968.

*Vietnam information—Maclear, *Ten Thousand Day War,* pp. 283–84.

*Bloody LBJ—Eldridge Cleaver, *Ramparts,* December, 1968, as reprinted in Goodman, *Movement Toward a New America,* p. 194.

*Revolutionary sabotage—Andrew Kopkind, *Temple Free Press,* as reprinted in Goodman, *Movement Toward a New America,* p. 577.

*Urban guerillas—Julius Lester, *Guardian,* February, 1969.

*Frustration—Lester, *Seed,* vol. 3, no. 6.

*Nonpolitical revolt—William Burroughs, *Rat,* October 4, 1968.

*Voluntary youth ghettos—Michael Rossman, *Express Times,* July 9, 1968.

*Ripoffs—*Seed,* vol. 3, no. 8.

*"The Bullshit Revolution"—Liza Williams, Los Angeles *Free Press,* as reprinted in the *Seed,* vol. 3, no. 7.

*Decline of Free City—Marjorie Heins, *Express Times,* January, 1969.

*End of LNS/Mass—Steve Diamond, *What the Trees Said,* pp. 46–52.

*Revolutionary letter—Diane diPrima, written in June, 1968, appeared in *Great Speckled Bird,* November, 1968.

*Marxism, Lenin, Marcuse—Herbert Marcuse, *The Aesthetic Dimension,* pp. ix–xiii, 12, 28, 57.

*Vagabond journalists—J.S. Thompson, "Literature and Ideology," Progressive Books and Periodicals (Spring 1969), as reprinted in Ethel Grodzins Romm, *The Open Conspiracy: What America's Angry Generation Is Saying,* p. 28.

*Problem with People's Art—Sandy Darlington, *Good Times,* January, 1970.

*Comics and revolution—Skip Williamson, in Mark James Estren, *A History of Underground Comics,* pp. 179; Harvey Kurtzman, ibid, p. 181; Paul Buhle at SDS convention, ibid, p. 178.

*Cheering announcement of cop's death—*Liberated Guardian,* July 14, 1970.

*Articles designed to propagandize—Allen Young, as quoted in Leamer, *Paper Revolutionaries,* p. 87.

*"This Article Is Propaganda"—San Francisco *Good Times,* October 2, 1969, as quoted in Armstrong, *A Trumpet to Arms,* p. 107.

*"Who Owns the Park"—Frank Bardacke, as reprinted in Goodman, *Movement Toward a New America,* p. 505.

*Covering People's Park—Max Scherr, *Barb,* 10th anniversary issue, 1975.

*Marshall Rosenthal—miscellaneous diary entries, 1969, as transcribed for author.
*Flash Gordon movement—Abe Peck, *Seed*, vol. 3, no. 12.
*SDS breakup—Sale, *SDS*, pp. 528, 557–58, 563–76; Abe Peck and Bernard Marshall, *Seed*, vol. 4, no. 1; Carl Oglesby, *Liberation*, August–September, 1969, as quoted in Goodman, *Movement Toward a New America*, p. 743.
*SDS breakup and impact on underground press—"The Situation Information Report: The Underground Press," as reprinted in Rips, *UnAmerican Activities*, p. 73.

Chapter 11: FROM COUNTERCULTURE TO OVER-THE-COUNTER CULTURE

Interviews—Jeff (Shero) Nightbyrd, Paul Williams, Jann Wenner, Jim Fouratt, Clive Davis, Jaacov Kohn, Greil Marcus, Dave Marsh, Abbie Hoffman.
*"Barber" story—recounted in Chicago *Tribune*, November 15, 1981.
Cheetah and *Eye*—Chet Flippo, "Rock Journalism and *Rolling Stone*," pp. 18–21.
*Intrinsic politics of rock—Franklin Rosemont, *Seed*, vol. 1, no. 10.
*Moby Grape review—*Rat*, March 4, 1968.
*Jimi Hendrix reviews—ibid, March 18, 1968.
*Janis Joplin review—ibid, August 9, 1968.
Rolling Stone on music—*Rolling Stone*, vol. 1., no. 1.
Rolling Stone vs. New Left—Jann Wenner, "Musicians Reject New Political Exploiters," *Rolling Stone*, May 11, 1968.
*Ralph Gleason on "Revolution"—LNS, as reprinted in *Seed*, vol. 2, no. 13.
Barb on "Revolution"—ibid.
*Irwin Silber on Beatles—*Guardian*, September 28, 1968.
*Silber—*Guardian*, December 6 and December 13, 1969.
*"The Man Can't Bust Our Music"—*Seed*, vol. 3, no. 3; Clive Davis, *Clive: Inside the Record Business*, pp. 106–107.
*"Know Who Your Friends Are"—*Seed*, vol. 3, no. 4.
*Sandy Darlington—*Express Times*, November 20, 1968, as quoted in Ethel Romm, *The Other Conspiracy*, p. 114.
*Bill Graham vs. Stephen Gaskin—San Francisco *Good Times*, December, 1969, as quoted in Steve Chapple and Reebee Garofalo, *Rock 'n' Roll Is Here to Pay*, p. 148.
*Bill Graham on rock not being revolutionary—*Rat*, October 18, 1968.
*Motherfucker poem—*Rat*, February 14–20. 1969.
*Motherfuckers vs. *EVO*—*East Village Other*, January 10, 1969.
*Cultural claim to music—ibid, November 1, 1968.
*Cultural revolution and "extinction of honkies"—John Sinclair, *Seed*, vol. 3, no. 5.
*"Rock and Roll Dope"—John Sinclair, *Fifth Estate*, December 26, 1968.
*MC-5 as "musical guerrillas"—Bob Rudnick and Dennis Frawley, *East Village Other*, September 13, 1968.
*Poetics, not politics—Jac Holzman, as quoted in Michael Lydon, "Rock for Sale," *Ramparts*, June, 1969, pp. 19–24.
*Black vs. White Panthers—William Leach, *Seed*, vol. 3, no. 6.
*White and Black Panther rules—*Seed*, vol. 3, no. 5.
*Sinclair vs. underwear—*East Village Other*, May 14, 1969.
*Groupie ad—New York *Times*, February, 1968.
*Need to be political—Jann Wenner, *Rolling Stone*, April 5, 1969, as quoted in Flippo, "Rock Journalism and *Rolling Stone*," p. 81.
*Phil Ochs—*Rat*, April 11–16, 1969.
*John Hoyland and John Lennon—*Black Dwarf*, May 1, 1969, as quoted in Romm, *Open Conspiracy*, pp. 106, 108.
*John Lennon on playing the establishment's game—*Rat*, June 12, 1969.

*End of Columbia ads—*Rat,* April 25, 1969.
*CIA and FBI memos—Angus Mackenzie in Rips, *UnAmerican Activities,* pp. 164–65.
*CBS and the CIA—William S. Paley, *As It Happened,* pp. 286–89.
*Frank Stanton denial—letter to author, October 21, 1983.
*Portions of my journey to Woodstock—Abe Peck, Chicago *Sun-Times,* May 13–14, 1979.
*Promoters as rock imperialists—LNS, as quoted in *East Village Other,* July 16, 1969.
*Protest against promoters—*Rat,* August 12, 1969.
*"Lemmings" and "real good"—New York *Times,* August 18, 1969.
*Woodstock as co-optable—Irwin Silber, *Guardian,* undated.
*Author on Woodstock—*Seed,* vol. 4, no. 5.
*"Hip Fantasy"—*Rat,* August 27, 1969.
*Contradictions at Woodstock—Gary Thiher, ibid.
*Hoffman vs. Townshend—Abbie Hoffman, *Soon to Be a Major Motion Picture,* p. 183; Dave Marsh, *Before I Get Old,* p. 300.
*Hoffman on Woodstock Nation—quoted by Irwin Silber, *Guardian,* June 6, 1970.
*No radical images in "Woodstock" movie—Abbie Hoffman, *Soon to Be A Major Motion Picture,* p. 184.

Chapter 12: UNDER FIRE

Interviews—John Wilcock, Bob Rudnick, Cheryl McCall, Art Kunkin, Max Scherr, Judy Clavir Albert, Stew Albert, George Kauffman, Suzanne Smolka, Paul Krassner, Jerry Rubin, Abbie Hoffman, Bobby Seale, Todd Gitlin, Harvey Wasserman, Jane Alpert, Jeff (Shero) Nightbyrd, Paul (Simon) Zmiewski.

*Conference background—*Rat,* late July (undated), 1969. See also John Burks, "The Underground Press," *Rolling Stone,* October 4, 1969, p. 14.
*Circulations—Glessing, *The Underground Press in America,* p. 124, 178; Burks, *Rolling Stone,* October 4, 1969, pp. 11–30.
Rising Up Angry—vol. 1, no. 1 (July, 1969).
*Vietnamization not the answer—Abe Peck, *Seed,* vol. 4, no. 2.
*Author's pre-Conference letter—files of John Wilcock.
*Harassment—Rips, *UnAmerican Activities,* pp. 84–85, 114, 125.
*FBI alert on Conference—FBI document, July 10, 1969.
*Police raid, reaction—*Rat,* late July, 1969.
South End—Detroit *Free Press,* July 12, 1969, *Detroit News,* July 12, 1969, and undated feature; New York *Times,* July 13, 1969, photocopy in FBI files; and Cheryl McCall.
*Tom Forcade—"His Highness, Citizen King," *Alternate Media,* vol 11, no 1, 1979.
*The *Barb-Tribe* split—Tim Leary's generational remark appeared in the *Barb*'s 10th anniversary issue, August, 1975. Steve Haines wrote "Capitalist Pig Max Scherr" in *Barb on Strike,* July 11, 1969. The egalitarian *Tribe* is described in Armstrong, *Trumpet to Arms,* p. 164. The nude Tribe and Stew Albert's attack on Scherr appeared in the *Tribe,* July, 1969. I also used my interviews and general sources.
*Leary on *Barb* and *Free Press*—*Flashbacks: An Autobiography,* p. 279.
*Drug arrest statistic—Abbie Hoffman, *Soon to Be a Major Motion Picture,* p. 176.
*Narcotics agent list—L.A. *Free Press,* August 8, 1969.
*Bust background—interviews; Leamer, *Paper Revolutionaries,* pp. 124–30; and the Los Angeles *Reader,* June 19, 1981.
*Bill Schanen—John Pekkanen, "The Obstinacy of Bill Schanen," *Life,* September 26, 1969, p. 59; San Francisco *Chronicle,* July 13, 1969; Leamer, *Paper Revolutionaries,* p. 131.
*Chicago Conspiracy trial—my own coverage of the trial; various issues of the *Seed;* Gene Mustain, Chicago *Sun-Times,* September 23, 1979.
*Quote from Deputy Attorney General Kleindienst—*Seed,* vol. 4, no. 7.

*Political defense—Frank Bardacke, "The Oakland 7," *Realist,* November–December, 1969, as reprinted in Goodman, *Movement Toward a New America,* p. 484.

*Purposeful disruptions—Harry Kalven, *Contempt: Transcript of the Contempt Citations, Sentences, and Responses of the Chicago Conspiracy 10,* pp. xviii–xix.

*Judge Hoffman on contempt—FBI Airtel 100-454662-422, October 7, 1969.

*Judge Campbell—FBI memo Chicago (100-48029) (176-5) (157-1291) 2P-Director (100-454652) (176-1014) (105-165706, Sub 9), October 29, 1969, and same-day memo from A. Rosen to Mr. DeLoach; Chicago *Tribune,* August 20, 1981.

*New York Press Service come-on—James Wechsler, New York *Post,* October 29, 1969.

*Salzberg's impact and LNS disinformation letter—SAC, New York (100-163303) to Director, FBI (100-449698), November 24, 1969.

*Authorization for letter—Director, FBI (100-449698-34-76) to SAC, New York (100-163303), December 1, 1969.

*FBI press critique—SAC, Chicago (176-5) to Director, FBI (176-1410), 176-141095(illegible), October 31, 1969.

*Juror's daughter and *Sun-Times* reporter—C. L. McGowan to Mr. Rosen, FBI memo 176-1410-1144, December 24, 1969.

*Seale Comments—Kalven, *Contempt,* pp. 8, 26.

*Stop the Trial—Abe Peck, *Seed,* vol. 4, no. 8.

*Seale on gagging—Bobby Seale, *A Lonely Rage,* pp. 190–91.

*Weathermen—*Seed,* vol. 4, nos. 6–7.

*"Sick Little Swine"—Chicago *Today,* October 13, 1969.

*Eldridge Cleaver on Weathermen—Berkeley *Tribe,* reprinted in *Seed,* vol. 4, no. 10.

*Liberals not radicals—*Rat,* October 29, 1969.

*Mobilization frustration—Abe Peck, *Seed,* vol. 4, no. 9.

*Effect of antiwar movement—Todd Gitlin, "Seizing History," *Mother Jones,* November, 1983, p. 35; Richard Nixon, *Memoirs,* p. 399; Henry Kissinger, *The White House Years,* p. 292.

*Nixon's Silent Majority speech—"Vietnam: A Television History," WGBH Educational Foundation, 1983.

*Agnew's media elite speech—William Paley, *As It Happened,* p. 313.

*John Chancellor—"Vietnam: A Television History."

*Operation Phoenix—LNS, as reprinted in *East Village Other,* October 23, 1969.

*Agent Orange—LNS, as reprinted in *East Village Other,* December 24, 1969.

*My Lai as continuation of radical journalism—Armstrong, *Trumpet to Arms,* p. 113.

*Seymour Hersh not interested in underground press—response to author's letter, August 9, 1982.

*Marshall Bloom's suicide—New York *Times,* November 3, 1969.

*Federal Building communiqué explanation—*Rat,* October 8, 1969.

*Allan Katzman on second-rate undergrounders—Glessing, *Underground Press,* p. 167.

Rat defense of Alpert—November 26, 1969.

*Bombings and Alpert's status—Jane Alpert, *Growing Up Underground,* p. 235.

Chapter 13: THE RAT WOMEN AND THE STONEWALL

Interviews—Robin Morgan, Claudia Dreifus, Al Goldstein, Bob Rudnick, Judy Clavir Albert, Jane Alpert, Paul (Simon) Zmiewski, Jeff (Shero) Nightbyrd, Alice Embree, Vince Aletti, Allen Young, Arthur Bell, Jim Fouratt, Steve Diamond, Harvey Wasserman, and Ray Mungo.

*Women's planks at the Ann Arbor conference—Glessing, *Underground Press,* p. 65.

*Stokely Carmichael—Robin Morgan, ed. *Sisterhood Is Powerful: An Anthology of Writings from the Women's Liberation Movement,* p. 37.

*White Panther Party Manifesto—*Seed,* vol. 3, no. 3. (LNS deleted this line, but retained the "Fuck God in the ass" that followed.)

*Sexism in mainstream news organizations—Lindsy Van Gelder in Morgan, *Sisterhood Is Powerful*, p. 89.

*NOW—ibid, pp. xxiv–xxv.

*Similarities to the gay rights movement—Marotta, *Politics of Homosexuality*, pp. 96–97.

*Sexism as core problem—Morgan, *Sisterhood Is Powerful*, p. xxxix.

*Miss America demonstration—Robin Morgan, *Rat*, September 20, 1968.

*Sexual revolution as phony—Roz Baxandall to Marge Stamberg, *Guardian*, March 29, 1969, as reprinted in Goodman, *The Movement Toward a New America*, p. 48.

*Male newsmen to be excluded from participatory coverage of Miss America Pageant—*Rat*, September 6, 1968.

*Women's liberation putdown—Marvin Garson, as reprinted in *Rat*, October 2, 1968; letter in *Rat*, October 18, 1968.

*No porno in underground—Richard Neville, *Play Power*, p. 76.

*"Dildo journalism"—Leamer, *Paper Revolutionaries*, p. 176.

Screw's "bad smut"—Barry Farrell, *Life*, November 21, 1969.

Kiss, New York Review of Sex, Pleasure—Leamer, *Paper Revolutionaries*, pp. 176–77.

*Marge Piercy—"The Grand Coolie Damn," *Sisterhood is Powerful*, pp. 473–74.

*Capitalism not sexism as "the enemy"—*Black Dwarf*, undated.

*"Women first"—"The Redstockings Manifesto," July 7, 1969, in Goodman, *Movement Toward a New America*, p. 50.

*Alpert on the *Rat* split—Alpert, *Growing Up Underground*, pp. 242–45.

*"Goodbye to All That"—*Rat*, February 9, 1970.

*"We Want to Work It Out" editorial—*Rat*, February 24, 1970.

*Male editor's critique—*Rat*, March 7, 1970.

*Letters on takeover—*Rat*, March 22, 1970.

*Women's movement and talent—Marge Piercy, "Symposium: From the '60s to the '80s," *Cultural Correspondence*, nos. 12–14 (Summer, 1981), p. 37.

*Venice sister piece—*Seed*, vol. 5, no. 8.

*International Women's Day editorial—*off our backs*, February 27, 1970.

*Discrimination vs. lesbians—Rita Mae Brown, *Rat*, March 7, 1970.

*Rita Mae Brown comments—letter to author, March 7, 1984.

*Feminists leaving underground press—Marilyn Salzman Webb, *off our backs*, April 25, 1970.

*Gay liberation movement background—in addition to my interviews, the key written source was Toby Marotta's *The Politics of Homosexuality*, especially pp. 27, 28, 53, 65, 71–76, 79, 89, 92–93, 96, 127, 147, and the specific media citations below:

> *One* magazine, p. 10.
>
> The *Ladder*, p. 16.
>
> *Rat* and *East Village Other* on Stonewall, pp. 71–76.
>
> The *Rat* and the GLF statement, pp. 88–89.
>
> *Come Out*, pp. 92, 140.
>
> "The Woman-Identified Woman," pp. 231, 242–43, 150. This manifesto first appeared in *Ladder*, no. 14.
>
> *Gay Power, Gay*, p. 109.
>
> *Gay Flames*, p. 131.

*The other general source on the gay press used here is Armstrong, *Trumpet to Arms*, pp. 238–40, 248–53.

*New York *Times* on the Stonewall—July 29, 1969.

Village Voice on Stonewall—Goodman, *Movement Toward a New America*, pp. 68–71.

*Eldridge Cleaver on homosexuality—*Liberation*, October, 1969.

*David McReynolds on homosexuality—*WIN*, November 15, 1969.

*Arthur Bell—interview with the author; the *Harper's* demonstration was also described in the *Village Voice*, June 26, 1984. See also Marotta, *Politics of Homosexuality*, pp. 151, 159.

Chapter 14: APOCALYPSE NOW

Interviews—Marshall Rosenthal, Tim Cahill, Greil Marcus, Jann Wenner, Ed Sanders, Lowell Bergman, Jerry Rubin, Paul Krassner, Cheryl McCall, Paul Williams.

*Fred Hampton—J.F. Rice, *Up on Madison, Down on 75th: A History of the Illinois Black Panther Party, Part I.*

*Wild gun battle—Chicago *Tribune*, December 5, 1969.

*Television reenactment—Chicago *Sun-Times*, December 12, 1969.

*All sides criticized—Mike Royko, Chicago *Daily News*, December 10 and 12, 1969.

*Radical coverage—*Seed*, broadside and vol. 4, no. 10.

*Altamont background—Anson, *Gone Crazy*, pp. 145–58; Armstrong, *Trumpet to Arms*, pp. 150, 177.

*Nation of sheep at Altamont—Sol Stern, *Ramparts*, as quoted in Anson, *Gone Crazy*, p. 150.

*Dots seeking a center—Todd Gitlin, LNS, December, 1969.

*Manson and police gloating—David Felton and David Dalton in David Felton, ed., *Mindfuckers*, pp. 27–28.

*Nixon accusation of Manson—Los Angeles *Times*, August 4, 1970.

*Threat of pogrom against longhairs—*Good Times*, February 27, 1968.

*Glorification of Manson—*Tuesday's Child*, February 7, 1970, and subsequent issues.

*Manson a hippie?—Felton, ed., *Mindfuckers*, p. 29.

*Jerry Rubin and Charles Manson—Jerry Rubin, *We Are Everywhere*, pp. 238–40.

*Weatherman song—Sale, *SDS*, p. 627.

*War Council—author; Sale, *SDS;* Skeets Millard, *Seed*, vol. 4, no. 11.

*Bernardine Dohrn on Charles Manson—Vincent Bugliosi with Curt Gentry, *Helter Skelter*, p. 296.

*Left criticism of violence—Hendrik Hertzberg, *Win*, February, 1970.

*Weathermen as the future—Skeets Millard, *Seed*, vol. 4, no. 11.

*San Diego *Street Journal* and violence against it—*Street Journal*, January 16, 1970, as quoted in Leamer, *Paper Revolutionaries*, p. 132; Rips, *UnAmerican Activities*, pp. 130–34; Larry Remer, *Alternative Press Review*, vol. 8, no. 11 (September–October, 1975); New York *Times*, June 27, 1975.

*Repression round-up—Rips, *UnAmerican Activities:* Legion of Justice at Second City, pp. 117–20; *Distant Drummer*, p. 108; Stoney Burns, p. 107; *The Black Panther* Airtel from SAC, Newark to Director, FBI, p. 83; and *The Revolutionary Worker*, April 3, 1981.

*Repression of *Om*—see *Rolling Stone*, June 11, 1970.

*Repression and distrust—Leamer, *Paper Revolutionaries*, p. 131.

*Conspiracy verdicts and contempt citations—Harry Kalven, *Contempt*, pp. ix, xx.

*Skull Statute of Liberty—*Seed*, vol. 4, no. 13.

*"Don't Bank on Amerika"—ibid, vol. 5, no. 1.

*Conspiracy verdict reconsiderations—Gene Mustain, Chicago *Sun-Times*, September 23, 1979.

*"Guilty as hell"—Chicago *Sun-Times*, March 8, 1976. The column was the idea of Bob Greene, who gave it over to Rubin for the day.

*People's militia in Berkeley—*Tribe*, March 6, 1970, in Goodman, *Movement Toward a New America*, p. 594.

*Jerry Rubin on his convictions—*Seed*, vol. 4, no. 13.

*Marshall Rosenthal's reservations—ibid.

*"Spring Equinox" supplement—*Seed*, vol. 5, no. 1.

*"Outlaws of Amerika"—*Seed*, vol. 4, no. 13.

*Radical zeal in face of beatings—*Leviathan*, February, 1970, in Goodman, *Movement Toward a New America*, p. 115.

*Extent of radical bombings—Sale, *SDS,* p. 632.

*"Responsible Terrorism"—*Tribe,* April 3, 1970, in Sale, *SDS,* p. 579.

*"Irresponsible Terrorism"—unsigned, *Rat,* May 8, 1970.

*Impending collision—Jaacov Kohn, *East Village Other,* April 14, 1970.

*Mainstream notice of underground press—New York *Times,* April 5, 1970.

**Guardian* split—*WIN,* May 15, 1970, pp. 4–6.

*Pre-Kent chronology and Kent State events—*Seed,* vol. 5, no. 4; *Rolling Stone,* June 11, 1970; Viorst, *Fire in the Streets,* pp. 507–11, 525–34, 536, 538–41. Gallup Poll—Jones, *Great Expectations,* p. 116.

*Mainstream response to Kent State shootings—Knight Newspapers, "Reporting the Kent State Incident," American Newspaper Publishers Association Foundation, January, 1971, pp. 20, 26.

*Richard Nixon and Mickey Mouse—*Seed,* vol. 5, no. 4.

*Chicago conspiracy issue—*Rolling Stone,* April 2, 1970.

*Clash at *Rolling Stone*—Leamer, *Paper Revolutionaries,* pp. 163–68; Anson, *Gone Crazy,* pp. 172–73; *New Times,* 1976, as quoted in Armstrong, *Trumpet to Arms,* p. 176; Jann Wenner letter of February 18, 1972, in Flippo, "Rock Journalism," p. 102; John Burks letter of October 14, 1970, ibid, p. 99.

*Kent State and Movement—Skeets Millard, *Seed,* vol. 5, no. 4.

*Continuation of war—*Seed,* vol. 5, no. 4.

Chapter 15: PRESSING ON, MOVING ON

Interviews—Chip Berlet, Bob Fass, Jerry Rubin, Flora Johnson, Ray Mungo, Sheila Ryan, Robin Morgan, Jaacov Kohn, Marshall Rosenthal, Eliot Wald, Michael James, Terry Sampson, Craig Pyes, Allen Young, George Cavalletto, Andy Marx, Bruce Brugmann, Danny Schechter, Jeff (Shero) Nightbyrd, Allen Katzman.

*Tom Forcade vs. obscenity commission—Rips, *UnAmerican Activities,* pp. 94–95.

*Alternate Media Conference—Richard Todd, "Alternatives," *Atlantic,* November, 1970, pp. 112–20; Estren, *History of Underground Comics,* pp. 294–300; Irwin Silber, *Guardian,* June, 1970.

*Workers and students—Jon Schwartz and Bill Callahan, *Old Mole,* March 5, 1970, in Goodman, *Movement Toward a New America,* p. 533.

*Tom Hayden on liberated zones—*Seed,* vol. 5, no. 6.

*Sabotage—"It's Just a Shot Away," *Rat,* April 17, 1970.

*Weathermen—"Declaration of War," *Seed,* vol. 5, no. 5.

*Chicago police shootings—Abe Peck, *Seed,* vol. 5, no. 8.

*Mayor Daley-sponsored rock concert—*Seed,* vol. 5, no. 7.

*Electric Circus bombing—*East Village Other,* June 2, 1970.

*Sly nonconcert—Marshall Rosenthal in *Seed,* vol. 4, no. 13, and *Seed,* vol. 5, no. 9; *Rolling Stone,* September 3, 1970; *Rising Up Angry,* Summer 1970.

*Berkeley police shooting—*Barb* response in Leamer, *Paper Revolutionaries,* p. 59; "Ariel" and casualty box, *Tribe,* August 28, 1970.

*Jonathan Jackson—New York *Times,* August 8, 1970; *Seed,* vol. 5, no. 10.

*Madison bombings and Mark Knops—*Seed,* vol. 5, nos. 6, 8, 10, 12, 13; Rips, *UnAmerican Activities,* pp. 121, 123.

*Pun Plamondon served 28 months in jail before being released because of an unauthorized telephone tap. He apologized—for the anti-ecological crime of tossing a beer can out the car window.

*Internationalist coverage—*Seed,* vol. 5, no. 7.

*Tim Leary, Richard Alpert—Bryan, *Whatever Happened to Timothy Leary,* pp. 198–203; *Seed,* vol. 5, no. 13.

**Old Mole*—a November, 1970, issue, as reprinted in Leamer, *Paper Revolutionaries,* pp. 118–23.

*Weathermen on nonviolence—*Seed,* vol. 6, no. 4.

*Allen Young—Young and Karla Jay, eds., *Out of the Closets*, p. 218; Young, *Gays Under the Cuban Revolution*, p. 74.

*Gay Liberation Front at United Front Against Fascism meeting—Marotta, *Politics of Homosexuality*, p. 123.

*GLF at Revolutionary People's Constitutional Convention—ibid, p. 129.

*Young on universal gay experience—Young and Jay, *Out of the Closets* p. 29.

*Leary vs. Cleaver—Bryan, *Whatever Happened to Timothy Leary*, pp. 203–14; *Seed*, vol. 6, no. 7, from Michael Zwerlin, *Village Voice*, January 28, 1971; *East Village Other*, February 9, 1971; *Tribe*, February, 1971; *Seed*, vol. 6, nos. 8–9.

*Start-ups of *Boston After Dark* and *Bay Guardian*—Armstrong, *Trumpet to Arms*, pp. 204, 205.

Rising Up Angry vs. *Chicago Free Press*—*Seed*, vol. 6, no. 2, and vol. 6, no. 4.

*Sandy Darlington—*Good Times*, as reprinted in *Seed*, vol. 6, no. 10.

*Karma Farm statement—*Seed*, vol. 6, no. 10.

*May Day—*Seed*, vol. 6, no. 12.

Chapter 16: THE HOWLING

Interviews—Chip Berlet, Eliot Wald, Julius Lester, Daniel Ellsberg, Geoffrey Rips, Tom Miller, Alan Young, Alan Howard, Jann Wenner, Craig Pyes, Danny Schechter, Cameron Crowe.

*Oyster River meeting—minutes furnished by Chip Berlet.

*Size of underground press—Craig Pyes and Ken Kelley, *SunDance* prospectus, late 1971.

*Seale-Huggins trial—New York *Times*, May 25–26, 1971, and various underground clips.

*Newspapers as substitute for organizing—Fruchter, "Games in the Arena: Movement Propaganda and the Culture of the Spectacle," *Liberation*, May, 1971, pp. 4–17.

*Lester on Panthers—*Liberation*, February–March, 1971.

*Pentagon Papers—Ellsberg on America eating its young—Maclear, *Ten Thousand Day War*, p. 301; underground press disinterest, Jaacov Kohn, *East Village Other*, June 23, 1971.

*FBI's Media, Pa., files—*Liberation*, June, 1971; *WIN*, March, 1972.

*Tom Miller and grand jury—Frank J. Donner and Eugene Cerruti, "The Grand Jury Network," *Nation*, January 3, 1972, pp. 5–20; and Miller interview.

*George Jackson—New York *Times*, August 22, 1971; Peter Collier and David Horowitz, "Requiem for a Radical," *New West*, March, 1981; *Seed*, vol. 7, no. 8.

*Attica—Bernardine Dohrn, *Village Voice*, September 9–15, 1981; *Seed*, vol. 7, no. 8; New York *Times*, September 13, 14, 21, 1971, and November 13, 1983.

*WPAX—Hoffman, *Soon to be a Major Motion Picture*, p. 269.

*Gay utopianism and Cuban gay letter—Young and Jay, *Out of the Closets*, pp. 29–30, 244–46; Cuban policy, ibid, pp. 246–47; Young, *Gays Under the Cuban Revolution*, p. 106; Richard Goldstein, *Village Voice*, July 24, 1984; Nestor Almendros, ibid, August 14, 1984.

*LNS critique—Howard et al, "Liberation News Service: Bourgeois or Revolutionary Journalism?", January 10, 1972; revised January 25, 1972.

Rolling Stone's severance with movement utopias—Jann Wenner, *Rolling Stone*, November 11, 1971.

*Critique of *Rolling Stone*—Craig Pyes, "*Rolling Stone* Gathers No Politix," first seen by author in *Space City*, as reprinted in David Horowitz, Michael P. Lerner, Craig Pyes, eds., *Counterculture and Revolution* (New York: Random House, 1972), pp. 103–11.

*Nobody reaching youth culture—Kelley and Pyes, "Rough Draft of a Perspectus for the Magazine," undated.

*John Lennon—Stuart Werbin, *Rolling Stone*, February 17, 1972, in Rolling Stone, eds., *The Ballad of John and Yoko*, pp. 126–34; Jon Weiner, *New Republic*, May 2, 1981; Joel Siegel, *Rolling Stone*, October 10, 1974, in *Ballad*, p. 132; Pete Hamill, *Rolling Stone*, June 5, 1975, in *Ballad*, p. 146.

*Vote for McGovern—Robert Scheer, *SunDance*, November–December, 1972.

*Forecast of success for *SunDance*—*Good Times*, April 7–20, 1972.

*Collapse of *SunDance*—Flippo, "Rock Journalism and *Rolling Stone,*" p. 105.

**Ms.*—10th anniversary issue, August, 1982; Armstrong, *Trumpet to Arms* pp. 242–47; Harry Reasoner mentioned in Chicago *Sun-Times,* July 18, 1982.

*"Enemy Bombs Hanoi" headline—*Nola Express,* December, 1972, as mentioned in Armstrong, *Trumpet to Arms,* p. 114.

*Police spying on author—Chicago Police Department intelligence files, p. 145716.

**Reader* history—Bob Roth to author, Chicago *Sun-Times,* December 6, 1978.

*CIA Situation Report—Rips, *UnAmerican Activities* p. 73.

Chapter 17: AMERICA DRINKS UP AND GOES HOME

Interviews with Art Kunkin, Chip Berlet, Tom Miller, Paul Krassner.

*Colorful shots of freaky glee—Thorne Dreyer and Victoria Smith, "The Movement and the New Media," *Orpheus,* vol. 2, no. 2.

*Conference coverage—Calvin Trillin, *New Yorker,* April 10, 1978; Berkeley *Barb,* June 22–28, 1973; *Northwest Passage,* July 9–30, 1973; New York *Times,* June 11, 1973; *Rocky Mountain News,* June 11, 1973; *Alternate Press Review,* November–December, 1973; *Underground Press Review,* July–August, 1973.

*Structural accomplishments of underground press—Daniel Ben-Horin, "The Alternative Press: Journalism as a Way of Life," *Nation,* February 17, 1973, pp. 238–45.

*Narrow-casting of media debate—Hodding Carter III, *The Wall Street Journal,* August 16, 1984.

*Bank stories—David L. Paletz and Robert M. Entman, *Media Power Politics,* (New York: The Free Press, 1981), as cited by Todd Gitlin, *Nation,* June 20, 1981.

*Effect of sixties—Herb Caen, San Francisco *Chronicle,* September 21, 1975.

*FBI on author's social graces—SAC Chicago to SAC Houston, 100-45153-33, August 7, 1972.

*"Extreme reformists"—Theodore J. Lowi, as quoted in "The American Left Still Searches for a Clear Political Direction," New York *Times,* September 26, 1982, p. E5.

BIBLIOGRAPHY

The first written sources were the primary ones—the underground papers that published from 1964 to 1973. I read through my back issues of the Chicago *Seed*—which was far easier than reading microfilmed black type over a 40 percent blue screen. Allen Cohen, the former San Francisco *Oracle* editor, kindly showed me his slide collection of covers and page spreads from that psychedelic paper. For the most part, though, papers were read in the microfilm room of the Chicago Public Library's central collection.

A full bibliography follows, but several works deserve special mention.

When it was published in 1970, I faulted Mitchell Goodman's underground press anthology, *The Movement Toward a New America*, for giving short shrift to the cultural side of things. On second reading, the book proved to be a valuable compendium that simplified my work.

Of the history-in-the-making books published about the underground press during its existence, Laurence Leamer's *The Paper Revolutionaries* has proved the most valid, and most important in doing this book. Leamer was especially good at depicting the tension between what he called "The Heads" and "The Fists," the cultural and political wings of protest.

Ray Mungo's *Famous Long Ago: My Life and Hard Times with Liberation News Service* and Steve Diamond's *What the Trees Said: Life on a New Age Farm* leaned toward the culture folk in the Liberation News Service split, but helped me capture the contending spirits of the split.

Chet Flippo's unpublished master's thesis on *Rolling Stone* provided a chronicle of the magazine that was the main alternative to the underground. Kevin McAuliffe's *The Great American Newspaper* did the same for the early days of the *Village Voice*.

Several more-recent histories helped inform my work. Though *Un-American Activities: The Campaign Against the Underground Press* may overestimate the role of repression in the demise of the papers, the work of Geoffrey Rips, Angus MacKenzie, and others augmented my own collection of repression documents, sixties damage reports, and the 1976 *Intelligence Activities and the Rights of Americans, Book II,* the Final Report of the Senate Select Committee to Study Governmental Operations with Respect to Intelligence Activities. David Armstrong's *A Trumpet to Arms: Alternative Media in America* may see continuity between generations of protest when dislocation might be more appropriate, but is another useful analysis. Toby Marotta's *The Politics of Homosexuality* helped me understand the contending factions of the gay liberation movement and their newsprint manifestations. Milton Viorst's *Fire in the Streets: America in the 1960s* is a substantive overview of the decade. A full bibliography follows:

Aaron, Daniel. *Writers on the Left: Episodes in American Literary Communism.* New York: Harcourt, Brace & World, Inc., 1961.

Alpert, Jane. *Growing Up Underground.* New York: William Morrow and Company, Inc., 1981.

Anson, Robert Sam. *Gone Crazy and Back Again: The Rise and Fall of the Rolling Stone Generation.* Garden City: Doubleday & Company, Inc., 1981.

Armstrong, David. *A Trumpet to Arms: Alternative Media in America.* Los Angeles: J.P. Tarcher, 1981.

Blake, John. *All You Needed Was Love: The Beatles After the Beatles.* New York: Perigee, 1981.

Blount, Roy, Jr. *Crackers.* New York: Ballantine Books, 1982.

Bryan, John. *This Soldier Still at War.* New York: Harcourt, Brace, Jovanovich, 1975.

Bryan, John. *Whatever Happened to Timothy Leary?* San Francisco: Renaissance Press, 1980.

Bugliosi, Vincent, with Gentry, Curt. *Helter Skelter: The True Story of the Manson Murders.* New York: Bantam Books, 1975.

Chappel, Steve, and Garofalo, Reebee. *Rock 'n' Roll Is Here to Pay: The History and Politics of the Music Industry.* Chicago: Nelson-Hall, 1977.

Cook, Bruce. *The Beat Generation.* New York: Charles Scribner's Sons, 1971.

Crumb, R. *R. Crumb Sketchbook: November 1974 to January 1978.* Frankfurt am Main: Zweitausendeins, 1978.

Davis, Clive. *Clive: Inside the Record Business.* New York: William Morrow, 1974.

Diamond, Stephen. *What the Trees Said: Life on a New Age Farm.* New York: Delta, 1971.

Didion, Joan. *Slouching Towards Bethlehem.* New York: Delta, 1968.

Estren, Mark James. *A History of Underground Comics.* San Francisco: Straight Arrow Books, 1974.

Felton, David, ed. *Mindfuckers.* San Francisco: Straight Arrow Books, 1972.

Flippo, Chet. "Rock Journalism and *Rolling Stone.*" Master's thesis, University of Texas at Austin, 1974.

Forcade, Thomas King, ed. *Underground Press Anthology.* New York: Ace, 1972.

Frith, Simon. *Sound Effects: Youth, Leisure, and the Politics of Rock 'n' Roll.* New York: Pantheon Books, 1981.

Gans, Herbert J. *Deciding What's News.* New York: Pantheon Books, 1979.

Gaskin, Stephen. *Amazing Dope Tales & Haight Street Flashbacks.* Summertown, Tenn.: The Book Publishing Company, 1980.

Ginsberg, Allen. *Howl and Other Poems.* San Francisco: City Lights Books, 1956.

Gitlin, Todd. *The Whole World Is Watching: Mass Media in the Making and Unmaking of the New Left.* Berkeley: University of California Press, 1980.

Glessing, Robert J. *The Underground Press in America.* Bloomington: Indiana University Press, 1970.

Goldman, Albert. *Elvis.* New York: McGraw-Hill Book Company, 1981.

Goodman, Mitchell, ed. *The Movement Toward a New America.* Philadelphia: Pilgrim Press/New York: Alfred A. Knopf, 1970.

Harris, David. *Dreams Die Hard: Three Men's Journey Through the Sixties.* New York: St. Martin's/Marek, 1982.

Hoberman, J., and Rosenbaum, Jonathan. *Midnight Movies.* New York: Harper & Row, 1983.

Hoffman, Abbie. *Soon to Be a Major Motion Picture.* New York: G.P. Putnam's Sons, 1980.

Hofmann, Albert. *LSD: My Problem Child.* Translated by Jonathan Ott. New York: McGraw-Hill Book Company, 1980.

Hopkins, Jerry, ed. *The Hippie Papers.* New York: Signet Books, 1968.

Howard, Mel, and Forcade, the Rev. Thomas King. *The Underground Reader.* New York: New American Library, 1972.

Jezer, Marty. *The Dark Ages: Life in the United States 1945–60.* Boston: South End Press, 1982.

Jones, Landon Y. *Great Expectations: America and the Baby Boom Generation.* New York: Ballantine Books, 1981.

Kalven, Harry. *Contempt: Transcript of the Contempt Citations, Sentences, and Responses of the Chicago Conspiracy 10.* Chicago: Swallow Press, 1970.

Kennedy, William V. *Press Coverage of the Vietnam War: The Third View.* Draft Report of the Study Group. Carlisle Barracks, Penn.: Strategic Studies Institute, 1979.

Kerner, Otto. *Report to the National Advisory Commission on Civil Disorders,* March 1, 1968. New York: E.P. Dutton and Co., 1968.

Kerouac, Jack. *On the Road.* New York: Viking Press, 1957.

Kissinger, Henry. *White House Years.* Boston: Little, Brown, 1979.

Kornbluth, Jesse, ed. *Notes from the New Underground: An Anthology.* New York: Viking Press, 1968.

Kowalski, Isaac. *A Secret Press in Nazi Europe: The Story of a Jewish United Partisan Organization.* New York: Shengold Publishers, Inc., 1969.

Leamer, Laurence. *The Paper Revolutionaries: The Rise of the Underground Press.* New York: Simon and Schuster, 1972.

Leary, Timothy. *Flashbacks: An Autobiography.* Los Angeles: J.P. Tarcher, Inc., 1983.

Lenin, V.I. *What Is to Be Done? Burning Questions of Our Movement.* New York: International Publishers, 1978.

Lens, Sidney. *Unrepentant Radical: An American Activist's Account of Five Turbulent Decades.* Boston: Beacon Press, 1980.

Lewis, Roger. *Outlaws of America: The Underground Press and its Context.* Baltimore: Penguin Books, 1972.

Maclear, Michael. *The Ten Thousand Day War: Vietnam 1945–1975.* New York: St. Martin's Press, 1981.

Mailer, Norman. *Pieces and Pontifications.* Boston: Little, Brown and Co., 1982.

Mao Tse-tung. *Talks at the Yenan Forum on Literature and Art.* Peking: Foreign Languages Press, 1967.

Marcuse, Herbert. *The Aesthetic Dimension.* Boston: Beacon Press, 1978.

Marotta, Toby. *The Politics of Homosexuality.* Boston: Houghton Mifflin Company, 1981.

Marsh, Dave. *Before I Get Old: The Story of the Who.* New York: St. Martin's Press, 1983.

Marsh, Dave, and Swenson, John. *The New Rolling Stone Record Guide.* New York: Random House/Rolling Stone Press, 1983.

McAuliffe, Kevin. *The Great American Newspaper.* New York: Charles Scribner's Sons, 1978.

McNeill, Don. *Moving Through Here.* New York: Alfred A. Knopf, 1970.

Morgan, Robin, ed. *Sisterhood Is Powerful.* New York: Vintage Books, 1970.

Morgan, Robin. *The Anatomy of Freedom.* Garden City: Anchor Press, 1982.

Mungo, Raymond. *Famous Long Ago: My Life and Hard Times with Liberation News Service.* Boston: Beacon Press, 1970.

Mungo, Raymond. *Return to Sender.* Boston: Houghton Mifflin Company, 1975.

Neville, Richard. *Play Power: Exploring the International Underground.* New York: Vintage Books, 1971.

Newfield, Jack. *A Prophetic Minority.* New York: The New American Library, 1966.

Nixon, Richard. *Memoirs.* New York: Grosset and Dunlap, 1978.

Norman, Philip. *Shout: The Beatles in Their Generation.* New York: Fireside, 1981.

Obst, Lynda Rosen, ed. *The Sixties.* New York: Random House/Rolling Stone Press, 1977.

O'Neill, William L. *Coming Apart: An Informal History of America in the 1960s.* Chicago: Quadrangle Books, 1971.

Paley, William S. *As It Happened.* Garden City: Doubleday & Company, Inc., 1979.

Parkinson, Thomas, ed. *A Casebook on the Beat.* New York: Thomas Y. Crowell Company, 1961.

Perry, Charles. *The Haight-Ashbury: A History.* New York: Random House/Rolling Stone, 1984.

Rice, J.F. *Up on Madison, Down on 75th: A History of the Illinois Black Panther Party, Part 1.* Evanston: The Committee, 1983.

Rips, Geoffrey et al. *UnAmerican Activities: The Campaign Against the Underground Press*. San Francisco: City Lights Books, 1981.

Rolling Stone, eds. *The Ballad of John and Yoko*. Garden City: Rolling Stone/Doubleday, 1982.

Romm, Ethel Grodzins. *The Open Conspiracy: What America's Angry Generation Is Saying*. New York: Giniger/Stackpole Books, 1970.

Rosenkranz, Patrick, and Van Baren, Hugo. *Artsy Fartsy Funnies*. Laren NH, Holland: Paranoia, 1974.

Rosenstone, Robert A. *Romantic Revolutionary: A Biography of John Reed*. New York: Vintage Books, 1981.

Rossman, Michael. *New Age Blues: On the Politics of Consciousness*. New York: E.P. Dutton, 1979.

Rossman, Michael. *The Wedding Within the War*. Garden City: Doubleday & Company, Inc., 1971.

Rothman, Stanley, and Lichter, S. Robert. *Roots of Radicalism: Jews, Christians and the New Left*. New York: Oxford University Press, 1982.

Rubin, Jerry. *Do It!* New York: Simon and Schuster, 1970.

Rubin, Jerry. *We Are Everywhere*. New York: Harper & Row, 1971.

Russell, J.P. *The Beatles on Record*. New York: Charles Scribner's Sons, 1982.

Sale, Kirkpatrick. *SDS*. New York: Random House, 1973.

Sanders, Ed. *The Family: The Story of Charles Manson's Dune Buggy Attack Battalion*. New York: Avon Books, 1972.

Sanders, Ed. *Shards of God*. New York: Grove Press, Inc., 1970.

Schoenbrun, David. *Soldiers of the Night: The Story of the French Resistance*. New York: E.P. Dutton, 1980.

Schudson, Michael. *Discovering the News: A Social History of American Newspapers*. New York: Basic Books, 1978.

Seale, Bobby. *A Lonely Rage*. New York: Times Books, 1978.

Seale, Bobby. *Seize the Time*. New York: Random House, 1970.

Senate Select Committee to Study Governmental Operations with Respect to Intelligence Activities, *Intelligence Activities and the Rights of Americans: Book II*. Washington: U.S. Government Printing Office, 1976.

Sheed, Wilfrid. *The Good Word and Other Words*. New York: Penguin Books, 1980.

Stapp, Andy. *Up Against the Brass*. New York: Simon and Schuster, 1970.

Tuchman, Gaye. *Making News: A Study in the Construction of Reality*. New York: The Free Press, 1978.

Viorst, Milton. *Fire in the Streets: America in the 1960s*. New York: Touchstone, 1979.

WGBH Educational Foundation. "Vietnam: A Television History," Boston, 1983.

Williams, Paul. *Pushing Upward*. New York: Links Books, 1973.

Walker, Daniel et al. *Rights in Conflict: A Report Submitted by Daniel Walker, Director of the Chicago Study Group, to the National Commission on the Causes and Prevention of Violence*. New York: The New American Library, 1968.

Wasserman, Harvey. *Harvey Wasserman's History of the United States*. New York: Harper & Row, 1972.

Watson, Francis M., Jr. *The Alternative Media: Dismantling Two Centuries of Progress*. Rockford: The Rockford College Institute, 1979.

Young, Allen. *Gays Under the Cuban Revolution*. San Francisco: Grey Fox Press, 1981.

Young, Allen, and Jay, Karla, eds. *Out of the Closets*. New York: Harcourt Brace, Jovanovich-/Jove, 1972.

Zinn, Howard. *A People's History of the United States*. New York: Harper & Row/Colophon Books, 1980.

INDEX

NOTE: A newspaper title is indexed under the place name when it seems inseparable from the title [as: *East Village Other;* New York *Times*]; otherwise, the place name is subordinate [as: *Actuel* (Paris); *Argus* (Ann Arbor)].

ABOUT THE AUTHOR

Abe Peck, now a professor of journalism at the Medill School of Journalism at Northwestern, was a founding editor of the Chicago Seed, and was on the coordinating committee of the Underground Press Syndicate. He has been pop music columnist for the AP; associate editor of Rolling Stone *(where he remains a contributing editor); and a reporter and weekly columnist for the Chicago* Daily News *and* Sun-Times. *His articles have appeared in a wide variety of magazines, from the* Progressive *to* Playboy, *from* Savvy *to the* New York Times Magazine. *He lives in Chicago.*

CITADEL UNDERGROUND

CITADEL UNDERGROUND provides a voice
to writers whose ideas and styles veer
from convention. The series is
dedicated to bringing back into print
lost classics and to publishing new
works that explore pathbreaking and
iconoclastic personal, social, literary,
musical, consciousness, political,
dramatic and rhetorical styles.

Take Back Your Mind

For more information, please write to:

CITADEL UNDERGROUND
Carol Publishing Group
600 Madison Avenue
New York, New York 10022

Take Back Your Mind

CITADEL UNDERGROUND books are published for people eager to stretch their minds around new and dangerous ideas.

CITADEL UNDERGROUND provides a voice to writers whose ideas and styles veer from convention. The series is dedicated to bringing lost classics back into print and to publishing new works that explore pathbreaking and iconoclastic personal, social, literary, musical, consciousness, political, dramatic and rhetorical styles.

We'd like to stay in touch with you. If you'd like to hear more about our plans for CITADEL UNDERGROUND, please fill out this card and send it to us. We're eager to hear your comments and suggestions.

CITADEL UN DERGROUND

"Challenging Consensus Reality Since 1990"

Carol Publishing Group • 1-800-447-BOOK
Sales and Distribution Center • 120 Enterprise Avenue • Secaucus, NJ 07094

Please keep me posted about Citadel Underground books!

Name (Please Print)_____

Address_____

_____

City_____ **State**_____ **Zip**_____

Title of this Book_____

Favorite Bookstores (and Locations)_____

Fax_____ **Electronic Mail Address**_____

_____

Comments_____

_____

_____

NO POSTAGE
NECESSARY
IF MAILED
IN THE
UNITED STATES

BUSINESS REPLY MAIL
FIRST CLASS PERMIT NO. 111 SECAUCUS, N.J.

POSTAGE WILL BE PAID BY ADDRESSEE

CAROL PUBLISHING GROUP

120 ENTERPRISE AVENUE

SECAUCUS, N.J. 07094-9899